THE VANISHING IRISH

THE PRINCETON ECONOMIC HISTORY
OF THE WESTERN WORLD

Joel Mokyr, Editor

*Growth in a Traditional Society: The French Countryside,
1450–1815* by Philip T. Hoffman (1996)

*The Vanishing Irish: Households, Migration, and the Rural Economy
in Ireland, 1850–1914*, by Timothy W. Guinnane (1997)

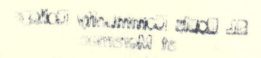

THE VANISHING IRISH

HOUSEHOLDS, MIGRATION, AND THE
RURAL ECONOMY IN IRELAND,
1850–1914

TIMOTHY W. GUINNANE

PRINCETON UNIVERSITY PRESS

PRINCETON, NEW JERSEY

Library of Congress Cataloging-in-Publication Data

Guinnane, Timothy.
The vanishing Irish : households, migration, and the
rural economy in Ireland, 1850–1914 / Timothy W. Guinnane.
p.   cm. — (The Princeton economic history of the Western world)
Includes bibliographical references and index.
ISBN 0-691-04307-8 (cl)
1. Ireland—Population—History.   2. Households—Ireland—History.
3. Ireland—Emigration and immigration—History.   4. Ireland—
Rural conditions.   I. Title.   II. Series.
HB3589.G84   1997   304.6′2′09415—dc21   97-5383   CIP

CONTENTS

LIST OF TABLES   ix

LIST OF FIGURES   xi

LIST OF MAPS   xiii

PREFACE   xv

ACKNOWLEDGMENTS   xix

CHAPTER 1
Depopulation in Post-Famine Ireland   3

CHAPTER 2
The Rural Economy in the Nineteenth Century   34

CHAPTER 3
The State and the Churches   59

CHAPTER 4
The Demographic Setting   79

CHAPTER 5
Households and the Generations   133

CHAPTER 6
Coming of Age   166

CHAPTER 7
The Decline of Marriage   193

CHAPTER 8
Marital Fertility and Fertility Decline   241

CHAPTER 9
Conclusion   272

NOTES   287

REFERENCES   305

INDEX   333

TABLES

4.1 Population indicators: size, celibacy, emigration, and fertility   89

4.2 Proportion never married in England and Wales, France, Germany, and Ireland   96

4.3 Proportion never married in the provinces of Ireland   97

4.4 Cohort-depletion measures, by province   102

4.5 Marital fertility and overall fertility in Ireland and England   112

4.6 Mortality estimates for Ireland   112

4.7 Urbanization measures: Ireland, England and Wales, France, and Germany   122

5.1 Distribution of household types, from local studies   141

5.2 Types of extensions in extended-family households   143

5.3 Transitions between household types, 1901 to 1911   145

6.1 Percentage of sons and daughters leaving household, by age   169

6.2 Number of sons, daughters, and servants in 1911, by household type   173

6.3 Relationship to head of household, 1911, ages 1–29   174

6.4 Household's perspective on children leaving home   175

6.5 Male household heads with co-resident siblings, 1911   177

6.6 Prevalence of servants, 1911   180

6.7 Ages of Irish emigrants   182

6.8 Evaluations of the waiting-time model   187

6.9 Evaluations of the probit model   190

7.1 Celibacy by age, Irish provinces and England, 1911   199

7.2 Relationship to household head of those never married, 1911   204

7.3 Male household heads and celibacy   205

7.4 Farm size and celibacy, 1926: Percentage never married for males aged 45–64   208

8.1 Distribution of number of children born and surviving, manuscript census sample   242

8.2 Marital fertility (I_g) for Ireland and other populations   249

8.3 CPA results for Ireland, 1911   256

FIGURES

1.1 The populations of Ireland and of England and Wales, 1821–1971   5

2.1 Growth of agricultural output in post-Famine Ireland   40

2.2 The disappearance of the agricultural laborer, 1841–1911   42

2.3 Changes in farm sizes, 1853–1902   43

2.4 The decline of agricultural employment, 1841–1911   56

4.1 Death rates by sex from tuberculosis in Ireland and in England and Wales in the early twentieth century   115

4.2 A comparison of male and female mortality in Ireland, 1901–1910 and 1951–1960   120

5.1 The household cycle for stem families   137

5.2 The household cycle for nuclear families   138

8.1 Convex costs, marriage, and fertility   266

MAPS

2.1 Distribution of small farms, 1901   45

2.2 Distribution of large farms, 1901   46

2.3 Prevalence of farm laborers, 1901   47

4.1 Depopulation, 1851–1881   90

4.2 Depopulation, 1881–1911   91

4.3 Internal migration by county of destination, 1911   123

4.4 Internal migration by county of origin, 1911   124

4.5 Locator map for manuscript census sample locales   131

6.1 Cohort depletion, males, 1861–1881   183

6.2 Cohort depletion, females, 1861–1881   184

6.3 Cohort depletion, males, 1881–1911   185

6.4 Cohort depletion, females, 1881–1911   186

7.1 Never-married women, 1881   200

7.2 Never-married men, 1881   201

7.3 Never-married women, 1911   202

7.4 Never-married men, 1911   203

8.1 Levels of I_g, 1911   250

8.2 Percentage decline in I_g, 1881–1911   251

PREFACE

SOME FORTY years ago John O'Brien edited a collection of essays entitled *The Vanishing Irish: The Enigma of the Modern World*. O'Brien and the other contributors drew attention to a central fact of Ireland's modern history: that the island's population by the mid-twentieth century was only about half what it had been prior to the Great Famine. This great depopulation reflected not just the deaths and emigration of the Famine years, but a slower and more drawn-out process during the sixty years that followed. This book focuses on the population decline of these six decades. My subtitle, while coupled with O'Brien's evocative title, signals a basic difference in approach and method. I argue that some aspects of Irish depopulation were unusual but that the basic forces leading to depopulation were similar to those at work all across Europe in the late nineteenth century. Ireland differed from some other places experiencing depopulation primarily in the particular combination of demographic forces that brought it about: high emigration rates, large families, and a large number of adults who never married. The Irish can be appreciated for the truly unique aspects of their history and culture, but we must remove from the list of things unique to Ireland most aspects of the population patterns that so exercised O'Brien. More recent history has also given good reason to rethink the views expressed in the O'Brien volume. Irish population growth has been slow and uneven since the 1950s, but there is little danger that the Irish will disappear.

Three aspects of this study are paramount. First, the focus throughout is on rural Ireland. The rural focus reflects the fact that Ireland was a very rural country even as late as 1914, and that depopulation was a primarily rural phenomenon. The contribution of urban areas to depopulation was to grow more slowly than was necessary to offset population decline in the countryside. Second, the focus is on the period between the Great Famine and the First World War, roughly 1850–1914. I stray outside these boundaries only rarely, in search of the historical roots of a post-Famine development or to trace the way a post-Famine development has worked itself out in twentieth-century Ireland. Third, this study aims at once to describe and explain Ireland's population history and to use that history to illuminate more general population-related phenomena both in European history and in today's world. This broader perspective reflects both my judgment that one cannot understand Ireland in a vacuum and my hope that this small island's history can offer more general lessons. Oversimplified versions of Irish population history have often figured in moralistic discussions of population problems today and in the past. On the grounds of equity alone it is time to let Ireland's population history speak to larger questions on the basis of a more nuanced understanding.

One of the pleasures of completing a book is the opportunity to thank those who assisted through their support, their encouragement, and perhaps most of all, their comments and advice. The list of people who have in some way aided this project is so long that any attempt to be exhaustive would be lengthy and still incomplete, but I would like to single out several individuals whose assistance was instrumental. Ireland's economic historians are a genial and helpful bunch, displaying a generosity of spirit and intellect that has materially added to this work. Joel Mokyr's vision and enthusiasm was crucial to completing the project; he encouraged me to write the book, showed great patience and insight as series editor, and read several drafts of each chapter, catching both errors and missed opportunities to make a larger point. Cormac Ó Gráda helped me to persist with views that often differ from his own, put up with a constant flow of questions and requests for help, and made insightful comments on many drafts. David Fitzpatrick did much to encourage my early research on this topic, and his tenacious skepticism was most useful. Fitzpatrick also shared several sets of unpublished demographic estimates for post-Famine Ireland. Paul David, Gavin Wright, and John Pencavel supervised the original doctoral dissertation, and were especially giving as advisors. Although the subject matter lies far from their own interests they have each made a profound mark on me and on this book. Stanley Engerman and David Weir each read the entire manuscript and provided thoughtful, helpful comments. David Miller shared his knowledge of Irish religion and provided assistance with the computer software that drew the maps. Others who have read all or part of the manuscript include George Alter, Charlotte Ellertson, Myron Gutmann, Barbara S. Okun, and Susan Cotts Watkins. I have not always taken their advice, but I appreciate their efforts to make me see things differently. Several students and colleagues over the years have provided assistance and suggestions on matters related to this book. Some show up as coauthors on related works; others made a less visible but no less important mark. I would like to thank Timothy J. Besley, Michael A. Boozer, John W. Budd, Anne Case, David Card, William English, Ronald I. Miller, Thomas A. Mroz, Christina Paxson, Robert A. Pollak, Samuel H. Preston, William Sundstrom, and James Trussell in particular.

The staffs of the Public Record Office and the Valuation Office in Dublin were unfailingly helpful during my stays there. I also owe thanks to the staffs of the National Library (Dublin), the Library of Congress, the Genealogical Society of the Church of Jesus Christ of Latter-Day Saints, and the university libraries at Pennsylvania, Princeton, Stanford, and Yale. The library at Princeton's Office of Population Research has no parallel for demographic issues, and I thank Maryann Belanger for whom no request was too obscure, no reference too sketchy. Support from the National Institute of Aging allowed me to pursue this research at the postdoctoral level. Several of Princeton and Yale's excellent undergraduates helped with library and data-gathering tasks. I am indebted to Edward Bernhard, Tracy Deblieck, Vanessa Grajwer, and Cheryl Gulden.

Last but not least, I owe a special debt to two Princeton University Press editors, Peter Dougherty and Jack Repcheck, whose diligence and support saw this work through to publication.

Critics have rightly noted that there is a tendency for American academics to write histories of the countries of their forbears or of the ethnic group to which they belong. Whether this proclivity is a good thing I cannot say. In my own case it is worth noting that surnames are imperfect indications of ethnicity. Guinnane is indeed a name found in some parts of the west of Ireland. But my maternal grandfather, Caspar Hochstetter, was no Irishman. My own children, to whom this book is dedicated, take this mix and add to it the rich heritage of Ashkenazi Jews. O'Brien worried more than was warranted: the Irish will not vanish, if for no other reason than their ability to thrive in other lands and to combine with other peoples.

ACKNOWLEDGMENTS

S OME OF the material discussed in this book was published earlier, in a different form, in scholarly journals. I am grateful for permission to reprint that material here. Portions of my essay (coauthored with Ronald I. Miller) "The Limits to Reform: The Land Acts in Ireland, 1870–1909," are reprinted from *Economic Development and Cultural Change*, copyright (c) 1997 by The University of Chicago, all rights reserved. Portions of my essay "The Poor Law and Pensions in Ireland" are reprinted from *the Journal of Interdisciplinary History* 34 (1993): 271–291, with the permission of the editors of the *Journal of Interdisciplinary History* and the MIT Press, Cambridge, Massachusetts, (c) by the Massachussetts Institute of Technology and the editors of *The Journal of Interdisciplinary History*. JAI Press, Inc., granted kind permission to reprint portions of "Re-thinking the Western European Marriage Pattern: The Decision to Marry in Ireland at the Turn of the Twentieth Century" from the *Journal of Family History* 16 (1991). JAI Press also granted permission to reprint portions of "Economics, History, and the Path of Demographic Adjustment: Ireland after the Famine" from *Research in Economic History* 13 (1991). The American Economic Association granted permission to reprint portions of "The Great Irish Famine and Population: The Long View" from the *American Economic Review Papers and Proceedings* 84 (1994). Portions of "Coming of Age in Rural Ireland at the Turn of the Twentieth Century," *Continuity and Change* 5(3): 443–472, are reprinted with permission of Cambridge University Press. Likewise, portions of "Age at Leaving Home in Rural Ireland, 1901–1911," *Journal of Economic History* 52(3): 651–674, (c) 1992 The Economic History Association, are reprinted with permission of Cambridge University Press.

THE VANISHING IRISH

Chapter 1

DEPOPULATION IN POST-FAMINE IRELAND

> I call heaven and earth to witness against you this day,
> that ye shall soon utterly perish from off the land.
> —*Deuteronomy 4:26a*

MANY COUNTRIES in the modern world face or will soon face one of two population problems. Some countries' populations are growing so rapidly that sheer numbers will endanger their ability to provide schooling, employment, and basic social amenities to their people. The physical requirements of the human population may overwhelm the environment's ability to provide for both it and local nonhuman populations. Other countries face a situation nearly the opposite. Their population is either growing very slowly or, in some cases, already declining. When growth continues at a slow rate, older people make up an increasingly large share of the society and eventually the population's numbers may begin to shrink. Rapid population growth now seems confined to the poorest societies, slow growth or decline seems the fate of the wealthier. Ireland faced both of these population problems during the nineteenth century: prior to the Great Famine of the 1840s, Ireland's population grew at unprecedented rates, while for over a century after the Great Famine the population shrank continuously. Part of this population decline reflects mortality and emigration during the Famine, but much of the depopulation occurred between 1850 and the First World War, after famine conditions had all but disappeared from the island. Most of the Irish decline, that is, reflects voluntary actions—emigration, postponing or avoiding marriage—rather than famine.

This book tells the story of that depopulation and why it took the form it did. Throughout I focus on rural Ireland because depopulation in Ireland was confined to rural areas almost exclusively. The ways in which the Irish were vanishing may be more noteworthy than the depopulation itself. To many writers the difference between Irish and other demographic regimes at the turn of the twentieth century has seemed an interesting, if quaint, illustration of the variety of ways populations can adjust to economic and social conditions. Here I examine the demographic differences from another perspective. My purpose is to understand why young Irish people made the decisions about marriage, emigration, and childbearing that produced Ireland's distinctive demographic regime.

The Famine's direct role in Ireland's depopulation over this period is less than one might think. Figure 1.1 shows the populations of Ireland and England from the early eighteenth century through the mid-twentieth century. Less than half of the total depopulation in Ireland from 1841 to 1911 can be attributed to the Famine itself. After the Famine the population declined without cease; by 1911 Ireland contained about half as many people as had lived there in 1841. Sustained reversal came only in the 1960s, and population growth since then has been modest. Population decline in Ireland along with rapid growth in Great Britain altered the weight of Ireland's population in the United Kingdom over the nineteenth century. In 1841 the Irish represented about a third of the United Kingdom's entire population. By 1911 Ireland formed less than a tenth of that whole.

Depopulation in the late nineteenth century was not confined to Ireland. Agricultural transformation at home and the pull of higher wages in cities and abroad also reduced the rural population in several regions of Great Britain and other European countries. In most other countries, however, depopulation was limited to specific areas (usually those most agricultural) and specific periods. One striking example comes from the United States, a country whose nineteenth-century population growth rates were extremely rapid for the day. Rural depopulation was under way in New England as early as 1860: between that date and 1920 the states of Maine, New Hampshire, and Vermont all experienced slow population growth overall coupled with an absolute loss of population in rural areas. Ogle (1889, table A) documents population declines in several of England's more agricultural counties for the interval 1851 to 1881. In his discussion of England, Scotland, and Ireland, Longstaff (1893, pp. 388–389) notes that only twelve of Scotland's thirty-three counties had experienced uninterrupted population growth since 1801. Nine counties had reached their maximum population (as of 1891) in 1851 or earlier. Depopulation continued in some areas into the twentieth century. Population growth in Scotland from 1861 to 1911 was largely confined to narrow areas around the cities of Glasgow, Edinburgh, Dundee, and Aberdeen. Without rapid growth in these urbanized areas Scotland's overall population would have declined, just as in Ireland (Anderson and Morse 1993a, b). Longstaff thought that rural depopulation was under way or at least imminent not only in the United Kingdom but in France, Norway, Italy, and elsewhere (p. 411). Rural depopulation in England owed more to migration from agricultural districts than to the low birthrates so important in Ireland. Elsewhere, as in the

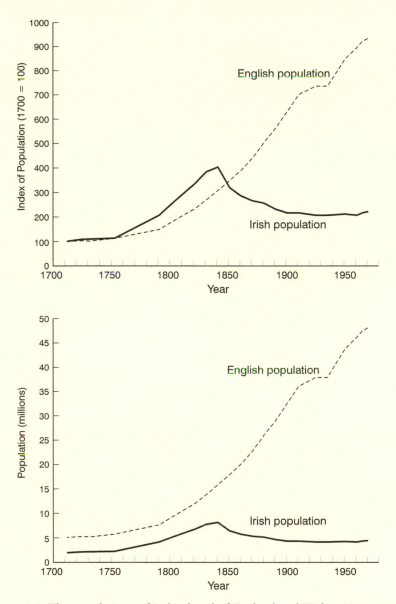

Figure 1.1 The populations of Ireland and of England and Wales, 1821–1971. The upper panel uses index numbers (1700 = 100) to compare the growth of the two populations. The lower panel is in millions of people to show absolute sizes of populations. (*Sources:* Ireland for pre-1821 data are Clarkson's estimates as reported in Mokyr and Ó Gráda 1984, table 1; for 1821 and later, estimates are from the official census, as reported in Vaughan and Fitzpatrick 1978, table 3. England and Wales, pre-1821 data are estimates by Wrigley and Schofield 1981, table A3.1; for 1821, estimates are from the official census as reported in Mitchell 1980, series B1.)

northern Portuguese communities studied by O'Neill and Brettell, population declines followed from emigration and reduced marriage, the pattern in Ireland. Today the rural regions of industrial countries find it increasingly difficult to keep their population on the land. Between 1980 and 1990 in the United States, for example, the state of Iowa lost over 8 percent of its rural population.[1]

Depopulation was thus not something specific to rural Ireland. The assertion or assumption of Ireland's uniqueness is, however, a quite general phenomenon. Rhodes (1992, p. xi), for example, begins her study of Irish women with the comment that "studies of Irish society show it to have characteristics which range from the unusual to the unique to the positively perverse." Every society is unique, almost by definition: no two societies share all the characteristics that define a group of people. As a literal description there is nothing harmful about claims of Irish uniqueness. Underlying the claim, however, is often an unstated assumption that we need not explain the demographic behavior of Ireland because, after all, it was populated by the Irish. Such an assertion, stated or not, is incorrect. Ireland's historical development was the result not of Hibernian perversity, but of the way the people there made their lives in often difficult circumstances.

The basic demographic facts at issue in Irish history are clear. Much of this study consists of looking more closely at details, or criticizing and reformulating explanations for those demographic facts. Since this process of refinement can become complicated, an overview of Ireland's demographic adjustment may help the reader keep basic issues in mind. Chapter 4 will return to nineteenth-century population history in a more detailed and systematic way.

Irish depopulation reflects the emergence after the Great Famine of a distinctive demographic regime. Western European populations always had relatively high ages at first marriage and a considerable proportion of adults who never married. In most of early-modern and modern western Europe marriage for women was rare before age 22 or so, and in each cohort some 10 to 20 percent of both sexes would never marry. The Irish took this western European marriage pattern to an extreme. Marriage had so declined in popularity that by 1911 about one-quarter of all adults in their fifties in Ireland had never married. This retreat from marriage may be the most famous element of Irish demographic behavior, and probably accounts for its unwarranted reputation as unique. A second feature of Ireland's distinctive demographic conditions reflects not change but a pace of change that was, relative to other European countries, very slow. The second half of the nineteenth century witnessed a dramatic fertility transition in most of western Europe. This transition, which refers to married couples' adoption of voluntary contraceptive practices, greatly reduced the number of children born to a typical marriage. Ireland's fertility transition was in comparison late and modest. The combination of large families but many unmarried adults gave Ireland a relatively low birthrate at the turn of the twentieth century, but this low birthrate was achieved in a way very different from the low birthrates obtaining in England, France, or Germany at the same time. Elsewhere more people married but had ever-smaller families; in Ireland families themselves became rarer, and their size declined more slowly. Another element of demographic systems in other countries, children born to unwed mothers, was very rare in Ireland. Finally, emigration from Ireland increased during the Famine and remained extensive afterward. The rate of emigration from Ireland was often higher than for any other European country during the second half of the nineteenth century. Though high by any standards, Ireland's emigration rates were very high for a country with such a low birthrate. Without emigration Ireland's population would have grown, albeit more slowly than many other places in Europe. But with such high emigration rates, the result was that in most years fewer Irish people were born than were lost to Ireland through death or through emigration.

None of the elements of this system—the rarity of marriage, large families, or extensive emigration—was unique to Ireland. As we shall see, one can always find counterparts to Ireland in each of these dimensions taken alone. Likewise, none of these elements represented any behaviors that were new or bizarre by European standards. The point warrants stressing because much of the historiography tries to find specifically Irish reasons for behaviors that were widespread. The only thing unique about Ireland's post-Famine demographic system was the combination of these three factors. And while the combination makes this period of Irish history fascinating, the fact that no single feature of Irish demographic behavior was unique undermines any case for Hibernian perversity and invites a more careful search for an explanation of Irish population trends.

DEPOPULATION AND ITS DISCONTENTS

After decades of concern about the world's rapid population growth, we may find it difficult to comprehend why low birthrates and depopulation were viewed as cause for alarm. Low birthrates and concomitant or potential depopulation emerged as an important political and social issue in western Europe toward the end of the nineteenth century. Worried discussion of this possibility has continued off and on virtually ever since. In most cases the debate concerned slow population growth, rather than depopulation as in Ireland, but the issues are similar. The French became acutely aware during the late nineteenth century that their rate of population growth was much slower than that of their neighbors—and sometime enemies—the Germans and the English. In works with titles like *Dépopulation et Civilisation* writers such as the influential French demographer Arsène Dumont called attention to two deleterious consequences of a smaller population. One danger was military. Slow population growth endangered the chance that the increasingly outnumbered French could ever enjoy their "hour of revenge" over the Germans (see Clément 1910, p. 46). Others argued from the position that a world with fewer French people was ipso facto a world less rich in cultural and scientific achievement. The historical demographer Hervé Le Bras (1991, p. 12) notes that French fear of population decline remains strong today, long after any military threat from Germany or other neighbors has disappeared and at a time when France's birthrates are no lower than those elsewhere in Europe.

A strong element in these population debates in some countries was a social Darwinist fear that the "wrong" people were reproducing and that the "right" people were not. In the United States this view took the form of concern that the somewhat higher fertility of African-Americans would turn a minority into the majority. This sort of thinking reached its hideous climax in the works of Nazi "intellectuals" who wrote of a *Geburtenkrieg* (war of births) or claimed that the Germans were, because of their declining birthrates, a *Volk in Gefahr* (a people in danger) (Danzer 1943; Helmut 1939). Nazi propaganda stressed the higher birthrates of some peoples considered inferior to Germans or otherwise enemies of the Reich. One can easily mock the crude racial stereotypes of Nazis and their sympathizers, but to do so risks missing the deep intellectual and cultural wells from which their population ideology drew. By the late nineteenth century Germany had a well-developed, intellectually and socially respectable eugenics movement, complete with university professors and other members of the upper middle class. Discussions of "racial hygiene" enjoyed the respect of prominent academics such as Schmoller and Sombart.[2] Germany was alone only in the horrifying consequences of this kind of thinking—not in the prevalence of the thinking.

Much of western Europe now has fertility patterns that imply eventual population decline (Bourgeois-Pichat 1986, table 1). Polish fertility, which so exercised Nazi propagandists, is nearing below-replacement levels, and recent projections assign Germany and Poland similar growth rates (UN Development Program 1994, table 45, p. 201). Concern over population decline today has somewhat different sources than in the nineteenth century. We worry less about military strength and more about the social and economic consequences of an older population. Reacting to possible depopulation, French demographers write of *La tragédie de la France* while Germans pose the question *Sterben Wir Aus?* (Are we dying out?). Yet the fact that population decline seems confined, at least now, to wealthy countries in Europe (or of European extraction) infuses even these discussions with overtones of racial or cultural chauvinism. One French writer, for example, claims that Europeans have a responsibility to themselves and to the world to produce more children. The loss of Germany would mean the loss "of the people who brought forth Luther, Göthe, Kant, Mozart, Planck, and Einstein" (Chaunu 1988, p. 147).

These population declines may well turn out to be small and temporary, and the histrionics surely reflect something other than serious fears of the disappearance of the Germans from central Europe. Yet underlying the melodrama are real issues concerning the implications of a declining population for social and economic conditions. A shrinking population will also become older. In 1980, half the population of the United States was 29 or older. According to one sober projection, if fertility rates persist at their current low levels, by the year 2100 half the U.S. population will be 50 or older (Coale 1986, table 2). The implications of this population aging for social insurance schemes is a topic of lively debate, one that is if anything too circumscribed. A population with this age structure calls into doubt the continued existence, at least in their current form, of many programs and institutions.

A few nineteenth-century Irish observers were concerned about the military implications of a smaller population. Irish soldiers had long been overrepresented in British armies, and Europe in the second half of the nineteenth century looked less peaceful to contemporaries than it does to us. The United States, moreover, its army swollen and confident after the defeat of the Confederacy, alarmed more than a few Europeans. The *Ulster Examiner* worried in 1874 that "[s]hould the Stars and Stripes ever appear in hostile form at Galway or Bearhaven," the graziers and bullocks who had displaced Ireland's people would be unable to defend the realm.[3] Concern over depopulation in Ireland more often focused on its consequences for life in the countryside and what it said about the Irish as a people. Many drew attention to the effects of reduced populations on the ability to maintain churches and schools. Rural depopulation was a vicious circle. A smaller population made it more difficult for a remote area to maintain an attractive social and cultural life for its people, particularly its young people, which made emigration all the more likely. Rural Ireland had become in some eyes, at least by the mid-twentieth century, bleak: "We were impressed by the unanimity of views presented to us in the evidence on the relative loneliness, dullness, and general unattractive nature of life in many parts of rural Ireland at present" (Commission on Emigration and Other Population Problems 1954, p. 175). A second theme is more specifically Irish. Irish leaders, including those of the Roman Catholic Church, displayed profound ambivalence about the emigration that was such an important cause of depopulation. Most leaders understood that emigrants were simply seeking a better life, and accepted the fact. At the same time, however, some ritual condemnation of the land-tenure system was heard, and the British government was widely viewed as the ultimate cause of Ireland's economic problems. Others viewed emigration in moral and religious terms. Anti-emigration propaganda stressed the moral dangers of a country such as the United States, with its large cities, anonymous society, and relatively small and uninfluential Catholic Church. If Ireland was holiest among nations then leaving it posed dangers for the soul. Schrier (1958, pp. 54–64) provides a good illustration of the ambivalence. He discusses the complicated view of emigration in the eyes of newspapers editors, politicians, and clergy. He also notes that newspapers often strongly opposed emigration but were happy to profit from carrying advertisements for ships that carried emigrants abroad (ibid., pp. 179–180, n. 1). Ryan (1955, p. 187) comments that even the Commission on Emigration and Other Population Problems, writing in the 1950s, "had some difficulty in passing judgement on the desirability of emigration."

Miller (1985, 1990) has constructed an interesting interpretation of this ambivalence as it played out during the nineteenth century. He argues that many Catholic emigrants in particular thought of themselves as having left Ireland not for the mundane reasons of increased economic opportunity overseas—the simple truth for the vast majority—but because they had been forced into a sort of exile. The putative powers behind the exile were the usual suspects of British misrule, landlords, and the Protestant ascendancy. We shall see in the next two chapters that to the extent these three powers played any role in Ireland's emigration, it was more subtle and indirect than might be thought. Miller argues that this misinterpretation of emigration's causes was both psychologically and socially important because it allowed the emigrant as well as those in positions of authority in Ireland to ignore the simple fact that people were leaving Ireland because of straightforward transformations in the Irish economy, much of it effected by and the source of economic advancement for middle-class Catholics.

Ireland's low birthrate caused similar ambivalence. French writers understood that their country's feeble population growth was due to small families rather than to the emigration or high celibacy rates that were so important in Ireland.[4] In Ireland there was widespread appreciation of the fact that the relatively low frequency of marriage, rather than contraception, was responsible for the low birthrate. Ireland's celibacy put the Roman Catholic clergy in an especially uncomfortable position. Catholic teaching advocated early and universal marriage for all lay people. But marriage in western Europe was nowhere early and universal, and Ireland's priests often came from the rural classes who were least likely to marry. Most clergy doubtless understood their parishioners' motivations in refraining from marriage. The available evidence on religion and marital status suggests that other Christian churches in Ireland experienced something quite similar.

Depopulation in Ireland, as in France, led to discussion of "race suicide": a population's extinction through its refusal to reproduce. Race suicide emerged as a prominent theme in several countries at the turn of the century. In the United States the term usually referred to the alleged slow reproduction of the "old immigrants" (those from western and northern Europe) and their descendants, which threatened to turn the country into a nation of eastern and southern Europeans. No such thing was happening at the time, of course (King and Ruggles 1990); as in the Nazi literature, fear of the consequences of demographic patterns had little or no basis in reality. The United States even spawned a brief discussion on the more focused question of whether the Irish in America were dying out.[5] In France, commentators blamed low fertility on those too selfish to place the nation above individual interests, who preferred social status or material goods to a third or fourth child. Bertillon (1911, p. 307) said for France, "[T]he nation is dying slowly, and individuals are not suffering from it."

A stronger theme in Irish discussions is one of profound disquiet, the sense that there was something very wrong with a society whose young people would rather leave or remain single than to marry and produce new members of that society. After castigating the usual villains—landlords, the English, sometimes members of nonfarming classes in Ireland—commentators lapse into brooding complaints to the effect that they simply do not know what is wrong with, or in, Ireland. In his contributions to *The Vanishing Irish: The Enigma of the Modern World* O'Brien sometimes resorts to hysterical recitations, often backed by cleverly drawn graphs, of the reasons for the imminent disappearance of the Irish people from the face of the earth. Consider, for example, the odd comparison: "Economists and sociologists are agreed that, if this ominous trend continues, in another century the Irish race will have vanished much like the Mayans, leaving only their monuments behind" (1953, p. 13). This claim by itself reflects O'Brien's preference for hyperbole. At the time he wrote, Ireland's population decline had slowed dramatically.

O'Brien's essays and those of his contributors also reflect a certain degree of Hibernian chauvinism. Yet behind the overstated claims of doom and the formulaic recitations of Ireland's unique virtues lies the more sober sentiment implicit in the suicide metaphor: why would the population of a country facing no overt economic crisis decline by a third?

MALTHUS AND IRELAND

No historian or social scientist interested in population matters can escape the intellectual influence, good or ill, of Thomas Robert Malthus. Malthus wrote numerous books, pamphlets, articles, and letters, but he is best known for his *Essay on Population*, first published in 1798. His influence in intellectual and policy circles today can be seen in many ways. Much recent historical demography, particularly studies of pre-industrial societies, draws explicitly on Malthus's thought. Perhaps the best example of this style of research is Wrigley and Schofield's masterly *Population History of England* (1981), which advances a frankly Malthusian interpretation of English population during the three centuries prior to the industrial revolution. Malthusian thinking also has a very strong influence among policymakers and academics—economists usually excepted, ironically—concerned with developing countries. Many claims about the danger of overpopulation boil down to agreeing with Malthus that living standards must decline as the number of people grows beyond a certain point. The U.S. National Academy of Sciences devoted an entire report to arguing that the evidence for Malthusian interpretations of population problems is less clear than one would think given the number of people who have been persuaded (National Research Council 1986). Malthus's influence on thinking about Irish population history can hardly be overstated. More than one historian has summed up Irish history as a sort of Malthusian morality tale (for example, Grigg 1980, chapter 10).

The term "Malthusian" has lost any precision as his name has been affixed to various political and intellectual currents. In one particularly ironic example, during the late nineteenth century Malthus's name was attached both to political groups agitating for the availability of contraceptives and for the general development of low birthrates themselves. Trying to be more consistent with his own argument, I will use the term Malthusian more narrowly. His statements come down to two assertions about the relationship between numbers of people and economic conditions. First, the number of people in a country affects living standards. A given territory with given resources can only produce so much food and other necessities of life. That is, an increased population adversely affects income per person. Second, economic conditions work to limit population size in two distinct ways. If a population grows too large, then the "positive check to population"—wars, famine, epidemic—causes an increase in death rates. The "preventative check" is more benign, and much of Malthus's writing concerns ways to strengthen the operation of this check. The preventative check works through marriage. As a population grows too large, living standards decline, and young people defer marriage out of concern about their ability to support a family. Later marriage reduces the birthrate. Malthus thought that contraception, the limitation of births within marriage, was morally wrong, and his model more or less assumes away contraception as a practical alternative. Less precise statements about Malthusian thought often neglect the important point that to Malthus, the only desirable way for the economy to influence numbers was through the preventative check.

Malthus paid little attention to the possibility that economic conditions could affect population growth through their influence on the biology of reproduction itself. In his model, biological forces only brought death, and reproduction was regulated by purely human agency. Some historical demographers question this view and its acceptance by later scholars. Komlos, for example, has argued that chronic malnutrition can significantly reduce fertility (Komlos 1989). Although this mechanism may be important in some contexts, evidence discussed below suggests that most Irish were relatively well fed after the Famine.

The operation of Malthus's preventative check presupposes a society in which young adults refrain from marriage until they can establish and support a household independent from their parents. This household-formation system is not common to all societies. Hajnal has noted that in a large area of northern and western Europe, household-formation practices were especially favorable to the preventative check. Marriage ordinarily entailed a new household and the severing of economic ties with both spouses' parents (Hajnal 1965, 1982). This household-formation system accounted for what Hajnal called the "western European marriage pattern" of a relatively late age at marriage for each sex combined with a significant number of people who never married at all. The need to establish economic independence before marrying produced a relatively late age at marriage, and some people never had the resources to marry. Because Hajnal's explanation for this behavior is an elaboration of Malthus's preventative check I shall refer to this explanation as "neo-Malthusian."[6]

Ireland's population history seems made to order as an illustration of Malthus's ideas. Writing before the Famine, Malthus claimed that the preventative check had little force in Ireland, so "the checks to population of course are chiefly of the positive kind" (Malthus 1927, I:278).

Had he lived to the late 1840s Malthus probably would have seen in the Famine a particular nasty form of the positive check made necessary by the extreme growth of population in Ireland since the mid-eighteenth century. And in the role of reduced marriage in the post-Famine depopulation Malthus would have seen the admirable, if belated, adoption of the preventative check. Kenneth Connell, Ireland's foremost demographic historian, put it this way: "Malthus defined his 'preventative check' as 'a restraint from marriage from prudential motives, with a conduct strictly moral during the period of this restraint.' He could scarcely have wished for a more meticulous or a more sustained demonstration of its effects than that experienced in the Irish countryside since the Famine" (Connell 1957, p. 88).

Writing later, Dupâquier (1981, p. 175) remarked that the post-Famine Irish behaved as if they kept Malthus's *Essay* at their bedsides. Despite its appeal, however, Malthus's view (and more recent versions of his model) does not provide an adequate account of much of Ireland's population history. Mokyr (1985) has cast serious doubt on Malthusian interpretations of the Great Famine itself. He has shown both that Ireland was not over populated in any simple sense at the time of the Famine and that the more densely populated areas of Ireland were not really the poorest. There have been several critiques of Mokyr's analysis, often focusing on the way he made adjustments to account for differences in the quality of land. Whatever the merit of these criticisms, however, Mokyr's research has made it much more difficult to tell simple Malthusian stories about the Famine.[7] A similar Malthusian interpretation of the post-Famine period is no more accurate. If Malthus was right about the working of the preventative check it would take a considerable deterioration in living standards to dissuade so many Irish from marrying. Yet the Irish economy did not deteriorate during the period between the Famine and the First World War. Although there were serious crises and some regions suffered badly at times, the incomes of average Irish people more than doubled between 1850 and 1914. A simple version of the Malthusian view, in other words, is simply wrong.

Malthusian interpretations of Irish population history are more than historically inaccurate, they are unhelpful. This seems an odd comment; if a theory is wrong, need one say more? Many theories serve the useful purpose of illuminating important features of a problem, even if they do not, in the end, provide a satisfying explanation of the facts. Malthusian models are unhelpful—for Irish history, at least—because thinking along the lines suggested by Malthus's model does not help us to isolate and explain the important features of Ireland's history. Imagine for a moment that the Irish population *was* too large for the economy to support. What would we expect to happen? Malthus would expect increased permanent celibacy, as took place. As economic conditions became worse, young people would find it harder to establish their own households. He might also expect to see some of the emigration that in fact occurred. Malthus was prepared to view emigration as a response similar to the preventative check, although he placed little faith in emigration's ability to provide lasting checks to population growth. But to say there would be both reduced marriage and increased emigration is hardly helpful. Would emigration increase slightly and half the population not marry? Or would half the population leave and most of those who remained marry?

Malthusian thought also provides little guidance in understanding why Ireland's population history was so different from that of France or England. By 1900 France and England had low birthrates that were a consequence of reduced family sizes. Ireland's low birthrates reflected a different set of choices. What can a Malthusian model tell us about why France and England went one way, and Ireland, the other? Given that a low birthrate is a good thing, can the Malthusian model help us to understand why a demographic adjustment would take place through emigration, reduced marriage, or changes in family sizes? The answer is plainly no; Malthusian models tell us nothing more precise than the two general statements of the relation between population and resources outlined at the outset.

Any interpretation of Ireland's population history must start by considering the research undertaken by Connell. In a book on pre-Famine Ireland and a series of articles on post-Famine society, Connell outlined a logically coherent, sweeping account of the economic and social forces underlying post-Famine economic adjustment. Connell's basic approach was Malthusian, but he grafted onto that scheme a more subtle tale that drew in specifically Irish themes such as the Famine, land tenure, and the role of emigration. Central to his account of post-Famine Ireland was the rise of a form of arranged marriage called "the Match." Subsequent research has not been kind to Connell's interpretations. In some instances his basic point of departure has been shown to be based on fragile evidence. In other instances he overgeneralized. Yet his interpretations warrant serious consideration. Much recent research has been motivated by attempts to confirm or refute his views, and in the absence of any other integrated interpretation Connell's story makes a useful starting point.

Central to Connell's story is land, particularly the inheritance of land and the laws and practices governing land tenure. Placing land at the center of Ireland's population drama was in many ways an extension to demographic history of land's central role in many other branches of Irish historiography. In Connell's view, changes in the way families transmitted farms from one generation to the next led to the creation of a distinct new form of post-Famine household organization. He thought the new inheritance regime reflected, in part, changes in the legal status of Irish farmers that gave them better property rights in their holdings. The result was a type of family that European historiography (though not Connell) called the stem family. Under this system the family's land was passed undivided to a single son. Given Ireland's large families the stem family implied a significant number of surplus siblings, many of whom would have to emigrate to find a livelihood. Connell argued that post-Famine demographic change reflected changes in property rights to land in Ireland and the way families reacted to those changes. The emerging stem-family system, in his view, accounted for both the widespread permanent celibacy and the extensive emigration of the post-Famine period.

POPULATION CHANGE, HOUSEHOLDS, AND THE LIFE CYCLE

My approach to population change after the Famine, in contrast, is based on thinking about demographic patterns as the outcome of individual behaviors motivated by Irish men and women's efforts to make their way in the world. Many historians and social scientists are uncomfortable with this explicit focus on individual behavior, grounded as it is in economics. They fear, with some reason, a mechanistic appeal to rationality and supposedly universal goals, divorced from much appreciation of the historical context in question. My contention is that by grounding the discussion in individuals and their behaviors one can formulate precise and meaningful arguments without ignoring historical or social context. Why the focus on individuals or couples? Because, quite simply, aggregate demographic patterns reflect the decisions of individuals. More than a truism, this statement is a prescription for avoiding at least some mistaken forms of argument. Consider an example. Some writers have claimed that the English used one way to reduce their birthrates (control of marital fertility), while the Irish used another (refraining from marriage). Neither statement is really true. Neither "the English" nor "the Irish" did anything about their society's birthrates. Individual and couples could only make decisions about their own birthrates. Young people in England were more likely to marry and to have small families. Perhaps some people in each society thought about overall birthrates (or, in Ireland, marriage rates), and there are doubtless some ways in which a high or low aggregate birthrate might influence a couple's fertility decisions. But in both countries young people were responding to signals about the implications of certain decisions for their own lives. To say that the Irish used a particular method to reduce their birthrates implies that young people decided to refrain from marriage because the national birthrate was too high, which imparts to individuals a willingness to make considerable sacrifice in the name of a social goal toward which their decision will make little contribution.

Some will argue that once one has adopted an approach based on individuals, one cannot give adequate credit to extra-individual factors such as cultural or social norms. The criticism is valid. Economists do not always have an explicit place for culture in their models, and are sometimes quite brusque about ignoring it outside their models. The most common approach to culture in economic works is to treat culture as a constraint, in the sense that devout Muslims do not eat pork. Yet this need not be the case. As Engerman (1978) notes, economists often employ a more subtle notion of culture without really acknowledging the fact.

I will refer to individuals who make decisions such as emigrating or marrying, and presume that their decisions reflect their evaluation of what is best under the circumstances. They emigrate if that will make them better off and marry if that will make them better off. This evaluation of what is best need not be as constricting as critics sometimes charge. We do not have to presume that the potential migrant had perfect knowledge of the future (either in Ireland or elsewhere) and later chapters discuss the implications of uncertainty for both migration and marriage decisions. A person can make rational decisions about issues on which she has incomplete information. Nor do we have to assume that the person in question is selfish in any simple sense. Many people doubtless remained in Ireland out of a sense of loyalty to family. Economists have little trouble understanding a person who sacrifices income for something else. In a related vein, treating individuals as the unit of analysis does not preclude dealing with the interactions among groups of individuals. Few economists would be surprised to hear that what other people thought and said influenced young people in Ireland, or that the number of people leaving Ireland in any year depended on the number of previous emigrants and the dense networks of information built up over the years. Nor do I assume that income is all that matters even in an economic sense. The central weakness of Malthusian models, in my view, is that they ignore the fact that many important "economic" goals have little to do with considerations such as income. Most important, our discussions of Irish households and people only makes sense if we visualize the decisions as the people of the day saw them. Thus to the extent social norms constrained thinking and decision making, those norms must be made part of the account. The analysis is only useful if it incorporates what Hammel (1990, p. 456) has called "culturally smart microeconomics."

Finally, I should make clear at the outset that saying a person chose X over Y does not imply that the person particularly liked X and did not wish there were some other choice available. That is, to talk about people choosing what is best for them under the circumstances is not to imply that they were excited about their options. This seemingly obvious point warrants repeating because it is often misconstrued. In this book I will argue that some seemingly unappealing demographic choices reflected the Irish people's evaluations of their best options under the circumstances. I do not mean to imply that they did not wish they had other options.

What Do Households Do?

The notion of a household lies behind much of what is discussed in this book. Before examining the particulars of households' structures and changes in those structures over time, it is worth pausing to consider several general issues about households. Here I outline two different but complementary visions of households, a combination of which inform later discussions.

I draw on several elements of Gary Becker's economic framework to understand demographic and household behavior. He views the household as a voluntary association of individuals who expect to be better off from their association through scale economies and gains from "trade." The decision to enter into this association forms the core of his analysis of marriage. Once formed, households allocate time and other resources to maximize the joint well-being of the household. One strand of Becker's analysis focuses on the trade-offs implicit in the various ways to produce a given good required by a household. To produce food, for example, one can combine market goods and household time in different combinations ranging from a restaurant meal (where the only time required is that needed to consume the meal) to purchasing unprocessed foods and making a meal in the home, from scratch. Changes in the relative costs of household time and of market goods and services will change not only the goods the household consumes and in what quantities, but also how it produces those goods.[8] A second strand in Becker's research focuses on the gains from household membership, and how changes in those gains imply decisions to join a household (marry) or to leave a household (for our purposes, children leaving home). Several aspects of Becker's theory of the household have been criticized, and the discussion here echoes those criticisms at points. His focus on the household as a maximizer of the joint well-being of all members presumes a benevolent dictator hard to reconcile with much of what we know about households and families. Some households may be run by benevolent dictators, but a more general approach sees household members as bargaining with one another for what they want. The bargaining reflects what each member wants, the power each member has within the household, and the limits of what people see as appropriate behavior within families—that is, the norms of family behavior. Other critics have noted that in discussing gains from trade in particular, Becker tends to assume that the sexual division of labor observed in twentieth-century urban societies is fixed by nature. Such thinking does not get us far in rural Ireland in the nineteenth century. The discussion of marriage in chapter 7 will pay more careful attention to substantive differences between men and women that affect potential gains from trade upon marrying. Some differences are biological, yes; men cannot bear children. Yet other gains from trade in marriage result from differential skills men and women acquire as they are raised in a given society.

A second way to think about a household is more concrete, focusing on what it does. The rubric "household" describes an institution that takes different forms at different times and in different places. Nonetheless we can distinguish several functions households can perform, without asserting that they do perform any particular function in a given society:

Consumption. Most consumption takes place within the context of a household, with goods and services allocated among household members and often consumed communally. The household usually provides the labor necessary to transform goods purchased from markets, or obtained from farms or through hunting, into edible food and other consumables (such as clothing). As consumption units, households create economies of scale and encourage a division of labor among individuals that allows greater efficiency in obtaining consumables and transforming them into final products.

Production. Households may be centers of production both for their own consumption and for markets, whether local or distant. Examples relevant to Ireland include farms and households controlling shops or performing artisanal activities such as black-smithing. Household production may provide the bulk of household income, or it may be a sideline for some members. Many rural Irish women of the nineteenth century, for example, raised poultry for eggs and meat to supplement household incomes.

Reproduction. Households that include a procreating couple are the locus of reproduction. This entails not just sexual intercourse and childbirth, but provision for child and mother while the latter's child-rearing responsibilities leave her unable to provide for herself. Again, as reproduction units households enjoy some economies of scale. A division of labor, whether it is sexual (women performing most child care) or generational (aged people caring for children while their parents do other tasks), may enhance the household's efficiency as a reproductive unit.

Intergenerational transfers. The human life cycle, with its beginning in dependency and with renewed dependency for many aged people, requires mechanisms whereby people who are not producing goods and services at a given time can still consume those resources. Households are often important for their role in managing these intergenerational transfers. Transfers from parents to children are important and have already been mentioned in discussing reproduction. Equally important are transfers from young adults to aged household members. Intergenerational transfers within households can be divided into two types: flows of goods and services primarily related to current consumption, and the transfer of assets from one generation to the next, sometimes in return for promises of support. A related function is provision for others who, because of disease or other infirmity, cannot provide for themselves.

In addition to these "economic" functions, households also serve as one of the places where people, especially children, are socialized, learning the "rules" of human society.

This chapter and the chapters to come emphasize the diversity of households and their role in performing these functions. Households in Ireland took many forms, from large multigenerational affairs to a middle-aged man with a sibling. Households' role in fulfilling their functions varied just as much. Many households, clearly, played no reproductive role, and the heterogeneity of farms and other household activities suggests as much diversity in households as in productive units. Some households consisted of one generation only, making it necessary (as is increasingly the case in the West in the late twentieth century) for intergenerational transfers to take place outside the household. These households are evidence that there are different ways to organize the tasks they undertake. Households in a given society organize consumption, production, reproduction, and intergenerational transfers in a specific way. Households in other societies may not play much of a role in one or more of these functions—households have lost most of their production role in industrial societies—and there are alternative or substitute ways of organizing each of these tasks. By the end of the nineteenth century many households in rural Ireland did not have a married couple or that couple's children, but they were households just the same, and played many of the roles played by households centered on conjugal couples.

Thematic Overview

The issues considered in the chapters to come are highly interrelated. Sketching them before delving into specifics will help us to bear in mind the whole as we examine the parts.

Marriage and Nonmarriage

Ireland's most distinctive demographic trait was its very high level of permanent celibacy. ("Celibacy" is a demographer's term meaning "never married." The term is not meant to imply that unmarried people never had sex, although that seems close to the truth in rural Ireland. Illegitimacy was rare. And by calling celibacy at age 45 or 55 "permanent" we do not intend to imply that marriage after this age never happened, although it too was rare.) By 1911 nearly one-quarter of both males and females in their late forties or early fifties had never married and were unlikely ever to do so. The decline of marriage forms the heart of what Birdwell-Pheasant (1992, p. 228) has so aptly called the "gloom and doom" school of Irish history. Ireland's marriage patterns during the late nineteenth century have struck some as evidence that Ireland was a peculiar place. Thus marriage forms a common starting point for exceptionalist views of Irish history.

Systematic discussions of Ireland's post-Famine marriage patterns tend to rely on Malthusian arguments. But Malthusian interpretations of Irish marriage patterns quickly encounter an empirical problem. To believe Hajnal, or Malthus, there is only one reason why young people would not marry: because they could not afford to do so. I have already noted some general qualms about this notion, and we shall consider them at several points in this study. This critique of Hajnal and Malthus arose with regard to Ireland's celibacy for the simple reason that celibacy became more and more common at a time when the Irish were becoming more and more prosperous. The historiography of Ireland's nuptiality patterns has proposed several explanations. Several observers have suggested that some of the change reflects subtle changes in regional population patterns as well as in changes in the distribution of income. More common, however, is the claim that tastes simply changed: that as the nineteenth century wore on, the income the Irish thought they needed in order to marry rose more rapidly than income. Economists are rightly suspicious of explanations that rely on changes in tastes. By claiming that aspirations rose more rapidly than income one can make an economic crisis out of virtually any experience. To the extent that historians have felt it necessary to explain this remarkable occurrence they have pointed to the fact that increasing numbers of Irish had family abroad and that economic and social change within Ireland itself increased the range of consumption goods available through the countryside. Both observations are potentially important, but neither explains why an Irish man or woman would remain in Ireland but not marry because he or she could not do so and live like his or her brother in New York. Nor do we know why the Irish grew to prefer bicycles and processed foods to children, sex, and family.

At a simpler level, it is difficult to reconcile this "change in tastes" argument with the easy emigration that created all those supposedly influential expatriate Irish communities. Emigration from Ireland was inexpensive by the late nineteenth century. Even those who could not raise the required passage money from relatives or friends could earn their way in a relatively short sojourn in Britain. So people who remained in Ireland and did not marry had in a real sense forgone the option to go to Liverpool, Boston, or Sydney. A man or woman who had never married and remained in Ireland at age 50 had made two important decisions: not to marry and not to emigrate. To understand these decisions we have to ask why staying seemed better than leaving, and why remaining single seemed better than marriage. This in turn suggests that the celibate life in Ireland held some attraction not obvious in the gloom-and-doom accounts. Chapter 7 considers this question in greater detail.

Migration and Emigration

Permanent celibacy may be nineteenth-century Ireland's most exotic demographic behavior, but emigration was certainly its most famous. At least since the early 1800s vast numbers of Irish people left their homes and made a new life in the many English-speaking countries overseas. The effect of emigration on Irish economic and demographic behavior can hardly be exaggerated. In 1900, people aged 45–54 who lived in Ireland represented less than half of those born in Ireland in 1845–1854. A proportion of those missing had, of course, died by 1900, but most were simply overseas.

Emigration influenced Irish demographic and economic behavior in several ways. Even without economic growth, depopulation would have raised the incomes of those who remained behind. Connell's argument about the effect of emigration on the development of the stem family after the Famine is echoed in more recent research. Emigration reflects the pull of a better life abroad, and this better life abroad made it easier for parents and children to agree that farms in Ireland would not be divided. More recent scholarship suggests that the "post-Famine" move away from subdivision had its origins before the Famine, but that distinction does not alter the fact that as opportunities abroad became better and better fewer young Irish people were willing to remain in Ireland for the sake of a tiny farm. Emigration also affected another famous aspect of Irish demographic behavior, family size. Although new research shows that fertility control was being adopted by Irish couples by the end of the nineteenth century, it is true that Irish marital fertility was high, by European standards, at the end of the nineteenth century. Several Irish scholars have argued convincingly that Ireland's fertility reflects the ease of sending surplus children abroad. French couples might have restricted fertility so that they could provide a good start in life for a smaller number of children. Irish couples simply had to buy the increasingly inexpensive passenger tickets for North America or Australia. This argument presumes, of course, that it was harder for French couples to send their children overseas to obtain that good life. I will argue that this was, in fact, the case.

Emigration had other, more subtle implications. Throughout this book I refer to the fact that those remaining in Ireland in the late nineteenth and early twentieth centuries were a "residual population." This phrase is not meant to agree with those who argued that emigration took from Ireland the best and most adventuresome, leaving behind people less able and fit to develop the country. Both historians and contemporaries have taken the latter idea seriously. Newspapers and parliamentarians alike often argued that those leaving Ireland were the best, "the same class who were the hope and the strength of other countries." The *Tipperary Advocate*'s complaint in 1883 that "the bone and sinew of the country [had] gone, gone to clear the forests of Nebraska and Ohio" was, aside from its fabrication of Nebraskan forests, boilerplate.[9] But the idea appealed to academics as well. In a 1914 essay on the implications of emigration, Professor Charles Oldham claimed that "there has been in Ireland a perpetuated survival of the unfittest, a steady debasement of the human currency—very similar to Gresham's Law, by which bad money continually tends to displace good money in circulation" (Oldham 1914, p. 214). Sir William Wilde's assessment of those who remained was more brutal, calling them "the poor, the weak, the imbecile and the insane."[10] Rather, any discussion of Irish culture must bear in mind that there were many Irish cultures, and that those who remained in Ireland had in some sense agreed to live within the confines of one variant on that culture. What we see in Ireland may be different from other countries in part because those who wanted to live a different type of life had left. Irish people interested in innovative behavior, in flouting conventional norms, were more likely to live in Irish-*America* or Irish-*Britain* than in Ireland itself: "The rebels left the country and the conformists were rewarded with dowry or land" (Connell 1968, p. 144). To the extent the Irish were distinctive, that distinctiveness reflects in part the decisions made by the large numbers of each generation who decided not to remain there.

Household Structure and Economic Objectives

A further theme of this book blends the concerns of economics and economic history with a long-standing interest of historical sociologists. Even when economists stopped treating households as black boxes whose formation and behavior could not be analyzed or understood, they remained uninterested in the structure of these important institutions. Historical anthropologists and sociologists, in contrast, have conducted long and spirited debates over the characteristics of household structure in Europe and elsewhere. And in recent years the lack of interest in household structure among economists and economic historians has largely changed. Problems associated with an aging population and its consequences for social insurance systems have brought economists to appreciate the importance of household structure, particularly as it relates to the way property is transferred between generations. Inheritance and bequests are now a central issue of debate among those interested in income and wealth inequality. Just as in nineteenth-century Ireland, it has become increasingly clear that a person's chances in life were strongly affected by who his parents were and what they were willing to do for him.[11] In a similar vein, economists interested in explaining bequests have come to the view that many "gifts" from parents to children resemble implicit intergenerational exchanges; parents reward children who provide them with assistance and care (Bernheim, Shleifer, and Summers, 1985). We shall touch on similar ideas as part of our consideration of Connell's stem-family argument.

The Aged and Relations between the Generations

A study of household dynamics raises another topical issue. All societies face a similar problem posed by a simple fact of the human life cycle. People require food, clothing, and other resources before they are physically capable of working, and many people live to an age at which they are no longer able to provide for their own needs. Thus any society has to organize some method whereby the young and the old can draw on resources when they are not actually producing. In most societies this problem is solved by means of a figurative intergenerational contract.

Parents care for their children as their parents cared for them. In modern industrial societies this intergenerational contract may be written into law, in the form of a social insurance system. In addition, in many societies (Ireland being a prime example), people control assets such as land that are crucial to being able to produce a living. Often the transmission of those assets involved a literal intergenerational contract. Even when it did not, the manner in which ownership and control of these assets is passed from one generation to the next is intimately connected both to support for children and the aged and to the demographic concerns at the heart of this book.

The problems of support for children and the aged are as old as human history. Recently, however, modern societies have faced a new and more difficult version of the problem, reflecting two fairly new developments. One is simply the aging of society noted earlier. Even if we ignore for a moment the particular mechanisms used to transfer resources to the aged, a population that has relatively more aged people will have less to spend for other ends. The second problem reflects the development of systems of public old-age support during the nineteenth and early twentieth centuries. Many European countries had, by 1914, some public system that provided at least a modicum of support for aged people. These systems were enacted when relatively small proportions of the population were old enough to qualify. Less than 3 percent of the English population was 70 years or older in 1911, just after the 1908 Old Age Pensions Act set 70 as the minimum age for a public pension. As populations have aged, these programs have become more expensive. In 1971 over 8 percent of the English population was 70 or older.[12] Clearly the expense of such programs depends on the level of benefits provided to the aged, and the precise economic impact of the system depends on subtle issues of how it is financed. The basic fact, however, is common to all countries with low birthrates: as populations age, old-age support systems enacted for earlier generations become more difficult to sustain.

The introduction of old-age pensions in the United Kingdom in 1908 brought to the fore another issue that seems strikingly familiar to people in industrial societies today. The old-age pension was financed out of general revenues, and eligibility depended primarily on age and on not being very wealthy. Ireland's poverty and age structure meant that Ireland had a much larger number of pensioners per capita than did England. The taxes that funded the pension were quite regressive. More than a few retired Irish farmers were probably wealthier than the English workers who paid the taxes to support the pension. Thus we see in 1908 an issue that forms the heart of many debates over social insurance schemes such as the U.S. Social Security system today. Programs based mostly on age imply transfers from one group to another. If the program is not designed carefully, transfers may be *from* the poor to those who are less poor.

Ireland's shrinking population resulted in a relatively aged population, producing these curiously modern problems in the nineteenth century. In 1901 over 6 percent of men and women in Ireland were at least 65 years old. The comparable figure for England and Wales was only 4.6 percent. The demographic patterns noted earlier entailed special problems related to old-age support. The high emigration rates meant that Irish parents saw many of their children leave Ireland and never return. Many parents received funds from their more prosperous children abroad, at least for a while. Out of sight was not necessarily out of mind. Yet parents of even large families could face the possibility of having none of their children alive and in Ireland when they needed assistance. More common was a lack of old-age support for people who did not marry and have their own children. People who lacked children had several other ways of arranging for support, including public programs (the Poor Law and later the old-age pension), and some relied on arrangements that I will call surrogate heirs.

New Departures

This is the first book-length treatment of the post-Famine population. Robert Kennedy's (1973) admirable study has a strong historical foundation and devotes some attention to the period covered here, but focuses more on the twentieth century. In the following chapters I discuss recent research that calls into question some of Kennedy's findings, but his achievement is still signifcant. Cormac Ó Gráda's *Ireland: A New Economic History*, which promises to be the standard economic history for decades to come, pays careful attention to demographic developments during the period covered here. But his study has a much larger scope and his discussion of some demographic issues is necessarily brief. This book tries as much as is practical to draw on and to integrate the findings of other scholars and to provide pertinent background for nonspecialists with the hope that it can serve as a comprehensive account of post-Famine demographic change.

This study is, however, first and foremost my own interpretation of population change in Ireland from the Famine to the First World War. In many respects my approach draws on and reflects the methods and ideas of other scholars. In other respects I have adopted a different approach.

New Sources

The most important aspect of this demographic history is the new empirical sources it uses. Much earlier Irish historiography failed to employ sources that were readily available, and recent revisionist histories have largely overcome this deficiency. Here much use will be made of a sample of households drawn from the 1901 and 1911 manuscript censuses of Ireland. This sample permits close study of households and household formation in four rural areas at the turn of the twentieth century. Unfortunately, few manuscript census schedules exist for earlier post-Famine decades, so this detailed look is confined to one specific period. To supplement this manuscript census sample I also use Ireland's published census. The printed census tables do not permit the same close examination of individual and household behavior, but they are invaluable for tracing long-term developments and examining geographical variation within Ireland.

Another important source of new empirical materials consists of the findings of the growing community of scholars interested in the issues considered here. These studies, some of which draw on the same 1901 and 1911 censuses to examine other regions in Ireland, yield crucial reference points for observations drawn from my own data. Modern research techniques that rely on amassing nominative data from census listings or other sources have opened up important doors to the past. Because no single scholar can adequately undertake this type of research for more than a few small areas, relying on other scholars' research permits a blend of the power of nominative sources with the need for sensitivity to regional diversity and distinctions. Furthermore, the disciplinary heterogeneity of those interested in this period of Irish history—some are social historians, some economic historians, others anthropologists—means that similar materials have been subjected to studies that have different disciplinary bases.

Comparative History

A second point of departure for this book is a firm comparative perspective. Assumptions of Ireland's uniqueness, as we have seen, cultivate an approach to Irish history that emphasizes exceptionalism rather than an attempt to understand Irish society.

The decline of marriage in post-Famine Ireland—a central issue here—makes an excellent example of the limitations of the exceptionalist approach. This demographic behavior was not unique to Ireland at the time. Several other European countries had very high numbers of unmarried adults at the turn of the twentieth century. No more unique to Ireland was Roman Catholicism, strong mother-son bonds, a dowry system, or many of the other factors that observers have claimed fully explain Ireland's demographic patterns. Yet historical accounts of Ireland's demographic patterns have, again and again, recited what are asserted to be completely singular patterns, and then invoked some form of irrationality to explain the otherwise unexplainable. Particularly troubling is a research methodology that identifies allegedly Irish demographic patterns and on this basis attempts to diagnose a uniquely Irish spirit, or even pathology, rather than ask how the pattern might reflect the ways Irish people met the exigencies posed by their situation.

Recent efforts in Ireland's social and economic history have quite usefully transcended this exceptionalist approach.[13] In the following chapters I seek to set Ireland's demographic experiences in their European context. The comparative perspective frees us from the search for a uniquely Irish spirit and leads to a search for forces and problems common to the history of Ireland and other countries. In addition, more careful comparative approaches serve to isolate that which truly was different about Ireland and thus aid in focusing more firmly on the details most worthy of attention. A comparative approach introduces its own problems, however. In the effort to compare Ireland with some other country or collection of countries there is a tendency to simplify Ireland almost to the point of stereotype to obtain a characterization of "Ireland" that lends itself well to clean comparisons with "England" or whatever the other place might be. The many local historical studies produced in the past twenty years or so demonstrate that Ireland—like, perhaps, anyplace—was a country of astounding regional diversity, making generalizations hazardous. Johnson (1990, p. 264) argues that this diversity can even be seen at the most local level, from "townland to townland." Thus in comparing Ireland with England we must beware that averages can deceive. Large regions of Ireland and England might be nearly identical. Yet England and France are at least as diverse as Ireland. The point of comparison is to highlight some feature of the Irish case, and not to draw literal parallels.

A comparative approach introduces another problem: with whom should we compare the Irish? The answer is not obvious, and I will try to make several comparisons wherever pertinent. England seems a natural comparison and was certainly on the minds of historical observers. Yet comparison with England may be as misleading as illuminating. By 1850 England was a very urban, industrialized country, its agriculture had a different structure, and the number of English people overseas was, in proportion to the Irish, very small. I suspect that much of Ireland's reputation for uniqueness comes from over-frequent comparisons with a country to which one should not expect much similarity. To avoid an overly "English" perspective we will keep in mind two sorts of comparisons. One comparison is with other large European countries, including France and Germany. The motivation for these comparisons is to contrast the Irish, who were by 1900 a tiny portion of all Europeans, with the experiences of larger countries whose populations might make more valid claims to European typicality. A second sort of comparison will be based on some a priori similarity to Ireland. Scotland naturally suggests itself, and will be mentioned frequently. Not only was Scotland also part of the United Kingdom, it shared certain elements of Ireland's cultural history. Scotland's demographic patterns were similar to Ireland's in many respects during the period discussed here, and recent research on Scotland's population history provides a firm basis for discussion. Several other European regions developed demographic patterns similar, at least in some respects, to those of the Irish. These regions will be mentioned from time to time to stress commonalities with Ireland.

Taking History Seriously

Writing demographic history makes special demands on the historian. The subject is inherently quantitative, and the data are often flawed or incomplete. Insufficient attention to statistical issues can, as we shall see, lead to serious errors of interpretation. Yet these requirements have sometimes led to a research style that emphasizes technical problems and sophisticated statistical methods over efforts to understand the history and society of the population in question. If we are to make progress in understanding demographic behavior in the past, that progress will emerge from research that views demographic events as outcomes of human behaviors, behaviors that require study as social scientists and historians.

   History in Ireland is fraught with special difficulties. Irish people have an unusual degree of historical awareness, which manifests itself most obviously in casual references to the historical roots of present-day political and religious conflicts. The modern Irish person's awareness of his history and his proclivity for thinking of his society in terms of its historical antecedents also extends to topics more central to the concerns of this book. Herein lies a subtle danger. Good historians are always both aware of historical continuities, such as the ways in which themes present in the eighteenth or nineteenth century continue in modern Irish life, and sensitive to the danger of anachronism, the assumption or assertion that a historical problem in one period is necessarily identical to the problem in another. Ireland's historians have nearly always blended this attention to continuity with the dictates of good history. Others—social scientists, journalists, and the person in the street—sometimes do not. Some observers, in particular, fail to recognize that behavior in the 1950s or 1960s, even if accurately described, may not tell us much about what transpired in the 1870s. In discussions of why people emigrated, or Ireland's marriage patterns, or the dynamics of rural households in the nineteenth century, even serious observers will sometimes attempt to justify their views by referring to their families in the 1950s or even later. Instead of analyzing the forces particular to a time and place—and, of course, considering the role of long continuities in the slow evolution of such behavior—one presumes that rural households in the 1950s are identical in their salient respects to those of the 1930s or even the 1870s. Sometimes this presumption is more or less explicit (if not at all defended). In *Inishkillane: Change and Decline in the West of Ireland*, Brody (1973) mixes discussions of the nineteenth century, the early twentieth century, and more recent periods, as if there was some "traditional" Ireland that remained unchanged for centuries, and is now not so much changing as dying. The genre is not unique to Ireland. Blythe's *Akenfield* (1969), a popular account of life in an English village in the 1960s, seems motivated by the presumption that the way of life under siege at that time had changed little for centuries. Sheehan (1989, p. 781) notes the generality of this phenomenon in a quite different context: "One of the characteristics of the modern condition seems to be each generation's belief that it stands just on the other side of a great divide between tradition and modernity."

This practice reaches its most egregious form in the uses for which various scholars have sometimes employed Arensberg and Kimball's *Family and Community in Ireland* (1968). This study is the product of fieldwork undertaken by two Harvard anthropologists in County Clare in the 1930s. As ethnography the work is magnificent.[14] Yet it is wise to recall that their study pertains to a specific farming region in a specific period. If we are to generalize from such observations, we must do so with due attention to the possible problems associated with such generalization. The historian can no more legitimately assume that Arensberg and Kimball's description of Clare farmers in 1930s would be an equally accurate description of Clare farmers in the 1870s than the sociologist can assert that Irish farming households were the same in the 1980s. Damian Hannan, an Irish sociologist whose work on change in rural communities shows great sensitivity to this problem, has rightly complained that "Arensberg and Kimball's study has been continuously reproduced as typical of Irish farm family and kin systems, even in the latest 'readers,' without clearly indicating its historical status and limited regional applicability."[15] Similar complications arise with uncritical use of sources such as Mogey (1947), which is an excellent study of rural life in Northern Ireland undertaken long after the period of our interest.

The greatest problem of anachronism for this book is failure to pay proper attention to the timing of economic and social changes that influenced demographic changes. Only by situating demographic behaviors clearly in the economic and social context of a period can we understand the causal connections between, for example, the selection of heirs and economic opportunities overseas. The nature of farm inheritance makes a good example. At the time of Arensberg and Kimball's fieldwork, the Great Depression in the United States had seriously reduced the attractiveness of the Irish emigrant's long-preferred destination. Thus Irish families could no longer so easily provide for noninheriting children by helping them to get started in the United States. The inheritance practices Arensberg and Kimball describe, and the roles for young unmarried people they found so unusual, are the products of a specific economic, historical conjuncture. The Irish family's basic normative framework—what parents and children expected from one another and for themselves, and how they tried to arrange their lives—probably evolved slowly, if at all, from the heyday of emigration in the 1880s to the 1930s. We must bear in mind that the Clare communities of the 1930s might have been subject to quite different forces than had been at work in the 1880s.

Women and Men

One of the great changes in historiography in recent decades has been the emergence of new subdisciplines focused on the history of previously neglected people such as women or racial minorities. Of this new historiography women's history is most relevant here. This book does not aim to be a contribution to women's history per se, but, given the subject matter, any discussion that failed to consider gender roles and their implications for young people's lives would be inadequate indeed. That said, one should not look here for a discussion of how gender roles are formed, which is beyond the scope of this study. Women and men are both clearly actors in any demographic story, and as Irish historians have emphasized, Irish women and men faced different options in life. Several recent studies of women in Irish society or among expatriate Irish communities have added considerably to our understanding of women's lives and their role in creating the demographic patterns of our study.[16] At the most obvious level, women's history has reminded all historians of the need to think about how differences between men and women—in status, in rights and responsibilities, in perceptions of what is important and what is not—shape both individual lives and relations between men and women.

Nineteenth-century Ireland was a place of profound differences in the roles accorded men and women. Women, as we shall see, were expected to take subordinate roles in virtually all aspects of life. This consideration must play some role in the way men and women viewed one another, and in particular, in the way Irish women viewed life as an Irish wife and mother. Chapter 5 examines the ages at which children left home and how this process was influenced by the child's gender, the gender of other children in the household, household wealth, and other factors. This examination shows that boys and girls were treated very differently by their households, and more interestingly, that the importance of other factors (such as household wealth) usually depended on the child's gender. Being male or female had a clear, substantive impact on one's life in Ireland.

An important and distinctive aspect of women's situations in post-Famine Ireland underlies much of the demographic story here. Unlike many women in some male-dominated societies, Irish women had an avenue of escape to societies that offered them comparative autonomy, if nothing like equality: the world of the emigrant. The representation of Irish women among emigrants was extraordinary. By the 1890s Irish female emigrants actually outnumbered male emigrants, a ratio nearly unknown among other emigrant flows at the time. One can hardly begin to understand demographic patterns in Ireland without an appreciation for the unusual role of Irish women in foreign labor markets. Consideration of this and other facets of female and male behavior will help us to understand Ireland's demographic transformation and the way it differed from changes taking place elsewhere.

ORGANIZATION OF THE BOOK

Much of this study will discuss the role of the economy in Irish demographic patterns. The next three chapters are background for the demographic story. Chapter 2 provides an outline of basic economic patterns in the period 1850–1914. Chapter 3 discusses two sets of institutions that figure heavily in discussions of demographic matters in Ireland, the state and the several churches. Chapter 4 surveys demographic patterns from the end of the eighteenth century through the First World War with the aim of fixing the patterns discussed in the following chapters. This chapter plays the double role of an extended essay on recent findings on the demographic history of this period.

Chapters 5–8 focus on the period toward the end of the nineteenth century and the beginning of the twentieth. These four chapters take advantage of sources available only late in the century to consider the central themes in post-Famine demographic change at the close of the period. Concentrating attention here is a bit like looking for one's keys under a lightpost because the light is best there, but with some care it is possible to take the specific lessons from the end of the period and tie them to the less complete evidence on the trends that characterize the entire period. Chapter 5 discusses the organization and dynamics of households and the way inheritance and the dispersal of children affected the conditions of the old and the young. Chapters 6–8 consider stages of the life cycle: leaving home (including emigration), marriage, and marital fertility. In the concluding chapter I tie these lessons into the experience of the entire post-Famine adjustment and Ireland's depopulation more generally.

A Word on Terminology

"Post-Famine" is one of those terms that is sufficiently vague so as to be widely used without authors being clear on what they and others mean by it. In this book it means the period between the Great Famine and the First World War. Other authors have used it to mean just the first few decades after the Famine. On a different matter, throughout this study I use nineteenth-century geographical place names. Thus the modern County Offaly is Kings, County Laois is Queens, and the city and county are Londonderry. Furthermore, by "Ulster" I mean the nine-county province of Ulster as it existed prior to the partition of Ireland. When I refer to the six Ulster counties that remain part of the United Kingdom I use the term Northern Ireland.

Chapter 2

THE RURAL ECONOMY IN THE
NINETEENTH CENTURY

> When I am tempted, as I sometimes am, to envy the extreme
> competence of colleagues engaged in writing ancient or
> mediaeval history, I find consolation in the reflexion that
> they are so competent mainly because they are so ignorant
> of their subject. The modern historian enjoys none of the
> advantages of this built-in ignorance. He must cultivate
> this necessary ignorance for himself.
> —Edward Hallett Carr, *What Is History?*

UNDERLYING the demographic developments that form the
subject of this book is a complex series of societal changes that
affected Ireland in the period under study. In this chapter and the
next, I briefly sketch the economic and social developments that set the
scene for our demographic story.[1] Three elements of Irish society are
most important to the story that follows. The first theme, Ireland's economic growth and transformation during the nineteenth century, forms
the subject of this chapter. This chapter also discusses two closely related
issues, agrarian conflict and land reform. The next chapter pursues two
further themes, the role of the state and of the churches.

BEFORE AND DURING THE FAMINE

The late eighteenth century witnessed two developments that would
force the Irish economy into a long process of adjustment. War disrupted
the production and shipping of grain in much of Europe, causing England to rely more heavily on Irish agricultural output. The increased
demand for Irish grain brought about sweeping changes in Irish agriculture. When those wars ended and Continental exports resumed, Ireland
was left with an agricultural sector inappropriate to the demands of the
time. The other important development was more specific to Britain. The
industrial revolution under way in Britain since the mid-eighteenth century lowered prices for a wide range of manufactured goods. Some man-

ufactured goods, especially cloth, had been produced for decades in Ireland by hand methods. This "proto-industry" was an important source of income for a large share of rural households. Eventually cheaper manufactured goods found their way to Ireland and deprived many in Ireland of their livelihoods.

Yet one of the paradoxes of the Irish economy at this time was that the same developments that caused so much pain also resulted in benefits for at least some. During the Napoleonic Wars English agriculture had undergone changes similar to those in Ireland. When peace returned in 1815 agricultural prices dropped, causing trouble for many English farmers. Parliament responded with the Corn Laws, tariffs on a wide range of (primarily agricultural) goods that succeeded in keeping agricultural prices in the United Kingdom above world prices until the laws' repeal in 1846. Irish farmers benefited from this tariff protection as did English farmers, and Ireland was spared an even more wrenching adjustment to the peacetime economy. The industrial revolution likewise brought benefits to some in Ireland. The prices of Irish manufactured imports declined relative to the price of Ireland's major export, agricultural goods (Ó Gráda 1994, table 7.7), which implies that trade with Britain increased Irish purchasing power over this period.

Despite imperfect evidence, historians concur that Irish agriculture had been primarily pastoral as late as the seventeenth century, meaning that most Irish land was devoted to raising sheep and cattle. The eighteenth-century disturbances in European grain markets drove prices much higher, making it more profitable to produce wheat, oats, and other grains. Solar (1987, app. table 2.17) shows that Irish grain prices more than doubled (in nominal terms) between the 1760s and the early nineteenth century. Some but not all of this price increase reflects a general wartime inflation.[2] Farmers responded by increasing grain acreage and to a smaller extent by bringing new lands under cultivation. By the time peace returned in 1815, Ireland was a major net exporter of grains and remained so in most years until the Famine (Solar 1987, app. table 6.11). Continued grain exports reflect the ability of the Corn Laws to shelter British and Irish markets from Continental competition (most Irish exports were to Britain). Reconversion of grain land to pasture up to the time of the Famine was slow, and did not become rapid until the repeal of the Corn Laws in 1846 and various post-Famine developments. In the absence of the Corn Laws Ireland would have been forced into a quicker reconversion of tillage to pasture, with a more rapid decline in the demand for agricultural labor, and a population crisis might have come to Ireland earlier in the nineteenth century.

The potato is central to any account of the pre-Famine economy and the impact of the Famine. The potato made its way to Ireland in the late sixteenth century and was widely diffused within the Irish countryside. Prior to the Famine potatoes accounted for about one-third of all the tilled land in Ireland. The potato was largely responsible for several features of the pre-Famine economy and for what occurred during the Famine itself. Potato cultivation played an important role in the crop rotations involving grains. The potato's second and indirect role was to support the large population of laborers necessary to work all the new arable land. The laboring population needed to eat something that would not displace more valuable crops. The potato filled in admirably: an acre's worth of potatoes produces far more calories than an acre's worth of any grain. No other crop known at the time could feed so many mouths on the output of an acre. But the potato had significant drawbacks that exacted a cost even before the Famine. Unlike most grains, the potato could not be stored for very long (Hoffman and Mokyr 1984, p. 134). Thus it was difficult to hold buffer stocks against the possibility of a poor harvest. Second, the potato is quite heavy in relation to its value, meaning that it cannot be transported very far (Hoffman and Mokyr 1984, table 1). The cost of transporting potatos discouraged the development of regional markets and removed an important form of insurance against local disaster.

The potato was widespread in several other European economies by the early nineteenth century. The same infestation that caused Ireland's Great Famine reduced potato yields and caused widespread misery in Scotland, France, Belgium, the Netherlands, Germany, and elsewhere. Yet potato failures there did not result in anything like the scale of starvation in Ireland. Part of the difference reflects the way governments responded to the Famine. But much of the difference also reflects the extreme dependence on the potato in Ireland: elsewhere it was an important food for the poor, but relatively few people outside Ireland relied so heavily on this single vegetable. Mokyr (1980a, p. 437) estimates that in the Netherlands, for example, per-capita production of potatoes was about one-fifth of the Irish level. Morineau (1970) discusses evidence on potato consumption in French-speaking regions of Europe at the turn of the nineteenth century, and all his figures imply maximum potato consumption well below Irish levels.

Pre-Famine Ireland was not entirely agricultural. Some economic historians have argued that in the early modern period, Ireland, like some other parts of western Europe, had experienced an expansion of "proto-industry": rural-based, nonagricultural activities, with output destined for international markets (Mendels 1972). The most common products of these proto-industrial activities in Ireland were textiles. Whatever the validity of the overall model of proto-industry, Ireland experienced a growth of rural industry at least into the late eighteenth century.[3] Some people employed in these activities had little or no connection to agriculture, but most were members of households that survived by combining proto-industry with farming small plots of land. Rural industry began to suffer badly during the early nineteenth century. A nationalist tradition in Irish economic history attributes this decline to the Act of Union, which gradually phased out tariffs between Ireland and Britain and so left Irish producers facing stiff competition from British factories (for the most famous example, see O'Brien 1921, pp. 415–434). The more important cause was the British industrial revolution, which so reduced the prices of many articles that only enormous tariffs could have sheltered Ireland's hand spinners and handloom weavers. Industrial decline was not immediate and universal, and a few Irish industries (including some textiles) succeeded in making the transition to modern industrial methods. But the decline of proto-industry in Ireland meant the loss of an important source of income for many rural people.

Visitors to Ireland prior to the Famine often came away convinced that the Irish were among the poorest people in Europe. The question of living standards in Ireland has an obvious connection to questions of the Famine's causes and severity. Just how poor were the Irish? Conventional national-income accounting suggests that they were very poor. Mokyr (1985, p. 11) estimates annual Irish per-capita income just before the Famine as about two-fifths of per-capita income in the rest of the United Kingdom at that time. But broader comparisons of the sort suggested by Ó Gráda (1994, p. 97) make Ireland's situation look better. England, after all, was the wealthiest country in Europe in 1841. Some claims about Irish poverty may reflect the visitor's disappointed expectations about what goods should be consumed. For example, the availability of low-cost fuel in Ireland, in the form of the ubiquitous peat or turf, meant that Irish houses could be less snug than their English counterparts but still comfortable in winter. Other evidence on living standards contradicts the notion that Irish people were extremely poor. The Irish, for example, tended to be rather tall in this period, which suggests that they were at least well nourished (Mokyr and Ó Gráda 1994, tables 3.4 and 3.5).[4] On balance the available evidence suggests that average incomes did increase in Ireland in the decades just prior to the Famine, but that many of the poor were at the same time becoming poorer.

The Great Famine of the 1840s, as the central event in Ireland's nineteenth-century history, has inspired many academic discussions. No serious historian denies that the Famine's impact on Irish population was important to later developments, political and otherwise. But scholars have sometimes debated how much of the strictly economic adjustment of the second half of the nineteenth century resulted from the Famine per se. Efforts to downplay the Famine's role run as follows. Even if the

Famine had not struck, changes in agricultural prices would have forced Irish farmers further along the path to grazing and away from tillage, reducing the demand for labor in Ireland. The reduction in labor demand would have provoked emigration and other population responses, leading to depopulation. In this counterfactual world, Ireland's future would have been much what it was in reality—agricultural adjustment and depopulation—but without the trauma of the Famine. This view has been advanced by revisionist historians such as Crotty (1966, p. 51). Cullen (1972, p. 132) wrote that "even if a famine had not interfered, a decline in population was inevitable."

The Crotty view implies that changes in prices paid to Irish farmers would have decreased the demand for labor in Ireland. But O'Rourke (1991a) has shown that the price changes alone would have increased the demand for Irish agricultural labor, contradicting Crotty's basic assumption. O'Rourke suggests two, more subtle ways in which the Famine marks a watershed in Irish economic history. First, the Famine dramatically reduced reliance on the potato. By 1908 potato acreage in Ireland was less than one-fourth its extent in 1840–1845 (Solar 1987, table 9.2; O'Rourke 1991b, table 4). Reduction in the potato crop reflects several factors, including the persistence of the potato blight (*phytophthora infestans*) until spraying methods were devised to control it in the 1880s. Reductions in potato cultivation altered the basis of Ireland's tillage economy and encouraged a shift to grazing quite independent of price changes. O'Rourke's second suggestion about the Famine's impact concerns Irish labor markets. The Famine helped to integrate the Irish labor market into the labor markets of Britain and North America. Henceforth, increases in wages in either of those two industrial economies would exert more upward pressure on wages in Ireland, forcing Irish farmers to economize on labor. Prior to the Famine Ireland had been linked to the world economy primarily through markets for its products. The Famine introduced (or at least greatly strengthened) a second link, through labor markets. This argument is closely related to an old argument about the Famine's long-term impact through its influence on emigration.

AFTER THE FAMINE

The period from the Famine to the First World War witnessed a long series of dramatic changes in the Irish agricultural economy. By 1914 the legal status, structure, nature of output, and incomes of Ireland's farms were quite different from what they had been just after the Famine. Some of these alterations reflected Ireland's adjustment to world markets. Other changes reflected Irish farmers' accommodations to economic development within Ireland. Still other aspects of agricultural change reflect legal adjustments that were spillovers from efforts to modify Ireland's constitutional status within the United Kingdom. Focus on land tenure and agrarian discontent has sometimes obscured the fact that Irish farmers did very well for some years after the Famine, and that on the whole the period 1850–1914 witnessed large gains in rural incomes. Figure 2.1 uses Michael Turner's (1996) new estimates of agricultural output to show the increase in output per worker and in output per member of the farm population over this period. Turner's estimates differ from other earlier estimates in several ways, but there is broad agreement among scholars on the picture outlined in figure 2.1: from the Famine to the First World War, output per person increased considerably. Turner's figures are in nominal terms, but making reasonable adjustments for changes in the value of money would not substantially alter this conclusion.[5]

The improvement was steady, and made a great difference in the lives of those who remained in Ireland. But the achievement must not be exaggerated. This was a time of great strides in European agriculture, and by international standards Ireland's experience was disappointing. A comparison of Ireland with several other European economies for the period 1870–1914 suggests that Irish agicultural productivity grew relatively slowly (Van Zanden 1991, table 4). This poor performance may account for some of the perennial complaints about the state of Irish agriculture during this period. And sustained long-term growth in agriculture did not mean an absence of bad years. Low prices paid to Irish farmers or bad weather in Ireland produced several episodes of reduced incomes. The early 1860s and most of the 1880s were two notable periods of poor results for Irish farmers (Turner 1996, tables 4.2 and 4.6). Irish agriculture's achievement during 1850–1914 was largely an ability to reduce the labor force by nearly half while keeping output (in real terms) roughly constant. Given the law of diminishing returns one would expect output per person to increase at least somewhat as the labor force declined. Despite these qualifications, however, post-Famine improvements left those remaining in agriculture with a much higher material standard of living than previously.

Three great adjustments in the agricultural economy during this period were all linked to one another and to changes overseas. From 1850 to 1914 there were substantial changes in the relative prices paid for various kinds of agricultural output, large increases in wages paid to agricultural laborers, and an even greater emphasis on livestock production that marked a fundamental reorientation of the agricultural economy away from crops and toward livestock. Cheap grains imported into

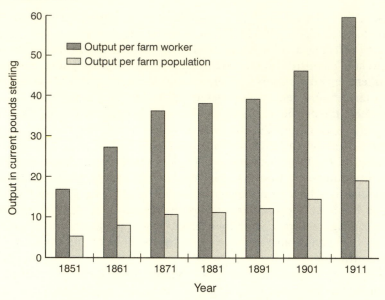

Figure 2.1 Growth of agricultural output in post-Famine Ireland. (*Source:* Turner 1996, table 5.2.)

Europe from foreign markets encouraged Irish farmers to grow fewer grains and to concentrate more on livestock production. Increases in real wages reflected the impact of foreign labor markets. As Ireland depopulated, labor became more scarce in the countryside, producing increases in wages for those who remained behind. Real agricultural wages more than doubled between 1854 and 1913.[6] This growth of Irish wages was part of a more general trend of convergence between the Irish and other economies, as we shall see. The changes in relative prices and increases in wages gave farmers two reasons to shift from growing grains to raising cattle and sheep on pastures. Turner (1996, table 4.2) reports that crops of all sorts accounted for 59.7 percent of the value of all Irish agricultural output in 1850. By 1914 this figure had fallen to 15.9 percent. In theory both lower prices for grains and higher wages for workers would give Irish farmers an incentive to shift from tillage to pasture. O'Rourke (1991b) argues that the wage increases were the force behind the move from tillage up to 1876, so that even without changes in the relative prices of grains and livestock Irish farmers would have made the switch under the pressure of labor costs. For the rest of the period (1877–1914) the issue has not received this careful scrutiny. Wages continued to increase, but the more severe relative price changes after 1876 suggest that price changes might have played a stronger role at the end of the century.

Laborers and Labor Markets

These general developments in Irish agriculture had profound implications for the organization of farms and markets. One trend Fitzpatrick (1980) has labeled "the disappearance of the Irish agricultural laborer." Figure 2.2 plots an index that Fitzpatrick has devised to show the importance in the Irish agricultural labor force of males who worked land but did not occupy it.[7] These people include the full-time laborers who worked for wages and who formed the bulk of the labor force in England, as well as the "assisting relatives"—brothers and sisters, nephews and nieces, and others—who made Irish farms a truly family enterprise. The index in Figure 2.2 does not include females, however, so the sisters, nieces, and other female assisting relatives are not reflected there. To convey some sense of the regional differences in this development, the much sharper decrease in the province of Connaught is also recorded.

This change in the structure of the agricultural labor force had two related causes. The shift from tillage reduced the demand for labor in aggregate. On large farms this meant less use of hired workers, and on small farms it reduced the household's ability to employ assisting relatives. Landless laborers also disappeared because small farmers provided the labor their wealthier neighbors needed. Farmers with too much land to work themselves hired the sons of smaller farmers rather than employing the full-time laborer so much a feature of British agriculture. Thus the "laborers" working on a large farm might themselves be occupiers of small farms. Many who worked for farmers in Ireland also occupied some land and might call themselves farmers when the census-taker called. The large proportion of the work force who were reported to the census as "assisting relatives" were in some sense landless laborers, but in another sense had an interest in the land formally occupied by their brother, father, or mother. As the nineteenth century progressed, the landless and near-landless became increasingly uncommon, which further blurred the distinction between laborer and farmer (Fitzpatrick 1980, p. 77). The disappearance of the Irish agricultural laborer, then, reflects both literal disappearance and the absorption of some laborers into the ranks of the farming classes.

The structure of the Irish agricultural work force by the end of the century contrasted sharply with that of England. In his report on agricultural wages in the United Kingdom Wilson Fox drew on the 1901 census to illustrate the relative unimportance of agricultural laborers in Ireland (Great Britain 1905). According to that census, in England and Wales about 66 percent of all male farm workers were laborers. The corresponding figure for Ireland was 18 percent, plus another 10 percent who were farm servants. In England 22 percent of agriculturalists were farm-

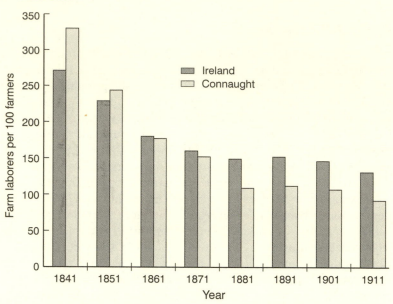

Figure 2.2 The disappearance of the agricultural laborer 1841–1911. (*Source:* Fitzpatrick 1980, table II, from census data.)

ers; In Ireland, 43 percent of male farm workers were farmers, and another 28 percent were their relatives. Wilson Fox may not have appreciated this, but in this comparison it is England that is distinctive. The structure of Ireland's agricultural work force was typical of European peasant economies in the late nineteenth century. In both France and the small-farm regions of Germany, most agricultural labor was performed by family members.[8]

The change in the Irish agricultural labor force's structure is related to another development, the reallocation of land among holdings of various sizes. Connell, like others, exaggerated both the frequency of farm subdivision prior to the Famine and the role of the Famine in calling a halt to the practice, but he was right to note that during the decades after the Famine subdivision of farms was much rarer than amalgamation of holdings after the death or emigration of a tenant. Connell relied on data abstracted from the decennial censuses. Unfortunately the farm-size data for 1841 are deficient in a number of ways, as Bourke (1965) has noted. Others have used various independent sources to try to correct the errors in the 1841 census data. For our purposes it is sufficient to focus on increases in farm sizes after the Famine, using the selection of years reported in figure 2.3. From 1853 to 1902, farms of one to five acres became steadily less common in Ireland, and larger farms became steadily

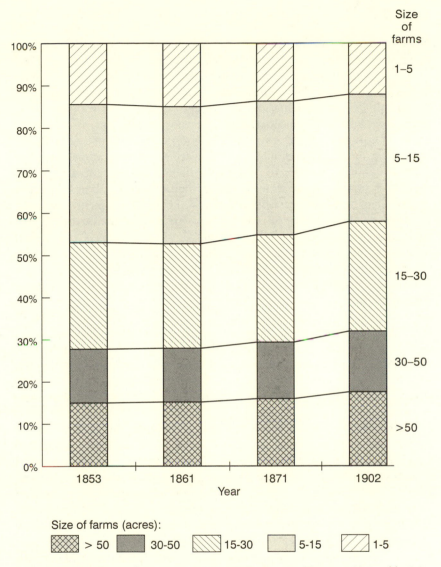

Figure 2.3 Changes in farm sizes, 1853–1902. (*Source:* Turner 1996, table 3.3, from annual agricultural statistics.)

more common. The Famine played a central role in the increase in average farm size. But the rest of the century witnessed its own, if slower, move from small holdings to larger holdings. By the early twentieth century tiny holdings were not unknown, but they had long ceased to be the most numerous farms and were most common in only a few regions.

Regional Diversity

No brief survey can do justice to the regional diversity of Irish agriculture. Varying weather and soils and different proximity to markets meant that some regions were better suited than others to particular forms of agriculture. The ability to take advantage of inherent differences in soil quality or other natural advantages depends on transportation costs. Kennedy (1981) has described the way that the extension of railroad networks in Ireland from the 1850s on increased the regional specialization in the rural economy. By lowering transportation costs, the railroad made it possible to locate activities in regions for which they were best suited. At the time of the Famine observers already noted a spatial division of labor within the island. Fifty years later this division of labor was much more pronounced. At the turn of the twentieth century most calves came from the southern dairying regions (Cork, Kerry, and so on) while most older cattle were to be found in the grazing districts centered on Meath and Kildare. Tillage was also more common in certain regions than in others. This division of labor reflects to a large degree the inherent qualities of soil and weather that make some parts of the country better for the pastures necessary for fattening cattle, or that leave only parts of the country with the rich but well-drained soils best for grains. One concomitant result of this increasing spatial division of labor in agriculture was a greater market orientation of farmers. Cuddy and Curtin (1983) stress that by the late nineteenth century even small farms in the more remote areas of western Ireland were commercially oriented.

Farm sizes also had a strong regional dimension. Maps 2.1 and 2.2 display the distribution of small and large farms in Irish counties in 1901. Farm sizes are defined here in terms of valuation. The valuation system was not directly comparable across Ireland, but using this definition makes it possible to make more meaningful comparisons of land in different parts of the country. The same number of acres could be a valuable farm in some regions and windblown mountain in another.[9] Small farms were heavily concentrated in a zone along the Atlantic and in central Ulster. The larger farms were more prevalent in Leinster and in south Munster. Using county-level data hides some important variation here, however. For example, central Mayo had a swath of large farms; in this and other instances there was nearly as much variation within a county as across counties.

The impact of changes in regional specialization on local labor markets may also be masked by confining our attention to aggregate measures such as those discussed earlier. Some areas of eastern Ireland such as County Meath had relatively little tillage even at the time of the

Percentage of farms with valuation of £10 or less

▨	Less than 40%	▨	50% to 60%
▨	40% to 50%	▨	More than 60%

Map 2.1 Distribution of small farms, 1901. (*Source:* Computed from Census of Ireland, 1901, *General Report*, table 66.)

Famine, and the shift to grazing documented by Turner was milder there than elsewhere. In other places such as County Mayo, the abandonment of tillage was more rapid than in Ireland as a whole. The impact on local labor markets was more extreme in such places. Using the Fitzpatrick index already discussed, consider the reduction in laborers. The ratio of farm laborers to farmers declined by 24 percent in County Wicklow between 1851 and 1911. The same measure declined by 61 percent in County Mayo. Map 2.3 displays the distribution of farm la-

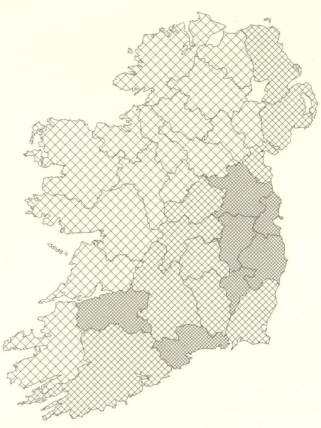

Percentage of farms with valuation of £50 or more

  Less than 10%   More than 15%

10% to 15%

Map 2.2 Distribution of large farms, 1901. (*Source:* Computed from Census of Ireland, 1901, *General Report*, table 66.)

borers in 1901. A comparison of maps 2.1 and 2.3 suggests a negative association between small farms and farm laborers. Every farm, however small, needs its "farmer." Only larger farms require the help of hired laborers.

Economic growth was also localized. Perhaps one reason Ireland's post-Famine economic growth did not receive its full due is that some regions of Ireland remained desperately poor well into the twentieth century. Along the Atlantic seacoast, from south to north, a consider-

Number of farm laborers per 100 farmers

 Less than 100   More than 200

100 to 200

Map 2.3 Prevalence of farm laborers, 1901. (*Source:* Fitzpatrick 1980, table II, from census data.)

able population tried to scrape out a living from a combination of fishing, some cottage work, and cultivating small amounts of poor-quality land. The government recognized the continuing poverty of this region by establishing the Congested Districts Board in 1891, an institution discussed more below. Price declines in the 1880s caused special suffering in these areas. On other occasions bad weather caused reductions in the yield of the potato crop, leading to severe if localized suffering (O'Neill 1989).

LAND TENURE AND LAND REFORM

For many generations of historians and Irish people the major player in any economic history had to be the land-tenure system, its alleged defects, and the alterations to that system effected by reform legislation of the period 1870–1909. Land tenure, as already noted, occupies a central role in Connell's account of post-Famine demographic change.[10] His view of land tenure owes much to nationalist critiques of landlords. Tenants, in Connell's view, had little security in the land, and in particular faced the prospect of rent increases whenever they showed evidence of being able to pay more rent without starving (Connell 1962, p. 521). Thus, according to Connell's interpretation, Irish farmers had little reason to work harder (as increased output would accrue to the landlord in increased rent) and little reason to accumulate material goods (as such accumulation would just spur the landlord to rent increases). Connell's account of demographic patterns prior to the Famine is based on this "elastic rent." The Land Acts function in Connell's interpretation as a change in the rules that prevented rent increases and thus guaranteed farmers the fruits of their labor and savings. Although more recent scholarship has downplayed the evils of the old system and land tenure's possible impact on rural life, for later discussion it is important to understand the argument of Connell and others.

Prior to 1903 a great majority of Irish farmers were tenants. Tenancy by itself was not necessarily troubling; the farmers who made England's agricultural revolution were by and large tenants. What bothered historians was that most tenants in Ireland were either yearly tenants or tenants-at-will. The first national data on tenancy-at-will date from 1870, and show two important facts. Most holdings in Ireland at that time *were* tenancies-at-will, but this form of tenure was most common among the smallest farms and was rare among the largest. For Ireland as a whole, about 84 percent of holdings valued at £15 or less were tenancies-at-will, and these amounted to 75 percent of all holdings. Of farms valued at £100 or more (which represented less than 2 percent of all holdings), only about a quarter were tenancies-at-will (Great Britain 1870b, tables 1–6). Another distinctive feature of Irish land tenure was the size of some landlords' holdings. Irish estates were huge by European standards. Vaughan (1989, p. 759) draws a telling parallel with Prussia, a country whose political history turned in part on the malign power of landed estates. In 1870 Ireland had 400 estates of 10,000 acres or more, and 2,000 estates of 2,000 acres or more. In that year only 100 Prussian estates were of 2,000 acres or more, and those of 10,000 acres were rare.

Critics of tenancy-at-will thought that without leases landlords could always raise rents or eject a sitting tenant, giving tenants little incentive to invest in their holdings or even to work them to their fullest. This view of Irish tenancy was widespread in the nineteenth century; even Alfred Marshall alludes to the defects of land tenure in Ireland (Marshall 1920, p. 545, n. 1). Recent research has not been kind to this view. Irish farmers occupied their holdings for surprisingly long times. Long occupation without a lease often reflected the landlord's recognition of tenant-right, or the "Ulster Custom." This practice has vexed Ireland's historians for generations and there is no consensus on how or why it emerged. Although most common in Ulster, the institution was widespread throughout Ireland even before the Land Acts. Under the Ulster Custom a sitting tenant could sell the right to occupy his holding to an incoming tenant. Prices paid for tenant-right were large, clearly exceeding the value of any improvements the tenant might have made or the value of any crops that might be left standing at the time of sale. Solow (1971) and Vaughan (1984, 1994) note that a new tenant's willingness to pay for a holding must imply that the rent charged by the landlord was not what the open market would fetch for the holding. With rent due to the landlord less than the market rent, the sitting tenant could find incoming tenants willing to pay a lump sum for the right to rent the land at the "fair rent," or what the tenant paid the landlord. Just why landlords would agree to the practice of tenant-right has always been a puzzle. The traditional view rests on fear of agrarian violence: if the landlord tried to charge the full rent, he would be attacked by one of his tenants. Guinnane and Miller (1996) note that this explanation is logically flawed, and stress a different explanation sometimes advanced in earlier times. This argument suggests that landlords respected tenant-right because a new tenant had to pay the landlord the purchase money, from which the landlord could deduct any outstanding rent before giving the remainder of the purchase money to the outgoing tenant. Thus tenant-right acted like a bond against nonpayment of rent.[11]

Vaughan has also shown that rent was not so "elastic" as Connell thought. Irish landlords after the Famine were remarkably reluctant to raise rents on sitting tenants. From 1850 to the mid-1870s, a period of great prosperity in Irish agriculture, the value of output increased much more rapidly than the value of rent (Vaughan 1994, app. 13). The farmers had to share some of this bounty with their laborers in the form of higher wages. But full-time laborers were becoming rarer. Most small farmers provided their own labor (that is, most small-farm *families* provided the labor necessary to run their farms), and thus the higher wages accrued to them in disguised form. Farmers owning tenant-right during this period experienced considerable capital gains at their landlords' expense, only to see these gains eroded with the price declines of the 1880s.

Land Reform

The alleged defects of Ireland's land-tenure system were a constant issue facing governments in the post-Famine period, and successive governments tried to pacify Ireland by making alterations to property rights in land. One such effort was an attempt to deal with the consequences of the Famine. During the Famine rents were not paid, and poor rates (taxes to support the Poor Law) skyrocketed. Some landlords were already in debt before the Famine, and even solvent landlords had difficulty remaining so during this crisis. To help satisfy creditors and with the hope of transferring land to new and more capable owners, the government established a special court charged with settling claims and transferring land to new owners, cleared of debt.[12] Later governments dealt with pressure of a different kind, for the regulation and eventual abolition of tenancy in Ireland. The considerable attention devoted to this issue was more a sign of Irish nationalists' ability to use land as an issue around which to rally voters than it was any sign of systematic government policy toward agriculture. The Land Act of 1870, which was confusing to all concerned, gave tenant-right the force of law where it had existed in custom before, and required compensation for improvements to all outgoing tenants as well as compensation for disturbance to any tenants who were ejected. In 1881 Parliament extended a version of tenant-right to all of Ireland and established a system to determine and enforce "fair" rents. Special Land Courts were set up to fix rents. The 1881 Land Act gave a statutory basis to what amounted to a co-proprietorship in Irish agricultural land. Landlords had the right to draw an income from land, but tenants had property rights in the same land. By 1919 at least 60 percent of the agricultural land of Ireland was let at a rate fixed by a land court (Great Britain 1920b, app. tables 52–54).

The regulation of rents was not the final step. Tenant ownership of the land had been a demand of some Irish parties from the start, although some leaders (such as Michael Davitt) advocated outright nationalization. Several late nineteenth-century land acts concerned primarily with the regulation of tenancy had also included provisions aimed at encouraging landlords to sell tenants their holdings. The former tenants of the Church of Ireland were given the chance to purchase their holdings when the church was disestablished in 1870, although few did. And the Congested Districts Board had the right to purchase estates and resell them to tenants. With the exception of the Congested Districts Board these early provisions had modest effects, as the terms on which land was sold were not attractive to landlord or to tenant. The Wyndham Act of 1903 and the Birrell Act of 1909 produced a large increase in the number of tenant purchases by improving the terms of sale. Tenant purchase was well under way when the outbreak of the First World War forced the government to stop making the advances required for the program to work (Hooker 1938, p. 92). By March 1919 the organs of the land-reform program, including the Congested Districts Board, had sold holdings amounting to about half the agricultural land in Ireland (Great Britain 1920b, vi; 1920a, iv).

The Land Acts occupy a central role in older histories such as Pomfret (1930). To Connell the 1881 act was decisive because it removed the threat of "elastic rent." Recently historians have questioned the importance of the Land Acts for agricultural improvement in Ireland. Earlier accounts exaggerated the drawbacks to tenancy-at-will as it existed before 1870. The insecurity hypothesis also fails as an explanation of overall productivity problems. By 1870 most of the largest farms in Ireland (and most of the land) were held on leases. And the stability of Irish rents suggests that the "elastic rent" was more a figure of political imagination than a fact of the Irish countryside. A second challenge to the importance of the Land Acts downplays the importance of tenure altogether, emphasizing instead the details of farming and changes in this practice over time. One result of this research has been to rescue Irish agriculture from its reputation as hopelessly backward and to try to reconcile its respectable growth in output per agricultural worker with changes in practice on the ground. A third line of argument emphasizes the limited economic implications of the Land Acts themselves. Guinnane and Miller (1997) note that on simple microeconomic grounds the Land Act of 1881 was more or less irrelevant for productivity, while the Land Purchase Acts of the early twentieth century contained provisions that were probably harmful to purchasers.

Finally, it should be noted that Ireland's land reforms did not contain one feature of some other famous episodes of land reform. In contrast to the English enclosures of the eighteenth century, Revolutionary France's confiscation of Church and emigré lands, or the Stein-Hardenburg reorganization of Prussian tenures in the early nineteenth century, little in the Irish reform aimed at redistributing land to create either larger farms or smaller farms. Most rents fixed under the 1881 act pertained to farms that had been in the same hands for years, while most tenant purchasers bought a holding they or their families had been operating for an equally long time. The Congested Districts Board did try to amalgamate and restructure holdings, but the board controlled a small fraction of the total land affected by the acts (Great Britain 1920c, 61). The later Land Acts contained redistribution clauses—some "untenanted lands" were made available to farmers' sons and others who had no land—but as politically important as these clauses were, they accounted for few of the total tenant purchases. Irish land purchase was mostly a redefinition of property rights for those already occupying the land.

AGRARIAN CONFLICT AND AGRARIAN DISCONTENT

Nineteenth-century Ireland had a reputation as a place with considerable crime and violence, motivated by both political and mundane concerns. Many crimes took place within the poorer strata, but what most attracted the attention of contemporaries was the Irishman's propensity to commit violence against his class betters. "If rural societies defined themselves by the crimes they committed, the English shot pheasants and gamekeepers, and the Irish shot landlords and agents" (Vaughan 1994, p. 138). Our concern with this reputation for violence is to understand the role of such activity in the demographic patterns that are our primary concern.

The Great Famine, not surprisingly, set off a wave of violence. The Famine-era annual murder rate of about 3 murders per hundred thousand (implied by Vaughan 1994, p. 138) was high indeed by contemporary European standards, but was low compared with the United States in the nineteenth century and nothing by the standards of the United States in the late twentieth century.[13] An Irish immigrant to the United States in 1900 entered a society where the murder rate was 6.4 per hundred thousand (Eckberg 1995, table 4). Crime statistics for earlier periods are not readily available on a national basis for the United States, but Lane (1979, table 8) suggests that in Philadelphia the murder rate for much of the nineteenth century remained at levels only reached in Ireland during the Famine. After the Famine Irish crime rates fell considerably, only to rise again during the Land War (1879–1882). Thus however violent Ireland was in the nineteenth century, it was a calm place compared with the United States.

Irish historians have debated whether this rural violence reflected primarily class conflict or other issues. In a famous paper Beames (1987 [1978]) outlined three interpretations of Irish agrarian violence. An old nationalist tradition viewed agrarian violence as grounded in motives as much patriotic as economic; the oppressed Catholic peasant was attacking his Protestant landlord. A second line of argument was first advanced by Lee (1973b). Lee argued that most conflict was actually between farmers and the poorer laborers and cottiers. Landlords might have been ultimately responsible for the plight of the poor, Lee reasoned, but they were difficult targets for the poor to attack. Beames argued that Lee overestimated the immunity of landlords from attack. A third, more recent line of argument stresses an element in rural violence that Beames also acknowledged was often present. Fitzpatrick (1982) emphasizes the familial context of many conflicts and insists on the difficulty of allocating crimes to those caused by "class" conflict as opposed to family conflicts.

Ireland's reputation for violence may also owe something to two concerted struggles between landlords and their tenants in the period that concerns us. Both incidents—the Land War (1879–1882) and its revival in the "Plan of Campaign" (1886–1887)—have names that sound unnecessarily ominous. Both incidents were rent strikes aimed at securing reductions in rents. Like any attempt at political change through violent means, the Land War had complex causes. One proximate economic cause was the combination of poor harvests and low prices in the late 1870s, an episode that seemed to bring to an end the good years of the post-Famine decades. The Land War witnessed an upsurge in both the frequency and the severity of violence. For the years 1880–1882 the number of homicides reported as agrarian outrages increased fourfold over the level of the 1860s, and the writing of threatening letters became a major literary occupation (Vaughan 1994, app. 19).[14] The Plan of Campaign was a less vicious renewal of the Land War, set off by depressed prices and bad weather in the mid-1880s along with the collapse of Gladstone's Home Rule effort in 1885. The agricultural crisis displayed the limits to the rent abatements granted under the Land Act of 1881, and in the areas affected the Plan of Campaign consisted of an effort to force landlords to agree to even further reductions. The Plan only affected 116 estates, and on 60 of these the landlord and tenants reached an amicable agreement (Lyons 1973, p. 189). The political and religious implications of this episode were in some respects as far-reaching as the Land War, however. As chief secretary for Ireland, Arthur Balfour made extensive use of coercive legislation to punish political crime. The Plan of Campaign also precipitated an open breach between the Irish Catholic Church and the Holy See. The religious dimensions of this episode receive more attention in the next chapter.

WOMEN IN THE RURAL ECONOMY

The economic history of Irish women has suffered considerable neglect. Part of this lack may reflect the frustration of using the economist's conventional categories—whether a person is occupied in the labor force, and if so, how—in a society where these distinctions often made little sense. We know that Irish women, wives, mothers, sisters, and daughters alike bore primary responsibility for household tasks such as childrearing, cooking, and cleaning. Descriptive sources also note that women were important contributors to labor for farming. Bourke (1993) has done much to overcome this neglect of women's economic history for the period 1880–1914, and in so doing has provided a much-needed study of the way social and economic change affected both women and men at the end of the nineteenth century. Bourke usefully divides women's work into three categories: work in the labor market, work at home producing goods for sale, and housework.

In rural areas the most important paid occupations for women were as farm servants. Farm servants, both male and female, usually lived with their employers and were rarely married, making this occupation for most a temporary stage in the life cycle. Detailed statistics of agricultural workers in Ireland collected in June of 1912 show that, especially on small farms, most workers were family members, and that a significant proportion of those family members were young people (Irish Free State 1928, table 22). But women most often worked on their husband's or father's farm; jobs as wage laborers in agriculture were rare for females. Of the million-odd agricultural workers in Ireland in 1912, only about 39,000 were women working on a farm other than their family's. Some 245,000 males were employed as workers in the same capacity.

A second type of work for women involved producing goods in their own homes for sale at local markets or to regional merchants. Raising poultry was an important activity for rural women. Precise estimates of income earned in this way are not available, but the Royal Commission on Congestion noted that poultry was a very important source of income for smallholders especially. Poultry raising experienced enormous growth between the Famine and 1914. Turner (1987, table 1) estimates that the total value of eggs produced in Ireland increased eightfold between 1850–1855 and 1906–1913, despite a reduced population (Turner 1996, table 4.2). That this was a primarily female activity can be seen in the reformers' insistence that the poultry industry in Ireland could never be serious until men came to be more important in it.[15]

Employment opportunities for young women contracted during the late nineteenth century. Institutional changes reduced the role of female labor in farming operations especially. Prior to the formation of cooperative creameries, for example, butter churning at home had been an important activity for women and especially girls. The cooperative creameries substituted machinery and male labor in the creamery for on-farm female employment (Fitzpatrick 1987b, p. 167; Bourke 1989, p. 32). Worries about the lack of rural employment for women led governmental and private organizations such as the Congested Districts Board, the United Irishwomen, and the Women's National Health Association to propose schemes for increasing income-earning opportunities for women in the countryside (Micks 1925, p. 78; Great Britain 1901, pp. 42–45; Bourke 1989, p. 30).

The meager paid employment opportunities for girls are reflected in the somewhat perverse form of their educational achievement. (By mid-century most areas of Ireland were served by nearly free primary schools; see chapter 3.) At the time of the Famine young men were much more likely to have achieved basic literacy skills than were young women. By 1911, however, women had closed the gap. The proportions literate at ages 15–24 was very high and nearly equal for males and females (Fitz-patrick 1986, table 1). This surprising interest in female education re-flects many influences, not least the knowledge that basic education made a woman more employable as a domestic servant in British and North American cities. Yet female educational attainment was also closely, and inversely, related to employment opportunities. When girls could not earn an income, they attended school.

Bourke notes that wealthier households, at least, offset the declining paid labor opportunities for women in the form of an increased demand for women's labor in their own homes. Why this change? Several late nineteenth-century developments conspired to produce the shift in women's work. Increased farm incomes encouraged the wives and daughters of farmers to work in the home rather than earn an income. This is a simple income effect—with their increased incomes rural house-holds purchased the female time necessary for clean and orderly homes. And if Bourke is right about declining paid work opportunities, then the price of a clean home (the opportunity cost of women's time) was also declining. And at the same time, Bourke argues that changes in housing and standards of household cleanliness, largely the result of campaigns by government officials and philanthropists, increased the time and ef-fort required to keep a home up to acceptable standards. The result was an increase in the amount of work women did in their own homes. In 1861, 29 percent of all female houseworkers were paid, compared with just 12 percent in 1911 (Bourke 1993, p. 203).

The Nonagricultural Economy after the Famine

Our story concerns rural Ireland, but rural Ireland and its rural popula-tion developed differently from other rural settings because of the rela-tive lack of industrial growth in the nineteenth century. Ireland's failure to industrialize is one of the central puzzles of its nineteenth-century eco-nomic history. Across the Irish Sea, England was the birthplace of the industrial revolution, and Scotland later became a significant center of manufactures. Ireland, despite its low wages and proximity to the rich

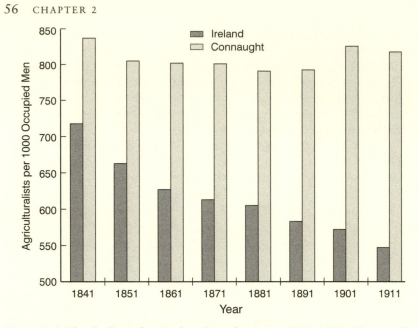

Figure 2.4 The decline of agricultural employment, 1841–1911. (*Source:* Fitz-patrick 1980, table I, from census data.)

markets of Britain and the Continent, saw only localized industrializa-tion. By the time of the Famine Ireland's cottage industry was long dying, and the only significant industrialization taking its place was occurring in East Ulster. Elsewhere in Ireland the nonagricultural economy ex-panded primarily in the areas necessary to service an increasingly prosperous rural populace. Most manufacture outside Belfast was the processing of agricultural output (including brewing and distilling), while many found employment in shipping, commerce, and government administration.

Once again we rely on indices devised by Fitzpatrick to examine trends in nonagricultural pursuits. Figure 2.4 plots the number per thou-sand of all occupied males who worked in agriculture for Ireland and its four provinces. (Again data limitations require a focus on males.) At the turn of the twentieth century some 45 percent of the male labor force worked in agriculture. By the standards of the day Ireland was quite agri-cultural. This figure is roughly comparable to Germany or France in 1870, and is much higher than the British figure for 1840.[16] The figures for Leinster are lower, largely a reflection of Dublin's importance as a commercial and administrative center. (In 1911 about one-quarter of the population of Leinster lived in Dublin and its suburbs.) For all provinces save Connaught, the second half of the century saw a substantial decline in the importance of agriculture.

What explains the lack of industry in Ireland? There is no consensus, and it is easier to show that some explanations are wanting than it is to show that others are satisfactory. The interested reader might start with Ó Gráda (1994, chaps. 12 and 13). Ó Gráda emphasizes that some industry did take root and grow in post-Famine Ireland, even outside East Ulster. He also succeeds in undermining some of the old chestnuts offered in explanation of poor industrial performance in Ireland. For our purposes it suffices to note the demographic implications of Ireland's sluggish industrialization: in contrast to many other European economies, Irish industry did not expand to offset declining employment in agriculture.

IRELAND CONVERGENT

The Irish economy of 1914 bore scant resemblance to its counterpart of 1850. The agricultural economy had shed much of its work force and made a transition to new crops and methods. The nonagricultural economy with some exceptions no longer had a significant role in industrial production, but had developed to serve the transportation, commercial, and administrative needs of the island. Most Irish people were much better off than their counterparts in 1850. Some were left behind by economic growth, of course, and a few (such as the poor in urban slums) might have had reason to envy their rural grandparents.

For many years the improvements in the Irish economy between 1850 and 1914 were downplayed in historical writing, hidden by a focus on land tenure, agrarian violence, and worries about the impact of British industrialization on Ireland. The pattern noted here, one of steady and cumulatively substantial growth, is now accepted by most historians. A broader comparative perspective suggests something a bit more surprising: the Irish economy not only grew during this period, by some measures real wages in Ireland actually caught up considerably with wages elsewhere. The "convergence" of Irish to British wages, or Irish to U.S. wages, is part of a much larger story about the increasing integration of the world economy, especially the Atlantic economy, in the second half of the nineteenth century. In a large and ongoing research project, Jeffrey G. Williamson, along with several collaborators, has studied this convergence and its causes. Overall, Williamson argues that the second half of the nineteenth century saw convergence between wages in the United States and wages in Europe. British wages, for example, were about half U.S. levels in the 1850s but nearly two-thirds U.S. levels by 1913 (Williamson 1994, p. 12). Ireland was an especially energetic player in this convergence story: wages for unskilled urban workers in Ireland were about 60 percent of British levels in 1852, but were 92 percent of British levels by 1905. Thus Ireland caught up, to a considerable extent, with both the leading European economy and the United States.

What caused this catch-up? In theory Ireland's wages could have converged for several reasons: more rapid technical change or capital accumulation in Ireland than elsewhere or certain types of international trade flows (that is, the Heckscher-Ohlin mechanism). The most obvious cause in Ireland's case would be migration. If large numbers of workers leave one economy to go to another, they will tend to drive up wages in the country they leave and depress wages in the country to which they go. Vast numbers of Irish men and women left Ireland for Britain and North America during the second half of the nineteenth century. Williamson (1994, p. 21) argues that emigration alone can account for half of the catch-up of Irish to U.S. wages between 1858 and 1908. The other half of the catching up remains unexplained, but these findings emphasize a central feature of the post-Famine economy: life improved in Ireland for those who stayed in large measure because so many left. In later chapters we shall see in more detailed ways the profound influence of emigration on life in post-Famine Ireland.

Chapter 3

THE STATE AND THE CHURCHES

> The cases of priests who take an improper part in politics
> are cited without reference to the vastly greater number
> who take no part at all, except when genuinely assured that
> a definite moral issue is at stake. I also have in mind the
> question of how we should have fared if the control of the
> different Irish agitations had been confined to laymen, and if
> the clergy had not consistently condemned secret associations.
> —Horace Plunkett, *Ireland in the New Century*

THIS CHAPTER provides a second element of the background necessary to our story. In the post-Famine period, two sets of institutions loomed large in the lives of Irish men and women. The first institution is the state. The decades between the Famine and the First World War were the high point of laissez-faire in the outlook of the British political elite, but Ireland's problems repeatedly forced policymakers to introduce interventionist measures despite their ideological leanings. The land-reform program of the late nineteenth century was discussed in the last chapter; here the poor-relief system, the schools, and several agencies that had responsibility for selected aspects of economic development will be considered. Churches form the second set of institutions to be discussed. To many Ireland's demographic patterns were the product of Catholic social teaching and a devout Irish population. This picture is at least too simple if not completely wrong. To clarify the role of the churches in demographic behavior, I outline their institutional status and development and describe their roles and influence in social and political life.

THE STATE

Ireland's government during the post-Famine period was essentially the United Kingdom's government, with administrative responsibility for Irish matters vested with imperial appointees in Dublin. A few important government tasks were performed by specifically Irish administrative

units, however. For example, the Poor Law and some other local responsibilities were under the direct control of local bodies such as the Poor
Law Guardians. Although responsible to officials in Dublin, within
broad limits these bodies had considerable discretion. During the century
local government became more democratic (as the franchise was extended to more people) and acquired additional responsibilities. Successive local government acts transferred increasing authority over local
taxation and expenditure to county councils and similar bodies. The taxation system consisted of local taxes destined for local (Irish) ends such
as the Poor Law and other taxes intended to raise funds for the Imperial
Exchequer. For some purposes the Imperial Exchequer made significant
net contributions to programs that were either specifically Irish (such as
land reform) or to the Irish component of a program in force throughout
the United Kingdom. Ireland's proper contribution to U.K. taxation was
a subject of some controversy during the nineteenth century. Ireland was
poorer than the rest of the United Kingdom, making it difficult to agree
on a just division of tax obligations. Vaughan (1989, p. 787) suggests
that the question of whether Ireland was fairly taxed is misplaced and
reflects the larger political concerns of the day. British taxation fell heavily on the lower classes. If Ireland was overtaxed it was in large measure
because it had fewer of the United Kingdom's lightly taxed wealthy.

The Irish Poor Law

The most far-reaching state program in nineteenth-century Ireland was,
as in England, the Poor Law. Poor-relief systems play a significant role in
arguments about demographic behavior. There are two arguments, one
implying that introduction of a poor law increases the incidence of marriage, the other, that a poor law decreases the incidence of marriage. The
first argument is Malthus's and is the more famous of the two. Malthus
argued that the English Poor Law encouraged "early and improvident
marriage" by providing support to laborers and their children. Boyer
(1989) found evidence to support Malthus's view for England in the
1830s. A second line of argument was advanced by Connell and also has
its echoes in some English discussions of the Poor Law. If families are an
important mechanism for ensuring against starvation in old age or in
times of adversity then the introduction of a poor law can, by providing
alternative guarantees, reduce the incentive to marry and to have families. My own views on the rise of celibacy in Ireland stress this second
view of the Poor Law.

Ireland had no formal poor relief system prior to 1838, in contrast to
England, which had had a poor law since the time of Elizabeth I. The
New Poor Law in England, an unevenly successful attempt at reshaping

the old system, was put in place in 1834. An 1838 act created for Ireland a system very much like that envisaged by the framers of the 1834 Poor Law Reform Act in England. The possible introduction of a poor law in Ireland was one of the great questions of the day. Some English observers advocated an Irish poor law out of fear that Ireland's poor would otherwise migrate to England in search of work. Others opposed a poor law for Ireland on the same ideological and practical grounds that led them to oppose the English Poor Law. Opinion in Ireland was also very divided. Some feared ruin by the taxes necessary to fund the new system; others saw a poor law as a positive step for the country's economic development.

The Irish Poor Law when instituted relied on the workhouse test, a central feature of the New Poor Law in England. Workhouses were large, centralized institutions designed to make life psychologically unpleasant for their occupants. The alternative to workhouses was called outdoor relief, and consisted of giving cash or food and other necessities to the poor who remained in their own households. Advocates of workhouses in England argued that this system would relieve the truly needy without reducing the poor's incentives to work and to save. One problem with the introduction of the Irish Poor Law goes back to the perception at the time that pre-Famine Ireland was desperately poor. If this was the case, then many Irish people might actually prefer the workhouse to what they could expect as a matter of course. Nassau Senior, to name only one, argued that a general poor law would not work in Ireland for this very reason (Black 1960, pp. 92–93). Sir George Nicholls, who became the first commissioner of the Irish Poor Law, acknowledged the concern but thought that he could use what he viewed as the Irish person's dislike of regimentation to make the workhouse an unattractive choice even in Ireland.

The original Irish Poor Law prohibited outdoor relief in any circumstances and thus was more draconian even than the English Poor Law. Before the Irish Poor Law could be put to any realistic test, however, the system was overwhelmed by the Famine of 1846–1848. To the extent the government had a relief policy during the Famine, that policy relied primarily on the Poor Law. But the relief system had never been intended to cope with a crisis of that magnitude, and the government was forced to authorize relief outside the Poor Law.[1] Famine-era legislation relaxed the system somewhat. An act of 1847 gave control of the Irish system to a specifically Irish body and permitted outdoor relief for the aged and infirm, the sick poor, and widows with two or more dependent children. Able-bodied adults could also receive outdoor relief in cases of "sudden and urgent necessity," opening an inviting loophole. Relief became subject to the "Gregory clause," which stipulated that any individual occupying at least a quarter acre of land could not be considered destitute and must be denied relief, along with his family.

Several changes during the nineteenth century relaxed regulations and extended relief to a larger segment of the population. The Gregory clause was amended in 1862 to pertain only to outdoor relief. In 1872 the Local Government Board for Ireland was created and took control of the Poor Law, the dispensary system, and a number of related programs. The Irish Poor Law (and later the Local Government Board) also had administrative responsibility for dispensaries and vaccination programs. Increasingly poor relief and medical relief were difficult to distinguish.

Despite the legal and administrative similarities, the English and Irish poor relief systems evolved very differently during the second half of the nineteenth century. In England the incidence of both indoor and outdoor relief declined steadily. The decline of outdoor relief in England was especially severe, reflecting in large part the efforts of the Charity Organization Society and its "Crusade Against Outrelief." This campaign to end outdoor relief for virtually any reason ultimately failed, but succeeded in making outdoor relief much less common in England. By 1901 the incidence of outdoor relief in England was less than half its 1861 level. Ireland experienced no counterpart to the English crusade, and on the smaller island outdoor relief became more common during the last decades of the nineteenth century (Guinnane 1993, table 3).

The Poor Law was in theory available to all, but the aged and the infirm were a major part of its clientele. No mid-nineteenth-century Irish Poor Law statistics clearly distinguish the aged from other groups of outdoor paupers, but the decennial censuses show a small increase in the proportion of aged cohorts who were indoor paupers in Ireland in the second half of the nineteenth century. Outdoor relief was more common than indoor relief for the aged in both Ireland and England. Aged men were more likely to be indoor paupers; aged women were much more likely to be outdoor paupers.[2] A special report from 1892 shows a similar pattern (Great Britain 1892). The same had also obtained for the few years the Poor Law existed prior to the Famine: Ireland had no outdoor relief, and had fewer indoor paupers per capita than did England (Ó Gráda 1994, p. 98). Only during the Famine did Ireland have more paupers per capita than did England and Wales.

Why did Ireland, the poorer country of the two, have fewer paupers? One explanation offered by contemporaries was based on the Poor Law's heavy reliance on local taxation. In areas with great poverty, many of those paying the taxes would not themselves be very well off; "in those counties they will not spend money on their workhouses or on outdoor relief" (Royal Commission on the Poor Laws 1910c, Q99615). A second explanation amounts to a theory of old-age poverty. Informants claimed that the Irish economy was easier on aged people: "In Ireland agriculture provides a living for a much larger proportion of the population than it does in England and Wales, and it is possible for people following that occupation to continue at work till a later age than people engaged in other industries. The system of land tenure is also the means of keeping down the rate of aged pauperism for the aged parents continue to dwell on the farm of their sons and daughters though able to perform little or no work" (Royal Commission on the Poor Laws 1909, §17). Other observers claimed that Irish families did a better job of providing for needy members, leaving fewer aged people who had to turn to the Poor Law for support. These arguments will be discussed in chapter 5. The early part of the twentieth century was another period of intense interest in poor laws and related matters. In Ireland a Vice-Regal Commission was appointed to investigate the Irish Poor Law and concluded that more and more outdoor relief had been extended to those who were merely poor— not destitute, as the law required: "Instead of outdoor relief being the sole support of the destitute, it has become merely an item in the receipts of the poor person. The relief is very often just enough to pay the weekly rent of a room or cabin, while support is obtained from the charity of neighbors or of the alms-giving public. In some cases relief is given to supplement small chance earnings, such as those of a charwoman, or as an addition to occasional sums of money sent by absent children" (Great Britain 1906a, par. 251).

The Old-Age Pension

In 1908 Parliament dramatically altered the form of state support for many of the aged. The Old Age Pensions Act of that year established a means-tested but noncontributory pension for men and women who had reached age 70. The maximum pension was 5 shillings per week, payable to husband and wife if both were eligible. In setting pension rates Parliament made no allowance for the lower wages and cost of living in Ireland. Most pensions paid 5 shillings per week in Ireland as in England, but 5 shillings was a far larger share of normal earnings in Ireland. For some aged people the pension amounted to more than they had earned while able to work, and for those previously on outdoor relief grants the pension was a substantial increase in weekly income. Five shillings per week was also so much more than the cost of upkeep for an aged person that this program implied that sheltering a pensioner could provide a substantial improvement in means for a poor household.[3]

By providing alternative support for the aged, the Old Age Pensions Act changed the character of the Poor Law, as was anticipated by its backers. The most obvious effect was a great reduction in the number of aged people receiving outdoor relief; average daily numbers on outdoor relief fell from 13 per thousand in 1907–1908 to 8.7 per thousand in 1913–1914 (Guinnane 1993, table 4.) The reduction in outdoor relief was larger than the reduction in indoor relief. This reflects both the aged's greater reliance on outdoor relief and other issues to be discussed in chapter 5.

The old-age pension in Ireland was more expensive than Treasury estimates had suggested it would be. One reason is that more people than expected were able to successfully claim that they had reached age 70. Establishing one's age in Ireland was difficult, because civil registration of births had only been introduced in the 1860s. The Local Government Board tried various stratagems for dealing with inventive applicants. Birrell (1937, pp. 210–211) notes that aged people in Ireland developed a tendency to forget their true ages but to remember the "Big Wind" of 1839. Just how many 68-year-olds succeeded in receiving a pension we will never know. Comparing the reported age distributions in the 1901 and 1911 censuses of Ireland, however, shows that many older people added a few years to their age and told the same thing to the census-taker as they did to the Local Government Board. The Scottish and English censuses for 1911 show little evidence of such inventiveness.[4]

Education and Schools

One of the most effective and pervasive aspects of government policy in Ireland was the national primary school system set up during the 1830s. The system consisted of a national board that supervised the use of a parliamentary grant. Local bodies—usually religious orders or parishes—would establish and run a primary school. At first the system was supposed to be explicitly nondenominational, although it was recognized that religious organizations would be the groups most likely to organize and run schools. By the end of the century "the system could be described as denominational in practice with a conscience clause" (McDowell 1964, p. 244). The system was impressive both for the financial contribution required and for its ability to provide basic education to the vast majority of young Irish people. In 1850 the system included about 4,500 schools, had more than a half-million children enrolled, and received a parliamentary grant of £125,000. The numbers enrolled are misleading, as measures of school attendance usually revealed a large number of students who attended infrequently. The number of schools in operation grew continuously, until by 1900 the system was supporting over 8,600 institutions. Attendance and enrollment measures peaked in the 1890s, however, which is not surprising in light of the declining number of children in Ireland.[5]

Education within this primary system was often rudimentary. Attendance was irregular, and despite the efforts of denominations and the national board alike, many teachers had inadequate training. But the system delivered basic education, and basic education meant a great deal for the mass of Irish people. According to the 1841 census of Ireland over half of Irish males aged 15–24 could read and write, and of females, three-quarters of that age were literate. By 1911 illiteracy was rare among both males and females of this age group (census data, from Fitzpatrick 1987b, table 8:3). Students did not have to pay school fees. The only out-of-pocket expense for a child's education was for books and materials. Probably the major cost to a family of educating its children was the possible alternative use of a child's time in household or farming tasks. Data on literacy mask a wide variety of educational levels, from those who could probably do little more than write their own names to those with considerable practical fluency with the written word. But basic literacy was significant nonetheless. Cullen (1989, pp. 4–5) notes the growth of newspaper readership during the decades after the Famine, a readership that presumably had political implications. From a strictly economic viewpoint, a literate population can gather and use information on new practices and techniques, on markets for inputs and outputs, and on job opportunities available in Ireland and elsewhere. Literacy was a valuable job skill for the emigrant; especially in North America, where the Irish immigrant was competing at first with the highly literate Germans and later with less literate eastern and southern European immigrants, the ability to read and write English must have made a difference in many cases.[6]

Economic Development

Despite a commitment to laissez-faire ideology, successive British governments tolerated and even provided significant financial support for initiatives intended to shape specific features of the economy. Several programs in Ireland were especially far-reaching. The Board of Works, formed in 1817, had a wide variety of responsibilities for the planning and upkeep of infrastructure and other government property. During the Famine the board planned and awarded funds for large-scale work-creation projects, and afterward the board's responsibilities were widened even more to include such disparate items as disused churches. McDowell (1964, p. 214) notes, "The board of works was for nearly half a century the principal agency through which the government influenced Irish economic development."

The late nineteenth century witnessed the formation of several new agencies with primarily economic functions. The Church Temporalities

Commission was established to supervise the former property of the Church of Ireland and to pay compensation to the disestablished clergy under the terms of the law. The second major land act in 1881 set up a new Land Commission with two distinct functions: to fix "fair" rents and to make loans to tenants who wanted to purchase their holdings under the terms of this and earlier acts. Later the Land Commission would supervise the land purchase programs described in chapter 2.

Two other bodies were very different in that each was intended to bring about changes in some aspect of the Irish economy. The Congested Districts Board was formed by a land purchase act in 1891. (The term "congested" denoted a zone of extreme poverty.) The original congested districts made up about one-sixth of the land and one-ninth of the people in Ireland. An act of 1909 extended the board's powers and with it the territory within which it could function. The Congested Districts Board had wide powers, and in its career launched a variety of initiatives. Its first step was to amass data on the conditions of people in the areas under its purview, resulting in the *Baseline Reports* that have told historians so much about poverty in the west of Ireland. To ameliorate this poverty the board first concentrated on a variety of projects intended to raise incomes. It tried to improve the quality of livestock and seeds used by farmers by introducing superior breeding stock and distributing new seeds. The board also tried to provide the capital, expertise, and shore facilities necessary to encourage fisheries in the west of Ireland. The Congested Districts Board also sought to encourage rural industry, partly out of concern for the lack of employment for rural women noted earlier. Here the board's efforts consisted of schemes to improve the quality and marketing of home-produced articles, as well as grants and loans to encourage new or expanded enterprises in the Congested Districts. Increasingly, however, the Congested Districts Board's time and funds were occupied by its special role in tenant purchase. Unlike the Land Commission, which enabled a tenant to purchase the holding he had farmed for perhaps years, the Congested Districts Board purchased large tracts, even entire estates, and resold them to tenants after rearranging and enlarging plots. The Department of Agriculture and Technical Instruction (DATI) was formed in 1899 with a similar eye to practical efforts to improve the lot of Irish people. The department had a wide range of responsibilities, often exercised in conjunction with local government bodies and private organizations. Its educational responsibilities were discharged through traveling educational exhibits and formal courses alike. The department (like the Congested Districts Board in its own way) tested and distributed seeds and arranged for the distribution of high-quality breeding stock. It also checked on animal disease and tried to advance knowledge of Irish farming by collecting statistics.

The creation and responsibilities of both the Congested Districts Board and the Department of Agriculture and Technical Instruction reflect, implicitly, developments in attitudes toward Ireland's economic woes. These initiatives were not the first involvement by the state in economic affairs, but they marked a departure from earlier programs in that the Congested Districts Board and DATI were self-consciously designed to improve certain features of economic performance. No less important, the support of these two groups by influential Irish people reflects the realization that land tenure was not Ireland's only economic problem and that land reform would not by itself cure all economic ills.

RELIGION AND THE CHURCHES

A repeated theme in many discussions of Irish demographic patterns is religion. A large majority of Irish people in nineteenth-century Ireland were Roman Catholics. Today the Catholic Church's social teachings, and especially those relevant to family life and demographic behavior, tend to differ from those of other Christian churches. The Catholic Church's more hierarchical organization and emphasis on dogma also give those teachings a force perhaps not true of the social teachings of some other religious groups. The Church's supposed power figures heavily in many discussions of Home Rule in the nineteenth century. Plunkett's comment about priests and politics, quoted at the beginning of this chapter, alludes to some of these criticisms. Historians have more nuanced views of the role of the Church in many areas of Irish life, including demographic behaviors. These views (plural, because there is no consensus) emphasize important points of similarity among the several Irish denominations and stress some obvious limits to the Catholic Church's influence.[7]

Perhaps the most basic observation is the number of adherents to the various religious sects as measured by the census. The first serious attempt to count church adherents took place in 1834. The decennial Irish census first asked questions on religion in 1861. Comparison of the 1834 with the 1861 figures shows the Famine's disproportionate effect on the poorer, predominantly Catholic, classes. Between 1834 and 1861 the Catholic population declined by 30 percent, while the Anglicans and Presbyterians declined by 19 percent (Connolly 1982, p. 25). The relative sizes of religious denominations shown by the 1861 census remained approximately steady through 1911. Catholics were about three-quarters of the population. Adherents to the Church of Ireland (Ireland's established church until 1869) numbered about 12 percent, and Presbyterians about 10 percent. Jews and members of smaller Christian groups (including Methodists) made up the rest. Change between 1861 and 1911 was slow, with the Catholics losing some ground relative to others because of higher emigration rates (Vaughan and Fitzpatrick 1978, table 13).[8] Adherence to religious groups in Ireland varied by region (as the partition of the country at least partially on religious lines suggests) and social class. Munster and Connaught were the most Catholic provinces, each with a population about 95 percent Catholic in 1911. Leinster's population was 85 percent Catholic, the balance made up largely of members of the Church of Ireland. Only about 49 percent of Ulster's people were Catholics in 1911. Presbyterians there made up 26 percent of the population, and the Church of Ireland 21 percent. Even these provincial differences mask some of the geographical variation in religious adherence. As a rule, Protestants outside Ulster were most common in cities and towns. Many of the Protestants in Munster, for example, lived in Cork or Limerick cities. In parts of Connaught Catholics were more than 97 percent of the population.

Roman Catholics, while a very large majority of the population overall, were thus never the entire population, and in some regions they were not even a majority. This simple point bears stressing because some discussions seem to presume that there were no Protestants, or at least none that mattered. For our purposes any exaggeration of the numerical importance of Catholics is important because it bears directly on the Church's potential influence on demographic behavior. Throughout the post-Famine period some regions of Ireland had Protestant majorities, and for the country as a whole adherence to Roman Catholic social teaching simply cannot explain the behavior of about one-quarter of the population. Only the partition of Ireland in 1921 created a state—the present-day Republic of Ireland—in which those who are not Catholic are a tiny minority.

The fact that many Irish people were not Catholics could permit an examination of the Church's influence in a compelling way, by comparing the behavior of Catholics with the behavior of others. Unfortunately our ability to do this for the nineteenth century is quite limited. Published census data sometimes provide cross-classifications by religion, but most of those tables have little demographic significance. Once again we are led to the manuscript censuses (see Appendices 4A and 4C). The design of the sample used in this book left it with few Protestants and almost no Jews, making it unsuitable for the comparisons of interest. Others have used the 1901 and 1911 census more explicitly for the study of religious differences, and I will discuss these studies in the relevant chapters below. Comparisons of Catholics per se to Protestants per se are usually of little use, as Akenson (1988) has stressed: Catholics and Protestants differed in many ways that affect demographic behavior within religious groups.

With a simple comparison we would not know what was the effect of religion and what was the effect of social class or occupation.

Those social class differences were large, although members of all social classes were represented in all denominations. In 1867, according to a recent reworking of a contemporary estimates, the average income for Catholics was £11.7 while for Protestants it was £21.8. Most of the difference comes from differences in rental incomes. Other forms of income were nearly equal for Protestants and Catholics on a per-capita basis.[9] Much of the income difference reflects the great underrepresentation of Catholics among the wealthiest group in Ireland, the landlords. The census consistently shows a relative underrepresentation of Catholics in the skilled trades, liberal professions, and among landed proprietors.[10] Since wealth, urban/rural residence, and farming status are all likely to assert independent effects on demographic decisions, simple comparisons of Catholics and Protestants do not tell us what we want to know. Meaningful inferences about confessional differences in demographic behavior can only be drawn from studies that control for these other factors through statistical means or by comparisons of similar individuals. Another way to state this problem is to compare it to a quite general problem of assessing causation in the social sciences. On the one hand, it may be that religious faith affected demographic behavior. On the other hand, it may be that some other factor, in this case most likely income or social class, affected demographic behavior, and that the empirical relation between religion and demographic behavior reflects not the influence of religion on demographic behavior but the relationship between income and religious affiliation.

The Catholic Church

The question is not just one of numbers: Catholicism supposedly matters for demographic behavior because of its distinctive teachings. The Catholic Church in the post-Famine period did not have enough political power in Ireland to affect state policies that might in turn affect demographic behavior, although that was probably the case later on in the twenty-six counties. The nineteenth-century Church's power relied on its ability to teach and persuade Ireland's Catholics. The decades after the Famine saw the emergence of a more disciplined and energetic Catholic Church, led by Paul Cardinal Cullen. To some degree the energy of Cullen's leadership was necessary to recover from over a century of legal impediments to the practice of Roman Catholicism in Ireland. The so-called Penal Laws were a series of statutory restrictions on Catholic civil and economic rights that had been enacted in the late seventeenth and early eighteenth centuries. These legal impediments to the practice of

Catholicism were never as total or effective as popular imagination would suggest, and by the mid-nineteenth century many of their most stringent features had been abolished or had fallen into disuse. During the period they remained in force they had serious economic effects on wealthy and middle-class Catholics, because the Penal Laws placed serious restrictions on the inheritance and acquisition of land and because they limited the ability of Catholics to engage in certain professions and occupations. Sometimes, however, the laws were ignored by those responsible for enforcing them, and at other times friendly Protestants lent their names to make it possible to Catholics to keep their property or professions. Popular memory exaggerates the scope of the Penal Laws and the uniformity of their enforcement. But their existence still informs both Catholic and Protestant understandings of the role of religion in Irish society.[11]

Although some reforms were clearly under way prior to the Famine, the first two decades after the Famine have been called a "devotional revolution" because of significant changes in the Church's organization and resources and in the behavior of Catholics. Larkin's (1972) account of this transformation has been challenged in the details, but the basic picture remains. Until this period the religion of Ireland's poor Catholics contained admixtures of folk practices and pagan influences. Many nominal adherents did not receive the sacraments and embarrassingly large numbers rarely if ever attended mass.[12] In part these pre-Famine deficiencies in Church practice reflected both the numbers and quality of the priesthood. In 1840 Ireland only had about 1 priest per 3,000 Catholics, making it virtually impossible for all Catholics to worship at weekly mass (Larkin 1972, p. 627). Certain priests also left something to be desired. Scandal and incompetence doubtless make a stronger impression than quiet piety in the sources available, but it seems clear that some Irish priests lacked proper theological training and that some indulged tastes incompatible with their vocation.

In its efforts at reform the Catholic Church was in part reacting to (and in its own way contributing to) a renewed and deepened hostility among the several Christian churches in Ireland. The bitter hostility that emerged in the early nineteenth century reversed earlier habits. During the Penal Era, Catholics and Protestants by and large got along well on the local level. Relations deteriorated with the emergence of a new and more aggressively Protestant Orange Order in the late eighteenth century, and with the development of Protestant missionary societies in the early nineteenth. These well-funded groups used the distribution of free Bibles and offers of free education to try to convert Roman Catholics. Despite considerable efforts they were rarely successful. They did, however, succeed in poisoning relations between Catholics and Protestants.

No doubt the effect on interfaith relations was not helped by aggressive counter-moves by Catholics, or by the millenarian prophesies, popular among poor Catholics, that predicted the destruction of all Protestant denominations in 1825.

The first Synod of Thurles (1850) and the appointment of Paul Cullen as archbishop of Armagh (1849) and later of Dublin (1852) ushered in more rapid and complete change in Ireland's Catholic Church. By the second Synod of Maynooth (1875) and Cullen's death in 1878 the Irish Church had succeeded in upgrading its priesthood, suppressing many folk elements in religious worship, and making available to all Catholics the services of priests and nuns. Cullen also continued a strong program of church building. The statistics on the religious alone are telling: in 1870 there was 1 priest per 1,250 Catholics in Ireland, and these priests were by all accounts better trained and more obedient to the hierarchy than their predecessors (Larkin 1972, p. 644). By 1900 priests were in surplus at 1 per 900 Catholics (and 1 nun per 400 Catholics) and Ireland was well on its way to its famous status as provider of religious for missions and schools overseas. The strengthened position of the Catholic Church also reflected the effects of the Famine. The Famine's demographic impact fell disproportionately on the poorer classes, people who were more likely than others to be Catholic and whose practice of Catholicism left something to be desired in the eyes of people like Cullen. The post-Famine Catholic Church had fewer adherents, but these adherents were both wealthier on average and more "respectable" than had been the poor rural people who died or were driven away during the Famine.

The Catholic Church as Political and Social Leader

However clear this bureaucratic and religious transformation of the Irish Catholic Church, it says little about the Church's ability to influence its flock on matters of social teaching. There is a tradition of ascribing to Catholics absolute obedience to the proclamations of Rome or local prelates. The historical record of the post-Famine period suggests that the Church's influence in political issues was much less direct and pervasive. Even when the hierarchy could come to a unified position on some social or political issue, local priests found ways to ignore or translate directives into a message more to their liking. And even when priests and bishops spoke with one voice, the mass of Catholics did not always follow.

One familiar charge was that priests played a direct role in local elections, in effect telling their parishioners how to vote. This charge is at least exaggerated. Catholic priests could play important roles in the selection of candidates and sometimes organized the transport and lodging necessary to get friendly voters from remote rural districts to polling places. But this influence was strictly limited: "[T]here is no doubt that there was a great fund of loyalty to the clergy in Ireland. . . . But, when this qualification is made, it seems to have been on the whole true that the Irish clergy could lead their people only in the direction that they wanted to go" (Whyte 1960, p. 248). The general elections of 1892 were an example of this phenomenon. These elections saw the split in the Irish nationalist party into Parnellites and anti-Parnellites, with many Catholic bishops and priests taking a strong public stand against the Parnellites. The reasons for the Church's position were complicated, and reflected more than Charles Stewart Parnell's relationship with Katherine O'Shea, at that time still Captain O'Shea's wife. Did the Parnellites' heavy electoral loss reflect the direct clerical intervention claimed by some Parnellites? Woods (1980) concludes not: priests, though influential in forming public opinion, were not the only relevant pressure group and were probably only exploiting splits that already existed within the body of those willing to vote for nationalist candidates.

The limits of Church power were especially clear in cases of popular movement such as the Land War. Popular agitation of any form made many Church prelates nervous, and their nervousness was not lessened by the prominence of Protestants (such as Parnell) or avowed socialists (such as Davitt) in the leadership of such movements. Balanced against this, however, was the plain fact that large majorities of Catholics supported the movements in question. Even priests could escape heirarchical discipline. Foster (1989, pp. 386–387) emphasizes more generally that whatever Cullen's ultramontane inclinations, even he had to accept this reality. To condemn popular positions might lead to an embarrassing if implicit denial of the Church's moral authority. The hierarchy's preferred solution involved substantial amounts of legerdemain—condemning the involvement of priests in politics, but ignoring involvement when it occurred, and splitting hairs on pronouncements concerning moral as opposed to political matters—all reflecting the perception that "when faced with widespread popular agitation it was best to bend with the wind" (Hoppen 1989, p. 163). The Plan of Campaign makes a telling example. In a rare display of clarity, the Church condemned boycotting and the Plan and forbade clerical involvement in either. Yet that condemnation did not end popular support, and even many priests ignored their hierarchy to provide assistance to the movement (Lyons 1973, p. 190). These examples could be multiplied many times. Historians ascribe to the nineteenth-century Church much less control over Irish Catholics than did those Unionists convinced that "Home Rule was Rome Rule."

In part the Church's inability to speak clearly on social matters reflects a social basis that put it at odds with some aspects of its theology. For its priesthood some moral teaching ran counter to all the values of the classes from which they sprang, while a too-zealous pursuit of some of the Gospels' social implications might alienate important Catholics. Connell (1968, pp. 122–126) has viewed the post-Famine priesthood as dominated by the sons of peasants and small farmers, as these classes became wealthy enough to afford the seminary for their sons and as wealthier families began to see the priesthood as below them in social status. Other backers of the Church were the shopkeepers and publicans, important members of the urban Catholic middle class. When faced with political decisions the Church found itself constrained by this social base. Consider the conflict over land. The land wars were not just quarrels between tenants and landlords, but involved complex struggles between small farmers and more prosperous farmers and between shop-keepers and their customers (and debtors). The Gospels and the Church's sympathies (and those of its priesthood) might have lain with the small farmers, but the Church could hardly side openly with them without alienating important parts of its own membership. One reason to forbid clerical involvement in these campaigns was simply to avoid exposing the Church's own social class fault lines. Another example of this problem arose in connection with the Church's attitude toward Horace Plunkett's cooperative movement. One would think that the Church would have supported these cooperatives whole-heartedly, and in fact many individual cooperatives were founded or otherwise actively assisted by priests. The case of the cooperatives is particularly instructive because the Church had no clear theological reason to oppose cooperation. Yet the Church hierarchy displayed oddly mixed feelings on cooperatives, as Kennedy (1978) has noted. Kennedy argues that cooperatives threatened to undermine shopkeepers and other members of the Catholic middle class, who were both politically powerful in their own right and influential within the lay structure of the Irish Church. Credit cooperatives—which did not threaten shopkeepers—did not arouse the Church's ire. Cooperative creameries, which did suffer repeated Church condemnation, were the most successful aspect of the Irish cooperative movement.

The Church on Sexuality and Family Life

Politics may be less personal than decisions about marriage or fertility, and it does not automatically follow that Catholics who supported the Plan of Campaign would also defy the Church on teachings regarding family life. But it should be no surprise that reactions to Church teachings on family life were also mixed. On the one hand, the Church advised Catholics to marry and to marry young, yet post-Famine Ireland was a land of increasing (lay) celibacy. On the other hand, the Church condemned contraception, and Ireland's fertility patterns suggest that this lesson was much better accepted—although even the teaching was increasingly ignored by the end of the nineteenth century. Here the social basis of the Church might have led to some moderation of the message between pastoral letter and priestly advice. Whatever the Church's teachings on lay celibacy, these priests fully understood the logic of the decisions that led to permanent celibacy. There may also have been some confusion over the finer points of St. Paul's condemnation of unmarried sex as opposed to married sex. Many historical and indeed modern accounts refer to priests (and nuns) doing everything they could to prevent young men and women from mingling in even the most innocent circumstances. This was supposedly to help the young avoid the occasion of sin. But one could hardly fault the young person kept carefully sequestered from the opposite sex for the suspicion that sex itself was evil: "[A] shadowy line divided godly chastity from sinful renunciation of marriage: the very success of this teaching—the stifling of 'impure thoughts,' wresting the mind from 'objects of temptation,' the avoidance of much social life, the wariness of mixed company—all this raised psychological (indeed, practical) barriers to marriage: all too readily the over-zealous confessor instilled in simple penitents not only a caution of marriage, but their reputed 'complete and awful chastity'" (Connell 1968, p. 129). All this said, few academic historians credit the Church with any ability to influence the demographic behavior of Irish Catholics. In his famous survey Lee contributed one of the more colorful statements in support of this position: "The Churches, particularly the Catholic Church, are frequently criticised for contributing to the unnatural marriage patterns in post-famine Ireland by treating sex as a satanic snare and exalting the virtues of celibacy. *The Churches, however, merely reflected the dominant economic values of post-famine rural society.* . . . Priests and parsons, products and prisoners of the same society, dutifully sanctified this mercenary ethos, but they were in any case powerless to challenge the primacy of economic man over the Irish countryside" (Lee 1973a, p. 5, emphasis added).

Ireland's Protestants

The two largest Protestant denominations in Ireland were the Church of Ireland, which was the established church until 1869, and the Presbyterians. Although formally united into one church by the same Act of Union that created one kingdom of Great Britain and Ireland, the Church of

Ireland in practice was distinct and autonomous from the Church of England. As noted earlier the Church of Ireland was a minority religion in Ireland, but counted among its members a disproportionate share of the very wealthiest. In the early 1880s over 70 percent of all justices of the peace were members of the Church of Ireland, and at about the same time 250 members of the church's general synod owned between them more than one million acres of Irish land (McDowell 1975, pp. 3–5). The Church of Ireland's influence was more extensive than numbers would suggest in other ways, as well. Many clergy found themselves materially comfortable but underemployed. Two-thirds of the Church of Ireland parishes had fewer than five hundred members at mid-century, and nearly one-third had fewer than one hundred members (McDowell 1975, p. 17). Some clergy reacted to the situation by cultivating leisure. Others assisted their neighbors, Protestant or not. One Church of Ireland clergyman told Gladstone that his Roman Catholic neighbors would be sorry to see him leave, as he managed the national school and frequently provided character references. However self-serving the claim, the Church of Ireland clergy functioned to some degree as local advisors and leaders for adherents to other religions.

The Church of Ireland's position as a minority but established church was always a cause of irritation to Irish Catholics and to other Protestants, and even to English liberals it seemed anomalous. The established church in England was the majority denomination. The Church of Ireland's position became increasingly tenuous as post-emancipation Catholics demanded the next step in religious equality, which would be the removal of the Church of Ireland from its privileged position. Like the Land Act of 1870, the disestablishment of the Church of Ireland with the Act of 1869 was largely an effort to secure the loyalty of Irish people through means other than coercion. Disestablishment did not sit well with many in Ireland or England, but realism prevailed and leaders of the Church of Ireland cooperated enough to secure the protection of their basic interests. The Church lost nearly all of its property, but most prelates and institutions drew incomes set up by the government. Compared with what could have been (or what had transpired elsewhere in similar circumstances) this revolution was civilized indeed. Taking advantage of the fortunate timing—the early 1870s were good times for Irish landlords—the Church reorganized and rebuilt itself. But it is fair to say that after its disestablishment the Church of Ireland as an institution exercised little direct influence over political and social affairs. Given its social basis the Church's membership would remain cohesive on matters such as Home Rule, and individual members continued to exercise considerable power because of their status as landlords and government and other leaders.

The established church in Scotland in the nineteenth century was a presbyterian Protestant church, but Presbyterians in Ireland suffered the double difficulty of being both a minority religion and of not enjoying the established status of the Church of Ireland. Although never subjected to the active disqualifications of the Penal Laws, Irish Presbyterians were acutely aware of their religion as a source of exclusion from the highest circles of social and economic power. The Irish Presbyterian Church, like other nineteenth-century Protestant denominations, felt the impact of evangelicalism. The revival of 1859 occupies a special place in the church's history not just for the thousands involved but because the revival helped boost Protestant self-confidence in the face of a demonstrably more powerful Roman Catholic Church. Presbyterians in Ireland also had a natural tendency to reduce their institutional power through frequent splits over doctrine, although in 1840 the major strands had been able to unite as the Presbyterian Church in Ireland.[13]

The Churches on Moral Issues

Ireland's churches had different histories, different relations with the state, and of course stressed different theological and social doctrines. But a somewhat surprising degree of similarity in outlook on some important matters, especially social teaching, should not be overlooked. In some ways Ireland's denominations had as much in common with one another as with coreligionists elsewhere in the United Kingdom. Hoppen (1989, p. 149) cites two telling examples. When England liberalized its divorce law in 1857, the new regime did not apply to Ireland. Failure to extend the law to Ireland did not bother the Catholic hierarchy, as one would expect, but there was also little protest from Protestants. Evidently there was considerable agreement among Ireland's religious leaders on this point.[14] In another example, the Catholic hierarchy's official 1875 denunciation of certain dances and amusements as leading to sexual danger could hardly be distinguished from the campaign of the Rev. Thomas Drew, rector of Belfast's Christ Church, against "plays that inflame the passions, excite the imagination, and depict vice." The Catholic Church's reputation for relative severity on certain matters may reflect its ability to police behavior more than its outlook. The Protestant Churches were more urban than rural, and in an urban environment even the most zealous prelate faces limitations to his authority. The Catholic Church was more firmly based in rural Ireland, where close personal contact and the limited movement of people gave priests the ability to know and, if they felt justified, denounce members of their flock.

We should leave the question of religion, then, with a more nuanced view than one typically hears in discussions of demographic behavior and the Catholic Church. The Catholic Church was large, but about one-quarter of Irish people professed another faith. The Irish Catholic Church was influential, but Catholics were not above ignoring it when they felt like it. And on some key issues related to family life and morals, the leadership of the Protestant denominations lined up in positions remarkably similar to those of the Catholic hierarchy.

MODERN IRELAND?

To some historians the decades between the Great Famine and partition is a period during which the Irish economy and Irish society became "modernized." The problem with the term modernization and all its uses is that it evokes a transformation without being very clear about the before, the after, or the nature of that transformation. Ireland clearly was a very different place by 1914, and those differences can be specified. In chapter 2 we charted the economic adjustments that left most Irish people considerably more comfortable in 1914 than their counterparts had been just after the Famine. The developments discussed here imply equally important changes of a different kind.

One set of changes concerns not the economy, but the state's role in the economy and the state's responsibility for those left behind by economic progress. By the turn of the twentieth century the Poor Law and later the Old Age Pensions Act provided minimal but certain support for those who might otherwise have starved. Various government initiatives had also placed the state in the position of assisting some of Ireland's very poorest and using government resources to improve entire sectors such as agriculture. The governmental relationship between Ireland and the rest of the United Kingdom had changed considerably, even within a fixed constitutional structure. The Irish did not have their parliament, but changes in local government produced a more democratic local order. Successive British governments had also increasingly come to use the carrot, even if they still at times applied the stick, to pacify Irish grievances.

The relations between Church and state and among Ireland's various churches had also witnessed important changes. Catholics were formally emancipated and the Church of Ireland had lost its established status. The Catholic Church had built itself into a cohesive institution more capable of at least attempting to guide its flock. More ominous were the hardening of attitudes among denominations. Each religious group seemed ever more inclined to view the others as too powerful.

These economic, political, and religious developments took Ireland from the disaster of the Famine to its position as a still troublesome but more prosperous part of the United Kingdom. The demographic developments of the same period, coupled with rapid population growth in England and Wales, made Ireland's population a much smaller part of that kingdom's populace. It is to those Irish demographic developments that we now turn.

Chapter 4

THE DEMOGRAPHIC SETTING

> It is becoming increasingly difficult in many parts of the
> world to keep the people on the land, owing to the
> enormously improved industrial opportunities and en-
> hanced social and intellectual advantages of urban life.
> The problem is better examined in Ireland than elsewhere,
> for with us it can, to a large extent, be isolated, since we
> have little highly developed town life.
> —Horace Plunkett, *Ireland in the New Century*

THE PRIMARY TASK of this chapter is to outline and discuss the major population developments of nineteenth-century Ireland. There is no single, convenient account of Ireland's population history during the nineteenth century. This chapter, by providing an account of the individual developments of migration, marriage, and fertility, as well as their connections to one another and to the economic and social developments of the period, seeks to fill that gap. In addition, the chapter serves as background for the more intensive discussion of households and the life cycle in chapters 5–8. It concludes with three appendices on sources and methods used both here and later in the book.

IRELAND'S POPULATION BEFORE THE FAMINE

Ireland's population history poses two serious intellectual challenges: why population grew so rapidly prior to the Famine, and why it declined for so long after the Famine. This book focuses on why and how Ireland's population declined during the second half of the nineteenth century. The other challenge has occupied numerous historians and forms a necessary prelude to this study's main focus: how did the Irish population before the Famine come to be so large?

Ireland's population grew rapidly for several decades prior to the Famine, although just how rapidly is not known precisely. Figure 1.1 presented figures on the total population of Ireland dating from the early eighteenth century. Any estimate of Ireland's population before 1841 is little more than an educated guess. The 1841 census was the first reasonably careful official count of the people in Ireland. Population at prior dates must be taken from adjustments to the flawed censuses of 1821 and 1831. Estimates prior to the nineteenth century vary even more. To appreciate just how quickly the Irish population was growing, consider the period 1750–1845, when the estimates are least speculative. France's population grew at an average annual rate of 0.4 percent over these years. England's growth rate was about 1 percent, Scotland's 0.8 percent. Ireland's population, in contrast, grew at about 1.3 percent per year. This seemingly small difference in growth rates implies large differences in population sizes after a century. Imagine, for example, that there were 100 French, 100 English, 100 Scots, and 100 Irish in 1750. With the growth rates cited above, in 1850 there would be 149 French, 270 English, 222 Scots, and 364 Irish.

Population growth in Ireland seems to have slowed down in the decades just prior to the Great Famine. Mokyr and Ó Gráda (1984, p. 476) propose a growth rate of 0.5 to 0.75 percent in the 1830s. Slower population growth in the 1820s and 1830s suggests that Ireland's population would have peaked and begun to decline even in the absence of the Famine. This possibility plays an important role in interpretations of the Great Famine. If the blight had hit Ireland later, after it had had more time to adjust to British industrialization, the end of the Napoleonic Wars, and the agricultural prosperity of that era, the economy might have been able to absorb the blow more easily. A slowdown in population growth in the 1820s and 1830s also sharpens the picture of very rapid growth in earlier decades. If the growth rate for the entire period 1750 to 1845 was in fact about 1.3 percent per year, and it had declined to 0.5 percent in the 1820s and 1830s, then between 1750 and 1820 the average annual growth rate must have been over 1.5 percent.

This growth accounts for much of Ireland's popularity in Malthusian discussions and has sometimes invited casual comparison to developing countries that today face problems of rapid population growth. But Ireland's pre-Famine experience is quite different from modern population growth in two instructive ways. Historical populations simply did not grow as rapidly as many developing countries have in the years since the Second World War. Between 1985 and 1990, for example, Africa's population as a whole grew at an average annual rate of 3 percent. At 3 percent growth per year, 100 people become 1,900 people in less than a hundred years. Thus we should bear in mind that Ireland's pre-Famine population growth was quantitatively quite different from the post–World War II "population explosion." Population growth in Africa and elsewhere in the developing world currently takes place for reasons that are, on a mechanical level, obvious: inoculation programs, the eradication of certain diseases, and other improvements in health have reduced death rates well below birthrates. The remarkable feature of Ireland's pre-Famine population is its rapid growth despite conditions very different from those underlying the rapid growth in some low-income countries today.

Pre-Famine Population Growth

What were the Irish doing that made population grow so fast relative to other countries? The considerable debate on this issue has been more successful in ruling out some possibilities than in firmly establishing an answer to the question. Much of the lack of consensus can be traced to imperfect sources that prevent rigorous testing of the various hypotheses. To grow rapidly a population must have considerable immigration, low mortality, or high fertility. (Rapid growth can result from combinations of these three, of course.) We can rule out immigration as a possible cause. Pre-Famine Ireland experienced extensive emigration. Connell (1950, p. 27) estimated that 1.75 million people left the island between 1780 and 1845, and Mokyr (1985, p. 230) estimated more precisely that in the period between Waterloo (1815) and the Famine at least 1.5 million emigrated. Mokyr's estimate implies an average annual outflow of about 0.7 percent. How could the Irish population grow at the rate it did while losing such large numbers to emigration? The answer must lie in some combination of low mortality, high fertility, or both.

Could mortality in Ireland have been so low as to bring about its population growth? We know even less about mortality than we do about other features of pre-Famine society, so we cannot answer with much certainty. Earlier writers thought that mortality conditions made little contribution to Irish growth rates. The 1841 census suggests a crude death rate of about 24 per thousand for Ireland overall (Mokyr 1985, table 3.2). This death rate is approximately equal to the rates that Wrigley and Schofield report for England in the same period (Wrigley and Schofield 1981, table A3.3). Viewed a different way, the expectation of life at birth in Ireland was about thirty-eight years just before the Famine. This figure is slightly below its English counterpart. Others have noted that death rates from important killers such as smallpox had declined markedly in the late eighteenth century in Ireland. The point has not received much stress, but it is possible that an unusually low death rate contributed to rapid pre-Famine population growth.[1]

So by process of elimination, and with some qualifications required by ignorance of various aspects of mortality conditions, the distinctive force underlying pre-Famine population must be fertility. Yet even scholars who agree that pre-Famine Ireland had unusually high fertility do not

agree on why. We noted earlier that fertility in western populations reflects two distinct forces. First, because women tend to marry late in
western populations and because some do not marry at all, marriage patterns make their own contribution to overall fertility. Second, there is the
number of children borne by married women, called "marital fertility"
by demographers. Thus Irish fertility could be relatively high because
Irish couples had relatively large families or because Ireland had unusual
marriage patterns. Which was it?

A long tradition in the historiography emphasizes nuptiality rather
than marital fertility. In his classic work *The Population of Ireland*
(1950), Connell claimed that pre-Famine Ireland had what amounted to
marriage patterns quite remarkable in Europe. The Irish, he proposed,
married at younger ages than did their European counterparts and virtually all of them married. Connell implied, in fact, that it was not uncommon for Irish women to marry in their teens,[2] which would have been
thoroughly extraordinary by European standards. Flinn's survey of reported ages at marriage from reconstitution studies shows very few populations with a female mean age at marriage less than 22 (Flinn 1981,
app. table 7). Connell argued that this early and universal marriage produced, in the absence of birth control within marriage, very high overall
fertility: "[T]here is little doubt that higher Irish fertility can be associated with earlier marriage" (Connell 1950, p. 39).

More recent research suggests that Connell was taken in by some unreliable evidence, although at least some social groups in Ireland tended
to marry earlier than was common elsewhere in Europe. Drake (1963)
first showed that Connell had seriously exaggerated the number of very
young brides in pre-Famine Ireland. Mokyr later computed ages at marriage from the 1841 census. These averages for women in rural areas
range between 25 and 27 (Mokyr 1985, table 3.3). Nor was Irish celibacy at this time particularly low. The proportion of women who never
married was virtually identical in Ireland and in England just prior to
the Famine. In contrast, some local studies do suggest lower ages at marriage, although how representative these areas are of Ireland as a whole
is not known. O'Neill's study of the parish of Killashandra (County
Cavan) finds a female age at marriage prior to the Famine of about 22
years for farmers' and laborers' wives (1984, table 5.9). Age at marriage
in Killashandra might have been unusually low because of the availability of earnings from textile production. Further evidence of relatively
early marriage comes from the Ulster parish of Killyman, studied by
Macafee (1987, pp. 152–156).

A study of Quakers in Ireland and Britain provides additional evidence on the issue, although that evidence is difficult to evaluate. Vann
and Eversley (1992) study the demographic behavior of this religious mi-

nority from the mid-seventeenth through the mid-nineteenth century. For Ireland especially their data are of exceptionally high quality. The problem with this evidence, of course, is that because it does pertain to a religious minority with distinctive economic and social characteristics, we cannot with any confidence extrapolate to the Irish population at large. Vann and Eversley show persistent differences between Irish and British Quakers. In the late eighteenth and early nineteenth centuries, the average age at marriage for Irish Quaker women was 24–25 years, somewhat lower than British Quakers but certainly well within European experience of the period (table 3.3).

Connell's claims about early marriage, then, seem almost without empirical foundation. Yet his explanation was accepted for many years. How are we to explain this? Connell did not simply make up claims about early marriage. He was relying on testimony given before the Poor Inquiry Commission of 1836, a body charged by Parliament with the question of whether to institute a poor law in Ireland or to adopt other measures to deal with Irish poverty, and other scholars found this evidence credible. There is something to be learned from examining the nature and acceptance of Connell's claim. Drake (1963, table 2) shows that the information on marriage ages contained in the census of 1841 does not agree with the Poor Inquiry's informants. Although witnesses claimed early marriage was common, the census says it was not. Why was the Poor Inquiry such an inaccurate source on marriage patterns? After all, most of the informants were well acquainted with the communities they were describing. There seem to be two reasons, one political and one cultural. The idea of introducing a poor law in Ireland struck terror into many hearts, as noted in chapter 2. Such a law was to be financed by a tax on land and buildings, a tax that would largely fall, ultimately, on landlords. A common strain of opposition to an Irish poor law (and, indeed, to its better-known English counterpart) was to argue that poverty was inevitable and could not be eradicated by government programs. And what better way to explain the inevitability of Irish poverty than to claim that the Irish were irresponsible about reproduction?

There is probably a deeper, less instrumental force at work, as Drake notes. Some of the Poor Inquiry's informants, when pressed, were unable to name a single case of early marriage. In one telling instance a priest was led to state a much higher age at marriage once he had consulted his marriage register (Drake 1963, p. 302). In these cases, as Drake points out, the informants seem to be reciting not evidence of specific people so much as a theory of Irish poverty. The influence of Malthusian thinking might explain why so many thought Ireland had a very low age at marriage. Malthus had been widely read and was very influential by the 1830s. To Malthus very rapid population growth must mean either a low age at marriage or a low death rate. To well-read but badly informed observers it would be quite natural to assume that the Irish married early, given that they were so manifestly poor. Houston (1992, p. 38) suggests that assumptions about Ireland were simply those of the English toward any foreign society. The claims about early marriage fit into a pattern of "literary conventions and ethnocentric cultural prejudices about all non-English societies—specifically, that the women would enter the loose bonds of marriage while still young, would be naturally fecund, and would bear large numbers of children with ease."

Marital Fertility

By a further process of elimination, we thus arrive somewhat tentatively at the conclusion that marital fertility in Ireland was the source of population growth; that pre-Famine Irish women, when they married, had extraordinarily large families. Few deny that Irish marriages were prolific of children, but the available evidence on pre-Famine fertility is thin. Vann and Eversley's study of the Irish Quakers is unfortunately the best detailed information available. Comparisons of Irish Quakers to British Quakers in the eighteenth century shows that the former had shorter intervals between their births, implying larger overall families (table 4.10). We do not know, of course, how Irish Quakers differed from their Catholic and Protestant neighbors. Eversley (1981, pp. 64–65) is probably right in arguing that Irish Quakers had lower fertility than other Irish people. Quakers in Ireland were more likely to be literate and were members of occupations and social classes that in other countries have been associated with low marital fertility.

The census of 1841 asked questions about recent births, and so allows us to examine marital fertility just prior to the Famine. To do this we employ a commonly used index of marital fertility known as I_g. Ansley Coale defined I_g in comparison with the fertility of the Hutterites, a religious sect whose fertility was the highest ever reliably recorded. The index lies between zero and one, with one indicating fertility as high as that of the Hutterites. It is convenient to multiply the index by 1,000 to remove the decimal.[3] Ó Gráda's estimate of I_g for Ireland as a whole in 1841 is 868; Mokyr's estimate of I_g for rural Ireland is at least 800 (Ó Gráda 1993, p. 207; Mokyr 1985, table 3.4). These I_g values imply very high marital fertility compared with other societies in Europe. England, for example, had an I_g of only 650 in 1851 (Mokyr 1985, p. 36). According to the Princeton study, fewer than one-quarter of the provinces of Europe had an I_g of 800 or more prior to the decline of fertility in that province (Coale and Treadway 1986, fig. 2.1).

We cannot say with any certainty why marital fertility in pre-Famine Ireland was so high. One interpretation is that the pre-Famine Irish wanted large families and took measures to ensure copious reproduction. Certainly many pre-Famine observers thought the Irish were unusual in the degree to which they enjoyed children. Mokyr (1985, pp. 60–61) echoed Connell in noting that in pre-Famine Ireland children would be an important source of insurance and old-age support for the poor. Whelan (1986, pp. 154–155) endorsed this view enthusiastically while dismissing another hypothesis: "Large Irish families may have as much to do with a canny assessment of the rigors of old age as they have to do with the supposedly positive effects of the spud on virility." Drake (1963, p. 311) thought the potato's nutritional qualities left Irish women unusually healthy and thus fertile. Another more recent and more sophisticated view suggests that reduced breast-feeding, linked to potato culture, could have caused Irish women to become pregnant again more rapidly after having a child (Schellekens 1993, p. 372). Breast-feeding is a mild contraceptive. His argument is based on the notion that potato culture requires relatively more female labor and that increased labor demands on women tend to reduce the amount of time they can breast-feed each child. Though entirely plausible, this argument is based on the observed correlation between potato culture and high marital fertility, which can have causes other than the one Schellekens suggests.[4] I shall pursue the entire issue of marital fertility further in chapter 7.

At the time of the Famine, then, Ireland differed from many other European countries and from its post-Famine experience in having a relatively high growth rate that seems to reflect high marital fertility and perhaps some differences in mortality and marriage patterns. Population growth would soon cease. But two other features of pre-Famine demographic behavior have important continuities with the post-Famine period. Emigration would become even more common during and after the Famine, but the pre-Famine Irish were already among the most migratory in Europe. And the correctives to Connell show that Irish marriage fit firmly into Hajnal's (1965) western European pattern of high age at first marriage and high proportions celibate. Later changes made Ireland a more extreme example of that pattern, but at the time of the Famine there was nothing at all remarkable about nuptiality in Ireland.

THE FAMINE AND IRISH POPULATION

The censuses of Ireland for 1841 and 1851 reveal in stark terms the human results of one of the last great subsistence crises in European history. In the space of ten years Ireland's population was reduced by some 1.5 million, or 20 percent, reversing the robust demographic expansion of the previous century. A famine like the one that occurred in Ireland in the late 1840s tends to reduce population in three distinct ways. First and most obviously, death rates increase. Although some people die from starvation per se, a more important cause of famine mortality seems to be increased incidence of infectious diseases. Dysentery and typhus were especially important in Ireland, aided by Ireland's version of a European-wide cholera outbreak in 1849. Two mechanisms are at work. People who are weakened from malnutrition contract diseases their bodies might otherwise resist. In addition, the starving beggars who walked Ireland's roads and even invaded the cities were effective carriers of germs that might otherwise have remained safely isolated. But mortality is not limited to famines. Even if famine had not struck Ireland in the 1840s, many people would have died of the causes typical of nonfamine years. To isolate the Famine's effects we must focus on excess deaths, or the degree to which death rates increased above what would otherwise have occurred. Second, famines may also reduce population by encouraging out-migration. Migration was an important cause of population reduction during the Irish Famine. The decades prior to the Famine had already witnessed the development of a substantial emigrant flow, but the Famine-era emigration was huge. Third, fertility ordinarily decreases during famines because marriages are broken through death or geographical separation, because few new marriages occur, and because couples are too ill or too weak to be interested in sexual relations.

Some think it important to know whether 1 million, 1.2 million, or 1.5 million died. The fascination remains undiminished because the statistics of the day do not support reliable estimates of that human toll. One careful accounting by Boyle and Ó Gráda (1986) places excess mortality at about 1.1 million deaths.[5] The Famine also, by their reckoning, increased emigration by 623,000 people and led to 315,000 fewer births.[6]

Total figures on deaths and emigration mask considerable regional variation in the Famine's impact. Just as reliance on the potato and the degree of the crop's destruction varied from place to place, so did the crop failure's impact on population. Hardest hit were the poorer western and southern counties: the population of Connaught as a whole fell by 29 percent from 1841 to 1851, and of Munster, by 22 percent. Ulster and Leinster did comparatively well with "only" 15 percent population losses in each province. Some individual counties were hit particularly hard. County Roscommon lost 32 percent of its 1841 population, and Counties Monaghan, Mayo, and Sligo lost 29 percent each. In relatively untouched rural parts of Leinster and Ulster, population losses ranged from 11 percent in Wexford to 16 percent in Armagh.[7] Even county-level figures do not adequately convey the regional variation in the Famine's impact. Several Galway baronies lost 40 percent of their population in ten years, while in the nearby Aran Islands the loss was only 9.5 percent (Ó Gráda 1993, p. 137).

The continuation of famines late into the twentieth century has recently provoked discussion of their larger causes and consequences. Malthus argued that in societies where the preventative check was not sufficient to keep a population from outgrowing the limits of the resources available, the "positive checks" of war, famine, and pestilence would periodically appear to reduce population more violently. Watkins and Menken (1985) raise a general question about whether famines can, in fact, check population growth as Malthus argued. They use a simple population projection model to ask whether famines of the severity we have observed recently can actually reduce population size enough to make a long-term difference. How much did Ireland's smaller 1911 population owe to the direct effects of the Famine? How much of the depopulation must have reflected either other causes (such as external economic development) or more subtle influences of the Famine on Irish institutions?

The Watkins-Menken model starts with a population of a given age structure and uses reasonable assumptions about fertility and mortality to "project" that population forward into the future. The authors then impose a stylized famine on their model and compare the hypothetical population subjected to a famine to their baseline population. Watkins and Menken use demographic parameters typical of South Asia in recent decades, so we cannot apply their results directly to the Irish case. The most important difference between the nineteenth-century Irish and their assumptions is that South Asian populations have early and universal marriage. Watkins and Menken also assume that the population has zero net migration. They show that recent South Asian famines are not enough, by themselves, to halt the growth of population. Their most severe set of assumptions (a five-year famine with a 150 percent increase in mortality, which reduces the population by nearly one-quarter) implies that fifty years later the famine's effects are barely noticeable (Watkins and Menken 1985, table 3).

These results hold a startling lesson for Irish history, because pre-Famine demographic conditions imply that the Watkins-Menken findings are an upper bound on the demographic effects of the Irish Famine. That is, the Irish Famine would have much less long-run demographic impact than the situation Watkins and Menken discuss. How can we draw this conclusion? First, by assuming early and universal marriage, Watkins and Menken assume that prior to their famine the population had no unused reproductive potential. In Ireland, in contrast, it would have been theoretically possible for women who survived the Famine to marry much earlier and for all of them to marry, leading to a large increase in fertility.[8] In a simple Malthusian model we would expect just such a change in marriage patterns, as a reduced population increased economic opportunities for those remaining. Second, it would have been theoretically possible for emigration to cease, requiring many fewer births to keep Ireland's population constant. Both points imply that if a South Asian famine cannot have long-term effects strictly through its impact on numbers, then the Irish Famine could not, either. The Watkins-Menken analysis serves as a useful warning: the Irish Famine killed thousands and forced thousands more to emigrate, but its impact on simple numbers would have been erased quickly. The Famine's long-run impact on numbers came not through its direct impact on population but through its impact on the social and economic organization of the country.

POPULATION DEVELOPMENTS AFTER THE FAMINE

Table 4.1 uses several simple indicators to summarize population changes in Ireland as a whole from 1841 through 1911. In the rest of this chapter each of those indicators will be discussed individually. First we pause to consider regional variations in demographic patterns within Ireland. Table 4.1 fails to show that post-Famine Ireland was a place of pronounced regional differences in demographic behavior. Verrière (1979, pp. 105–112) notes an interesting feature of this geographical difference in depopulation. Over the long term, from 1851 to 1966, depopulation was quite uniform across Ireland. All regions of Ireland had, in 1966, a population percentage similar to that of 1851. Yet maps 4.1 and 4.2 show that the pace of decline varied significantly. Population increases after the Famine were limited to Dublin and Belfast. Outside these two cities depopulation was the norm. The very rapid decline from 1851 to 1881 was heaviest in the Midlands and south Leinster, but with the exception of a few counties along the Atlantic coast depopulation reduced numbers by at least 20 percent. After 1881 the Atlantic counties lost more of their population than before, and a diminution of the hemorrhage in Leinster moved the center of depopulation west.

In two famous papers Cousens (1961, 1964) noted the regional differences in depopulation. Post-Famine development in the eastern regions of Ireland—particularly the increase in celibacy—was noticeable right after the Famine, and probably represents trends under way even before the Famine. Parts of western Ireland, in contrast, underwent comparatively little demographic change until the 1870s and 1880s. Marriage patterns remained relatively unaltered, and Cousens (1964) claimed that emigration rates were surprisingly low given the poverty and population density. Part of Cousens's analysis turns out to be wrong, however. The

TABLE 4.1
Population Indicators: Size, Celibacy, Emigration, and Fertility

Year	Population	Percentage Never Married[b]		Emigration[c]		Marital Fertility[d]
		M	F	M	F	
1841	8.2	10	12	—	—	868
1851	6.5	12	13	—	—	—
1861	5.8	15	14	34.3	27.7	—
1871	5.4	17	16	18.1	23.6	—
1881	5.2	17	17	30.7	29.2	841
1891	4.7	20	18	25.6	21.1	—
1901	4.4	24	22	21.5	21.4	—
1911	4.1	27	25	—	—	769

Sources: Population: Vaughan and Fitzpatrick (1978, table 3); marriage: decennial censuses of Ireland, 1841–1911, as reported by Fitzpatrick (1985, table 1); emigration: calculated from population by age, as reported in Vaughan and Fitzpatrick (1978, table 25); I_g: unweighted means of county measures, as reported by Ó Gráda (1993, table A5).

Notes:

[a] In millions.

[b] At ages 46–55 for 1841, 45–54 for later census years.

[c] Measured as the percentage of the cohort aged 5–24 in that census year missing from the next. See text for discussion of biases and justification for this measure.

[d] I_g an index lying between zero and one, one indicating maximum fertility. See text for definition and discussion of this measure.

emigration statistics he used to study regional patterns of emigration were seriously flawed for the decades just after the Famine, and in particular seemed to have missed many emigrants from the west of Ireland who went to Great Britain.[9] In fact, "the regional distribution of net outward migration was largely determined during the 1840s and replicated throughout the remainder of the century" (Fitzpatrick 1989c, p. 571). The western counties did tend to differ in their marriage patterns, however. The striking levels of celibacy that were typical of Leinster in the 1860s emerged in Connaught, and parts of Munster, only in the 1880s. Ó Gráda (1973, 1980) has offered what is probably the correct interpretation of these regional differences, namely, that a tradition of seasonal migration to Britain provided sources of income to support families on holdings that would otherwise, by post-Famine standards, be viewed as too small and poor to permit a couple to marry. Reductions in opportunities for seasonal work helped to break down this system.

The components of Irish depopulation were mirrored in Scotland. Anderson and Morse (1993a, pp. 12–16) discuss the regional aspects of Scottish depopulation. Unlike the Irish case, Scotland as a whole experi-

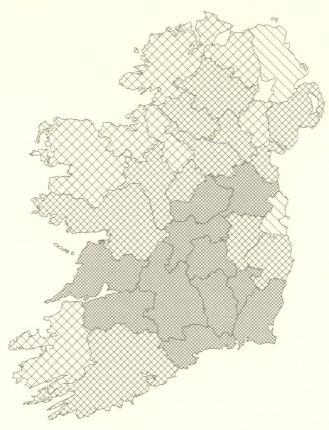

Population Loss of

 Less than 20%   More than 30%

20% to 30%   Population Gain

Map 4.1 Depopulation, 1851–1881. (*Source:* Census data as reported in Vaughan and Fitzpatrick 1978, table 6, with corrections against the original census reports.)

enced population increase from 1861 to 1911. But this increase reflects fairly rapid growth in a few regions, most notably in the urban and industrial areas centered on Dundee, Aberdeen, Glasgow, and Edinburgh. Most other areas of Scotland experienced either population loss or feeble population growth. Scotland's depopulation differed from Ireland's mostly in that a few rural Scottish districts did experience population increase, and Scottish urban growth was rapid enough to compensate for overall rural depopulation.

Population Loss of

 Less than 20%   More than 30%

20% to 30%   Population Gain

Map 4.2 Depopulation, 1881–1911. (*Source:* Census data as reported in Vaughan and Fitzpatrick 1978, table 6, with corrections against the original census reports.)

Connell on Post-Famine Developments

Connell's story of post-Famine demographic change is the logical place to start in any explanation of this aspect of Irish population history. The next few paragraphs are a sympathetic exposition of his argument. Later I will note some empirical and logical flaws in the account and explicitly draw out a different view. In his account of post-Famine change Connell traces the process by which the Irish changed their marriage behavior.

He focused his attention on the arranged marriage called "the Match." In this idealized family system one child, usually a son, remains at home, and when he marries he brings his bride into his parents' household. Upon the heir's marriage his siblings could remain so long as they did not marry, but if they were to marry they had to "travel": leave the household, perhaps Ireland itself. The Match in Ireland was, according to Connell, a post-Famine development. Though not unknown in pre-Famine Ireland, he argued, the stem family had been confined to the more prosperous sections of the farming community. Before the Famine, for the rest, early and universal marriage of sons was the norm. Fathers were willing to subdivide their farms, permitting all their sons to set up their own households on land nearby. The sons did not have to wait for their parents to retire or die before marrying. Thus local marriage was not restricted to one son and to one daughter from each family. Early and universal marriage produced large numbers of children who themselves grew up to marry young.

The Match, if it really was as prevalent as Connell claimed, and worked as he claimed, would be a coherent explanation for post-Famine Ireland's population patterns. If only one son (and perhaps a daughter) could marry, and if each couple had six or more children on average, then the stem family would create large numbers of surplus siblings at each generation. Some of these surplus siblings would emigrate; others would remain in their natal households as bachelor uncles and spinster aunts. Connell understood that he could not invoke this form of household organization as a *deus ex machina*. He had to explain why the stem family came to be the norm. For him the explanation centers on changes in the value and availability of land, which in turn determined the aspirations and options of young people in Ireland and the power their parents (for Connell, chiefly fathers) had over them. Before the Famine living standards and material aspirations were both low, leading peasant children to "marry whom they pleased when they pleased" (Connell 1968, pp. 114–115). The enormous productivity of the potato meant that tiny holdings, perhaps acquired through splitting a father's farm, could produce enough calories to sustain life. Land enough to marry and start a family was easy to obtain. If a young man's father would not split off a scrap of land from the main farm, the young man could recover new land from bog or mountain. And the great demand for labor inspired by the tillage economy of the day meant that even the landless could earn an income. The result, according to Connell, was a striking departure from the typical European marriage pattern discussed above.[10]

Crucial to this interpretation is Connell's belief that pre-Famine Irish peasants were unwilling to place the accumulation of material goods over the pleasures of marriage and family. He offered two reasons for the emphasis on family. One relates to the discredited view, discussed in chapter 2, that landlords extracted every last shilling from their tenants. "Rent, in general, was elastic: if a man worked harder he was more likely to enrich his landlord than himself; there was little reason, in consequence, to defer marriage in the hope that a family might be more comfortably reared" (Connell 1962a, p. 521). The second reason Connell offered for early and universal marriage was the lack of public support for the poor. Irish people had to count on family connections for insurance against infirmity and old age: "In a community which lacked so largely institutional provision for sickness, widowhood, and old age, common prudence pointed to the virtues of early marriage" (Connell 1957, p. 76). Once again we see the hint that lack of a poor-relief system could affect marriage decisions.

The emergence of the stem family came in two stages, in Connell's view. The horrors of the Famine warned some of the dangers of demographic profligacy. "No peasant survived the Famine unchastened by it; nor can we believe, however venomously he imputed blame elsewhere, that he shook off a nagging guilt that drove him to question his own feckless ways" (Connell 1957, p. 87). Then land reform in the 1870s and 1880s brought regulated rents. Landlords could no longer raise rents without judicial approval, ending the problem of "elastic" rents: "It was the land legislation that eventually subdued rent, first restraining it, then making it a falling real charge. Essentially, therefore, it was the land legislation which re-united industry with its reward, and which made of acquisitiveness a rational (if not altogether estimable) rule of life" (Connell 1958, p. 4).

Connell's description of the Match emphasizes control over land and the possibility of emigration. His argument at this point seems a bit odd: his view amounts to claiming that land became more scarce after the Famine, but that the Famine reduced the Irish population considerably, making land less scarce. To follow him we have to understand post-Famine land scarcity as relative to what peasants wanted to accumulate. Fear of renewed crisis and the late Land Acts' fixing of rent gave rural people a stronger interest in accumulating land and so made land more scarce relative to the smaller post-Famine population. The scarcity and value of land after the Famine placed fathers in a strong position with respect to their children. Unlike the pre-Famine period, a son unwilling or unable to endure his father's discipline could not replicate his living standard on bits and scraps of land. Thus fathers were in a position to dictate who would take over the farm and when, as well as whom that son would marry. That is, the farm's value as a "prize" gave parents considerably more influence over their children's marriages. The system also required good emigration possibilities. Emigration became easier and more attractive over the century, as less expensive and safer ships brought emigrants more rapidly to foreign economies with abundant work opportunities. The result was not just the increased Irish wages noted in the previous chapter, but endorsement of the new marriage system. "It is unlikely that the arranged marriage would have met with an acceptance so widespread or so willing unless provision were elsewhere available for the brothers and sisters to whom it denied any chance of a place on the land" (Connell 1957, p. 85; see also Connell 1962a, p. 522).

Connell's account has the considerable merit of trying to integrate specific institutional and historical features into the Malthusian framework. But we have already seen that two features of his analysis have been undermined by more recent historiography. With the exception of an unusually high level of marital fertility, pre-Famine demographic patterns were distinctly less exotic than Connell claimed. And his account of the Match's rise also rests on an exaggerated notion of the insecurity of tenure both prior to the land reforms of 1870 and later. More generally, whatever its historical virtues or faults, Connell's view still amounts to the preventative check with a Hibernian twist.

Marriage

Nuptiality in western European populations encompasses two related ideas: the age at which people marry and the proportion who ever marry. Demographers conventionally measure these two dimensions of nuptiality by the mean age at marriage and the proportion who did not marry by some advanced age. Hajnal (1953) devised an appealing and simple way to estimate the average age at marriage from census reports. This measure, the Singulate Mean Age at Marriage (SMAM), has been widely used. Extensive out-migration, unfortunately, may play tricks with SMAM and for the Irish we must use the measure with caution. Measuring the number who ever marry is simpler, although with extensive out-migration this figure, too, may not be what it seems. Most Irish census reports give the number of people married, widowed, and single in several age groups. Formal divorce was quite rare in the nineteenth century and can be ignored for statistical purposes.

Some discussions of marriage patterns after the Famine tend to confuse changes in the extent of celibacy with changes in the age at marriage. Permanent celibacy in Ireland did become much more widespread between the Famine and the First World War. But age at marriage in Ireland was not distinctive, nor did it experience much change during this period. This confusion as to what actually occurred may account for the variety of interpretations of the behavior. Fitzpatrick's (1985, table 2) calculations of SMAM for the cohorts born between 1821 and 1861 are the best place to start. Men born in 1821 married for the first time on average at 30.3 years, women at 26.2. These figures may seem remarkable to modern eyes, but as we have seen the Irish were not marrying much later than their counterparts elsewhere in Europe. Age at marriage rose very slowly throughout the post-Famine era. Age at marriage for the cohort born in 1861 was 31 for males, 27.5 for females. Thus in the period after the Famine age at marriage increased only slightly. The increase in age at marriage during the century, in fact, was less than the regional differences in evidence just after the Famine. Male ages at marriage for the cohort born in 1821 ranged from 29.1 in Ulster to 31 in Munster. For females, the range was from 25 in Connaught to 26.8 in Leinster. The differences narrowed over the century. For the cohort born in 1861, the high and low for males is 31.7 (Connaught) and 30.3 (Ulster) and for females, 27.8 (Ulster), and 26.9 (Connaught).[11]

Confusion about increases in age at marriage may be traceable to folk wisdom about the role of inheritance and dowries in forcing young people to wait to marry. Unfortunately, this confusion has made its way into several widely read general histories. A reader of Lee's venerable survey would be forgiven for thinking that changes in age at marriage were more pronounced than changes in permanent celibacy (Lee 1973a, pp. 3–6). Similarly, Cullen's survey also speaks of an "apparent sharp rise in the age of marriage in post-Famine Ireland" and does not mention any changes in the proportions who married (Cullen 1972, p. 136). In a more recent work Rhodes (1992, pp. 88–89) also deduced an increase in age at marriage from an increasing number of older bachelors and spinsters.

Literary accounts might also bear some responsibility for exagerated notions of age at marriage in rural Ireland. The poet Patrick Kavanagh's prose works *The Green Fool* and *Tarry Flynn*, both set in the early twentieth century, suggest an average age at marriage much higher than is consistent with statistical sources. In *The Green Fool*, for example, he remarks at one point that "the marrying men were usually hairy-faced farmers of around forty-five or fifty years of age" (Kavanagh 1939, p. 156). Later he implies that a typical age at marriage for a rural man would be 55 or 60 (p. 240). The protagonist in his poem "The Great Hunger," which has been cited as illustrating some features of rural life, was still waiting to marry at age 65 when the protagonist's mother died.[12] Kavanagh himself married for the first time in 1967, shortly before his death at the age of 63. Mid-twentieth-century Ireland had, according to official sources, an average age at marriage for males of about 32.[13] Kavanagh's purpose was not statistical description, to be sure. But his considerable literary influence may have contributed to an unwarranted view of Irish marriage patterns.

TABLE 4.2
Proportion Never Married in England and Wales, France, Germany, and Ireland (in percent)

Year	England and Wales		France		Germany		Ireland	
	M	F	M	F	M	F	M	F
1841	—	—	—	—	—	—	10	12
1851	12	12	—	—	—	—	12	13
1861	10	12	11	13	—	—	15	14
1871	10	12	11	12	9	12	17	16
1881	10	12	13	13	8	11	17	17
1891	10	12	12	13	8	10	20	18
1901	11	14	10	11	8	11	24	22
1911	12	16	11	11	9	12	27	25

Sources: Ireland: Fitzpatrick (1985, table I); England and Wales: Kennedy (1973, table 51); France: *Statistiques de la France*, D.S. XIII, 1861–1991: Maison and Millet (1974, table 1), 1871–1911. Germany: *Statistik des Deutschen, Reichs*, E.R. vols. 14, 57, N.F. vols. 68, 150, 240.

Notes: Irish and English figures are percentage never married at ages 46–55 for 1841, and 45–54 for later years. French figures average the percentages never married at ages 45–49 and 50–54 for 1871–1911; 1861 is for those 45–54. German figures are for the Reich, and are the percentage never married at ages 45–54 for 1871–1901, 50–59 for 1911. Actual dates of German censuses are 1871, 1880, 1890, 1900, and 1910.

Ireland did experience a very large increase in the proportion who never married between 1851 and 1911. This increase was sufficient to propel the country to the edge of European demographic patterns. Table 4.2 reports the proportion of each cohort that never married for Ireland, England and Wales, France, and Germany. Viewed in this light the Irish were completely unremarkable at the time of the Famine, but by 1911 had celibacy levels twice those of the other countries. The Irish difference at the turn of the twentieth century reflects for the most part increases in celibacy in Ireland. Age at marriage declined somewhat in European countries over this period, but the proportions who did not marry remained relatively constant.

Increases in celibacy occurred at different paces in the different regions of Ireland. Table 4.3 reports a celibacy measure for the four provinces of Ireland in 1841 through 1911. Two differences are immediately apparent, seen most clearly by comparing Leinster to Connaught. Prior to the Famine celibacy was already more common in Leinster. But recall the European marriage pattern; if anything Leinster was more typical of western Europe, and Connaught had an unusually low proportion of

TABLE 4.3
Proportion Never Married in the Provinces of Ireland (in percent)

Year	Leinster		Ulster		Munster		Connaught	
	M	F	M	F	M	F	M	F
1841	13	14	10	14	9	11	7	8
1851	15	14	13	15	10	10	7	8
1861	19	17	16	16	12	12	10	10
1871	21	19	19	19	13	13	12	12
1881	22	20	19	20	14	13	11	9
1891	25	22	21	23	17	13	14	10
1901	28	25	24	26	20	17	19	14
1911	31	28	26	27	26	21	25	18

Source: Decennial censuses of Ireland, 1841–1911, as reported by Fitzpatrick (1985, table 1).
Note: At ages 46–55 for 1841, 45–54 for later years.

those who never married. Increases in celibacy proceeded fairly steadily in Leinster and Ulster. In Munster and especially Connaught, the change was more abrupt. Celibacy had become only slightly more common in those two provinces until the 1880s, after which the celibate proportion increased sharply. Here we are seeing the delayed post-Famine adjustment that Cousens noted in his research, and discussed earlier here. By 1911 regional variation in celibacy had abated considerably.

Irish Nuptiality in Comparative Perspective

Figures such as those reported in table 4.2 have led some to argue that Ireland was unique. This conclusion flows from the selection of comparisons. The proportion of never-married adults in Ireland was larger than in the large, industrialized countries represented in table 4.2, but a broader and more appropriate selection of comparisons shows that Ireland was not unique. In 1900 the percentage of all males aged 45–49 who had never married was 20 in Ireland, but 19 in Iceland and 16 in Belgium. More strikingly, the same figure for females was 17 each in Ireland, Switzerland, and Belgium, but 29 in Iceland, 20 in Portugal, and 19 in Sweden (Hajnal 1965, table 2). Anderson and Morse (1993a, table 2) report that 21 percent of Scots women aged 45–54 in 1911 had never married. (The comparable figure for males was 16 percent.) Several European regions were also famous for their permanent celibacy. In five of the twenty districts into which Livi-Bacci (1971) divided Portugal for his study, at least 25 percent of women aged 50–54 in 1911 had never married. All of these districts were in northern Portugal.

Several regions of Germany and Austria also had very low levels of nuptiality during the nineteenth century. Ehmer (1991, app. table 3) reports the results of parish studies that imply that in 1890, 31 percent of men aged 45–49 had never married in the province of Salzburg, and 38 percent in the same age and sex cohort had never married in the province of Kärnten. Official statistics for all of Austria show these two provinces to be extremes, but in several other provinces in 1880 more than 20 percent of men aged 45–49 never married (app. table 5). No German regions can rival these levels of permanent celibacy, but the population census for 1880 showed that in the rural areas of both Oberbayern and Niederbayern over 16 percent of men and women aged 45–49 had never married; women in Franken (Bavaria) and the Oberpfalz were nearly as likely to be celibate (Knodel and Maynes 1976, app. table A.2). These south German marriage patterns were part of a different demographic system—illegitimacy rates were also very high in these regions—but reinforce the point that the rural Irish were not the only celibates in Europe.

Another type of comparison serves as a useful warning about monocausal explanations involving the Catholic Church. Rural Québec was overwhelmingly Catholic, and this Catholicism shared some features of the Irish Catholic Church. After the British took over the province in 1759 French-speaking Catholics viewed themselves as a relatively powerless group, and the Church has remained a rallying point for Québeçois sentiment. But permanent celibacy in rural Québec was relatively rare during the nineteenth century. For example, in 1891 in the rural areas of the province only 7.4 percent of males and 10.4 percent of females aged 45–54 had never married.[14]

Did the Famine Directly Cause the Increase in Celibacy?

Before proceeding we must also confront an explanation of changes in marriage patterns that is widespread in the historiography, but that does not appear to be correct. According to some, the Famine simply removed, by death or emigration, a disproportionate share of the rural lower classes, laborers and cottiers. These people tended to marry relatively early in life, and almost all of them married. Thus, from this perspective, changes in marriage after the Famine were due not to behavioral changes within any strata of rural society, but to the decimation of the poorest strata of rural society.[15] The Famine did much to reorder the class composition of rural Ireland, but the available information does not support the view that it had a direct and appreciable impact on marriage patterns. The only systematic exploitation of pre-Famine manuscript census sources shows that laborers in the parish of Killashandra, County Cavan, married earlier in life than farmers, but reveals no appreciable differences in the proportions who ever did so (O'Neill 1984, table 5.10). Even the published census does not support this interpretation of the Famine's role. There was no large increase in the proportions of those never married at the time of the Famine, as this claim implies. The discontinuity in the series for Munster and Connaught, the two provinces hit hardest by the Famine, comes in the 1880s and 1890s, if at all. Furthermore, the proportion who never married remained at elevated levels well into the twentieth century, long after any shifts in weights within the rural population should be showing their results. The influence of the Famine on later developments was profound, but worked through a mechanism more subtle than a shift in population weights.[16]

A final notable feature of rural Irish celibacy is its unusual relation to urban marriage patterns. In most historical circumstances celibacy is more common in urban areas than in rural areas. For Ireland this relation was reversed. In 1911, for example, some 27 percent of all men and 25 percent of all women aged 45–54 in Ireland had never married. For the city of Dublin, the same figures are 21 and 22 percent. In Belfast male celibacy was very uncommon (by Irish standards): about 13 percent of men aged 45–54 there had never married, and about 21 percent of the women. In the United States in 1910, in contrast, celibacy was more common in urban than in rural areas (U.S. Census, 1913, table V, p. 585). The Irish pattern was true of men in only a few other European countries, according to the compilation by Knodel and Maynes (1976, table 1), and in none of the countries they list were rural women more likely to remain unmarried than urban women.[17]

Widowhood and Remarriage

This chapter focuses on first marriages, largely because Ireland was most distinctive in this regard. We should briefly consider another feature of marriage patterns that is important in European history: the possibility of remarriage following the death of one's spouse. The relatively high mortality rates of centuries past meant that many husbands and wives could expect to lose their spouse fairly early in life. In most societies remarriage became less common during the eighteenth and nineteenth centuries. In sixteenth-century England, for example, widows and widowers probably accounted for 25 percent or more of all brides and bridegrooms, but by the mid-nineteenth century this proportion had fallen to about 11 percent (Wrigley and Schofield 1981, pp. 258–259). Official statistics for the second half of the nineteenth century show a decline in remarriage over the relevant period for most countries; see, for example, Italy (Bellettini 1981, table I), Norway (Dyrvik 1981, table I), or Hungary (Horvath 1981, table I). Knodel's work (1988, chap. 7) on couples married in German villages between 1700 and 1899 is one of the most detailed studies of remarriage patterns. Knodel shows that the decline of remarriage has two proximate causes. Better mortality conditions meant that marriages lasted longer. Equally important, however, was a second trend. Widows and widowers became much less likely to remarry, even when widowed. About one-third of marriages in the first half of the eighteenth century involved a widow or widower. By the second half of the nineteenth century, this figure had declined to about one-fifth (Knodel 1988, table 7.4). Remarriage was usually more common for males than for females. In Knodel's villages, men were more likely to remarry following their spouse's death at virtually every age and in every time period. During the eighteenth and nineteenth centuries as a whole, nearly 50 percent of all men would remarry within ten years of being widowed, compared with only 20 percent of women (Knodel 1988, table 7.5). The same holds for most populations for which the relevant information is available.

Irish sources do not permit us to study remarriage until the 1860s, when the Registrar-General began to report the conjugal status of brides and bridegrooms each year. By then remarriage was somewhat less common in Ireland than in many other places, especially for women. In the 1880s, for example, some 11 to 12 percent of all bridegrooms and 5 to 6 percent of all brides had been married previously (Great Britain 1890, table V). These figures declined slightly to about 8 percent of men and 4 percent for women by 1910 (Great Britain 1911c, table VI, p. x). In contrast, in Knodel's villages 14.6 percent of bridegrooms marrying between 1850 and 1899 were widowers, and 5.4 percent of the brides were widows (Knodel 1988, table 7.4). Livi-Bacci (1981, table I) reports similar figures for a large number of European countries for a slightly earlier period, showing that in Ireland the widows and widowers accounted for a smaller proportion of marriages than in most other European countries, although not by a large margin. Within Ireland the Registrar-General's reports suggest some interesting, but fairly weak, regional patterns. Remarriage was most common in the large cities. In 1910 about 8 percent of new husbands had been widowed previously, although in Belfast the same figure was 10 percent (Great Britain 1911b, pp. 2–3). Remarriage was least common in eastern counties such as Meath and Wicklow that had large fractions of never-married adults. Birdwell-Pheasant (1993, p. 25) reports that in her study area of Bally-duff (County Kerry), only 3.5 percent of men and even fewer women were known to have remarried.

The literature on remarriage elsewhere offers several different explanations for why men were more likely to remarry than women. Some theories focus on property relations in a peasant society. If land is associated with a male lineage, a remarrying widow who has children with a man from outside that lineage endangers the control of her first husband's family over the holding. Beames (1987, pp. 274–277) notes instances in which rural violence occurred when a dead husband's family attempted to prevent his widow's remarriage. Other explanations focus on the sexual division of labor within a household and the need to replace a dead wife's contribution to the household economy. A widower with young children, some argue, had a particularly strong need for a new wife to care for those children; a widow could more easily hire farm laborers and others to replace her dead husband's contribution to the household. These arguments have not received much systematic scrutiny, and in all likelihood the real reason for the sex difference in remarriage depends on the institutional context.

Emigration

We shall never know the precise numbers, but certainly more than four million people left Ireland for good between the Famine and the First World War. Many European countries experienced significant emigration during the second half of the nineteenth century, but the Irish outflow was extraordinary for its size and duration. This four million total translates into average annual gross emigration rates of nearly 19 emigrants per thousand persons during the 1850s, and 16 persons per thousand during the 1880s. Even in the 1890s and the decade prior to the First World War, when Irish emigration was low by post-Famine standards, the average annual gross emigration rate stood at 9.7 and 7.9 per thousand (Hatton and Williamson 1994, table 1). To appreciate how large these numbers are, consider the outflow from Gemany, another country famous for its emigrants. In 1881 Germany had three emigrants for every emigrant from Ireland. Yet Ireland's population at the time was only one-ninth of Germany's.[18] Only Norway had an average annual gross emigration rate of over 10 per thousand in any decade between 1850 and 1913 (Hatton and Williamson, table 1).

Table 4.4 gives some idea of the impact of this outflow on each cohort by showing the fraction of those aged 5–24 in Ireland in one census who would not be counted by the next census. The numbers in table 4.4 are called "cohort-depletion rates," and will be used in this study as a proxy for the sometimes badly flawed official counts of emigrants. Cohort-depletion measures have both advantages and disadvantages. Their primary disadvantage is that they can be confused by regional variations in mortality and by internal migration. That is, if mortality is worse in County Mayo than in County Meath, a cohort-depletion measure will make it appear as if County Mayo had higher emigration rates. This,

TABLE 4.4
Cohort-Depletion Measures, by Province

Decade	Leinster	Ulster	Munster	Connaught	Ireland
1861–1871					
Males	28.64	33.47	36.05	41.57	34.29
Females	22.74	23.41	32.55	36.50	27.69
1871–1881					
Males	19.90	30.83	27.68	34.83	28.07
Females	17.45	21.79	26.76	31.53	23.61
1881–1891					
Males	22.50	30.17	32.96	39.65	30.73
Females	20.81	24.96	34.64	40.91	29.23
1891–1901					
Males	16.64	24.03	28.26	37.40	25.58
Females	12.60	15.51	27.02	35.73	21.07
1901–1911					
Males	12.21	21.69	23.82	32.47	21.49
Females	12.62	17.97	25.32	37.49	21.44

Sources: Census of Ireland, 1861, Provincial Summaries; 1871, Provincial Summaries Table XIV; 1881, Provincial Summaries Table XIII; 1891, Provincial Summaries Table XIII; 1901, Provincial Summaries Table XV; 1911, Provincial Summaries Table XV.

Note: Figures are the percentage of the cohort aged 5–24 in the first census who are not returned in the next.

fortunately, is probably not a serious problem in rural Ireland in the post-Famine period. Similarly, a cohort-depletion rate can only count net movements, and so in the case of simultaneous in- and out-migration would be powerless to tell us how many emigrants there were. Ireland, however, experienced relatively little return migration during this period. For our purposes the drawbacks of these cohort-depletion measures are more than compensated for the fact that they are based on the census rather than on the flawed counts of emigrants, and so offer the possibility of reasonably accurate comparisons of emigration rates across regions and over time.[19]

Emigration from Ireland can be divided, somewhat imprecisely, into three types: seasonal migration, migration to Britain, and overseas migration. Since the introduction of steamer service on the Irish Sea in the early nineteenth century, thousands of Irish men (and some women) had yearly gone to England and Scotland to harvest crops. The harvest migration was an extension of a long-standing internal migration of harvesters. This seasonal flow to Britain probably paved the way for the

Irish navvy, famous for his work on railroads, docks, and other construction projects, and later for the Famine-era outflow (Handley 1945, 1947). Seasonal harvesters (or *Spailpíní*) originated primarily in the poorer western and northwestern counties. Harvesters traveling to Britain were part of a larger, geographically widespread movement of agricultural workers, many of whom remained in Ireland on their travels.[20] Earnings from these yearly forays supported a way of life that had, in most other areas, vanished with the Famine (Cousens 1964; Ó Gráda 1973). By the end of the nineteenth century the seasonal harvester had become much less common, as agricultural machinery displaced his labor in Britain (Ó Gráda 1973).

The second flow consisted of more or less permanent migrants to Great Britain.[21] Some migration to Britain had existed for centuries. In a famous remark, Adam Smith marveled at the health and beauty of Irish men and women in Britain (Smith 1976, pp. 179–180). But permanent emigration on a mass scale originated in the nineteenth century. Emigration to Britain was quantitatively much more important than one might think, given the historiographical focus on overseas emigrants from Ireland. In 1851 the number of Irish-born people in the United States and in Britain was nearly equal, with about 500,000 Irish living in England and Wales and another 200,000 in Scotland (Fitzpatrick 1989b, p. 625 and app. table 1). And though the numbers of Irish-born in Britain peaked in 1861, Britain remained an important destination for Irish emigrants. In 1911 there were about a half-million Irish in the neighboring island, constituting 1 percent of the resident population in England and 3.6 percent of the population in Scotland (Fitzpatrick 1989b, table 1.1).

With the waning of the seasonal harvester, most Irish migrants to Britain lived in cities. The geographical concentration of Irish migrants in cities, in fact, made them seem more numerous than they in fact were. Persons born in Ireland were about 4 percent of the population of London in 1841, and did not fall below 2 percent of all Londoners until 1891 (Shannon 1935, pp. 81, 83). In other cities the Irish were an even greater relative presence. In 1871 over 15 percent of Liverpool's population had been born in Ireland, and 14 percent of Glasgow's (Fitzpatrick 1989b, table 1.2).

The final migratory flow has been the most famous. Officials drew a distinction between migrants who left Ireland for Britain (who were, after all, remaining within the same kingdom) and those who left the United Kingdom altogether—"overseas" emigrants. Several million people left Ireland for the United States, Canada, Australia, and elsewhere between the Famine and the First World War. Both the destinations reported to the keepers of the emigration statistics and the statistics on birthplace reported in the census of the United States show that throughout the post-Famine period the United States claimed the lion's share of Irish emigrants who went somewhere other than Britain. The share varied with economic conditions in the United States and in other destination countries. Eighty-four percent of all overseas emigrants went to the United States during the period 1861–1870, a figure that rose to 93 percent for 1891–1900 and fell slightly during the first decade of the twentieth century.[22] In 1850 the number of Irish-born people living in the United States was nearly a million, and this figure peaked at almost 1.9 million in 1891. The numbers living in Canada peaked at 286,000 in 1861, and at 227,000 in Australia in 1891. The total number of Irish-born people living in England and Wales and Scotland peaked at about 800,000 in 1861.[23]

One consequence of this enormous outflow was that by the end of the nineteenth century a substantial fraction of all people who had been born in Ireland were living elsewhere. In 1881 nearly 40 percent of Irish-born people were not living in Ireland. Even in 1911, after a decade of relatively slow emigration, about 33 percent of all people born in Ireland were living elsewhere.[24] The prevalence of emigration and its consequence, the large number of expatriate Irish, is a theme to which we shall return several times. But it is worth repeating two comments that form the basis of many early studies of the Irish. First, the very definition of "the Irish" is somewhat problematic. Clearly we want to count those living in Ireland, and perhaps even those who were born there but lived most of their lives elsewhere. But how do we count the many children of the Irish-born overseas? At some level this is the question of ethnic identity that concerns so many social histories of immigrant groups. Second, for the Irish who remained at home the outflow of people meant that Ireland was an extraordinarily outward-looking society. Few young people could not have had a relative or at least acquaintance who left Ireland to spend his life abroad.

Migrants' Characteristics

Emigration was not a new phenomenon after the Famine, but several features of post-Famine emigrants were quite new. Before the Famine and during the cataclysm, a substantial proportion of Irish emigrants were families and their children. In her sample of Irish emigrants to the United States in 1831 and 1841, Erickson (1989, table 13) found that about 60 percent of Irish migrants were traveling as families. Families were also a large majority of Famine-era emigrants. But Irish emigrants after the Famine consisted overwhelmingly of single, young adults. From the 1860s on people under 15 never make up more than 14 percent of all emigrants. The same can be said for people 35 or older.[25] The post-Famine Irish migrated alone, or with friends or siblings.

Another feature of Irish emigration, especially after the Famine, was both distinctive and important: Irish males and females emigrated in nearly equal numbers. During the 1860s there were about 800 female emigrants per thousand males. This ratio rose until by the 1890s women actually outnumbered men at 1,150 female emigrants per thousand male emigrants.[26] No other country's emigrants included so many women. Among Italian emigrants the number of females per thousand males ranged from the mid-teens to about 300 (Ferenczi and Wilcox 1929, p. 820). Even the Germans, who like most northern Europeans had relatively more females among the emigrant outflow, never saw more than about 850 female emigrants per thousand males (Ferenczi and Wilcox 1929, p. 698). The sex ratio of Irish emigrants was sometimes less balanced in a particular region than for Ireland as a whole. But even at a more local level the outflow of Irish emigrants was more balanced by sex than among many other European emigrations.

The sex ratio of Irish emigrants is central to the character of post-Famine demographic developments.[27] On a mechanical level this balance between the sexes among emigrants meant that Ireland's very high emigration rates did not produce very unequal numbers of men and women either in expatriate Irish communities or at home. In Australia in 1870, for example, there were about equal numbers of Irish-born men and women, while among Scottish and the English-born people males outnumbered females by a ratio of five to three (Fitzpatrick 1980, p. 137). In the United States at the turn of the twentieth century there were even more dramatic contrasts between the nearly equal numbers of Irish men and women and the other immigrant groups in which males far outnumbered females. To take just one example, the 1910 Census of the United States reported that among the foreign-born population as a whole in that year there were 131 men for every 100 women. For the Irish-born, however, this number was 83 men per hundred women, or more women than men. The excess of men was especially severe among eastern and southern European groups; among the Italian-born there were 191 men for every 100 women (United States Bureau of the Census, 1913, table 39, p. 866).

In other countries, with their male-dominated emigrant streams, high emigration was synonymous with expatriate communities that had excesses of men and a population remaining at home that had more women than men. The demographic impact of such sex imbalances could be profound. In her study of the Portuguese parish of Lanheses, which she aptly titled *Men Who Migrate, Women Who Wait*, Brettell noted the implications of unbalanced emigration. For most of the later nineteenth century Lanheses annually lost three to four times as many men as women to emigration. The result for marriage patterns was stark: at the turn of the twentieth century at least 25 percent of women dying over age 50 had never married, compared with fewer than 10 percent of the men (Brettell 1986, tables 1.1, 3.9). We have already seen that Ireland escaped this fate. Although the extent of permanent celibacy rose steadily in Ireland, it increased at rates very similar for men and for women. Irish men were more likely to remain single than Irish women, but not by much. Celibacy in Ireland was not a condition for one sex or the other, as in some countries experiencing mass emigration.[28]

Being mostly single young adults, Irish emigrants would seem well positioned to take advantage of expanding economies in North America and Oceania. Young people unburdened by dependents can move within their new country to take advantage of job opportunities and can afford to invest in the new skills required to prosper in a new land. Irish emigrants also had an important advantage over many other newly arrived Europeans: most spoke English. Precise statistics on the language ability of emigrants are lacking, but we do know that the Irish language became increasingly less common after the Famine. Certainly a large majority of Irish emigrants spoke English, either as their only language or as the language they had learned in school. In a country such as the United States speaking English set an immigrant apart and helps account for ability of the Irish immigrants to move rapidly into positions that required social contact with the native population: domestic service, the police, and so on. Yet Irish migrants to the United States did not do all that well economically, and this feature of the Irish-American experience is one of the enduring points of debate about the Irish in the United States. The Irish emigrant's occupational background was less useful in industrial countries. Many emigrants had skills most applicable to the farm but would be looking for work in cities. The emigration statistics record the emigrant's occupations, although these figures may reflect as much hope or intention as reality. Emigrants generally listed an occupation that implied few skills that would be of much help in the urban and industrial world to which they were moving. Of the nearly 19,000 males who emigrated from Ireland in 1902, more than two-thirds stated their occupation as "labourer." Three-quarters of the 21,000 females who emigrated that same year were servants.[29] For the two sexes combined, laborers and servants made up at least a majority, and usually more like two-thirds, of all emigrants to the United States in the period 1875–1914 (Thomas 1973, app. table 82).

Fitzpatrick has argued that for Irish women, at least, this lack of skill might be more apparent than real. English-speaking and literate, young

Irish women were especially prized as servants in North American cities (Fitzpatrick 1986). Still, this relative lack of skill contrasts sharply with English or Scots emigrants. During the nineteenth and early twentieth centuries the number of Irish immigrants to the United States who claimed a professional or skilled occupation never topped 25 percent. Professional and skilled workers among English immigrants to the United States, in contrast, ranged between 40 and 60 percent for the same period.[30]

Another feature of Irish emigration that was distinctive, although less so than the sex ratio of emigrants, was the chance that an Irish emigrant would return home. Return migration was a common feature of many European emigrant streams. Returning to Ireland from overseas was less common. Unfortunately the only detailed study of return migration focuses on the period 1858–1867 (T'Hart 1985). According to T'Hart's study, those who returned to Ireland seemed to have done so not as part of the original plan to leave, but because something changed while they were away; someone died unexpectedly, making a farm available, and so on. Schrier notes that in some cases an emigrant would send money to his family, who would buy an "American out-farm" intended for his use. But few emigrants ever returned to take the farm, and the property eventually fell to a relative (Schrier, 1958 pp. 119–120). More common, perhaps, were Irish women who went abroad in their teens and earned sufficient funds to form an attractive dowry back in Ireland.[31] This dearth of planned return migration contrasts with the pattern of many southern European migrants to North America who went with the intention of acquiring savings and then returning home. The Dillingham Commission reported the number of people who left the United States in the fiscal years 1908–1910 compared with the number from the same group who entered in those years. Seven Irish people left the United States for every hundred who entered. For North Italians, the figure is 63 per hundred (United States Immigration Commission [1907–1910] 1970, I:182, table 16). The Commission on Emigration and Other Population Problems virtually dismissed return migration as an important feature of Irish population dynamics (1954, p. 115).[32] The reasons for these higher return emigration rates are diverse, but in cases such as the Italian reflect, in part, the difficulty of marrying a woman from one's country without returning home. Irish people who wanted to marry other Irish people could easily find a partner from among other emigrants.

Most aspects of emigration, from the size of the flow to the destination to the emigrant's characteristics, had a regional dimension. Emigrants to the United States tended to originate in Connaught and other areas of the west. Other destinations had stronger Scots, and so Ulster, traditions. Emigrants to Canada were more likely to be from Ulster, as were emigrants to New Zealand. Australia and Canada also drew a slightly more skilled migrant and were more likely to attract family groups. The marital status of emigrants also differed by their origins in Ireland; the few married emigrants, for example, were most likely to come from Leinster and Ulster.

Migration decisions were strongly correlated with economic conditions in Ireland and abroad. Migrants probably chose their destinations on the basis of family ties and other issues that are not strictly economic. And for some, of course, Ireland's political and constitutional status was one reason to leave. But evidence shows that the overwhelming majority of emigrants were simply seeking a better life abroad. A recent study examines the econometric determinants of migration in the later nineteenth century. The year-to-year outflow depended heavily on economic conditions both in Ireland and in the major destination countries. A shock to agricultural output in Ireland, such as occurred in the early 1880s, led to a swelling of the outflow. Improvements in economic conditions abroad had the same effect (Hatton and Williamson 1993, table 2). County-by-county emigration rates over the period 1881–1911 show that emigration rates were highest in areas that were poor, agricultural, had relatively small farms, and had families that were relatively large.

Chains of Migrants

Students of migration, whether traditional or modern, frequently note the importance of migratory "chains." The individual links in the chain metaphor are most often family members, but can be connected through village ties or in other ways. First one member of a family goes abroad. Especially if the trip is expensive, this first migrant's travel may be financed by members of his family, pooling their funds. Once settled and earning enough income to save, the first migrant repays those who sent him by financing the passage of another migrant, perhaps a sibling. Through this mechanism entire groups of siblings and even families may move from one country to another. The important implication of these migratory chains is that once a country or region has settled a substantial number of its people elsewhere, migration to the new place becomes more common.[33] Chain migration was certainly a feature of Irish life:

> If emigration became a custom among the Irish, it also became a tradition to go to America. The reasons are not far to seek. As Adams has shown, a considerable number of Irishmen already had established themselves in the United States long before the ravages of the famine descended upon the home country and opened the flood gates of the later emigration. Once the road to America had been laid down it became the principal highway out of Ireland

and few would deviate from it. The existence of a prospering Irish community in the United States acted as a powerful magnet upon the overburdened Irish at home. Then the famine struck, the destitute fled by the thousands to the land they knew best and further swelled the American-Irish community. From that time forward there was hardly a family remaining in Ireland which did not have a friend, relative, or near neighbor somewhere in America. (Schrier 1958, p. 16)

Schrier underrated the importance of destinations other than the United States, but the basic point is solid enough: the large Irish communities who settled overseas before and even during the Famine, particularly in the United States, made it easier for later migrants to follow. Throughout the century such chains remained important. Siblings assisted siblings, uncles brought out nieces and nephews, each repaying his or her own benefactor with transfer in the form of passage money (see, for example, Rhodes 1992, p. 290). The practice of sending prepaid tickets is simply one more way to help family members remaining at home, and in some respects is the fulfillment of an expectation that each one who was brought out would bring out others. Helping an emigrant aided both the individual in question and his or her family, contrary to Schrier's curious comment that passage money "never contributed in any way to the welfare of those at home" (Schrier 1958, p. 110).

These chains of migrants help to explain how such poor people could travel so far. But part of the Irish people's extraordinary mobility lies in the cheapness of travel, especially to Britain. The cost of passage between Ireland and Britain declined rapidly after the introduction of steamer service. During fare wars passage could be inexpensive indeed. In 1867, steerage fare from Belfast to Glasgow (including the rail portion) was briefly 6 pence (McNeill 1969, p. 40).[34] Even the normal steerage fare of 3 shillings was modest, about half a week's wages for an agricultural laborer. Later, railroads organized special train/ship fares that saved migrants the need to walk to an Irish port for the trip to Britain. Travel to North America and Australia was more expensive, but the cost declined over the nineteenth century. The costs of these trips varied with the season, the port of embarkation and debarkation, and the migrant's ability to scout a good price. Passage from Ireland to North America varied between £2 and £6, depending on the season, with passage to Australia running £10–£15 (Fitzpatrick 1984, p. 22). Prices could go even lower, as in 1894, when one could travel from Ireland to North America for £1 16s. (Miller 1985, p. 355). Such sums were not hard to save for even an unskilled Irish worker in the Unites States at that time. An average "lower-skilled" worker would earn about $8.70 per week (£1 16s.) in 1890, a figure that increased to about $10.65 (£2 4s.) by 1910 (U.S.

Bureau of the Census 1975, ser. D778). Nor were passage costs prohibitive when compared with the dowries of £70 and £100 that even modest farms could demand by the early twentieth century. Viewed another way, the cost of passage to North America by the late nineteenth century was roughly equivalent to the cost of a heifer or the annual rent of a typical Mayo farm (Fitzpatrick 1984, p. 22).

But even these sums had to come from somewhere. After all, most people left Ireland because they were poor. Banks and other regular lenders might have been unwilling to lend such people money for any purpose, but migration is an especially difficult project to finance from conventional sources. The migrant, after all, wants to borrow money so he can leave. Assistance from the state and from other institutions helped a few. Several efforts to assist Irish emigrants emerged both before and during the Famine, and after the Famine local Poor Law officials were permitted to raise loans to assist paupers and their families to emigrate. Emigration assisted by the Poor Law was responsible for getting some 45,000 Irish people to Canada and elsewhere during the period 1849–1906. Another state-assisted project helped remove about 25,000 from poor western districts during the economic crisis of 1883–1891 (Fitzpatrick 1984, p. 18). For the aspiring emigrant who could neither earn nor borrow the funds required on his own, however, two sources of assistance were more important: landlords anxious to clear their estates of smallholders, and colonial and foreign funds in territories seeking to encourage the immigration of English-speaking whites. Ten major landlords were responsible for financing the emigration of 30,000 emigrants as part of efforts to reorganize their estates. Many Irish settlers in Australia received some sort of government assistance, and similar schemes aided migrants to New Zealand, South Africa, and Latin America (Fitzpatrick 1984, p. 18).

More important, however, were funds sent from overseas by earlier emigrants and their families. The state and various private sources provided something like £2 million in assistance during the nineteenth century. In contrast, official estimates show that U.K. emigrants sent home £34 million between 1848 and 1887 alone (Schrier 1958, table 18). Official statistics do not report how much of this went to Ireland, but the proportion must have been considerable. Given that two-fifths of the remittances were in the form of prepaid tickets and at least some of the remainder would have been used for the same purpose, assistance by earlier emigrants dwarfed all other sources of finance. State and private assistance was not unimportant, however. By sending out considerable numbers of Irish people before the Famine and during the crisis years, these sources established the overseas Irish communities that would later bring out their own relatives.

Chain migration can also be important because those who travel first are able to report home on conditions in the new country. Later, potential migrants have a more accurate source of information. They may either decide not to go or can make better decisions about when and how to travel, which place in the new country to go to, and so forth. Irish emigrants after the Famine had a rich variety of information on both Great Britain and overseas destinations, including not just letters and testimonials from returned emigrants, but newspapers, special broadsheets, and other printed sources. Plunkett (1970 [1904], p. 56) recounts a telling anecdote. The daughter of a Galway small farmer chose emigration to New York over settling with relatives some thirty miles away in Galway. She chose New York "because it is nearer"—because of the many emigrants she knew in New York, the daughter felt more at home there than in another part of the county in which she was born.

Fertility

We have already seen that Irish marital fertility was high by European standards prior to the Great Famine. Marital fertility in Ireland became even more remarkable during the nineteenth century as fertility declined in most other western European countries. Most of western Europe experienced a dramatic decline in marital fertility. In countries such as England and Germany this transition was well under way by the 1880s. Irish fertility did decline at the end of the nineteenth century, but by 1911 an Irish wife would still bear more children than most of her counterparts in western Europe. The measurement of marital fertility is complicated both by thorny conceptual issues and by the familiar problems of poor-quality data. Table 4.5 presents estimates of the index I_g of marital fertility for Ireland and England in 1881 and 1911. By 1911 Ireland's I_g was among the highest of all the countries studied by the European Fertility Project (discussed in chapter 8). But table 4.5 illustrates an important point: overall fertility (here measured by I_f) was very similar in Ireland and in England. The difference between marital and overall fertility reflects Ireland's marriage patterns.

Mortality

Irish mortality has not been well studied. Table 4.6 brings together the several estimates of the expectation of life at birth available for the nineteenth and early twentieth centuries. Each of these individual estimates is in itself reliable, but given that the figures were arrived at using different methods and that the 1926 estimate pertains to the Irish Free State only, one should not take the comparison as any more than approximate.[35]

TABLE 4.5
Marital Fertility and Overall Fertility in Ireland and England

	Index			
Country and Year	I_f Overall Fertility	I_g Marital Fertility	I_h Nonmarital Fertility	I_m Proportion Married
England 1911	.234	.467	.019	.479
England 1881	.355	.674	.034	.501
Ireland 1911	.267	.769	.010	.339
Ireland 1881	.312	.841	.011	.370

Sources: Teitelbaum (1984, tables 4.3, 5.4, 6.1, and 6.8). I_g for Ireland computed as unweighted averages of the thirty-two counties from Ó Gráda (1993, table A5).

Note: The I_h Teitelbaum presents for Ireland is most likely flawed as well, but is used here in the absence of other information. See chapter 8 for a full discussion of these issues. I_f is computed from the measures presented in table.

TABLE 4.6
Mortality Estimates for Ireland

Period	Males	Females
1821–1841	38.3	38.3
1890–1892	48.8	
1900–1902	50.2	
1910–1912	54	54
1926 (Irish Free State only)	57.4	57.9

Sources: For 1821–1841, Boyle and Ó Gráda (1986, app. table 2); for 1890–1902, Preston and Haines (1991, table 2.3); for 1926, "Saorstat Life Table Number 1" (Irish Free State 1926).

Note: Because geographical basis and methods differ, comparisons across years should be viewed as approximate only. Separate estimates for males and females are not possible with the method employed by Preston and Haines.

The available evidence does show two important facts. Mortality in Ireland was not appreciably worse than in other countries at the time. At the turn of the twentieth century the expectation of life in Ireland was about the same as in the United States or England and Wales, and higher than in Germany. Ireland also compared well with other poor countries of the time (Preston and Haines 1991, table 2.3). Ireland's relatively good mortality may simply reflect its very rural population. Cities were extremely unhealthy places to live during the nineteenth century. In about 1906, the typical Irish child living in one of the six county boroughs (cities) stood about a 20 percent chance of dying before his or her fifth birthday. In the rest of Ireland (the rural areas and smaller towns) that risk was only about 12 percent. Fitzpatrick's unpublished estimates show that this urban/rural difference held for adults as well. As late as the early twentieth century, slightly more than half of people living in County Dublin would survive from age 15 to 55, compared with more than 70 percent survivorship in adjoining counties. These estimates imply much better mortality in the province of Connaught, which was poor but very rural, than in the wealthier but more urban provinces of Ulster and Leinster. Comparisons with England and Wales suggest that at the turn of the twentieth century rural mortality in Ireland was somewhat lower than in England and Wales, while urban mortality was higher (Preston and Haines 1991, p. 184 and table 5.2).

Tuberculosis

One cause of death deserves particular attention for its prevalence in Ireland and its impact on those afflicted with the disease: tuberculosis. This disease in its several forms was the leading cause of death in Ireland for much of the late nineteenth and early twentieth centuries. According to official sources, the death rate from tuberculosis in Ireland rose slightly from the 1860s until about 1900, declining only after 1905. This was in marked contrast to the rest of the United Kingdom, and indeed much of the rest of western Europe. Death rates from tuberculosis in Scotland and in England and Wales had begun to decline, steadily, in the 1870s. In 1900 the annual death rate from tuberculosis in Ireland of 2.8 per thousand was significantly higher than in Scotland (2.2 per thousand) or in England and Wales (1.9 per thousand). The improvement in the Irish experience after 1905 was slower than in England and Wales or Scotland, and tuberculosis remained a serious health problem in Ireland into the 1950s.[36]

Tuberculosis had been a major killer in Europe since at least the seventeenth century. Theories of the disease's origins and transmissions were legion, with many authorities stressing either inheritance per se or a more complex theory of inherited predisposition to acquire the disease by other means. In 1882 Robert Koch, a German bacteriologist, discovered a bacillus (Mycobacterium tuberculosis) that was eventually understood to be the cause of all the various manifestations of tuberculosis. The implication that tuberculosis was a communicable disease caused by an infectious agent did not meet with immediate and universal agreement, however. Treatment based on Koch's finding did not come until late 1890, and even then the first results from Koch's tuberculin were disappointing. Slow medical progress against tuberculosis meant that for much of the period of interest the only effective measures taken against the disease were unpalatable efforts to prevent transmission from persons already known to be infected. The reasons for tuberculosis's widespread incidence and eventual decline are only imperfectly understood. Most people are exposed to the bacillus when an individual with an advanced infection coughs, spraying clouds of bacilli-laden droplets. Infection usually requires prolonged exposure to an infected person. The body mobilizes defenses against this initial infection and may succeed in destroying the bacilli. Understanding cross-national differences in death rates from tuberculosis and changes in death rates from tuberculosis requires an understanding of the factors associated with the original infection as well as why some individuals go on to become ill and others do not.

Historical information on deaths by cause is especially imperfect. Assignment of cause of death reflects at least three problems. First, those reporting cause of death were not always trained medical personnel, and even doctors' attributions could reflect their expectations as much as any meaningful diagnosis. In 1906, for example, the second leading cause of death in Ireland was "old age." Age is strictly speaking not a cause of death, and most deaths reported as age related were probably due to tuberculosis, heart disease, or something else that would have been recognized in younger people. Second, other causes of death may mask the primary disease's incidence. A chronic wasting disease such as tuberculosis weakens the patient, leaving him or her more vulnerable to other infections. The Irish Registrar-General noted in 1894, "There are considerable difficulties encountered in dealing accurately with the statistics of deaths from phthisis [tuberculosis] as many persons affected by phthisis have their lives terminated by other forms of disease, especially . . . bronchitis and pneumonia."[37] Finally, the widespread belief that tuberculosis was hereditary led many to prefer that their relative's death be ascribed to some other cause.

These reservations noted, we can better appreciate aspects of the disease by looking closely at official data on its incidence. Figure 4.1 summarizes information reported by Ireland's Local Government Board (1908, tables 33 and 35 for the period 1901–1905, from the reports of the Registrar-General in Ireland and in England and Wales). The levels alone are appalling: about one in two hundred Irish men and women aged 25–34 died every year of tuberculosis. Several additional regularities are apparent in comparing the Irish data with the English and Welsh. The Irish death rates, as we already know, were considerably higher at all ages. Female death rates were relatively higher at lower ages and relatively lower at older ages in both countries. The death rates for young Irish females are especially striking: girls aged 10–19 in Ireland

Figure 4.1 Death rates by sex from tuberculosis in Ireland and in England and Wales in the early twentieth century. (*Source:* Local Government Board 1908, tables 33 and 35.)

had TB death rates that were high compared with both Irish boys of the same age and girls in England and Wales. This prevalence among young females is a special feature of tuberculosis in Ireland, quite apart from the overall level.

Why was tuberculosis so serious in Ireland? The disease became unusual there in the 1870s and later, when death rates began to fall significantly elsewhere in the United Kingdom while remaining roughly constant in Ireland. We do not yet have a careful study of tuberculosis in Ireland, and even accounts of other countries' experience do not come to definite conclusions. Many explanations were advanced during the period and since, and several probably played some role. Transmission of the bacillus favors repeated exposure to an infected person in an enclosed, poorly ventilated space. This naturally focuses attention on poor housing and slums. Dublin, it is true, had some of the worst housing in the United Kingdom in the early twentieth century. Over 10 percent of Dublin's inhabitants lived in dwellings where five or more people shared a single room. This was far worse than other major cities in the United Kingdom; in Belfast the comparable figure was 0.1 percent, and in the worst British city, Glasgow, it was 5.2 percent. Slums cannot be the entire story, however, as Belfast had TB death rates about four-fifths as high as Dublin's in 1905, despite much better housing.[38] Poor housing might help to explain the prevalence of tuberculosis in rural Ireland, where the disease was less common than in Dublin or Belfast but still serious. Rural housing standards improved dramatically over the nineteenth century, but many families still lived in small, cramped dwellings that favored the spread of infection. Similar logic, coupled with the unusually high incidence of tuberculosis in school-aged children in Ireland, led the Local Government Board (1908, p. 50) to argue that "[t]he crowding of large numbers of children at a susceptible age, into badly ventilated schools . . . has had on the whole . . . a bad effect on the young people of our race." The board noted that female school attendance had increased markedly over the last few decades of the nineteenth century, a period during which death rates for girls aged 5–14 had risen significantly in contrast to a small decline in tuberculosis mortality for boys of the same ages (Local Government Board 1908, table 35, p. 36). A similar factor not mentioned in contemporary sources may account for some of the unusually large excess female mortality from tuberculosis at young ages. The sexual division of labor in rural Ireland implied that young boys would be outside with their fathers, young girls inside with their mothers. The latter condition, we know, made it easier to contract tuberculosis.

But just as important for Ireland's poor progress against the disease was the difficulty of employing contemporary medical interventions. The establishment of sanitoria and special wards for people with tuberculosis reflected many ideas about how to heal the sick, but these measures were probably most effective in removing a sick person from his home and preventing the infection of other family members. In accounting for Ireland's relatively poor progress against the disease, the Local Government Board pointed to two factors. First, "Ireland has suffered more from the acceptance of the theory of heredity as applied to Tuberculosis than probably any country in the world" (1908, p. 30). The board noted with reason that the hereditary theory discouraged efforts to prevent the disease by making those related to consumptives unnecessarily convinced that they were destined to become ill themselves. Second, Irish people had, according to the board and many other observers, a profound dislike of institutions and a fear of dying away from home. This fear militated against the use of separation and isolation. Infected people remained at home, even when highly contagious, spreading the disease to others whose counterparts elsewhere would have been spared infection.

Tuberculosis caused special horrors because it concentrated on young adults and because many who survived the disease were left permanently disabled. Numbers alone cannot convey the impact of this disease on the people who lived in fear of it or with it: "Tuberculosis was inscrutable as Providence. In its pulmonary form it prodigally disabled and killed men and women at all ages and especially at the peak of their early maturity between 15 and 35. In its various manifestations in other parts of the body it was a major destroyer of young life. Tuberculosis wrecked hopes, broke courtships, crushed breadwinners as they neared their maximum earning capacity and bereaved young families" (Smith 1988, p. 1). The nature and incidence of this disease make it directly relevant to two of the major decisions that underlie Irish demographic patterns. A young person contemplating marriage in Ireland could never forget tuberculosis. Marriage to an infected person could mean a short marriage or, worse, a long marriage to a disabled spouse. The acceptance of the theory of heredity meant that many young people could be dismissed as unsuitable candidates even if not infected; a cousin with tuberculosis might suffice to earn a family the label of "consumptives." The disease also affected decisions about migration. Leaving Ireland meant, for one ill or concerned about contracting the disease, risking death or disability far from home and kin. We shall never know how many, but probably more than a few people who remained in Ireland did so in part because they were worried about the possibility of coming down with the disease once overseas.

The Mortality of Irish females

The estimates of the expectation of life reported in table 4.6 also hint at a pattern that led Robert Kennedy to emphasize the harshness of life for women in Ireland. In most western European populations the expectation of life at birth for women was longer than men. In Germany, for example, the expectation of life at birth in 1901–1910 was 48.3 years for women, 44.8 years for men (Marschalck 1984, table 3.15). Kennedy (1973, table 4) points out that in 1911–1912, women in England and Wales lived about four years longer than men. In Ireland the expectation of life for men and women in Ireland was nearly the same.[39] Kennedy rightly interpreted this lack of a difference in Ireland as unusually high female mortality.

Several causes for this high female mortality are plausible. Recent authors tend to follow Kennedy (1973, pp. 51–65), who attributed the poor female mortality to an unequal division of resources within household and the relatively greater work shouldered by women and girls. The direct evidence on this unequal division is slight, however. Arensberg and Kimball noted, as have others, that in many households males ate before females, leaving females with less nourishment. Observers of rural life were also impressed by how very hard Irish women worked, implying that they needed more nutrition, perhaps, than women in other contexts. The somewhat thin basis of Kennedy's view receives corroboration from studies of sex differences in mortality in developing countries today. There, reliable evidence points to unequal allocation of resources as the main culprit. In many low-income countries the mortality risks for women are much worse than for men. By one estimate, because of excess female mortality several countries, including China, India, and Pakistan, have between 5 and 8 percent fewer females than they would have if males and females faced similar mortality risks (Coale 1991, table 1). The differences discussed here for Ireland are not nearly this large, but what they suggest about the status of women in Ireland is important nonetheless.[40]

Akenson (1988, pp. 40–41) raises the issue of excess female mortality and offers explanations that differ from Kennedy's. Akenson noted first that childbirth was more dangerous for women in the nineteenth century than now. Perhaps Irish women did not live long because many died in childbirth: "[T]he relatively low Irish female life span may largely have been a result of frequent exposure to the risk of child bearing." This intriguing suggestion does not, unfortunately, survive closer scrutiny. Many women in Ireland were not married and never had any children. According to Akenson's logic these women would have been especially long-lived. The Irish data do not support separate mortality estimates by marital status, but we can note that Kennedy was using life tables that pertained to all Irish women. For Akenson to be right, childbirth would have to be so dangerous that married women's mortality experience could pull down longevity for all women. Furthermore, despite Akenson's assertion that "until very recently, childbirth was the single most common cause of female death," historical statistics on maternal mortality suggest that women faced considerably less risk from this source than from other risks equally faced by men. Life tables by cause of death are not available for Ireland for the late nineteenth or early twentieth centuries. But we can use information on maternal mortality elsewhere to form a rough idea of the seriousness of this problem in Ireland. In England and Wales in 1901, women aged 25–34 were more than twice as likely to die of tuberculosis than in childbirth. Eliminating deaths from childbirth in that year would have added only about five months to the average woman's life, an improvement nothing like the apparent discrepancy between male and female life expectancy in Ireland. Clearly fertility in 1901 was much higher in Ireland than in England and Wales.[41] But even doubling the risk of death in childbirth from the English level (to approximate the effect of the fertility difference) would not support Akenson's argument. More concretely, life tables by cause of death for another country with high fertility—Italy in 1881—shows once again that tuberculosis dwarfed maternal mortality as a cause of death. Overall fertility in Ireland was only 80 percent as high as Italy's in that year, while marital fertility in Ireland was 30 percent higher. Elimination of maternal mortality in 1881 would have lengthened Italian women's lives by less than half a year.[42] The risk of death in childbirth was certainly significant for Irish women, and could account for some of their unexpectedly short lives. But even after accounting for this cause of death, much remains unexplained.

Akenson notes another possibility: perhaps female Irish mortality was relatively poor because the emigrant ship took the strong and healthy. His point is that what distinguished Ireland was not how women were treated there, but the fact that so many left. If emigrants were healthier than those who remained, then the remaining population would suffer higher mortality than if there had been no emigration. How this observation becomes an explanation for relatively poor female mortality is unclear, however. Women and men emigrated in roughly equal numbers, as we have seen, with slightly more women emigrating in the late nineteenth and early twentieth centuries. If the selection by health status works the same for each sex, then emigration simply reduced life expectancy for both males and females who remained. To reconcile Akenson's claim with Kennedy's observation it would have to be the case that selection for emigration by health status worked more strongly for women; that is, that unhealthy males were more likely to migrate than were unhealthy females. One can imagine reasons why an unhealthy male would do relatively better as an emigrant than his unhealthy sister, but there is no evidence on the point.

We cannot resolve this issue, but one feature of Irish mortality patterns, stressed by the Local Government Board in its 1908 report, is notable. Figure 4.2 takes us back to the specifics of relatively poor female mortality. I make use of data from one of Kennedy's tables in the figure to draw attention to something he mentioned only in passing: the unusually high mortality of females aged 5–19. In most populations at the time female death rates at these ages are either lower than male death rates or only slightly higher. Female death rates that are 140 percent of male rates at these ages are not unknown, but are unusual. Figure 4.2 provides information for two dates to show that the bulk of the relative improvement in female mortality between 1901–1910 and 1951–1960 took place at these younger ages. This finding is inconsistent with Akenson's maternal mortality hypothesis. Very few women in Ireland had their first child before age 20. The figure is slightly more consistent with his emigration story, although, once again, few girls aged 5–9 emigrated. Nor does Kennedy's explanation provide a very satisfying account of this age pattern of male-female differences. If Irish women died young because of

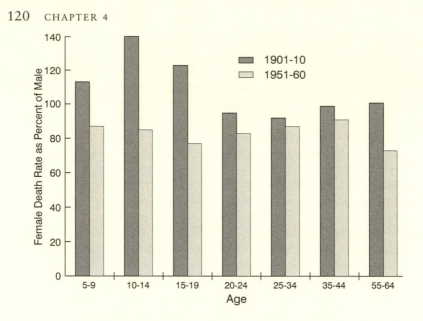

Figure 4.2 Comparison of male and female mortality in Ireland, 1901–1910 and 1951–1960. (*Source:* Kennedy 1973, table 12.)

unequal treatment, why did that unequal treatment stop having much effect on death rates once the women reached age 20 or so?

Tuberculosis may provide both a partial answer to the age pattern of excess female mortality and a way to understand more deeply some of the consequences of the way girls and young women were treated. Much of the excess of female over male mortality at these ages reflects the much higher female death rate from tuberculosis at these ages. If tuberculosis had been eliminated female morality would have been reduced much more than male, and the more common longer female life expectancy might have been found. Noting this does not invalidate Kennedy's observation, of course, and it is not the same as claiming that tuberculosis alone caused poor female Irish mortality, which is clearly false. But the role of the disease in female mortality in Ireland raises interesting questions. The Local Government Board wondered whether increased female schooling was harming the health of girls. Another factor, also mentioned by the Local Government Board, was stress in the form of poor nutrition and overwork. Many people are exposed to the bacillus that causes the disease. Those who actually become ill are those whose bodies cannot resist the disease. Perhaps Kennedy's comments about unequal division of household resources were just too general. The poor treatment of women Kennedy claimed might have worked primarily by increasing the death rate from tuberculosis for young women.[43]

Another possible role of the disease in this matter gives more credence to Akenson's discussion of maternal mortality. Pregnancy was known to be one of the stresses that could exacerbate active tuberculosis or even precipitate the onset of illness in a woman who had been exposed to the bacillus.

Before leaving this discussion of mortality I must lay to rest a possible false impression created by table 4.6. The expectation of life at birth is an average measure, and in a population such as Ireland's in this period it reflects the heavy mortality of infants and children. The 1926 life table, for example, implies that about 11 percent of boys and 10 percent of girls died before reaching their fifth birthday. The life tables do not show that living past 57 years was rare in 1926. About half of those living to age 15 would also see their seventieth birthday. Thus even with expectations of life at birth that seem low by our standards, most young adults would see themselves as living a long life and so make preparations for that possibility.

URBANIZATION AND INTERNAL MIGRATION

The severity of Ireland's overall depopulation reflected two distinct forces. First, rural depopulation in Ireland was especially pronounced. Second, the growth of Ireland's cities was so slow that they did not offset population losses in the countryside. In 1911 there were 125 urban Irish people for every 100 urbanites in 1841, on the eve of the Famine. But in 1911 there were only 41 rural Irish people for every 100 rural people in 1841.[44] The slow growth of urban centers, and a related lack of internal migration, is another distinctive feature of Ireland's population history.

Table 4.7 compares urbanization in Ireland with urbanization in England and Wales, France, and Germany. As late as 1911 Irish cities accounted for only 35 percent of the population as opposed to 78 percent in England and Wales or 60 percent in Germany. Of Ireland's major urban centers, only those in Ulster grew rapidly during the post-Famine period. Belfast more than trebled in size between 1851 and 1901; Londonderry grew by 50 percent over the same period. The three largest Irish cities in 1851 were Dublin, Belfast, and Cork. Dublin's population grew from 247,000 in 1851 to 305,000 in 1911. Dublin had been a center for some "traditional" industries, but as those activities were supplanted by (largely British) manufacturers Dublin failed to develop alternative industrial employment (Daly 1981, pp. 222–224). Belfast grew from 98,000 to 387,000 over the same period, overtaking Dublin as Ireland's largest city during the 1880s. Clarkson (1985, table 4.2) shows that the growth of urban centers was widespread in Ulster, and not just

TABLE 4.7

Urbanization Measures: Ireland, England and Wales, France, and Germany

Year	Ireland	England and Wales	France	Germany
1851	19.5	50.1	25.5	26.8[a]
1861	20.2	54.6	28.9	—
1871	22.9	61.8	31.1	36.1
1881	25.0	67.9	34.8	41.4[b]
1891	27.5	72.0	37.3	47.0[b]
1901	32.2	77.0	40.9	54.4[b]
1911	34.7	78.1	44.2	60.0[b]

Sources: For Ireland: Commission on Emigration and Other Population Problems (1954, table 3); for England and Wales, France: Commission on Emigration and Other Population Problems (1954, statistical app. table 3); for Germany: Marschalck (1984, table 5.5).

Note: "Urban" for Ireland is a place of 1,500 or more persons. Definition varies for other countries.

[a] Prussia, 1852.

[b] Previous year (1881 is 1880, etc.).

confined to Belfast and Londonderry. Cork actually lost population, declining from 83,000 to 77,000 people between 1851 and 1911. Cork never had significant industry, and as it lost its important role as a commercial center it lost population (Murphy 1981, pp. 126–127). Elsewhere in Europe, the second half of the nineteenth century was a period of extraordinary growth for cities. Düsseldorf increased its population by nearly eight times, Hamburg by over five times. Even older, larger cities such as London and Paris more than doubled in size.[45]

The relative dearth of urban growth in Ireland is closely related to Ireland's low rates of internal migration. Most of Europe experienced considerable internal migration during the nineteenth century as growing industrial regions drew their work force from dispersed rural areas. European urbanization, indeed, owed much of its rapidity to rural-urban migration. Yet in Ireland, only about 13 percent of people in 1911 had been born in an Irish county other than the one in which they lived. This is not to say that Ireland had no internal migration at all. Maps 4.3 and 4.4 use birthplace data from the 1911 census to make a simple point: those who stayed in Ireland did not always stay put. The two large cities of Dublin and Belfast drew the lion's share of internal migrants. Those who moved elsewhere in Ireland avoided the Atlantic seaboard. And the Atlantic counties contributed few of their number to internal migration, as map 4.4 shows. As the maps suggest, for young people born in the western counties migration within Ireland was relatively unlikely. But for

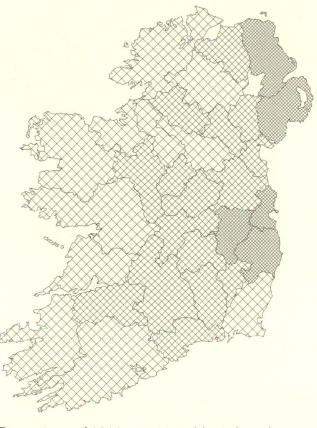

Percentage of 1911 county residents born in
another Irish county

Less than 10%   More than 20%

10% to 20%

Map 4.3 Internal migration by county of destination, 1911. (*Source:* Census of
Ireland, 1991, *General Report*, table 74.)

some eastern counties movement to Dublin took a significant proportion
of all those who left their county of birth. Women from Wicklow, in fact,
were more likely to move to Dublin than to emigrate.[46]

To ask why internal migration and especially rural-urban migration
was so meager is to pose, in indirect form, the question of Ireland's feeble
industrialization discussed briefly in chapter 2. The Irish did not move
within Ireland because, East Ulster excepted, no place in Ireland experienced the rapid industrial and commercial development and growth of
labor demand that drew people to the north of England, to the Ruhr

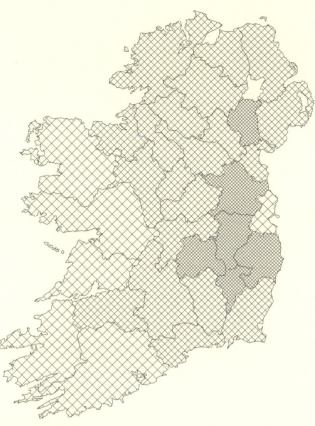

Percentage of those born in county residing in
another Irish county

 Less than 10%   More than 20%

10% to 20%

Map 4.4 Internal migration by county of origin, 1911. (*Source:* Census of Ireland, 1991, *General Report*, table 74.)

Valley, and to the other great centers of urban growth. But the lack of
urbanization does not mean that the Irish as a people did not become
urban. Most Irish emigrants (at least in the post-Famine period) ended
up as city dwellers in Britain or overseas. The difference between rural-
urban migration in Ireland and in Germany during the late nineteenth
century was that to become urban most Irish left their country. Thinking
about Irish rural-urban migration in this way does not increase the size
of Dublin or Cork, but it does place the apparent lack of urbanization in

some context. The four British cities of London, Liverpool, Manchester, and Glasgow had some 280,000 Irish-born people living within their borders in 1871. Dublin city proper had only 246,000 residents in that year, meaning that there were more Irish-born urbanites in four large British cities (combined) than in Ireland's largest city.[47] About one-quarter of the Irish-born in the United States in 1910 lived in New York City, meaning that this single American city had more Irish-born people than Dublin and slightly fewer Irish-born people than Belfast. If we expanded this list to include the Irish-born in urban centers in the United States, Canada, and Australia, we would see that the Irish countryman or countrywoman often moved to a city, but not an Irish city.

SUMMARY AND LOOKING FORWARD

The sixty-odd years between the Great Famine and the First World War witnessed in Ireland the emergence of a new demographic regime. The immediate demographic consequence of this new regime was rapid population decline in the countryside and only slow growth in the cities. Some aspects of Ireland's post-Famine demographic arrangements were common throughout Europe. Permanent celibacy was a long European tradition, and at the turn of the twentieth century several European regions had levels of permanent celibacy rivaling or exceeding Ireland's. Some other countries, such as Germany, also experienced heavy out-migration. For most of the nineteenth century uncontrolled marital fertility was the norm rather than the exception. Ireland's demographic differences turn on differences of degree and not kind, and on the unusual combination of elements often found in isolation in other times and places.

APPENDIX 4A
THE SOURCES FOR IRISH POPULATION HISTORY

At various points in this study I invoke the time-honored historian's lament that something is not well understood for lack of appropriate sources. Compared with England and with most Continental countries, sources for the study of Irish population history are thin indeed. Sources for the study of demographic history can be divided into two groups, official and unofficial. The former are those collected by governments, the latter, by nongovernmental groups (often but not always religious organizations). Prior to the nineteenth century there are virtually no official sources that bear directly on Irish population history. For the nineteenth century the most important official sources in Ireland are the decennial censuses that began in 1821 and ran through 1911 and then resumed in 1926. The first two censuses, in 1821 and 1831, were seriously flawed, but the 1841 census is a thoroughly admirable piece of nineteenth-century data collection.[48] The 1841 census established a reasonably accurate count of Ireland's population and also yielded considerable insight into fertility, mortality, and marriage patterns at the time. Later censuses were taken in years ending in "1" (as in England and Scotland) until 1911. After the partition of Ireland the Irish Free State undertook the census of 1926 for the twenty-six counties under its jurisdiction. This census is much more detailed than those taken during the nineteenth century.

Irish history has been less well served by another important type of source, the parish register. In many places in Europe the clergy kept records of all births, marriages, and burials in their parish. Historical demographers have been able, for many countries, to use these records to reconstruct the demographic behavior of parishes and regions as far back as the sixteenth century. The church records are extremely important for most countries because they are often the only information available. The systematic collection and publication of official population data did not begin in most countries until the nineteenth century. Several important research projects are based at least in part on these sources, including Wrigley and Schofield's *Population History of England* and the project initiated by Louis Henry at the Institut Nationale d'Études Demographiques in France.[49]

The surviving parish records for Ireland do not have the same scope, quality, and coverage. This is not to say that Irish parish registers have not contributed to our understanding of Ireland's population history. Some useful research on pre-Famine population patterns has been undertaken for County Antrim, and Eversley's (1981) valuable study of Irish Quakers is based on their registers. But Catholic registers are quite deficient, and Catholics made up the majority of the population. Even high-quality registers might not be very useful in Ireland. Registries report demographic events, such as marriage, and are silent about "nonevents," such as the failure to marry. And parish registers are not as useful for highly mobile populations. Given the lack of alternatives, Ireland's historians have used other sources to study population developments, including hearth tax returns and registries of land transactions. These sources all suffer from the somewhat obvious drawback that they were not intended to be used to study population and so often provide only indirect answers to the questions of interest.[50]

Many European governments created formal systems during the nineteenth century to count and record vital events. Ireland's system, run by the Registrar-General, did not begin to count births, deaths, and marriages until 1864. In its early years the Irish registration system provided a very incomplete count of these events. In his first report the Registrar-General warned, "I consider that many Births, Deaths, and Marriages have not been registered."[51] Uncritical reliance on the Irish registration data led one author to conclude that marital fertility in Ireland actually rose between 1881 and 1911. He mistook improvement in the system's coverage (the system counted a larger fraction of the births that actually took place) for an increase in the number of births. Throughout this study I employ or refer to proxies for the information given by the Registrar-General, or provide ways to assess the quality of that information.

Emigrants are notoriously difficult to count, and the circumstances of Irish emigration make these counts even more difficult. Many Irish people would leave Ireland to work in Britain before moving on to North America or elsewhere. Counting these people accurately as emigrants from Ireland required knowing both that they were leaving the United Kingdom and that they were originally from Ireland. There were actually two distinct systems of counting emigrants, although only one was tolerably complete. The emigration commissioners tried to enumerate "overseas emigrants," or people leaving the United Kingdom entirely, from 1825 on. The Registrar-General also kept a tally of emigrants, including those to Great Britain. The Registrar-General's tally was incomplete, missing, in particular, many migrants to Great Britain (Ó Gráda 1975; Fitzpatrick 1989b, p. 12). But because only these statistics provide information on the sex, marital status, age, and occupation of emigrants, I make cautious use of them. If I am interested in only some gross measure of the total number of migrants, the preferred measure is cohort depletion: the complement of the number of people who should be in Ireland if all had remained between censuses, divided by the number at the start of the period. For example, the cohort-depletion measure for those aged 15–19 in 1861 is:

$$\frac{P^{1861}_{15\text{-}19} - P^{1871}_{25\text{-}29}}{P^{1861}_{15\text{-}19}}$$

where $P^{1861}_{15\text{-}19}$ is the number of people aged 15–19 in 1861, and so forth. This index simply tells us how much smaller the cohort is in the second census than in the first. The index does not tell us why it is smaller. Some of the people "missing" have died, and if we are looking at a smaller unit such as a county, some may have moved elsewhere in Ireland. These are minor problems, however. Mortality tends to be much more constant across time and space than migration. We can usually estimate or at least approximate the fraction who have died, and for young people mortality is relatively unimportant anyway. We cannot do the same for internal migration or for return migration. The cohort depletion measure does not tell us whether 25 percent of the cohort left but were replaced by an equal number of people who moved into the area in question between the censuses.

The census is the most important source for nineteenth-century population. Census data are very useful, but since they were not designed to address some of the questions of interest to modern historians, we must often use them in ways their creators never intended. This book relies heavily on two such extensions. First, I use samples of households drawn from the manuscript census, that is, the forms for each household that were filled out as the first step in compiling the census. Nearly all the manuscript census schedules were kept from the 1901 and 1911 enumerations, and for some parts of the country there are also schedules from earlier censuses. Some of my research has been based on a sample of households from the 1901 and 1911 census, and I draw on other published studies that have used the same sources for other parts of Ireland. Using the census manuscripts requires considerable labor but is the only way to answer some important questions. Were we to rely on the published census alone, we could only look at information cross-classified in ways of interest to those in charge of the original census. With the manuscript census one can examine the relationship among any two (or more) pieces of information included in the form.

A second extension draws on the first. A census only captures a population's characteristics at a point in time; strictly speaking, on the single day of the census. But often questions of interest to us concern changes over the life cycle. The most reliable way to examine change with census data is to compare two successive censuses. With manuscript census data, one can compare information on the same household, or individual, at two different dates, such as 1901 and 1911. In chapter 6, for example, I examine the ages at which young people left home. The census does not say when a person left the household, but by comparing the census schedule for the same household in 1901 and 1911 one can infer whether someone left between 1901 and 1911. Thus comparison of two individual views of the same household can tell us about changes in the intervening years.

APPENDIX 4B
DEFINITION OF THE PRINCETON INDICES

The European Fertility Project developed a number of fertility indices that are useful in certain circumstances and have come to be used quite widely among historical demographers.[52] The index of marital fertility I_g is defined by:

$$I_g = \frac{B_m}{\sum\limits_{a = 15 - 19}^{a = 45 - 49} m_a F_a}$$

where B_m is the number of births to married women in a given year, m_a is the number of married women in age group a, and F_a is the fertility schedule of Hutterite women aged a.[53] The Hutterites, as noted earlier, were a North American Anabaptist group known for their high and accurately recorded fertility. I_h is defined analogously to I_g except that the numerator is the number of births to *non*married women and the term in the denominator is the number of nonmarried women. A fourth index, I_m, measures nuptiality:

$$I_m = \frac{\sum\limits_{a = 15 - 19}^{a = 45 - 49} m_a F_a}{\sum\limits_{a = 15 - 19}^{a = 45 - 49} w_a F_a}$$

where w_a is the total number of women at age a.

Note that this index is weighted by the Hutterite fertility schedule, so it places much more emphasis on age at marriage (that is, how many young women are married) than on the proportions who ever marry, which was necessary for the purposes of the Princeton project. I do not make significant use of I_m in this study for this reason. These four indices have the convenient property of breaking down overall childbearing into its components:

$$I_f = I_m I_g + (1 - I_m)I_h$$

In words, the three indices show that overall fertility (I_f) is the weighted sum of marital and nonmarital fertility, where the weights are the index of nuptiality I_m.

APPENDIX 4C
MICRODEMOGRAPHIC SAMPLES FOR IRISH HISTORY

Unlike their counterparts in the United Kingdom, the Irish manuscript census schedules for 1901 and 1911 are open for public inspection. (Most earlier census schedules were destroyed; the few to survive have been used by Carney 1981 and O'Neill 1984.) These census schedules are a valuable source for the study of virtually any question in Irish social and economic history of this period. For many years some scholars apparently believed that the census schedules were destroyed in a fire in the Dublin Public Record Office. This proved not to be the case, and in recent years the schedules have been put to good use by a variety of historians.[54] Here I discuss this source with an eye to drawing information from it in later chapters.

Underlying both my sample and several others are three distinct sources: the manuscript census schedules for each census (1901 and 1911) and the information on tax valuation from the revisions to the General Valuation of Ireland. These three sources are most powerfully used in conjunction with one another. Combining the two censuses permits a glimpse at changes over time. The next chapter will use that feature of the data to study changes in household structure and to study inheritance patterns. In chapter 6 this two-census structure underlies our study of age at leaving home. Combining the census information with the valuation information allows us to differentiate households according to the size and value of their farms, which is useful for studying the effect of farm size and household wealth on virtually any behavior.

Combining these three sources makes for a priceless source, but imposes an important drawback: the need to match three sets of records on a single household. Other historians who have attempted to match census returns across two censuses have found this to be a difficult task, and they usually report that only a fraction of those in the first census could be definitely matched to a record in the second. Matching to a third source (as with the valuation records here) only exacerbates the problem. In some cases introducing a third, noncensus source reduces the percentage of matches to a very small number indeed. This problem is especially acute in rural Ireland, where a large number of persons share common surnames as well as common first names. For example, in the small region of County Clare included in my data there are several men named John McMahon, several of whom were married to a woman named Mary. In addition, some Irish names are spelled differently in different census returns. Finally, some matching techniques used elsewhere are inappropriate for purposes here. For example, one might use other characteristics such as age and marital status to differentiate between two individuals with the same surname. Yet age-misreporting in the 1901 and 1911 censuses makes age a poor tool for this task; not a few people claim to be 50 in 1901 and 67 in 1911. Moreover, using variables such as marital status to identify people is not, in my view, a wise practice: because this practice makes it easier to match married people, one could easily end up biasing those included in favor of married people.[55]

To reduce these matching problems I chose, following several others, to employ a "cluster" sampling technique. This amounts to including

Map 4.5 Locator map for manuscript census sample locales. (Black rectangles in Counties Mayo, Clare, Meath, and Wicklow show approximate location of locales for manuscript census sample. Rectangles not drawn to scale.)

every household in several small regions, rather than trying to draw a random sample from the entire country. The great advantage of this method is that it considerably eases the tasks of matching households across the censuses and the valuation information. My dataset contains about 1,200 households drawn from Counties Clare, Meath, Wicklow, and Mayo.[56] Map 4.5 shows the approximate location of each locale within the respective county. I am confident that in this dataset virtually every household included in the 1901 census was matched to a household in the 1911 census if that household was still present in the area in 1911.[57] Thus I have tolerably complete matches for four small regions of rural Ireland.

Historians do not always have the opportunity to draw samples based on any optimal statistical criterion. In many cases one simply has to use the information available; either what has survived, or, as is often the case in historical demography, the examples of what has survived that seem reasonably complete. Neither my census data nor the data underlying the other studies to be discussed here were drawn as a random sample. Fitzpatrick and I each studied every household in several small regions of Ireland. We each chose our study areas with an eye to the regional variation noted above. Birdwell-Pheasant's study differs in that it is a more intensive analysis of a single region. The drawbacks to this approach are real but easy to exaggerate. At the simplest level we should ask whether the ten locales in all covered by my study, Fitzpatrick's (1983), and Birdwell-Pheasant's (1992, 1993) are so idiosyncratic as to seriously misrepresent the Irish experience. Because (as we shall see) the empirical patterns in these several studies are similar, this possibility seems unlikely.

Chapter 5

HOUSEHOLDS AND THE GENERATIONS

> Fathers that wear rags
> Do make their children blind;
> But fathers that bear bags
> Shall see their children kind.
> —The Fool in *King Lear*, II, iv

CONNELL'S ACCOUNT of demographic change after the Famine places alterations in household structure at center stage. Although he was primarily interested in marriage, and so stressed the Match over other aspects of household behavior, Connell's account amounts to a description of inheritance practices, the dispersal of siblings, and provision for the aged—in short, a complete theory of household behavior. Other accounts of post-Famine change center less explicitly on the household, but nonetheless involve the same basic themes. This chapter considers the rural Irish household system and evidence of changes in that system over the post-Famine period. Our central focus is the issue raised by Connell: did changes in inheritance practices imply restricted marriage opportunities for young people in Ireland? Also considered are broader questions concerning household structure, inheritance, and relations among the generations. Here we are interested in the implications of Connell's story for other behaviors, such as emigration.

A problem posed by the available sources must be acknowledged. To address Connell's account more detail on households is needed than is contained in the published sources discussed in chapter 4. Manuscript census schedules exist for some years prior to 1901, but they are patchy. The best evidence on households comes from the end of the post-Famine period, not long before the First World War. But Connell's story is explicitly historical; how can his account of change be discussed by looking only at households at the turn of the twentieth century? I will adopt the somewhat unusual procedure of going backward in historical time. The rich information available from the early twentieth century will be used to study households as they existed then, and subsequently, at the end of the chapter, we will consider the evolution of Irish households over the nineteenth century.

THE RURAL IRISH HOUSEHOLD SYSTEM

Connell's account of demographic change after the Famine centered on the emergence of a household system that limited marriage in Ireland to a single favored son and daughter in each generation. Arensberg and Kimball's (1968) study of Clare farmers in the 1930s first systematically described the household system implicit in Connell's later analysis although there are some differences between this account and Connell's. Connell based his description of household dynamics on materials gathered by the Irish Folklore Commission during the twentieth century. Because many of the folklore informants were very old, and because in some instances their stories refer to practices described by their own parents or grandparents, Connell's materials in principle refer to the time period of interest (Connell 1958, 1962a). Gibbon and Curtin (1978, pp. 433–434) noted both that Connell was influenced by Arensberg and Kimball and, perphaps more important, that the Irish Folklore Commission materials tend to stress the more exotic features of rural life. The basic descriptive account of household dynamics has not been questioned, however, and historians since Connell have confirmed much of his story using a variety of other sources, including wills, newspaper accounts, diaries and other memoirs, and parliamentary reports.

The idealized stem-family household described in these accounts functions as follows. An Irish farming father would decide to retire and to turn the farm over to his chosen successor. Often this transfer was accompanied by formal legal documents providing for the son's possession of the farm and guarantees of support for the elder couple. This moment marked the point of transformation in the household's history: the heir married, his siblings left home, and the elderly couple retired from active control of the farm. Siblings might choose to stay, but did so with the understanding that they could not marry and remain in the household.

Before considering whether this basic tale is true, let us consider some ambiguities and points of disagreement. A first point of contention concerns the timing of the farm's transfer from the older to the younger generation. In some versions the successor married and brought his wife into the household before formally taking control. This probationary period, which Arensberg and Kimball regarded as normal practice in the Clare communities they studied, implies a household with two married couples of different generations living together. Because that morphology has been identified as the crucial distinguishing feature of a stem-family household system, the timing of transfer is central to the debate over an Irish stem family (Arensberg and Kimball 1968, chap. 7; Laslett 1972, table 1.1). Connell thought it more common for Irish fathers to maintain control for as long as they lived, usually preventing the marriage of the heir during his father's lifetime. "For all the exceptions, it is probably true that a family's land normally fell to a son only when his father had died" (Connell 1962, p. 510). Connell's description of the Irish household system does not, then, fit Laslett's definition of a stem family, because Laslett's definition is restricted to households containing two co-resident married couples. I return to this distinction below.

A second issue concerns the treatment of children, both sons and daughters, who do not take control of the family farm. In Connell's simplest account one daughter might receive the dowry that would permit her to marry a local man of the proper social rank. The rest had to sacrifice their future to the farm and the family it signified. That sacrifice could take the form of remaining in Ireland without ever marrying and assuming the fully adult role that marriage implied, or it could mean taking whatever sum the family could afford and going to Britain or overseas to start a new life. Connell's version implies great inequality among children enforced by powerful fathers in the name of keeping a holding intact and viable. If this account is not accurate, then Connell's tale loses much of its power to explain celibacy and emigration from Ireland. Connell does mention instances in which children married and remained in Ireland without being either the direct successor or the daughter favored with a dowry.

Finally, what about households that did not control farmsteads? The stem-family story seems to turn on the existence of a farm. Farm transfer gives the older generation power over the young, and the farm's income and labor requirements both permit and require a larger number of mouths—and arms—to be grouped under one roof. Not all rural households had farms. How did these households behave, and what are the consequences of their behavior for demographic patterns?

The Stem Family and Debates about European Households

Discussion of the rural Irish household has not taken place in a vacuum. Scholars had long believed that in most of Europe, households were historically large and "complex"—they included, in addition to a married couple and their children, other kin such as aunts and uncles, cousins, and grandchildren. The nuclear household of parents and children supposedly reflected modern society's assault on the extended family. Laslett and several colleagues challenged this orthodoxy in the 1960s (Laslett and Wall 1972). They drew on large numbers of household listings to show that English households were historically small and simple. The nuclear family household in Laslett's view was the norm, and other household types were the outcome of unusual circumstances.

Laslett has noted that families are always an emotional topic, and that those who live in times of confusing change for the family cherish an image of the "good old days" when large, extended families lived together harmoniously (Laslett 1972, p. 8). The stem family conveys an image of a large family controlled by a powerful, propertied father, and thus had considerable appeal to nineteenth-century reactionaries. LePlay, an early advocate of both stem families and the idea that this form of family organization had traditionally been the norm in Europe, saw in the stem family an appealing image of patriarchal power. LePlay's book is frankly partisan. To him the *famille souche* (stem family) was the "[t]rue model shown by history for all peoples and times," a phrase that serves as the subtitle of his book. In his view, modernization had brought about the degeneration of the stem family into nuclear families—which he called "unstable families"—and in so doing had undermined respect for patriarchy, authority, and other foundations of the world he cherished. Connell's views on the rise of the stem family in Ireland form an interesting contrast to those of LePlay. Connell claimed that the stem family asserted itself in Ireland in the second half of the nineteenth century, when LePlay saw the world falling apart. Patriarchy in LePlay's view was threatened by the modern world; patriarchy in Connell's post-Famine Ireland was for the first time unconstrained by a predatory land system.

The stem family is not the only type of complex household historians have unearthed in European history. Other examples include the *zadruga*, a Balkan household that could become quite large and complex. At its most elaborate, such households would include parents in addition to several of their married children, along with other kin (Hammel 1972). But for western Europe the debate has been cast as nuclear versus stem. The difference between the stem-family and nuclear-family cycles can be illustrated using the simple diagrams familiar to anthropologists. In figure 5.1 a triangle denotes a man, a circle denotes a woman. Connecting lines under a triangle or circle denote relationship by marriage, connecting lines over the symbol denote siblings, and a diagonal slash through the symbol indicates a deceased household member. A square drawn around the symbol means the person has left the household. The stem-family developmental cycle begins (stage 1) with a married couple and their children living together without other relatives. In the second stage one child, usually a son, has married and brought his spouse into the household. This second stage—the co-residence of two married couples—is the distinguishing feature of the stem family's developmental cycle. In stage three the noninheriting siblings have left their parents'

The Stem Household

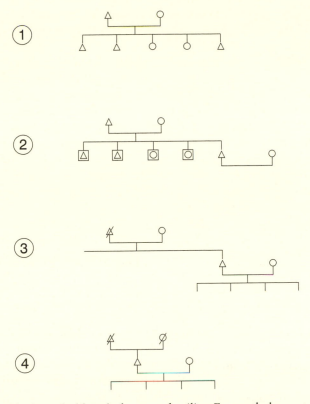

Figure 5.1 The household cycle for stem families. For symbols, see text.

household and the married son's father has died. With the death of the widowed mother (stage 4), the household completes the cycle and looks identical, in the schema, to a household at stage 1.

The nuclear family household (figure 5.2) has only three distinct stages. First, the household is formed by a newly married couple who have their children living with them. At stage 2 some or all of these children have left home. In the final stage one widowed partner is living alone, and when this person either moves into an institution or another household, or dies, the household ceases to exist. Comparing figures 5.1 and 5.2 indicates an important cause of the continuing debate over the nature of households. at some stages a nuclear-family household takes on a form *identical* to that of a stem-family household. A household taking on the stem-family forms of stage 1 or 4 (figure 5.1) cannot be distinguished from a nuclear-family household.

The Nuclear Household

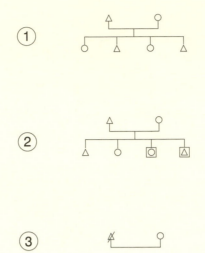

Figure 5.2 The household cycle for nuclear families. For symbols, see text.

Partible and Impartible Inheritance

At the heart of Connell's account of the rise of the stem family lies an end to the practice of subdividing farms at each generation. Impartible inheritance is a theme common to most accounts of European stem-family systems. The term itself is used in a confusing way in the literature. Some writers seem to think that impartible inheritance means that all family property was concentrated on a single child. Others use the term to mean that a farm was kept intact, although other children might receive other forms of family property. In a famous study Berkner (1976) compared two neighboring regions of Germany and showed that stem-family households were more common in the region of impartible inheritance than in the region of partible inheritance. Others have reached the same conclusion. Fauve-Chamoux (1985, 1987) discusses regions of the Pyrenees with strong stem-family traditions. Cole and Wolf's (1974) classic study of two Alpine villages notes the association of impartible inheritance with stem families, although the authors' focus is to question "ecological" views of inheritance systems. Verdon (1979) and Goldschmidt and Kunkel (1971) offer models of the stem family that require impartible inheritance.

A long tradition in European historiography places great stress on inheritance practices. Historians argue that the way property was passed from one generation to another influenced fertility, migration, agricultural productivity, capital accumulation, and through these economic development more generally. Habakkuk's (1955) speculations on the influence of inheritance systems have been influential. Connell's account of Ireland differs from Habakkuk's analysis, and from much of the other early European literature, in viewing inheritance practices as the outcome of social and economic conditions rather than the direct product of laws regarding inheritance. Close study of inheritance systems has usually demonstrated that law was less important than Habakkuk thought. The law might require division of all property equally among children, but did not usually stipulate how that division was to take place. The farm could be kept intact for one son, other children taking their portion in cash or in future obligations charged to the farm. Depending on local financial markets, farms could be mortgaged, permitting departing children to take cash and require the heir to repay the lender. In some cases historians have found that even when the law did require physical division of a property, siblings would sometimes arrange to sell one another their portions to re-create an undivided holding. Flandrin (1979, pp. 77–78), for example, found that inheritance law in the Pyrenees gave fathers no freedom in the disposal of their property, yet that region appears to be one of impartible inheritance—in practice.[1] A legal code, though not irrelevant to inheritance outcomes, should not be viewed as a literal description of actual practice.

In Ireland the law was nearly irrelevant in any case, because in our period a testator could dispose of his property as he pleased (Ó Gráda 1993, p. 184). Farm sizes, as noted in chapter 2, increased considerably during the nineteenth century, reflecting the near-cessation of the subdivision of farms. More direct evidence on subdivision confirms that the increases in farm size owed much to the cessation of the practice. Ó Gráda (1988, p. 157) found little physical subdivision in his study of wills, and subdivision was virtually unknown among the households included in my census sample. The Land Purchase Acts that turned so many tenants into owners forbade subdivision as a condition of sale, but these provisions were probably irrelevant, given the voluntary retreat from subdivision. We can thus confirm that Connell was right about the basics of changes in this aspect of inheritance practice. Whether he was right about the underlying causes of those changes, or their effects on household behavior, remains to be discussed.

Evidence on Household Structure in Ireland

Much can be learned by looking at the number of households that fell into each of several types of structure. A classification system that can group historical households into a manageable number of similar types is required. The most commonly used classification system, that devised by Hammel and Laslett, has been criticized in various quarters but remains useful.[2] This system has special utility because it has been used by so many other scholars, allowing us to make comparisons to other places in Ireland and to other societies. Laslett's classification is based on conjugal family units (CFU) and the relationship of other household members to those units. He identifies five major household types. "Solitaries" (type 1) consist of individuals living alone. An example of this would be stage 3 of the nuclear-family cycle as displayed in figure 5.1. "No-family" households contain several people not related by marriage. They could be siblings, cousins, or be not related at all. "Simple-family" households consist of a couple or widow living with children and correspond to stages 1 or 4 of the stem-family cycle or stages 1 or 2 of the nuclear-family cycle. "Extended-family" households differ from nuclear-family households in that they contain someone related to the conjugal family unit other than the married couple and their children. That someone else could be the married man's mother, or his father-in-law, an uncle, brother, or other, more distant kin.[3] The fifth or "multiple-family" type is Laslett's preferred definition of a stem family: two married couples of different generations living together under the same roof, one partner in the younger couple ordinarily a child of the older couple. For this fifth type of household, as with the fourth, the household head's generation does not matter.

These definitions are static. One problem discussed below reflects a confusion of the classification of a household at a static point in time with the experience of a single person over time, or, more directly, with statements about the household system. A person born into one of Laslett's multiple-family households could spend the majority of his or her own lifetime in a household lacking any aged people. A child born after the death of his grandfather and shortly before the death of his grandmother would experience a household very similar to a nuclear-family household. People we observe living in a no-family household were most likely born into a nuclear-family household.

Table 5.1 combines information on household structure from my own research and from reports by Birdwell-Pheasant. The definitions are Laslett's, and so are directly comparable. One source of change underlying the differences between 1901 and 1911 deserves brief comment. The Old Age Pensions Act of 1908, outlined in chapter 2, is probably responsible for some of the change in households between 1901 and 1911. Aged people and their families could use the additional resources to purchase privacy for each generation (the aged and their children could live apart), or the pension could make the aged welcome in households that might not otherwise find a place for them (the aged could live with their children, nephews, and so on). The latter effect implies an increase in both multiple- and extended-family households such as observed in the

TABLE 5.1
Distribution of Household Types, from Local Studies

Locale and Date		Percentage of Households				
	Solitary	No Family	Simple Family	Extended Family	Multiple Family	Number of Households
Ballyduff 1901	3.5	4.5	63.7	21.8	6.6	289
Ballyduff 1911	4.7	5.4	54.4	27.7	7.8	296
Clare 1901	7.3	3.3	56.4	32.2	0.7	273
Clare 1911	9.5	0.7	54.7	32.5	2.6	274
Meath 1901	12.6	1.5	57.1	28.4	0.4	261
Meath 1911	11.3	1.2	51.4	34.8	1.2	247
Wicklow 1901	9.2	3.4	58.0	29.0	0.4	262
Wicklow 1911	9.4	1.8	62.3	24.3	2.2	276
Mayo 1901	3.3	7.0	63.3	25.6	0.9	215
Mayo 1911	2.3	3.3	64.3	26.8	3.3	213

Sources: For Ballyduff, Birdwell-Pheasant (1992, table 1); for all others, Guinnane (1992b, table 1).

Clare, Meath, and Mayo locales of my study and Birdwell-Pheasant's. The drop in multiple- and extended-family households in Wicklow in the data, with an increase in no-family and simple-family households, may reflect the former effect of the old-age pension.

Because the principal difference between the 1901 and 1911 classifications is found in the proportion of multiple households, I focus on the 1911 data for the remainder of this discussion. The most striking feature of the Irish data is the high proportion of extended-family households. In the Meath subsample, over one-third of all households take this form. Fitzpatrick (1983, table 7) does not report results in the same format, so those results were not included in table 5.1. Yet he, too, reports relatively large numbers of extended-family households. Though certainly not unique, the proportion of extended-family households in the Irish data is much higher than in many other communities. Solitaries and nonfamily households are rarer in the Irish data than in Laslett's English communities, although they are more numerous in Ireland than in his Continental and Asian communities. Simple family households are the most common in both the Irish and the English communities, although they are relatively less numerous in Ireland. Debates about stem families aside, Ireland's households were definitely more complex than in England.

One persistent criticism of Laslett's position has been that he pays insufficient attention to differences in occupation and household wealth. To the extent that household structure reflects the household's consumption and production roles, we would expect household structure to vary with the nature of household operations, if any, and with the resources available to households. If households were in part economic enterprises, running farms, shops, and other businesses, one would expect that household size and complexity would reflect labor requirements. Other writers have suggested a relationship between household wealth per se and household structure. There are two possible relationships between wealth and household complexity, paralleling the possible effects of the old-age pension. On the one hand, wealthier people may be able to afford to shelter more of their kin. On the other hand, poorer people may be forced by circumstances to double up in housing. Ruggles (1987, pp. 58–59) notes that there is no a priori basis for asserting either a positive or a negative relationship between wealth and the size and complexity of a household. Aggregate data from the 1911 census of Ireland show that mean household size increases steadily with farm valuation (reported in Fitzpatrick 1983, table 4). Household complexity tends to increase with wealth: the two more prosperous classes have more multiple and extended family households, fewer solitary and no-family households. Simple family households form only a bare majority of the wealthiest group (Guinnane 1992b, table 2). Birdwell-Pheasant (1992, table 6.4) also found that complex households were more common among more prosperous farmers, though not unknown for others.[4] And in Fitzpatrick's five communities, once again, the simple households tended to be those of smallholders (Fitzpatrick 1983, table 7). There is a similar strong association between occupation and household structure. Multiple and extended households are much more numerous among farmers than among others; solitary households are most numerous among those who are neither farmers nor laborers (Guinnane 1992b, table 3). Other studies show a similar relationship between household wealth and structure.

So far we have seen that the real Irish departure from a nuclear-family model is reflected not so much in a large number of multiple-couple households as in a large number of extended-family households. Table 5.2 takes a more detailed look at the latter.[5] In Laslett's scheme such households are extended upwards if they contain a relative of a generation earlier than that of the conjugal family unit, such as a parent; extended downward, if they contain a relative of a later generation than that of the conjugal unit, such as a niece or nephew; and extended laterally if the person creating the extension is of the same generation as the conjugal unit. Households with more than one type of extension are tabulated in the "combinations" row. Table 5.2 reveals a great diversity in the types of extensions. Households in Meath and Wicklow are relatively more likely to be extended downward or laterally. Upward extensions are more important in Clare and Mayo. Clare and Mayo households, as table 5.1 indicates, are also more likely to contain two conjugal couples.

TABLE 5.2
Types of Extensions in Extended-Family Households

Extension Type	Clare	Meath	Wicklow	Mayo	All
Up	37.1	11.6	13.4	31.6	23.4
Down	28.1	36.0	38.8	40.4	35.1
Lateral	28.1	45.3	37.3	14.0	32.4
Combinations	6.7	7.0	10.4	14.0	9.0
Number of Households	89	86	67	57	299

Source: Irish manuscript census sample.
Note: Households in 1911, with head present. For definitions, see text. Figures are within-locale percentages of all extended-family households.

Who are all these extended kin? Some, including parents and parents-in-law, siblings of the household head, or some grandchildren and other young kin, are probably in the household for sheltering, either out of a sense of kinship obligation or as part of the agreement that led to the heir's marriage. Others are functioning as servants, whatever their relation to the household head.[6]

What can we make of all these extended-family households? Recall that in Connell's account, fathers rarely gave up control of the farm, thus denying a son permission to marry while the father was still alive. Connell's account implies extended-family households (in Laslett's scheme) rather than multiple-family households. A married couple and the husband's widowed mother is one type of extended-family household in Laslett's scheme, as is a household containing the household head's sibling. Some extended-family households, such as those containing nieces or nephews, do not play any real role in Connell's story. Yet others—those with widowed parents or resident, unmarried siblings—are precisely what Connell's story would imply.

The Household's Structure and Its Developmental Cycle

Relatively few multiple-couple households are found in the 1901 and 1911 census schedules, but this does not necessarily mean that most households did not, at one time or another, have two married couples living together. Like all households, a stem-family household would go through a cycle over time. At many points in that cycle, a stem family would be indistinguishable from a nuclear-family household. Berkner (1972, 1975) criticized Laslett's methodology on the grounds that the snapshot contained in a single census listing could yield a misleading view of what happened over time. Berkner's criticism refers to a common problem: the confusion of a stock (the number of multiple-family households on a given date) with a flow (the number of households moving through that stage).[7] For example, assume that in every household in a given society, a son married and brought his wife into his parents' household before either parent died. In a single listing, how many multicouple households should we expect to see? Not as many as had taken this form at some time, Berkner notes. A son could marry in 1908, his father die in 1910, and the 1911 census would not be able to tell us whether the son had married before or after the father's death. Berkner is clearly right in theory, but there is no way to know how important the stock/flow problem is in practice. For his criticism to be serious there must be many stem-family heirs whose fathers die shortly after the son's marriage.

There are in principle three ways to study household structure without becoming confused by the developmental cycle. The first approach is not possible with census data, and therefore for Ireland, but has been used in other contexts. Some European cities maintained continuous population registries, requiring that all residents register their address with the authorities and notify the authorities of any moves.[8] These sources make it possible to reconstruct household structure on a daily basis. Thus we know precisely how many households ever had a stem-family form, and for how long. Few places in Europe had such systems, however, and unfortunately Ireland was not among their number.

A second approach produces less specific information on any given population but provides insights into household formation more generally. One can view the stem-family or nuclear-family models as a set of stylized rules. The rules tell people when to marry, when to have children, when to leave home, and so forth. Wachter, Hammel, and Laslett (1978) draw on this observation to examine the relationship between household-formation rules and household structure under controlled conditions. Their approach is often called Monte Carlo simulation because it is based on a computer program that creates "people" with birth, death, and marriage dates assigned randomly, but in a fashion that mimics what was known about real historical populations. The fictitious people form households according to the rules specified in the program. By employing realistic mortality tables the program assigns a number of people to die each year. The Monte Carlo approach shows that a population experiencing marriage, fertility, and death rates similar to those obtaining in early modern Europe, and who were following stem-family formation rules, would have many more multiple households than Berkner anticipated. If the Irish were adhering rigidly to a stem-family household system, then we would expect to see many more multicouple households than are actually in the 1901 and 1911 censuses. Berkner was right in principle, but he exaggerated his case (Wachter, Hammel, and Laslett 1978, pp. 80–81).

TABLE 5.3
Transitions between Household Types, 1901 to 1911

	Laslett Type in 1911					
1901 Type	(1)	(2)	(3)	(4)	(5)	Number of Households
Solitary	47.2	2.8	13.9	33.3	2.8	36
No Family	9.4	6.3	50.0	34.4	0.0	32
Simple Family	3.1	1.2	74.1	18.3	3.1	487
Extended Family	5.4	2.5	31.8	58.3	2.1	242
Multiple Family	0.0	0.0	50.0	16.7	33.3	6

Source: Irish manuscript census sample.
Note: Limited to households matched between censuses. Households of servants only excluded. Table reads horizontally, for example, 47.2 percent of solitary households remained so until 1911; 18.3 percent of simple-family households became extended by 1911.

A final way to approach the ambiguity inherent in single census listings uses two successive listings to see how many households undergo the changes stipulated in the stem-family model. If a population truly has a stem household system, at least some of the apparent simple-family households in the first enumeration will take in a daughter-in-law and exhibit the multiple-family form by the second census. Nuclear households will not undergo this change. Table 5.3 follows households from one census to the next, and so captures some change over the household's developmental cycle. The majority of solitary and no-family households take on another form in 1911. Fully a third of the solitary households become extended. This is expected, given that a household consisting of only one individual is likely to suffer extinction unless other members join the household. More interesting are the final three household types. About one-quarter of the simple-family households go on to some other form in 1911. A fifth of simple households become complex. Half of the six multiple households revert to the simple family. The persistence of extended-family forms over the ten-year interval suggests that such forms are more than the product of casual or haphazard arrangements.

Focus on household survival offers another way to examine the stem-family view. Recall that stem-family households can persist forever, while a nuclear-family household undergoes extinction when both parents die and their children leave home. Thus household survival offers a second way to see whether stem-family households were the norm in Ireland. We can classify households by their structure in 1901 and by whether the household could be located in the 1911 census. Extended-family households, which we might take to be at some stage of stem-model development, are little more likely to persist than are either the simple-family or no-family households. Roughly 85 percent of those households survived from one census to the next. The extended-family households are, instead of stem households at a particular stage of development, either a variation on the nuclear family household or something else altogether. Fewer than half the solitary households, in contrast, are present in the second census. All of the multiple-family households survived, although there were only six in 1901 (Guinnane 1992b, table 4).

Household structure is not the only influence on household disappearance, of course. Some occupations required geographical mobility, implying that some households would leave an area between censuses. And even some stem households will disappear because of the early death of household members or the peculiarities of sibling dispersal. To isolate the effects of household structure per se, I estimated a regression model in which the explanatory variables are household structure, occupation, wealth, and the head's age. Holding these other influences constant, household structure had little effect on whether the household survived the ten-year interval. Solitary households had little chance of surviving, but for other households structure was unimportant.[9]

The rural Irish household at the turn of the twentieth century does not seem to fit cleanly into either the stem-family or the nuclear-family model. Households tend to be too complex to be nuclear-family arrangements as Laslett envisaged them. Yet multiple-couple households are rarer than they should be if stem families were really the norm. What are we to make of this? First, the Irish case may be of interest in that it illuminates a problem inherent to the entire debate. Laslett and his critics have both confused residence, which produces a given household structure, with succession, which determines how and whether a household will persist across the generations. Marriage and residence practices in Ireland rarely led to multiple-couple households, but that is not the central feature of Connell's story. His story turns on transferring household resources from one generation to the next—which the rural Irish clearly did—and the ways that process shaped the fortunes of young people.[10]

Parents and Their Heir

Connell saw the father's decision about the farm as an attempt to ensure the survival of the holding, and so the "name on the land." More recently, interest in the social and economic consequences of population aging has led economists and others to a more careful study of inheritance and related phenomena. With this attention has come the appreciation that economic relations between parents and children are more complex than that of dominators and dominated. Obviously, parents and children are bound together by emotional ties that make the transfer of a farm from one generation to the next more complicated than a simple land sale. Nonetheless transfers of property between parents and children often involve a considerable element of transaction. What Connell and other historians once viewed as the gift of a farm by a man anxious that his name live on the land, and the son's willingness to provide unpaid labor for many years out of devotion both to his parents and to that same belief in the importance of continuity on the land, looks in the light of more recent scholarship like the implicit sale of a farm from the father to the son. True, this is not just any sale, as we shall see, but considering the transfer as a transaction helps clarify numerous issues. This perspective has now become almost commonplace in modern economics (for example, Pollak 1985; Bernheim, Shleifer, and Summers 1985).[11]

Three features of household succession bear on household structure and the demographic behaviors of interest: the heir's identity, when he is permitted to take over from his parents, and what obligations the heir incurs in return for taking the farm. In Connell's account the identity of the chosen successor determined his future and that of any other siblings (usually brothers) who had hoped to have that role. Historians and writers of fiction have also adopted this view, placing the fate of children firmly in the hands of their parents, for good or for ill. The timing of the generational transition is also important. We have seen that the difference between an extended-family household and a stem-family household lies in when the successor marries, whether before or after a parent dies. Connell virtually ignored the final question, the heir's obligations, but this issue features prominently in later accounts of Ireland and in discussions of inheritance in other European countries.

Any transaction is a form of cooperation; each party agrees to the deal because each has something to gain by so doing. Conflict arises because each party has something additional to gain by having the transaction take place on the terms most favorable to himself or herself. This is equally true of transactions within farming families. Farming parents and their successor had much to gain by a smooth transition from one generation to the next. Parents hoped to live to an advanced age when they could no longer run the farm. At this point they would need labor to operate the farm and to provide for their personal needs. Although parents could use their assets to hire labor to run their farm, their children might be preferable on economic grounds alone. Their own son knew the farm well, after having worked it for many years himself, and any agreement made with him would enjoy considerable social sanction.

A son had similar reasons to prefer inheritance to the alternatives. If a young man wanted to remain in rural Ireland, his parents' farm was his best chance to set himself up as an independent farmer.

There are other reasons for the transfer to take place within the family rather than through sale on a market. The evidence suggests that maintaining the "name on the land" mattered in rural Ireland. For many families, inheritance would be restricted to sons even if that restriction imposed some cost. And economists have also noted that in some strictly economic dimensions transactions with family members are preferable to transactions with others. Family members know one another better. A man is a better judge of his son's farming ability than of a stranger's, assuming that emotional issues have not clouded his judgment. Family members can also enforce agreements without recourse to formal legal means. Shame or even expulsion from the family is both inexpensive and perhaps viewed more seriously by the potential miscreant (Ben-Porath 1980). Yet not all farms were passed to sons. Irish farmers seemed willing to pass their property to a daughter when a male heir was not available. And what happened to childless couples, or to those with a family but no children suitable for running a farm? Alternatives were available, and they were used. Restricting a transaction to a small group such as family members has its drawbacks. Even having two or three sons is no guarantee that any one of them has the ability to farm successfully. Family affection can also work the other way. One party to a transaction may well abuse the other's willingness to indulge irresponsibility in a family member. These considerations suggest that heirship and farm transfer were, at least potentially, more a matter of discussion and negotiation than has been implied by the autocratic fathers (and mothers) of literary accounts.

The choice of a successor is the first important issue. Some accounts imply a hard-and-fast rule that required the eldest male to inherit the farm. Other accounts stress the conflict between brothers who wanted a farm for themselves. Still others, including Connell, recognize that sometimes being chosen as successor would be a burden undertaken out of filial devotion rather than out of self-interest. Another issue fraught with potential conflict is the age at which an heir could expect to take over his parents' farm. Literary works often refer to a conflict between a son who wants to take over the farm and marry, and a parent—often the mother—who is not prepared to cede control. The conflict in interests here is direct: every year a man has to wait to take control is a year he is working for little or nothing on his parents' farm, and another year he has to wait before he can marry and have his own family. Patrick Kavanagh's often-quoted poem "The Great Hunger" turns partly on this point. Ó Gráda (1988, p. 155) quotes the poem as evidence that sometimes the heir was viewed as the unlucky sibling. The situation in the poem is a bit extreme, and reflects Kavanagh's obsession with very old bachelors, but conveys the sense of the problem:

> Maguire was faithful to death:
> He stayed with his mother till she died
> At the age of ninety-one.
> She stayed too long,
> Wife and mother in one.
> When she died
> The knuckle-bones were cutting the skin of her son's backside
> And he was sixty-five.[12]

For the aged parent, every year he or she can force the successor to wait is another year that does not require sharing household resources with a younger woman and grandchildren, and another year that does not involve the possibility of mistreatment at the hands of a son and daughter-in-law.

Intergenerational Contracts

Thus far I have discussed farm transfer as if it automatically involved old-age support for parents, and in some cases "retirement" for an aged father. This affair seems curious to those accustomed to thinking of retirement as an institution created by modern pension and social-insurance systems. Even more curious is an institution the rural Irish called "the writings," a written agreement that spelled out the conditions of the farm's transfer to the younger generation. This agreement was at its core a literal intergenerational contract. In other instances a man's will stipulates that a son inherit the farm, subject to certain obligations to the man's widow and other children. How common were these arrangements, and what did they provide?

Many descriptive accounts mention these contracts and the fact that the contracts (or wills) included "reservations" for a parent, sibling, or other kin. Arensberg and Kimball (1968) refer to such agreements, as does Connell. Perhaps more convincing are the Poor Law inspectors who were asked to report on the state of landlord-tenant relations in 1870. These inspectors usually referred to the practice with some combination of surprise and disapproval. Their surprise is not inexplicable; most remarked that the farmers who wrote these documents did not own the land, they owned tenant-right, and so the practice amounted, in the inspector's eyes, to bequeathing a property one did not own. Samuel Horsley, inspector for parts of Munster, wrote "I need scarcely say that such wills are valueless in law." Dr. Brodie, an inspector for several western counties, probably understood the enforcement mechanism better than did Horsley: "Such arrangements are incapable of legal enforcement, and therefore dependent on the good faith of the members of the family to each other."[13]

Further confirmation of this practice comes from efforts to administer the Old Age Pensions Act of 1908 in Ireland. One requirement for eligibility was a means test, so dealing with the act in Ireland brought out the entire question of peasant retirement and the economic relations between Irish parents and children. Especially controversial was the issue of "intentional denial of means." The act specifically denied benefits to anyone who had given away assets in order to qualify for the pension or to qualify for a larger pension. In the first years of the pension's operation a number of Irish farmers were denied a pension on the grounds that they had signed their farms over to their sons only to make themselves look poor. The Local Government Board, which had the responsibility of administering the pension, on inquiry came to the following conclusion about this practice:

> [O]ne of the most perplexing questions coming under our notice in connection with Irish agriculturalists arises from the custom, which has obtained for generations past, of the nominal assumption by the eldest son (or daughter, where there is no son) of the ownership of the farm, either on marriage or when the head of the family is advanced in years. . . . These formal transfers, which are now taking place all over the country, would, beyond all question, disqualify claimants for pensions . . . were it not for the fact that they represent a continuance in valid form of an old standing custom. (Local Government Board 1910, p. xiii)

This ruling did not settle the matter. In a letter to the *Catholic Bulletin* in 1913, Padraig O'Shea cites a case in which a farmer had been denied a pension on the grounds that the transfer of his farm to a son had been solely to obtain the pension.[14] Intentional denial of means was closely related to problems associated with another common practice, the support of aged parents by children. Regular income provided to parents was supposed to count toward "means," although officials recognized that it was pernicious to assume that aged people could regularly count on such income (Hoare 1915). The Departmental Committee charged with estimating the potential costs of old-age pensions in 1899 noted that in a country of small peasant holdings such as Ireland, the legal occupier of a farm was not necessarily the individual doing the farm labor (Great Britain 1900, §69).

Thus we need not rely on Arensberg and Kimball or anecdotal accounts. Two government reports, including one where much money was at stake, agreed on this aspect of parent-child economic relations in Ireland. Examples of the agreements themselves also exist. Considering a number of them in an admittedly anecdotal manner gives a flavor of the commitments agreed to on both sides.[15] Legally the contracts are a series of stipulations placed as contingencies on the transfer of a farm. One typical agreement was struck between Daniel McCarthy and his son William, of Youghal, County Cork. The agreement, dated July 1911, states that upon his marriage (and the payment of a dowry by his wife's family, also stipulated in the contract) William receives his father's farm, in return for which he agrees to "diet, clothe, and support" his parents in "a suitable manner" for life, and to pay his father 5 pounds annually for life. Both the room and board and the cash are "charges" on the land, meaning that his parents can recover damages at law.[16] The McCarthy farm was quite large. A more typical farm is transferred in the agreement between Bernard Harvey and his son Brien, both of County Tyrone. Brien paid his father 10 shillings, in return for which he obtained a twenty-seven-acre farm and the obligation to permit his parents and sister to remain on the farm for life "in all respects as they had theretofore lived thereon during their lives."[17] Many agreements are simpler still, as in the case of Elizabeth Clegg, a widow in County Down, and her son James. They agree that James will receive the land formerly farmed by his father, and care for Elizabeth for life.[18]

These arrangements were by no means unique to rural Ireland. Elsewhere the agreements go by a variety of names, including *Altenteil* and *Ausgedinge* in German-speaking areas and *kårkontrakter* in Norway (Held 1982; Gaunt 1983), but are similar in form and purpose. Gjerde (1985, p. 85) notes that the institution in Norway dated back to the fourteenth century but became more common in the eighteenth century. According to Gaunt, such intergenerational contracts were a common feature of farm transfers in northern Europe until the late nineteenth century, when they fell out of use. Irish parents often turned their farms over to a child in return for old-age support and guarantees for their other children. That they did so, and that they sometimes wrote out formal contracts governing the relationship, says nothing in particular about relations between parents and children in rural Ireland.

The Choice of Successor

Who was ordinarily the child favored to take over the household, marry, and continue the line? Economists and others seem to consider primogeniture—the choice of the eldest son as heir—as one of the fundamental "stylized facts" of peasant households and peasant inheritance. Even some Irish historians—for example, Whelan (1986, p. 160)—claim that primogeniture was "standard practice" in Ireland. Yet historical accounts of peasant inheritance often stress that the choice of heir followed no strict rule. Berkner noted, "'Impartible inheritance' does not specify *which* child will become the heir. . . . Peasant customs may favour the eldest (primogeniture), the youngest (ultimogeniture), or leave the choice open" (Berkner 1976, p. 89). Connell himself emphasized the power of parents to select their heir, which Arensberg and Kimball explained to mean "[i]n choosing the son to remain upon the farm, the father has full power of decision. His interest lies in choosing among his sons the one he thinks will carry on most successfully" (Arensberg and Kimball 1968, p. 63).

Primogeniture or any other fixed rule is implausible for the simple reason that it might be costly to follow. There are three distinct drawbacks to primogeniture. One has already been alluded to: what if the eldest (or youngest) son has no aptitude for farming? Yet a set inheritance rule would be costly even if all potential heirs were identical. There are two further drawbacks in this case. Imagine for the moment that the successor is chosen simply to maximize total family income. (This is one way to interpret the emphasis on smooth transition from one generation to the next.) Maximizing income provides the largest possible "pie" to divide among parents and children, both successor and outgoing siblings alike.[19] We should be surprised to find that primogeniture is the rule in a peasant society because in many circumstances primogeniture requires that the family give up income. Maximization of total family income requires choosing the son who will waste the least time as a productive worker waiting for his father to retire. Unless the father and son are far apart in age, if the eldest son is the successor, the period when the son is at his greatest work potential will overlap considerably with his father's. In the Irish case, forcing an eldest son to wait a long time amounted to wasting his considerable capacity to earn a higher income abroad, as an emigrant. Thus the logic of income maximization would suggest that younger sons inherit after their older brothers have left.[20]

This need not be a general result. Whether primogeniture is the best outcome in any given case depends on three factors: how rapidly a farmer's productivity declines with age, the difference between emigrant and domestic wages, and the relative ages of fathers and sons. The last point implies a certain number of years that a first-born son would have to wait for the farm. A farmer whose first son is born when the farmer was 25 would have an adult son by the time the farmer was 45. That son could spend many years at home with a father who was fully capable of running the farm. If, however, the son was born when the father was aged 35, then the overlap would be much less. Of course for a second or third son born five years later, there might be no father-son overlap at all. Similarly, under extreme mortality conditions (much worse than the conditions obtaining in Ireland in the early twentieth century) parents might fear that they would outlive their eldest son, and choose the youngest as heir to minimize the chance of spending their last days without offspring to run the farm. Thus we should not be surprised to find that the heir was in fact the eldest son on farms where the father married relatively late in life, or died relatively early; where mortality was especially severe; or where the first few children were girls. Otherwise, adhering to a rule of primogeniture would be costly.

The third drawback, and a second reason not to have primogeniture even with identical potential heirs, is that it dramatically reduces the bargaining power of parents. A parent who can play off two or more potential heirs against one another can drive a hard bargain. Statements to the effect that parents engaged in this sort of bargaining, setting one son against another, are not common in accounts of Irish inheritance. Yet this process can be very subtle, and may be part of the sibling rivalry that colors accounts of childhood in peasant regions. Parents need not use their advantages "selfishly." Parents could use their bargaining power to get the best arrangements for themselves, to be sure, but they could also strive to protect their daughters or to meet some other goal. This ability to play off one son against another was probably a rare source of real power for farmer's widows. Thus a rule that specifies a particular child as heir leaves the parents with only one dimension in which to negotiate, the timing of farm transfer.

This simple discussion illustrates the improbability of peasant households adhering to a fixed heir-selection rule such as primogeniture. Four empirical studies of farm succession have used a variety of methods to demonstrate that primogeniture was, in fact, not the rule. My own study relies on changes in household headship and household structure between the two census dates. Census data do not provide complete information on birth order, because we do not know the birth order of any children absent on the day of the census. But several indirect tests demonstrate the frequency of departures from primogeniture. Sons attain headship in seventy-seven households in my sample between 1901 and 1911. Of these, all but 9 percent were the eldest son present in the household in 1901. But this does not imply primogeniture. Of all eldest sons present in 1901, and aged 10–14, 35 percent are gone by 1911 ($N = 68$). This figure rises to 44 percent for eldest sons aged 15–19 in 1901 ($N = 106$). Young men left home as they achieved adulthood. When it came time to select an heir, parents might select the oldest remaining son, but he was by no means always—or even usually—the eldest son in the family.[21] Líam Kennedy used the 1901 and 1911 manuscript census schedules for another four regions to arrive at a similar conclusion. Inheritance by the first son occurred in a minority of cases in all four of his study areas, although primogeniture was relatively more common among the wealthiest farmers (Kennedy 1991, tables 1 and 2).[22] Birdwell-Pheasant (1992) reports a similar finding.

Ó Gráda (1980) used a different method to arrive at a similar conclusion. He compared the age of the eldest son in the household with the duration of the parents' marriage as of 1911. The difference between the two, he points out, can be interpreted as a rough test of the primogeniture hypothesis. The larger the gap, the more likely an older son has already left the household, and so the less likely it is that the eldest son inherits the farm. In the four locales he studied, the mean gap is at least 5.9 years, and in one area it is 7.5 years. He concludes that this is strong evidence against primogeniture.[23]

The Timing of Succession

Even after agreeing on a successor, families had to face the issue of when that successor would take over the farm. On the one hand, parents had reasons to want to prolong their period of control, as well as ways to encourage their successor to wait. On the other hand, the successor had good reason to want to take over sooner rather than later, and he, too, was not powerless in this conflict. Most sources stress the parents' power. Parents controlled the farm that would permit their successor to marry and remain in Ireland. The son was unlikely to abandon such a prize, and the parents knew that even if deserted, they could run the farm and arrange for old-age support without the son's assistance. Yet sons were not powerless. The son could voice a serious threat against a parent who insisted that he wait for the farm. The son would leave Ireland, forcing the parent to run the farm with hired labor and depend on others for care in old age. This threat only worked if this son was the last remaining acceptable heir in the household, and if parents had reasons strongly to prefer their own son as successor. To the extent hired labor could provide the services parents wanted, the son's threat would mean little.

Is it plausible to think sons would abandon their parents if forced to wait too long for the farm? The strength of family bonds in literary and historical accounts makes this seem implausible, just as implausible as parents letting the son run off and settling instead for hired labor. But both parents and their children knew this was always a possibility. One source claimed that such threats were made explicitly and taken seriously. Judge Johnston, who was a county judge for Fermanagh and Monaghan in the early twentieth century, referred to just such a threat in his testimony before a body taking evidence on the old-age pensions in 1919. Johnston viewed farm transfer as occurring when a son convinced his father that the son would leave for America unless farm transfer occurred soon (Great Britain 1919, Q8464). Going to America might not mean complete abandonment. A son who left in frustration could send home remittances, thus satisfying himself that he was aiding his parents. Johnston's comment is all the more interesting given his other testimony to the effect that Irish people felt unusual respect toward the aged, sometimes even taking in and caring for unrelated older persons (Great Britain 1919, Q8425).

These considerations suggest some scope for bargaining over the timing of succession to household headship. We can test this notion empirically. As a practical matter the timing of succession often came down to whether a son inherited upon his father's death or whether after his father's death the son would have to wait while his mother had her day as household head. This was her customary right, and some wills explicitly guarantee the widow's status as the farm's controller, if not owner, after a male farmer's death. The census schedules show many cases in which a father died and left control in the hands of his widow rather than of his adult son. We can expect that parental bargaining power would be strongest on the most valuable farms, and weakest on the least valuable, with later succession on the more valuable farms. Two indirect tests using my manuscript census data support this assertion. The sample contains twenty-two households in which a son became head between 1901 and 1911, and in which either his mother or his father is still alive. Another thirty-six households contain a son at least 25 years old in 1911, in which headship transferred from his father to his mother (that is, not the son) between 1901 and 1911. These two kinds of household are the crux of our comparison. The successor's age when he took over depended more on whether his mother had an intermediate period of control after his father's death than on his father's behavior. Our argument predicts that the second group, widows who have sons denied succession, occupy larger farms. A formal statistical test confirms this. Another way of approaching the same question yields a similar result. Thirty households have as head a man aged 35 or more in 1911, whose mother is still alive. Another fifty-six households have the reverse situation: a resident son aged 35 or more, but still listed as "son" to his mother. A statistical test again confirms that widowed mothers retained household headship on larger farms.[24]

A second way to test this assertion uses the heir's age at marriage as a proxy for age at succession. The relationship between succession and marriage is tenuous, because so many male household heads never married. Yet for those males who did marry, age at marriage might be taken as a rough indicator of when they attained headship of the household. Median age at marriage is higher for male farmers than for male non-farmers, 33 ($N = 351$) compared with 31 ($N = 291$); among farmers, age at marriage increases with farm size. Those occupying farms rated at zero to four pounds have a median marriage age of 31 ($N = 125$); those occupying farms rated at twenty pounds or more, 34 ($N = 79$).[25] A more complete statistical analysis of the relationship between marital status and farm size, discussed in chapter 7, qualifies this picture somewhat but does not obviate the basic finding.

One of the Irish Folklore Commission's informants stated this case: "It is mostly the eldest son who gets the farm if the people are rich. If poor, it is usually the youngest son who gets it because the elder ones have to emigrate" (quoted in Rhodes 1992, p. 94). Rather than attribute this evidence of hard-headed bargaining to something uniquely Irish—perhaps reflecting the alleged primacy of farms over family, a theme in more than one standard account—we should ask whether similar behavior characterized other peasant regions. Without making an exhaustive survey, one can establish that the relationship between farm size and age at succession does not arise from distinctive conditions peculiar to Ireland. In his study of similar transfers in the Württemburg Oberland during the early twentieth century, for example, Brugger found that heirs to large farms married later in life than did heirs to smaller farms (Brugger 1936, table 9).[26]

This discussion of heir selection and the timing of household succession has yielded several results salient to our larger demographic concerns. I have argued that strict efficiency militates against primogeniture and shown that the Irish evidence demonstrates an absence of primogeniture. This finding alone suggests more flexibility in succession practices than many, including Connell, have appreciated. In particular, there is solid evidence of intrafamily bargaining. Rather than Connell's autocratic father, we see parents who need something from their children and have to give up more or less time in control of the household in order to obtain it. The only remaining actors are the siblings denied succession.

HEIRS AND THEIR SIBLINGS

The stem-family account explains emigrants and celibates as the result of an inheritance system that concentrated most family resources on a single son and daughter. Connell's view of noninheriting children fits well into a longer tradition of viewing stem families as ones that sacrificed the adult well-being of all but one child to the goal of maintaining an undivided property worthy of the family name. At its most extreme this view implies that the heir received all of the family's wealth and that the other children were deprived of any inheritance. To advocates such as LePlay this was one of the stem-family's virtues, in that it placed considerations of the lineage above the well-being of individual family members. (This perspective on the treatment of siblings also bears on discussions of fertility, discussed in chapter 8.) However improbable this view might seem, and however contrary to the complaints of contemporaries to be discussed below, it has been accepted even by some of Ireland's best historians.

How true was it? Even the "impartible" inheritance regimes of continental Europe ordinarily included provision for children who did not inherit the farm. Such provisions were, in fact, the source of much criticism of impartible inheritance regimes. The criticisms have their echo in Ireland. The Poor Law inspectors complained that obligations to siblings sometimes posed considerable burdens to heirs. In addition, discussions of inheritance in Ireland have not always taken account of two related questions.[27] First, what obligations did the heir incur as part of the general agreement to take over the farm? What looks like a valuable prize, a large and well-stocked farm, might look less attractive if heavily mortgaged, if the heir incurred obligations to his parents in return for taking the farm, or if he had to provide many years of free labor while waiting for his chance to inherit. Second, should we consider the value of what noninheriting children received from their parents, or instead consider the lives they could start with whatever bequests they received? Inexpensive passage abroad bought for many Irish emigrants a more comfortable life than they would have known in Ireland.

According to Connell the children who did not inherit the family farm faced three options. A lucky daughter or two might assemble a dowry and so be able to marry and remain in the locale. The others faced emigration or remaining at home for life as an unmarried assisting relative. The last option Connell viewed as bleak indeed: "[T]hey became professional aunt or odd-job uncle, despised, a little ridiculous, working away for food, clothing and shelter and a shilling on a fair day, never to work, accidents apart, for husband or wife of their own" (Connell 1968, p. 117). The system provided ways to avoid this fate, however. As we have seen, in Connell's account, an incoming wife usually brought with her a dowry. In chapter 7 some worries about the place of this dowry in the entire drama will be noted, but for now let us simply trace its implications. What would become of this new cash injected into the household? Connell mentions several uses, including the repayment of old debts that might otherwise encumber the farm and the purchase of new household items or farm stock. In some cases the intergenerational agreement for taking over the farm specified cash payments to the parents every year, and the dowry could be put to this purpose. Still, according to Connell, the dowry's "real purpose—certainly its commonest use—was to provide for one or more of the groom's brothers and sisters." He mentions several ways to distribute dowry wealth to siblings, including education and paying for emigration (Connell 1962a, pp. 507–508). Thus even by Connell's account the treatment of siblings was more egalitarian than it would at first blush seem.

For a more general picture of the treatment of siblings we need something more than anecdotes. Unfortunately, probate records are the only reliable sources for the study of the division of family wealth among children, and these records are notoriously difficult to interpret. We have to wonder why people would write a will. Were they unusually wealthy, or unusually worried about family discord after their passing? Moreover, a will may tell us nothing about *inter-vivos* transfers. A son who left home years before the will's writing might have received a generous transfer at that time. The will, considered alone, would imply that he had been excluded from any family patrimony.

These caveats aside, if we are to learn how children were actually treated, we have no choice but to examine probate records. Ó Gráda (1993) constructed a sample of wills from the 1890s and 1900s, focusing on County Cork and South Ulster. His results should dispel any doubts about a general practice of disinheriting those who did not receive the farm. He first confirms that physical subdivision of holdings was rare. Compensation for siblings took forms other than land (p. 186). In strict money terms, sons as a group received no more than did daughters as a group, with the exception of the largest Cork farms (Ó Gráda 1993, table 41). Birdwell-Pheasant's efforts at tracing all children in her study area provides further evidence against the disinherited-siblings view. She cites a number of practices that permitted nonheirs to remain in the locale, including construction of second dwellings on farms. She sees the emigration of all surplus siblings as exceptional rather than as an integral part of the household system: "Permanent emigration of all nonheirs must be seen as a short-term, self-terminating strategy pursued primarily by those farmers whose farm enterprises were so marginal as to offer little future for heirs and no future at all for siblings" (Birdwell-Pheasant 1992, pp. 221–222).

The evidence available thus does not support the view that, at least by the 1890s, all but one child was being treated badly in the financial aspects of the division of the family estate. But financial equality may not be the right consideration. In modern society an equal treatment of children is fairly straightforward. Parents who favor equality may try to ensure that all children receive roughly equivalent educational opportunities and distribute any other wealth in cash or as assistance in purchasing a house. In rural Ireland in the nineteenth century this issue is complicated by questions of running a farm and caring for aged parents. Suppose we find that in a particular family one son received a farm with a value of £100, while each of his siblings received only £10—enough for travel to North America and not much more. Should we conclude that the siblings were treated unfairly? Several considerations suggest that this conclusion is not obviously true. Consider first what the heir has to do to acquire his £100 farm. In all likelihood he was much older when he obtained the farm than were all his siblings who went off to America with their £10. The heir had invested in the holding a greater portion of his life, in both labor and submission to his parents, than had his siblings. So part of the £100 should be seen as back wages and some compensation for lost independence. At earnings of £20 per year, about average for a farm laborer, this could be an expensive way to purchase a farm. In addition, the heir probably incurred obligations to his parents along with the farm. If his inheritance requires that he care for his aged parents—meaning provide them with food and other necessities, care for their needs directly, and perhaps endure differences of opinion about farming and other issues—then the real net value of that £100 farm could be considerably less. Finally, recall the discussion of encumbrances in the 1870 Poor Law inspectors' report. The inspectors suggest that (in 1870) it was common for the intergenerational agreement to place additional obligations on the heir, and in some cases at least the heir to the farm faced serious difficulties in meeting these obligations.

Connell's simplest story is also inconsistent with another of his observations on rural households. Connell himself emphasized the role of dowries in the arranged marriage system. In Ó Gráda's probate data dowries were over half the entire probate value for small farms in the 1870s through 1910 (1993, table 41). Fewer daughters than sons received bequests, but this may simply reflect the fact that girls left home earlier than boys and thus had already received their share prior to the father's death. (Age at leaving home is discussed in the next chapter.) Irish daughters, even when they did not inherit the family farm, were not ordinarily disinherited.

So on strictly financial grounds the division might not be so unequal. And once we move from the value of the bequest to the desirability of the life it would buy, things might look even more equal. Some children wanted to remain as farmers in Ireland, and some did not. For someone who desperately wanted to remain, failing to be named as heir could be devastating, and £10 would not make it right. Yet for others life in the countryside was seen as something to escape, and many would not trade places with their brother the heir even if offered the chance. The emigrant's £10 bought him passage to a number of dynamic, growing economies, one that afforded him the chance to earn as much as or more than his brother at home. O'Rourke (1995, fig. 2) estimates that in the late 1860s an unskilled Irish worker could expect to double his real wages by migrating to the United States, and at no time in the nineteenth century were Irish wages much more than 60 percent of U.S. levels. Connell notes, "Indeed, in these years, the disinherited may have felt that it was they, not their brothers, who were favoured; that all too soon the heir to Irish land might more conspicuously be the heir to Irish disaster" (Connell 1957, p. 86).

Treatment of the Aged

One of the features of the rural Irish household system was a clear place for the aged in households. How were aged people treated in this society? How was life different for those who did not have families? The literature on Central European retirement agreements conveys the impression that parents feared mistreatment at the hands of their successor, even with the written contract. Gaunt (1983, pp. 260–268) notes that retired parents could be a burden, or at least perceived as a burden, and that legal enforcement of such contracts was not always perfect. In Ireland accounts of intergenerational conflict associated with retirement center on trouble between a mother and her new daughter-in-law. This stress may reflect the real points of tension in the Match, but it also may reflect male perceptions of power struggles among females. We have already seen two observations that imply that rural Ireland was relatively benign for the aged. The Royal Commission on the Poor Laws, quoted in chapter 3, argued that the rural economy made it easier for aged people to live with their children. Others made the parallel argument that it was easier for people with the infirmities of old age to perform certain agricultural tasks, making them more useful on the farm. The implicit contrast in both cases was with urban, industrial life, as in English cities, where, it was thought, the aged were unable to compete in the labor market and could not find a role in their children's homes. Above I mentioned a Judge Johnston who told the Departmental Committee on the Old Age Pensions (1919) that many aged people were taken into households to which they were completely unrelated. This was the same Johnston who claimed that sons would threaten to run off to America unless their father yielded the farm. Together these comments imply a society in which people are willing to be fairly hard-nosed about their interests, but in which there is also an ethos of caring for those unable to care for themselves.[28]

The changes in public support for the aged debated at the end of the nineteenth century, and enacted in the Old Age Pensions Act of 1908, give us more direct information on the economic status of the aged. This information pertains, of course, not to how aged people were treated within private households so much as to whether the aged needed to rely on state support. The pension reduced the number of people receiving both indoor and outdoor relief from the Poor Law, but the reductions were larger for outdoor relief than for indoor relief. Why? Aged people in workhouses before the pension was instituted were those for whom outdoor relief was not enough to keep body and soul together. They might have had medical problems that required institutional care. More likely, they did not have kin willing to shelter an aged person in return for the 2 shillings or so the Poor Law was likely to pay each week. Those in workhouses prior to the old-age pension were more likely to be the hard cases for whom 5 shillings per week could not buy life outside an institution. Comparing information on indoor paupers in 1901 and 1911 confirms this impression and shows an interesting difference between aged men and aged women. The census only counted indoor paupers, and it used age classifications that did not correspond to the pension's rules, so we can only look at workhouse inmates aged 75 and over in the two census enumerations. The percentage of all men and women aged 75 plus who were indoor paupers fell between 1901 and 1911. But the decline was largest for never-married men and widowed men (a decline of about 55 percent) and considerably smaller for married men and women and for single women.[29] The smaller declines for married men and women and for single women suggest that those in the workhouse prior to the institution of the pension had some problem that meant 5 shillings per week would not make them welcome in a private household. The Royal Commission on the Poor Laws asked about the feasibility of a system whereby aged indoor paupers were "boarded-out" or placed in private homes with support from the Poor Law. One response (from a member of the Tyrone County Council) said the plan was unworkable because "the aged and infirm who are able to be boarded out are really the same persons who now get outdoor relief, and there are a certain class that are not suitable for outdoor relief, and you must have some refuge to bring them into."[30] Viewed the other way, prior to the pension married men and women and single women were unlikely to end up in a workhouse unless their circumstances were unusual. Simple poverty did not lead to the workhouse. This fact reflects some combination of the Poor Law's policy (its generosity, if that word may be used in this connection) and the behavior of private households.

The Vice-Regal Commission considered a proposal to create separate Poor Law institutions for the aged. The idea was a small number of more centralized "Almshouses" where aged people could live in relative comfort, freed from the discipline of normal workhouses. But the commission was worried that by removing someone from the relatively local workhouse to an almshouse that might be many miles from where the aged person had lived his life, the new institution would cut people off from visits by friends and family. This fear reflected a misperception: "We found that, while the acutely sick were visited by their friends, the infirm and aged received very few visits from friends or relatives. This, we were informed, is because large numbers of these old people are among the last remaining survivors of their generation. In other cases the old people are unmarried men and women in touch with few, if any, relatives. Again, some are fathers or mothers of children who have emigrated but have not done well" (Vice-Regal Commission 1906a, report §141). Reactions to this proposal, by highlighting the characteristics of aged people who lived in workhouses, also illustrate the character and degree of support for the aged in this society.

HISTORICAL EVOLUTION: FROM BEFORE THE FAMINE

Thus far we have not really addressed the heart of Connell's story: that the stem family became increasingly common in the period between the Famine and the early twentieth century, and so can account for the rise of permanent celibacy over that period. Unfortunately here we are on less firm empirical ground. Agricultural statistics show that subdivision of farms became less common, but that does not necessarily imply any particular household structure. Sources for the family are thin indeed before 1901. The published census does contain some hints. From 1841 through 1911, one can construct consistent measures of the average household size and the number of households. The average size of a household tells us nothing about its structure, much less whether a son is waiting to take over and marry, but in the absence of any other information it warrants examination. Fitzpatrick's compilation of the mean household size in the four provinces from 1841 through 1911 shows no dramatic changes anywhere. Average household size in 1911 was about 85 percent of its 1841 size in Ireland as a whole, with little variation across the provinces. Households had become somewhat smaller, but depopulation took its heaviest toll on the number of households: Ireland had only 62 households in 1911 for every 100 households in 1841, and Munster and Connaught had only half as many households in 1911 as in 1841 (Fitzpatrick 1983, table 1).

We can also examine changes in how people were related to the head of the household in which they were living. The Irish censuses report number of persons under three broad headings: natural family, visitors, and servants. (Recall that the term "visitor" in the census is ambiguous.) From 1841 to 1911 the number of family members per household declined most, from 4.47 to 3.81 for Ireland overall. The number of visitors declined much less, from 0.73 to 0.7 per household, while servants declined from 0.34 to 0.19 per household (Fitzpatrick 1983, table 2). Shrinking households reflect fewer family members. Once again these changes are not evidence for the emergence of a stem-family system—many changes could produce a reduced number of family members per household, and it seems unlikely that a LePlay-style stem system would have fewer family members per household than any other—but it does support Connell's basic assertion that some transformation was taking place in Irish households over the period.

The only study to try to compare households in the same areas of Ireland before and after the Famine uses census schedules from 1821 and 1911. Carney (1981) drew random samples of households from Counties Meath and Galway in the two periods. Unfortunately he does not present his results separately for the two counties, so we cannot assess the degree to which changes over this period reflect changes in one or both of the areas. Carney's results do not confirm Connell's views. Whether we examine all of his households or only his rural households, extended-family and multiple-family households were less common in 1911 than in 1821 (Carney 1981, tables 6 and 7). Yet Carney notes, correctly, that the family-cycle problem raised by Berkner may be complicating the interpretation of his results. When he retabulates his information on household structure by the age of the household head, he finds more subtle changes. The 1821 data show the developmental cycle Berkner expected. Young household heads live alone or with a simple family, and older household heads have extended- or multiple-family households. By 1911 there is little relationship between the head's age and the household's structure. Much of this reflects the fact that the household heads are older in general, rather than any necessary change in the household cycle (Carney 1981, tables 9 and 10).

O'Neill's (1984) detailed study of pre-Famine County Cavan is the only one to use the manuscript census schedules from 1841. His study area warrants some caution. As he notes, pre-Famine Cavan had considerable textile employment and an unusually developed capitalist agriculture. Comparison of his 1841 data with information for 1901 or 1911 is comparing across both time and some important social and economic differences. That said, his findings provide more support for Connell's interpretations. O'Neill finds higher proportions of households fitting the "simple-family" definition than in any of the studies for 1901 and 1911.[31]

So is there any reason to believe that the rural household system of 1911—whatever we might want to call it—differed considerably from that of 1821 or 1841? Connell's story of an emergent stem-family household system does not receive strong support from the information available. Moreover, the changes that we do find, especially in Carney's study, are inconsistent with some of Connell's themes and with our discussion of the Irish household at the turn of the twentieth century. Carney's 1821 data show a household system that already has large numbers of people not associated with a nuclear-family system. Nuclear-family households became even less common during the nineteenth century, but the reallocation of households was not toward the classic stem forms of multiple- or extended-family households. Rather, the decline in households with any family reflects the increase in households without any family.

This suggests an interpretation different from Connell's. The major change in Irish households was not that they developed a new tendency to take on exotic forms, but that on the death of a member of the older generation a new couple was less rapidly formed by the marriage of a member of the younger generation. Succession became more problematic, and with it more heirs never married, producing the large number of solitairy and no-family households that are the real innovation in the 1911 data.

Connell's account emphasizes a shift from equal inheritance prior to the Famine to unitary inheritance by the early twentieth century. Even given our discussion above, his account may not be all that incorrect. The evidence on the subdivision of holdings during the post-Famine period is robust. Few farms were subdivided, and an increasing average holding size suggests rather that the amalgamation of holdings was more common. As Ó Gráda suggests, Connell went wrong only in confusing the nature of bequests with bequests at all. The Match and related practices reflect not new assertions of patriarchal power but a change in the strategy of providing for young and for old. In the 1830s many Irish parents could afford to give their children little more than a chance at a small scrap of land, and the children could expect little more. Equality meant sharing out the holding equally. As emigrant opportunities increased, the meaning of equality changed. By giving one son a solid farm and the others a chance at a good life elsewhere, parents were able to provide for both themselves and their children. Doubtless sometimes this system involved bitter disappointment for the son or daughter not favored to remain in Ireland, and considerable anguish for the son who would rather leave but was expected to stay. But it is more accurate to view this situation as changes in the ways families divided their properties than to cling to the notion that parents disinherited all but one or two of their children. Nor should we accept the view that post-Famine household change "signalled the breakdown of the collectivist mentality" (Whelan 1986, p. 161). Irish families found that the post-Famine economic order offered new ways to manage the process of transferring property and getting the young started in their own adult lives. This was not necessarily a change of mentality, just a change in opportunities.

The family system Connell saw emerging in the post-Famine decades has by most accounts broken down since then under the weight of other forces. Hannan (1979) studied this process in the west of Ireland, and concluded that "[o]ver time, but particularly since the 1950s, the [peasant] system has gradually and cumulatively disintegrated." Mogey (1947) did not focus on household structure per se in his study of rural Northern Ireland during the early 1940s, but his examples consist mostly of either nuclear-family households or families lacking a conjugal couple entirely. Other local studies have come to similar conclusions (for example, Symes 1972). Birdwell-Pheasant (1992, pp. 228–229) has aptly noted that the classic stem family in Ireland existed, if at all, briefly, but that its figurative and emotional appeal was such that many writers have equated its demise with the demise of rural culture more generally. Why the stem family holds such a strong fascination is, as Laslett noted long ago, more than somewhat puzzling, and bears study in its own right. For our purposes the rural family's more recent history simply bears out our main conclusions. Concentration of land on one heir and the dispersal of most of his siblings reflected a delicate balance of economic opportunity, and so particular economic circumstances. The system worked best when the small amount necessary to go abroad purchased a life that parents and child alike could view as roughly equivalent—in terms of who was well treated, and who was not—with remaining on the farm. But as life in cities in Ireland and abroad became more attractive relative to life in the countryside, the balance was upset.

Chapter 6

COMING OF AGE

> I was over twenty years then and according to the standards
> of many countries a man fit to assume responsibility. But
> this was Ireland.
> —Patrick Kavanagh, *The Green Fool*

T HE YOUNG PERSON coming of age in rural Ireland during the decades following the Famine faced a future unlike those in store for most of his European neighbors. Young Irish people knew they were likely, like many before them, to experience adult life not in Ireland but in Britain, North America, or Australia. Young people also knew that should they remain in the Irish countryside, they were increasingly unlikely to marry and to rear their own families. This chapter traces the process by which children became adults in this environment. A close look at this part of the life cycle illustrates several features of the demographic transformation that is our concern. Certain behaviors such as migration are largely the outcome of decisions young people make as they grow up and try to find their place in the world. More generally, looking at the world that shaped and constrained the transition to adulthood teaches us much about the decisions that shape other patterns such as marriage. Common themes in Irish history and in economic and social history will be considered throughout, but each time with a view to its relation to the way children became adults.

Economists and economic historians have as of yet devoted little attention to the issues discussed in this chapter. The omission is difficult to understand, given the centrality of households in much research in these fields. Focusing on this stage in the life cycle highlights several features of the household as institution discussed in chapter 5. For the household the departure of young members is an adjustment in its size and composition. The adjustment may entail changes in its consumption role (it has one less member to feed and clothe, and one less person capable of helping to feed and clothe those too young or too old to help themselves) and its production role (the household has lost one potential worker). For some households the departure of a child may require recourse to the labor market to continue essential consumption or production tasks. A child's departure marks the end of the household's reproductive role, at least for that child. Finally, the departure of children may mark a change in the way that particular household plays its role of transferring goods, services, and wealth across the generations. A departing child will no longer consume what his parents and others have prepared, and will no longer work on his parents' farm. He may, however, take with him assets transferred to him from his parents, and may help to support remaining family members through remittances sent home.

Leaving home, for the young person, marks the beginning of independent life. He or she takes what life (and the household) had to offer so far—education (formal or not), connections and relations that may ease entry into domestic or foreign labor markets, and perhaps some wealth that will enable the young person to acquire more education, to migrate, or to purchase his or her own enterprise. The young person begins to make the decisions about migration, work, and marriage and family that will determine the conditions of his own life. Aggregating over all the young people leaving all the rural Irish homes, we have the decisions that eventually produced the demographic patterns at issue in this book.

We can, once again, profit by setting the Irish experience in a broader historical and comparative context. Social historians have devoted increasing attention to the process of growing up in the past. This research has helped observers to understand not only how children fit into households and the societies in which they were raised, but also to understand how the process of growing up shaped the lives they would live as adults.[1] Thinking about Ireland in this more general context helps to clarify what was really different about youth and the coming of adulthood in Ireland, and how those differences might lead to differences in marriage and other behaviors.

An important difference between coming of age in Ireland and the process as it took place in many of the other times and places that have been studied should be noted. Many studies rightly refer to the general issue as simply "leaving home." Equating the young person's entry into adulthood with leaving home rests on two assumptions about households and about relations between parents and children. These assumptions are not necessarily appropriate in the Irish case. First, leaving home may not imply the severing of all economic connections between parents and children. The remittances discussed in chapter 4 show that many people would leave home, and even Ireland, without fully severing economic ties to their families. Second, Irish inheritance practices imply that some people became adult without ever leaving home. In farming households normally at least one child, the heir, never left home. In addition, the heir's siblings sometimes remained with him in the household. Thus, although we too will examine the process of leaving home and the more specific issue of when in the life cycle children left home, we must bear in mind that in Ireland leaving home and becoming adult were not necessarily the same thing.

HOUSEHOLDS AND CHILDREN

Many studies have focused on the age at leaving home. Examining on this event provides a convenient way to compare the experience of young people from various backgrounds, and suggests several natural questions. What is the most common age to leave? Who leaves earlier, boys or girls? How is age at leaving home influenced by household and family traits and other features of the young person's circumstances? The timing of children's departure bears directly on the way growing up affected both household dynamics and the young people raised in those households. Leaving home represented both a milestone in the young person's life and an important change in the household he or she left behind.

Differences between boys and girls are a theme prominent in studies of leaving home. We have already alluded to demographic conditions that imply different life cycles for boys and for girls. In many (if not most) western European societies girls tended to leave home earlier than boys. Ireland appears to have been no exception. Table 6.1 shows that at every age, daughters were more likely to leave home than were sons.[2] Emigration statistics also show that women were younger when they left Ireland than were male emigrants. This difference between the sexes is pervasive but, as we shall see, is partly a result of the statistical bias created by the large number of sons who never left home. Much of the gender difference in table 6.1 reflects not age at leaving home, but the chance that someone ever left home. Once this problem is accounted for, it becomes clear that other variables such as household occupation and local labor market conditions have a strong influence on age at leaving home and do not always affect males and females in the same way. Certain household characteristics induce a girl to remain at home longer than her brother.

I refer throughout this chapter to the "decision to leave home." This language raises an issue mentioned in chapter 1. Whose decision was this—did the individual young person choose, or did the household (meaning a child's father, or perhaps mother) decide when children should leave, ignoring the child's wishes? Doubtless there were instances in which a child left home over parental protests, or when an unwilling child was ushered to the door or train station when an uncle wrote from abroad offering a job. But both the household system described in the

TABLE 6.1
Percentage of Sons and Daughters Leaving Household, by Age

Age in 1901	Expected Dead[a]	Remain in Household	Exit Household[b]	Household Disappears	Number of Persons
5–9					
Males	4.42	70.3	19.4	10.2	283
Females	4.16	59.3	27.4	13.3	263
10–14					
Males	4.72	51.5	37.0	11.5	305
Females	4.05	35.4	53.5	11.1	243
15–19					
Males	5.95	47.3	44.4	8.2	243
Females	4.71	33.0	54.8	12.2	197
20–24					
Males	6.69	57.7	36.8	5.5	182
Females	5.47	37.0	49.3	13.7	140
25–29					
Males	7.20	60.6	26.9	12.5	104
Females	6.27	37.0	49.3	13.7	73

Source: Manuscript census sample.

Note: The sample is restricted to those reported as a son or daughter of the household head in 1901.

[a] Computed from Coale-Demeny model "North" level 14 ($\overset{\circ}{e}_0$ = 49 for males, 50 for females).

[b] "Remain in Household," "Exit Household," and "Household Disappears" sum to 100 percent except for rounding. "Expected Dead" can be subtracted from "Exit Household" to obtain a mortality-corrected measure. Expected deaths equals

$$1 - \frac{{}_5L_{x+10}}{{}_5L_x}$$

last chapter and other accounts of rural society suggest that such disagreements were exceptions rather than the rule. Parents and children had similar values and aspirations and would usually be able to agree. The complex economic ties between parent and child make it unlikely that one party could force the other to do something truly unwanted. (This is another facet of the bargaining discussed in the previous chapter.) Children reluctant to leave or in a hurry to leave could be reminded of their parents' control over the distribution of the family patrimony. And children were not entirely powerless should they disagree with their parents. Children unable to persuade their parents directly might find other ways, such as sloppy performance of farm or household chores, to convince others it was time to depart.

Viewed by the child, the decision to leave home would be similar to a decision to migrate. Implicitly, the child would compare the costs and benefits of remaining with his parents with the costs and benefits of leaving. Remaining, of course, includes the option of leaving next year instead of this. Earlier studies and the Irish historiography suggest four major influences on the costs and benefits of remaining at home:

1. *Household resources.* In poorer households children leave home earlier both because the child may hope to be able consume more if on his own, and because what the child does consume takes resources away from other family members.

2. *Local employment opportunities.* Children can contribute to household income without leaving home, and perhaps save for their own futures, if there are employment opportunities in the locale. These opportunities may be outside their own home or may consist of helping their parents with a family operation such as a farm. Or, if local employment chances are poor, the child may have to leave home to earn for his family or his future.

3. *Adult opportunities.* Some investments toward their own futures may require children to leave home at a certain age or forgo long-term benefits. Examples include formal education or on-the-job training not possible locally. The chance to obtain a farm or marry in Ireland, we shall see, induced some young people to remain at home longer than those unlikely to obtain an adult position in Ireland.

4. *Intergenerational transfers.* A child's share of any family patrimony may depend in part on the age at which he or she leaves home. Parents may encourage a child to leave early by offering to pay for a dowry, education, or emigration. Other parents may encourage a child to remain longer with a promise of a larger dowry or alternative resources.

Just how these four general forces affect young people depends on the specific features of the situation in which they are raised. Household size and structure, the nature and amount of household wealth, and the characteristics of local markets for youth labor, local schooling opportunities, and local adult opportunities will all produce different effects. Each of these four forces can affect males and females differently.

Children in the Household Economy

Children's material experience while at home depends on many things. The first and perhaps most obvious consideration is how many mouths a family has to feed. Irish families could be very large. The manuscript census sample includes 278 women who had been married at least twenty years by 1911. These women had borne on average 7.3 children, of whom 5.9 survived at the time of the census. About 10 percent of couples had ten or more surviving children after twenty years of marriage.[3] Some biographical accounts suggest that in poor families children

left home earlier to relieve pressure on household resources and to contribute some of their own earnings. One of Breen's informants, Johnny
Cronin, left home at age 12 (in 1925) to work for a farmer as a live-in
servant. Cronin's wages were paid directly to his father, and Cronin
claimed that many poor children left home at this age in his district
(Breen 1983, p. 91). Patrick Gallagher told a parliamentary committee
(in 1913) that in his district (County Donegal) families who became indebted to moneylenders or "gombeen men" sent their children out to
farm service at age 8 or 9, and that he had left home at age nine for this
reason (Great Britain 1914a, Q13569).

Another important consideration is the degree to which a young person's labor contributed to his own family's income on a farm, in a shop,
or in some other capacity. Virtually every description of rural farm life
emphasizes the contribution of young people to farming and household
labor in tasks such as minding livestock, running errands, watching
younger children, and churning butter. Family labor also played an important role in rural labor markets. As noted in chapter 2, after the Famine full-time laborers became less and less common in Ireland, until by
the end of the nineteenth century much hired labor was provided by the
sons and daughters of small farmers. Depending on the local economy
young people might not be able to make much contribution to the household budgets of families lacking land. The problem could be worse for
girls because of the changes in the organization of some traditionally female activities. To some extent the employment problem for young
women reflected a larger pattern of the fairly rigid division of tasks according to sex. According to Arensberg and Kimball, "Each learns his or
her part in farm economy, not as a vocational preparation but as a making ready for marriage. The boy acquires his man's skills and techniques
for the farm and farm family he may head himself some day; the girl
learns the woman's role as an integral part of her future state of wife and
mother" (Arensberg and Kimball 1968, p. 47). This division of labor
would make it more difficult to substitute young men and women in each
other's roles, and seems on balance to have limited employment opportunities for girls especially.

The local availability of educational opportunities also influenced the
age at which children left home. In a study of age at leaving home in the
United States, Galenson (1987) found that opportunities for formal
schooling and on-the-job training affected the decision to leave home.
Educational opportunities also mattered in Ireland, although they had
complex, opposite effects. The National School system meant that most
children could acquire a basic education without leaving home. More
advanced education, however, could require leaving home to go to a
town, city, or even abroad. This necessity was not limited to those seek-

ing formal education. Young men who expected to emigrate found little opportunity to acquire job skills in the Irish countryside, which could not provide the industrial training most relevant to their futures in Britain or North America. The relatively few Irish emigrants who acquired such skills did so overseas. In the late nineteenth century over half of Irish-born men in the United States were laborers or operatives.[4]

Another consideration affecting when a child would leave home is closely related to the inheritance system discussed in chapter 5. Some young people could not be sure what life in Ireland would hold for them and had to wait at home to know whether they would inherit, be able to marry locally, or need to pursue other options. Recall that relatively few emigrants ever returned from overseas. The inheritance system limited local marriage to at most a single male heir and usually to one daughter. Many of the surplus children emigrated, but the economy allowed some scope for young people to make their place without the parental farm or dowry. Males denied their own parents' farm could hope to obtain a tenancy in other ways. Arensberg and Kimball report that farms without heirs were sometimes given to "friends" or to the farmer's nephew (Arensberg and Kimball 1968, p. 133). A young man denied his own family's farm might wait on in Ireland, hoping to acquire another farm. One Meath farm in the manuscript census sample passes from uncle to nephew in this way between 1901 and 1911. A young woman might remain, hoping to acquire her own dowry or otherwise be matched without her parents' resources, in ways discussed below. Individuals hoping to remain in Ireland this way may account for some of the children who remained at home into their twenties before leaving.[5]

Children in Households

The manuscript census sample can help us better understand the role of children and young people in rural households. Table 6.2 introduces some basic regularities by reporting the average number of sons, daughters, and servants present in a subgroup of rural households in 1911. The households are subdivided by several relevant characteristics, including the household head's age and, for households headed by males in two age groups, the conjugal status of the household head. Table 6.2 follows census designations exactly: a son is a son even if he is 45 years old, and servants are those who call themselves such, regardless of their relationship to others in the household. (Some who report the occupation "servant" also claim to be the nephew or niece of the household head. Table 6.2 considers such persons to be servants.) The age panel in table 6.2 shows the role of children in the household's developmental cycle. The number of children rises until the household head is in his or her late forties and early fifties, then declines as children leave home. The more

TABLE 6.2
Number of Sons, Daughters, and Servants in 1911, by Household Type

	Mean Number of			Number of Households
	Sons	Daughters	Servants	
Age of Household Head				
35–44	1.5	1.3	0.2	156
45–54	1.7	1.4	0.3	226
55–64	1.6	1.2	0.3	180
65+	1.3	0.8	0.1	345
Occupation of Household Head				
Laborer	1.6	0.9	0.0	221
Other	1.0	0.8	0.4	282
Small Farmer	1.6	1.1	0.0	173
Medium Farmer	1.5	1.2	0.1	252
Large Farmer	1.0	1.0	0.9	92
Marital Status of Male Household Heads				
Age 45–54				
Married	1.9	1.6	0.3	171
Widowed	1.2	1.7	0.3	6
Age 55–64				
Married	1.7	1.6	0.3	98
Widowed	1.4	1.5	0.2	18

Source: Manuscript census sample.

striking difference is in the number of sons and daughters at home, and is not surprising given what we have already seen about age at leaving home. Boys outnumber girls in nearly every instance.[6]

Subdividing households by occupation and wealth shows even more pronounced gender differences. Sons at home outnumber daughters markedly in households most likely to judge a child by an income-generation criterion, laborers and small farmers. The gender difference is smallest, and the number of servants largest, among the wealthiest farmers and the residual occupation group. The retention of children in these households reflects less the role they play in the household economy and more the opportunities in the wider world afforded by those households' wealth. The differences between widowed and married male household heads also reflect the role played by boys and girls in rural households. Girls are more likely to remain at home when their mother has died, taking her place in domestic duties. Households headed by widowed men are, in fact, the only category of household to contain more daughters than sons.

TABLE 6.3
Relationship to Head of Household, 1911, Ages 1–29

Age	Percentage of Males Related to Household Head as					
	Head	Child	Sibling	Other Relative	Not Related	Number of Persons
1–4	0.0	83.3	0.0	14.4	2.3	174
5–9	0.0	84.8	0.0	15.2	0.0	244
10–14	0.0	85.3	0.0	10.4	4.3	279
15–19	0.0	80.6	1.4	4.2	13.8	283
20–24	3.8	74.1	4.1	2.3	15.8	266
25–29	15.5	63.8	3.4	7.2	10.1	207

Age	Percentage of Females Related to Household Head as					
	Head	Child	Sibling	Other Relative	Not Related	Number of Persons
1–4	0.0	78.8	0.0	19.6	1.6	184
5–9	0.0	84.6	0.0	14.6	1.4	214
10–14	0.0	86.0	0.4	9.2	4.4	228
15–19	0.8	73.2	1.9	5.1	19.1	257
20–24	11.4	61.4	3.0	6.6	17.5	166
25–29	27.4	43.0	5.6	16.2	7.8	179

Source: Manuscript census sample.

Table 6.3 examines the relationship to the household head of all young people in the sample in 1911. In examining this table we need to bear in mind that a child's relationship to the household head depends both on what the child does and on what others do. The small number of older "daughters" in the table reflects the fact that women over 25 were relatively unlikely to remain in a household unless they were married to the household head. But whether a 14-year-old girl is the daughter or sister of the household head depends entirely on whether headship has passed to her brother. Once again we observe important differences in the experience of boys and of girls. Over 25 percent of females aged 25–29 in the sample are the head or spouse of the head, compared with the 15 percent of males in that age group who head their own households.[7] This reflects both the later male age at marriage and the tendency of girls to leave home earlier. Few married men do not head their own households. The "other relative" column includes grandchildren, nieces and nephews, cousins, and some called simply "relative." Females are nearly always more likely to fall into this category, for reasons related to the ambiguities in the kinship terms employed by the census.

The table also shows an aspect of rural Irish life that has received considerable attention in literary and folklore accounts and that underlies

TABLE 6.4
Household's Perspective on Children Leaving Home

| Age of Household Head in 1901 | Percentage of Households Losing at Least One Child, 1901–1911 | | | | Mean Proportion of Children Leaving Home, 1901–1911 | | Number of Households | |
| | All Households | | Households with Same Head in 1901 and 1911 | | | | | |
	Sons	Daughters	Sons	Daughters	Sons	Daughters	Sons	Daughters
35–39	32.6	41.0	36.6	41.7	0.15	0.22	46	39
40–44	52.4	63.6	54.4	61.6	0.28	0.43	84	77
45–49	61.7	69.0	64.8	67.3	0.33	0.44	60	58
50–54	62.1	68.3	66.7	76.3	0.34	0.49	87	82
55–59	58.8	59.1	56.4	55.6	0.31	0.40	51	44
60–64	42.0	63.9	43.8	61.3	0.26	0.44	100	83
65–69	29.7	47.4	36.4	43.8	0.17	0.35	37	19

Source: Manuscript census sample.

Note: The sample is limited to households present in both censuses. "Sons" is restricted to households with at least one resident son in 1901. "Daughters" is restricted to households with at least one resident daughter in 1901.

Kavanagh's remark quoted at the outset of this chapter. Young Irish people found themselves in subordinate, nonadult roles well into a period in life that in other societies would entail full adulthood. Sixty-four percent of the males aged 25–29 not only do not head their own households, they are still reported to the census-taker as the household head's child. The comparable figure for women, 43 percent, is low only by Irish standards. Perhaps more remarkable is the high proportion of men who are still "sons" at ages 40–49, 11.1 percent ($N = 135$).[8] In an oft-quoted remark Arensberg and Kimball (1968, p. 55) noted that a male who did not yet head his own household was called a "boy." This prolonged period of social childhood in Ireland surely weighed on the minds of those considering emigration.

Finally, did households shed children gradually, or did the exit of a household's younger members occur in a short space of time? Connell (1958) conveys the impression that children left home en masse when one of their brothers married and took over the household. The financial aspects of these arrangements seem to imply that the household would undergo several changes nearly simultaneously. The use of dowries to finance emigration has led some to believe that other children would wait at home, however anxiously, until the sister-in-law's dowry appeared (for example, Miller 1985, p. 405). Table 6.4 suggests something different. The departure of children is not limited to households experiencing headship transfer between 1901 and 1911. There seems to be a regular progression of children out of the household. Fitzpatrick (1983, table 6) shows something similar. He finds that on average, the children born to marriages of twenty years duration are neither entirely in nor entirely out of the household, again implying that children did not leave home en masse. The death of one parent or the marriage of an heir would naturally require some alterations in property arrangements, and might seem a propitious moment to ask for one's passage money. But a parent's death need not always lead to a child's departure. The early death of one parent might induce a young person to remain, taking the dead mother's or father's place in the household economy.

Remaining

Three paths would lead a young person to remain near the place where he or she was raised. An heir would not leave home at all. His sister who was able to marry locally would leave home but would likely settle in a place not far from where she was raised. And some of their brothers and sisters alike would remain in the same household more or less for life. Heirship was discussed in chapter 5; here we discuss two other ways young people remained in Ireland even if they did not inherit the family property.

The available sources give little precise information about the young women who left home to marry in Ireland. Such women were, as a group, a minority. Just 27 percent of all women aged 15–24 in Ireland in 1901 would remain and be counted as either married or widowed in the 1911 census.[9] Accounts of two fathers bargaining over a "match" imply that young women who married and stayed in Ireland remained in their natal household until marriage (Connell 1962a, pp. 511–513; Arensberg and Kimball 1968, pp. 107–108). Because the average age at marriage for women in the sample is about 26, this seems unlikely, as girls usually left home earlier than that. Other references to women who worked as servants or who emigrated temporarily to earn their own dowry imply a lower age at leaving home still consistent with late marriage. In another passage Connell (1962a, p. 506) claimed that it was not unknown for young women to earn their own dowries this way.

A final way to remain locally in Ireland was also to remain in the household, this time not as heir but as the heir's sibling. Table 6.5 shows that many young people in fact stayed on in this type of position. In discussing intergenerational transfers of property in the previous chapter we noted that parents usually tried to make some provision for all their children, not just for the one who acquired the holding itself. For many siblings this provision amounted to the right to live in their natal household if they so chose. Table 6.5 suggests that this practice was most common where the sibling was not competing with a new wife and her family.

TABLE 6.5
Male Household Heads with Co-Resident Siblings, 1911

	Brother	Sister	Number of Households
	Percentage of Households with at Least One Co-Resident		
Age of Household Head			
35–44	7.7	12.0	142
45–54	8.7	9.2	195
55–64	3.0	8.3	133
65+	5.0	7.3	218
Household heads Aged 45–54			
Never-married	22.2	50.0	18
Married	7.6	4.7	171
Widowed	0.0	16.7	6
Household heads Aged 55–64			
Never-married	0.0	41.2	17
Married	4.1	4.1	98
Widowed	0.0	0.0	18

Source: Manuscript census sample.

Brothers in general were less likely to stay on, and remaining sisters were most common where a brother did not have a wife. Some accounts, in fact, refer to such brother-sister pairs as replicating aspects of the household arrangements of married couples. In the next chapter I discuss this point in detail in examining the reasons for widespread permanent celibacy in Ireland.

Life-Cycle Service

Social historians of western Europe have emphasized the prevalence in the lives of young people of an institution that has now disappeared: life-cycle service. Under this arrangement, young people left home in their early teens and spent several years living with and working for a succession of employers, usually on yearly contracts.[10] Servants were employed much more broadly than the modern sense of the word would imply. Many if not most were live-in farm laborers. The institution of service figures heavily in discussions of the transition to adulthood in modern Europe. Laslett and others have stressed the role of life-cycle service in the household system of early-modern English society.[11] Mitterauer and Sieder (1982) and Sieder (1987, pp. 48–59) show that service was an important feature of life in rural areas of continental Europe as well. Hajnal (1982, tables 13 and 14) notes the high prevalence of servants in western European historical populations. Some 30–40 percent of males and females were servants at ages 15–19 in his Icelandic, Norwegian, and Flemish communities, and over half of all 15- to 19- year-olds were servants in some rural Danish parishes. Laslett calls the institution "life-cycle" service because for most people service occupied a brief part of their lives between leaving home and marrying. Moreover, service did not always entail class differences between master and servants. Many young people would leave their parents' home to work for a farmer of similar social class (Laslett 1977, p. 45; Kussmaul 1981, chapter 5). Laslett argues that while in service young people were treated as family members, as social equals. Life-cycle service has an additional significance in the role it plays in Hajnal's model of the western European marriage pattern. According to Hajnal, life-cycle service was a stage before marriage during which young people acquired assets and skills needed to establish and run their own households. Western Europe's relatively advanced age at marriage reflects the length of this stage in the life cycle.

The institution of service had dual significance. For young people, it provided a way to accumulate skills and savings in preparation for marriage. For farmers and others who needed labor, hiring servants was a flexible way to guarantee the labor needed through an agricultural production cycle. Since servants were not day laborers, the farmer could be more nearly assured that he would have the labor necessary for critical times such as harvest. But because servants usually worked on yearly contracts, this source of labor was easily adjusted to balance changes in family labor supplies. In his classic study of an Austrian region that, like Ireland, practiced impartible inheritance of farms, Berkner noted the role of life-cycle service in matching the changing availability of household labor to the unchanging labor demands of a farm:

> In Austria the peasant holding was impartible and was transferred en bloc from generation to generation. The amount of land belonging to a family remained relatively constant, but the amount of labor provided by the family went through [a cycle determined by the number and ages of children in the household], creating a labor shortage in the first years of the family's existence. The obvious solution was to expand the labor force by hiring servants in the early years of marriage to replace the labor of retired parents and the brothers and sisters who had left the farm to do the work for which the children were still too young. As the children grew up they replaced the servants. (Berkner 1972, p. 414)[12]

In their studies Symes (1972, p. 33) and Breen (1983, pp. 96–97) both find evidence of this use of servants to substitute for family labor in Ireland.

Life-cycle service was also an important life-cycle stage for many rural Irish youths. The most common forms of service were as farm servants or, especially for women, as domestic servants. The manuscript census also lists some girls who work as servants for a shopkeeper or publican. But Breen (1983) has called attention to several differences between service in early twentieth-century rural Ireland and the institution described by Hajnal in early-modern Europe. Irish farm servants were of inferior social status to their masters. Servants in Breen's County Kerry sample came from households on average much poorer than those in which they worked. Accounts of the treatment of farm servants differ, but Kavanagh's story of hard work and at least mild mistreatment seems typical.[13] In addition, service in Ireland and the institution described by Laslett differ in what followed. Irish service for young men was, according to Breen, usually a stage before emigration (1983, p. 101). The difference between the early twentieth-century Irish and the early-modern populations discussed by Hajnal may simply reflect the relative ease of emigration for the Irish. Breen has little to say about girls who entered service, for whom the next stage might not always have been emigration. For the rest, life-cycle service in Ireland stemmed more from the need to leave home before leaving Ireland and to acquire funds for passage.

Servants made up substantial portions of all young people in three of the four sample locales, as table 6.6 shows. But the figures in this table require explanation. Many young people had already emigrated by their early twenties. Servants at that age are a large fraction of a cohort heavily depleted through emigration. In addition, the three locales with many servants had considerable demand for adolescent labor, but this demand was not necessarily filled by those born and raised in the locale. Servants were more likely than other young people to have been born outside the county in which they resided at the time of the census. The available evidence also says nothing about the number of servants born in the same county as the subsample locale but outside the locale itself. Some locales, that is, might have been net importers of adolescents.[14] The Mayo locale, in contrast, lacked both the nonfarm activities and the large farms that employed servants elsewhere, and was presumably a net exporter of adolescents.

Moving within Ireland

Internal migration, especially rural-urban migration, was less common in Ireland than elsewhere. As noted earlier, British and North American cities, rather than Irish cities, provided the bulk of new job opportunities for young people in rural Ireland. One source of urban labor demand that did produce significant internal migration was the demand for domestic servants in larger Irish towns and cities. Many of the young female migrants who moved within Ireland were domestic servants, work-

TABLE 6.6
Prevalence of Servants, 1911

	Clare	Meath	Wicklow	Mayo
Percentage Who Were Servants				
Males				
15–19	30.5	22.6	11.4	7.6
20–24	31.5	17.6	28.4	1.3
Females				
15–19	25.6	31.8	36.2	8.2
20–24	23.5	38.2	34.1	2.7
Percentage of Servants Aged				
15 to 24 Born in County				
Males	78.3	94.7	82.1	57.1
Females	78.8	66.7	75.0	14.3
Percentage of Nonservants				
Aged 15 to 24 Born in County				
Males	96.1	92.5	89.8	94.6
Females	99.0	90.2	80.3	94.2
Number				
Males				
15–19	95	31	79	79
20–24	54	68	67	77
Females				
15–19	82	44	58	73
20–24	51	34	44	37

Source: Manuscript census sample.

Note: The table employs a "relationship" definition of servant. See text for explanation.

ing either alone or as part of a large domestic staff for Dublin's middle- and upper-class households. The same would be true in Belfast, Cork, or any other Irish city. The published census shows that about 70 percent of domestic servants in Dublin 1911 were from the province of Leinster. This was a short-distance migration. A recent study of domestic servants in Dublin argues that life as a domestic servant in Dublin held several advantages for the young women so employed. Servants received board and lodging (as did farm servants), and although their formal pay could be meager, many had the opportunity to supplement that income through tips or gifts from their employer and their employer's guests (Hearn 1989, pp. 161–162). Perhaps more important, working as a domestic servant did not conflict with "the ideology of the time which considered the home, albeit someone else's home, the natural place for a girl or woman" (ibid., p. 149). Working as a domestic servant did not threaten a young woman's desirability as a wife.

Emigration

Chapter 4 surveyed general aspects of emigration during the nineteenth century. The focus here is on the process by which young people left Ireland. Emigrants from other European countries often migrated in steps, moving first from their rural homes to a nearby town, and then on to a larger city in their own country before migrating overseas. If we are to believe the personal reminiscences and folklore accounts, this practice was less common among Irish emigrants, many of whom speak of being accompanied from their rural homes to a ship that would take them abroad. The ability to move in this way speaks of two important features of the young emigrant's situation. First, he or she was often, by the end of the nineteenth century, the beneficiary of a system that provided the intending emigrant with passage money rather than forcing him or her to earn it himself. Whether the money came from a relative already abroad or was part of a new sister-in-law's dowry (disbursed as "portions" to her new husband's siblings), the intending emigrant was saved the necessity of earning it before departure, an important reason for step migration in other contexts. Second, the large Irish communities in several other countries eased the problem of settling into a foreign economic and social environment. Other Europeans used step migration to ease gradually from rural Europe to urban North America.

For some Irish emigrants, however, the transition from rural Ireland to urban North America, or whatever their final destination, did take several steps. One common strategy was to spend a period of time in Great Britain. We will never know how many of the Irish who went to Britain at the turn of the twentieth century intended to stay there and how many viewed it as a convenient way-station while contemplating moving overseas or while waiting to see what their options might be in Ireland. Harris (1994) argues that many pre-Famine migrants to Britain did not intend to stay, either seeing the neighboring island as a way-station on the trip to North America or intending to return to Ireland. For those lacking funds to proceed directly abroad, employment in England or Scotland offered the chance to work for a few years and earn what was necessary to proceed overseas. Certainly these intentions contributed to the character of Irish communities in Britain, which for much of the nineteenth century had a transient, unsettled nature not true of their North American or Australian counterparts. The earl of Donoughmore said in 1854, "I think that the whole aspirations of the people are turned towards America, and that they come to England as a temporary expedient."[15] Passage from Ireland to Britain was much cheaper than passage overseas, meaning that it was easier to get to Britain and that going to Britain made it easier to return home.

TABLE 6.7
Ages of Irish Emigrants

	Percentage of Emigrants Aged						
	0–14	15–19	20–24	25–29	30–34	35–54	55 or Older, or Age Not Specified
Males							
1852–1854	22.6	14.7	28.1	21.2		12.2	1.2
1861–1870	13.7	8.4	33.7	20.1	9.0	9.9	5.2
1871–1880	13.5	10.2	31.7	20.9	10.5	11.8	1.4
1881–1890	13.7	15.0	38.3	15.5	6.6	9.5	1.4
1891–1900	8.5	11.0	41.6	23.4	6.2	7.9	1.4
1901–1910	9.0	11.6	42.1	21.3	7.8	7.2	1.0
1911–1921	9.3	12.7	41.6	28.1		7.5	0.8
Females							
1852–1854	22.0	18.8	28.4	16.8		12.6	1.4
1861–1870	16.1	13.1	34.0	13.3	6.9	10.9	5.7
1871–1880	15.7	17.8	33.8	13.6	7.6	10.0	1.5
1881–1890	13.9	26.0	35.5	10.0	4.8	8.5	1.3
1891–1900	7.3	22.1	44.1	14.1	4.6	6.7	1.1
1901–1910	8.8	25.2	39.5	14.0	5.1	6.2	1.2
1911–1921	8.7	26.5	39.5	18.2		6.1	1.0

Source: Commission on Emigration and Other Population Problems (1954, table 91, p. 122).

This said, table 6.7 shows that few had to wait long. (Table 6.7 relies on the official emigration statistics that we know to be faulty, but the undercounting of emigrants in the statistics is unlikely to affect the age distributions at issue here.) If they were to leave, most Irish people left early in life. In any year the preponderance of emigrants from Ireland were under 30 years old, and the highest emigration rates were for people in their early twenties. The table also illustrates a point noted in the introduction to this chapter and to which I return below. With regard to male and female emigration rates, the women had a tendency to leave even earlier. What can account for this preponderance of youth, especially among females? Several factors were at work. First, migrants in any society tend to be young. Students of migration usually give two reasons for this phenomenon. Migration and assimilation into a new economic and social environment require considerable flexibility and are probably easiest for the young. In addition, migration is like an investment. It makes most sense to give the investment in migration a long time to pay off—that is, a long time to earn the higher wages available in a foreign labor market. These considerations may account for the emphasis on the importance of youth that Schrier (1958, p. 25) detected in some

Percentage of the cohort aged 5–14 in 1861
absent from county in 1881

Less than 50%		60% to 70%
50% to 60%		More than 70%

Map 6.1 Cohort depletion, males, 1861–1881. (*Source:* See Table 4.4.)

letters from Irish emigrants. Second, the youth of Irish emigrants also testifies to many emigrants' ability to raise the funds they needed to emigrate without actually saving it themselves. Few 17-year-olds could have saved passage costs out of their own earnings. The even greater youth of female emigrants is an issue explored below.

Maps 6.1 through 6.4 use the cohort-depletion measure of migration to show the geography of emigration for two different cohorts. (The periods 1861–1881 used in the first set of maps is shorter than the period 1881–1911 used in the second set. The age cohort 10–14 in 1861 is shown as it was depleted by age 30–34, while the age cohort 10–14 in

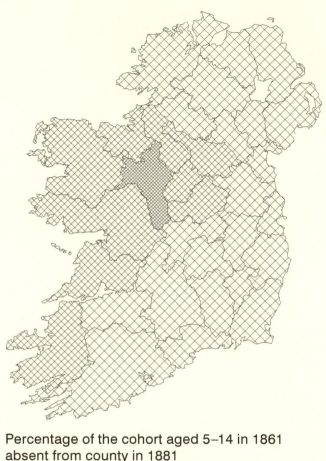

Percentage of the cohort aged 5–14 in 1861
absent from county in 1881

☒	Less than 50%	☒	60% to 70%
☒	50% to 60%	▨	More than 70%

Map 6.2 Cohort depletion, females, 1861–1881. (*Source:* See Table 4.4.)

1881 is shown as it was reflected at age 40–44. The periods were chosen deliberately to avoid using the 1851 census data, which still show the effects of the Famine, while still using 1881 as a mid-point. The choice of years introduces some unavoidable awkwardness.) The maps show, first, the rarity that someone born in Ireland would remain in Ireland. In many counties a majority of males aged 10–14 in 1861 were gone by 1881. The maps also show the much heavier rates of emigration in the west of Ireland. (Some of this impression stems from internal migration, which confuses the cohort-depletion measure, but comparing these maps with maps 4.3 and 4.4 shows that the effect of internal migration

Percentage of the cohort aged 5–14 in 1881
absent from county in 1911

Less than 50%   60% to 70%

50% to 60%   More than 70%

Map 6.3 Cohort depletion, males, 1881–1911. (*Source:* See Table 4.4.)

is slight.) The depletion of the second cohort is less dramatic in the eastern counties. The maps also show changes in the relative numbers of
male and female emigrants. For the second cohort female cohort-depletion rates are much higher in several counties, especially those on the
Atlantic seaboard. The increasing female emigration from western counties reflects the decline of female employment opportunities there as
well as the relatively stronger demand for Irish females in urban labor
markets in Britain and North America. The next chapter considers
the implications of these sex differences in emigration for marriage in
Ireland.

Percentage of the cohort aged 5–14 in 1881
absent from county in 1911

Less than 50%		60% to 70%
50% to 60%		More than 70%

Map 6.4 Cohort depletion, females, 1881–1911. (*Source:* See Table 4.4.)

AGE AT LEAVING HOME

Having described the ways young people left home, we return to a question originally posed at the outset. Who left home earlier, boys or girls? Children of laborers or children of prosperous farmers? Elsewhere I have used the manuscript census sample and two different econometric models to get at these questions. The nature of the data and these questions involve some fairly complicated statistical issues, but the major results

TABLE 6.8
Evaluations of the Waiting-Time Model

	Probability of Remaining at Home				Mean Age at Leaving Home[a]	
	At Age 20		At Age 30			
	M	F	M	F	M	F
Farmers						
Mayo: house points = 4;	.72	.34	.10	.04	23.2	18.8
farm value = £7	(.08)	(.06)	(.05)	(.02)		
Meath: house points = 10;	.28	.58	.15	.32	15.9	23.8
farm value = £25	(.09)	(.15)	(.09)	(.09)		
Meath: house points = 10;	.18	.48	.04	.29	14.9	21.5
farm value = £50	(.14)	(.17)	(.06)	(.08)		
Clare: house points = 10;	.20	.63	.01	.29	17.2	24.3
farm value = £25	(.06)	(.07)	(.01)	(.05)		
Nonfarmers						
Mayo: house points = 4	.24	.20	.15	.06	24.7	15.1
	(.12)	(.09)	(.14)	(.03)		
Meath: house points = 4	.26	.16	.19	.09	13.4	11.1
	(1.03)	(.12)	(.68)	(.06)		
Wicklow: house points = 4	.85	.26	.24	.13	26.1	15.2
	(.10)	(.09)	(.12)	(.04)		
Clare: house points = 4	.71	.33	.07	.07	22.7	18.5
	(.16)	(.09)	(.06)	(.04)		

Source: Computed from estimates reported in Guinnane (1992a, app. table 1).

Note: Standard errors are shown in parentheses. Evaluations assume that the individual is "leaving prone."

[a] Mean number of years lived in the parental household before age 39.

from these exercises can be summarized rather simply, which I do in the remainder of this section. Guinnane (1992a) explains the econometric models used, the potential pitfalls associated with either the modeling or the data, and discusses more technical features of the estimation procedures. Here I discuss only the major results. Two distinct models are used, the first a waiting-time model and the second a binary-probit model. In both cases the idea is to allow the data to speak more clearly by using statistical techniques to isolate the effect of one variable while holding others constant. In this case, for example, we want to see how farmers' sons differ from sons of laborers in the same sample locale. This requires holding locale constant so we are not comparing the sons of Meath laborers with the sons of Clare farmers.

Tables 6.8 and 6.9 summarize the results. Table 6.8 shows the implications of the waiting-time model, which is designed to estimate the chance that a young person would leave home at any point in childhood or adolescence. The statistical model allows us to study how the chance of leaving home depends on not just the child's age and gender, but on household wealth, father's occupation, and where the household is located (which sample locale). The numbers in table 6.8 summarize the results by taking a hypothetical individual and calculating, based on the statistical model, the chance that this person would still be at home at age 20, still be at home at age 30, and the average age at leaving home for this person. Thus the first row in the table says that a relatively poor farmer's son in Mayo would have a 72 percent chance of being home at age 20. This boy's sister would have a 34 percent chance of remaining at home at that age. All the figures presented in table 6.8 assume that our hypothetical individual has some chance of leaving.[16] The summary measures show clearly that boys did not always leave home later than girls. The later male age at leaving home originally suggested by table 6.1 is largely spurious, reflecting in part differences in the propensity ever to leave home that have been taken care of by the statistical model, and in part an averaging of individuals with different behaviors. Table 6.8 supports two generalizations. First, females do leave home earlier in nonfarming households. Daughters of men who are not farmers cannot be employed in family-run operations, and are unlikely to be matched to a farmer's son. Such girls have little to hold them in the countryside. Note, however, that even among nonfarming households some within-gender differences are larger than most of the differences between genders. Now consider the farmers' children. Daughters leave home later than their brothers in all but one of the instances selected for illustration here. Meath sons from both farming and nonfarming backgrounds leave home relatively early. In the Clare example (and in a similar Wicklow farming example not shown), males leave home earlier than their sisters.

Table 6.8 also shows an important result for males: wealthier farmers' sons who do not remain to inherit the farm leave home rather early, pursuing the educational and other opportunities that their family's wealth can buy them. Their sisters remain at home somewhat longer. This difference reflects two features of the difference between male and female opportunities. The Meath locale imports more female servants than male servants, suggesting a stronger local demand for female labor. This area also has some nearly landless laborers, so a farmer could depend on hired labor rather than on his sons. But the finding also reflects the nature of female opportunities. Young women who expected to marry locally could remain at home, acquiring some earnings while waiting for their day.

The locale effects are very large. Even after we have controlled for influences such as gender, household wealth, and household occupation, the locale in which a young person is raised has a strong influence on age at leaving home. The locale most likely reflects the importance of labor markets for young people. As noted earlier, in discussing servants, some of our sample locales have a strong demand for adolescent labor; others do not. Gender and household wealth and occupation may shape a young person's adult opportunities, but opportunities available while he remains at home play a strong role in determining when he leaves to take advantage of those opportunities.

The Effect of Household Composition

One would think that the timing of a child's departure from the household would depend on various features of his family—number of siblings, whether his parents are living, and so on. Connell, Arensberg and Kimball, and the other Irish evidence described above actually suggest a series of related questions: Does birth order affect leaving home? How does a glut of siblings affect the chance of leaving home? And what role does transfer of household headship, actual or expected, play in children's departure? To address the impact of household structure on age at leaving home I use a binary-probit model. Unlike the waiting-time model, the probit model cannot account for the statistical problems associated with an heir who never leaves home. But it provides a simple and convenient way to study the impact of these forces on when a child leaves home.

Table 6.9 uses hypothetical individuals to summarize the results from the binary probit model. Here the figures are the chance that a person with the stated characteristics would leave home between 1901 and 1911. Birth order has some effect on the chance that a girl leaves homes, but hardly matters for boys. This should not be all that surprising—chapter 5 showed the absence of any strong birth-order effects in inheritance. The effects for females aged 15–24 are somewhat surprising, because there is no direct counterpart to the alleged primogeniture for males. Why should birth order affect the order in which daughters leave home? A folk expression reported by Connell may explain the finding: "No girl should make a bridge of her elder sister's nose" (Connell 1958, p. 518).

The number of siblings in the household had a complicated impact on when a child left home. More brothers makes a son more likely to leave, and more sisters makes a daughter more likely to leave. Departure is not influenced by the number of siblings of the opposite sex. In this respect

TABLE 6.9
Evaluations of the Probit Model

| | Implied Probability that a Child Leaves Home between 1901 and 1911 | | | |
| | Males | | Females | |
Characteristics	Probability	Standard Error	Probability	Standard Error
Baseline[a]	51.09	6.59	60.55	7.69
Meath	40.23	9.63	44.31	10.55
Meath: farm value = £25; house points = 10	45.44	10.01	32.14	9.32
Aged 25–29	43.44	12.80	86.06	9.81
Eldest	49.18	6.73	78.74	6.21
Headship transfers to wife	37.31	7.88	60.82	9.93
Headship transfers to son	57.20	8.59	62.39	9.40
Household head: female 65+	37.93	21.62	23.75	15.15
Household head: male 65+	49.20	8.74	59.77	10.78
Number of other family members = 1	49.80	7.58	55.45	8.98

Source: Computed from estimates reported in (Guinnane 1992a, app. table 2).
Note: Both probabilities and standard errors are multiplied by 100.
[a] The baseline person is 15 to 19 years old; is the child of a Mayo farmer whose farm is worth £7 and whose house scores 4 house points; is not the eldest; has two siblings of the same gender; and has three other family members in the household. The household head is less than 65 years old, and household headship has not changed between 1901 and 1911.

the model provides striking confirmation of the comments, noted above, about the rural Irish being rigidly divided by sex. Households' behavior toward a particular child depended not on the total number of children in the household, but on the number of the same sex as that child. Males and females did not compete for the same part of the family patrimony; males ordinarily got the farm. This is striking confirmation of Arensberg and Kimball's (1968) finding that males and females were viewed as poor substitutes for each other in household and farm tasks.

The Irish historiography implies that the timing of departure for all children would be closely related to the time at which an heir took over the farm and married and his living parent or parents retired from active control. The statistical results support a more complicated view. Males were less likely to leave home when headship had transferred to their mother. This may reflect the death of a father and an expectation that their widowed mother would eventually cede control. Household transfer does not affect the chance that a daughter leaves home. Aged parents, in contrast, have no influence on sons, but having an aged mother as household head reduces the chance that a daughter leaves.

These statistical investigations produce three important results. First, the gender differences in table 6.1 are partly spurious, resulting from differences in the propensity ever to leave home. Males are much more likely never to leave, because of the inheritance system. Once we have taken into account the inheritance system's effects, we find that gender differences in age at leaving home are often smaller than other systematic differences, and do not always imply that males leave home later. Second, locale—which here proxies for the characteristics of local markets in labor, in tenancies, and in mates—has a very strong effect on age at leaving home. For nonfarmers, especially, locale sometimes produces larger differences in age at leaving home within a sex than between sexes. Finally, household structure and composition affect males and females differently. Age at leaving home for members of each sex is influenced by the number of siblings of the same sex in the household, but not by the number of siblings of the opposite sex in the household; and a male's departure from the household is more closely tied to transfer of household headship.

SUMMARY

This discussion of coming of age in Ireland reiterates, in a different way, a point first made in the previous chapter. We saw there the way ostensibly noneconomic behaviors such as inheritance or household residence were shaped in part by a household's economic circumstances. The analysis of age at leaving home shows something broadly similar. Leaving home was not in any simple sense an economic undertaking. Leaving home signaled both young persons' separation from their household's economy and the deep emotional significance of separation, perhaps permanent, from their family. But once again the timing and incidence of this event were influenced by the practicalities of everyday life—the number of mouths a household had to feed, what a son or daughter could earn locally, a son's evaluation of how long he would have to wait to inherit the farm.

This discussion of age at leaving home also echoes some of the recent historiography of rural Ireland and that of other societies. We saw sharp differences between boys and girls in whether they would leave home and, if so, when they would leave. This finding matches up well with the comments in Arensberg and Kimball, in folklore accounts, and in other historical studies of Irish households. We also saw the more interesting interaction of gender with other traits, such as household wealth, that meant that the significance of being a boy or a girl depended very much on whether one's father was a rich farmer or a poor laborer, whether one lived in remote Mayo or in Wicklow. In a very real way, the combination of gender and "class" is more important than either taken alone. The gender differences we have first seen here, as we examined the way young people became adults, will return in different forms as we examine the way they lived out their lives in Ireland or abroad.

Chapter 7

THE DECLINE OF MARRIAGE

> Of such was Neary's love for Miss Dwyer, who loved a
> Flight-Lieutenant Elliman, who loved a Miss Farren of
> Ringsakiddy, who loved a Father Fitt of Ballinclashet,
> who in all sincerity was bound to acknowledge a certain
> vocation for a Mrs West of Passage, who loved Neary.
> "Love requited," said Neary, "is a short circuit."
> —Samuel Beckett, *Murphy*

MARRIAGE after the Famine may be the most often noted but least-analyzed element in Irish history. To shape our discussion of marriage patterns it is useful to begin with some remarks on what an explanation should look like. Social changes over time or differences across groups of people at the same time can reflect variations in the constraints people face or in the things they desire. An explanation of Irish celibacy might say that the Irish wanted the same things as everyone else but faced economic and social circumstances that led them to different marriage choices—the constraints explanation. Or an explanation might say that Irish circumstances were similar to circumstances elsewhere but that fewer Irish wanted to marry—the preferences explanation. Elements of both explanations may be important, and in a long historical process constraints may eventually influence preferences, and vice versa. We must also consider what an adequate account of Ireland's marriage patterns has to be able to explain. Suppose we say that Irish people refrained from marrying because of something we will call factor X. For the "X theory" to be adequate, it must not only be inherently plausible (X must have something to do with marriage), we must also be able to show that changes in X correspond to changes in nuptiality; X must have become more common in Ireland after the Famine, so the rise of X corresponds with the rise of celibacy. X must also be distributed across the country and across social groups in the same way as celibacy. In 1861, X must be more common in Meath than in Mayo. Finally, if X is to explain celibacy in Ireland, X must be more common in Ireland than in the other countries that had less celibacy.

We can divide earlier explanations of Ireland's nineteenth-century nuptiality patterns into three groups. These three views are not logically exclusive, and some discussions advance a combination of at least two. The most prominent is the Malthusian interpretation that lies at the heart of Connell's model. Others, including Walsh (1970a), Kennedy (1973), and McKenna (1978), also fit into this category. The remaining two interpretations are less clearly articulated and are often mentioned in combination with some other style of argument. One, which I will term "institutional," views marriage in Ireland as impeded by the complicated institutions of inheritance and the Match. The Malthusian and institutional explanations share the trait of explaining Irish celibacy in terms of constraints rather than preferences. The Malthusian explanation says that marriage was limited by incomes; the institutional explanation says that marriage was limited by the difficulty of transferring properties and locating mates. Finally, some writers make cultural difference the centerpiece of their explanation.

A weakness common to most of the earlier literature is a failure to take seriously what marriage meant to the young men and women in question. To marry in nineteenth-century Ireland was to assume a complex new set of rights and responsibilities, including not just sexual relations and child rearing, but property rights in land and other assets, and connections to kin. Young people in Ireland had to make important decisions about how they wanted to live their lives, whether in Ireland or elsewhere, whether married or not. If we do not try to understand how these decisions appeared to the young people in question, we cannot hope to understand why so many decided to remain in Ireland without marrying. My approach is, in its structure at least, simple. The implications of marriage depend on time, place, and one's personal circumstances. To some marriage requires giving up a great deal in return for relatively little that one values. For others, as Connell maintained in his explanation of early nineteenth-century marriage practices, marrying and rearing a family may be the only practical ways to attain aspirations such as security against starvation. These differences in the implications of marriage are connected to differences in the motivation to marry. Understanding the motivations is the key to understanding changes in behavior over the nineteenth century.

To be more concrete, consider the possible benefits of marriage to an individual. These are potential benefits because not every marriage would entail each item, and for some individuals the item would not matter:

> *Sexuality and companionship.* Given the paucity of illegitimacy in rural Ireland, we can assume that sex outside of marriage was rare. Marriage may also be a source of companionship and emotional intimacy.
>
> *Labor.* Marriage brings another adult capable of helping with household tasks, farming operations, and related work. The upbringing of men and

women emphasized different practical skills, so differential abilities would mean one's spouse could do some tasks better than one could oneself. Work by family members of any kind are relatively free of agency problems, making this source of labor preferred to others.

Offspring. Children are valued for their own sake, and in a peasant society may be valued for their ability to "keep the name on the land." Children are also another source of relatively problem-free labor. Finally, children (unlike spouses) are by definition younger and so able to provide support in old age.

Economies of scale in consumption. The costs of many household goods (housing itself, fuel, and so on) is not strictly proportional to the number of household members, so per-person costs are lower with a spouse and with children.

How much any of these potential benefits is an actual benefit depends on the person's circumstances prior to marriage. Someone who has a small holding that requires little labor will get little benefit out of another worker in the household. More generally, many of the benefits of marriage can be had in alternative ways. In a society with arranged marriages, companionship may come more from same-sex friendships than from spouses. Satisfactory labor arrangements can be provided by other relatives, or even through long-term arrangements in the labor market.

We begin by laying out the Malthusian explanation in greater detail. At the same time the empirical implications of the Malthusian view will be used as a framework in which to present more detailed information on patterns of nuptiality in Ireland. Next we discuss the institutional and cultural interpretations. Finally, we turn to a discussion of the incentive to marry in rural Ireland and how this view can account for Ireland's marriage patterns.

THE MALTHUSIAN INTERPRETATION OF RISING CELIBACY

Anyone who advances a Malthusian interpretation for the rise of celibacy in post-Famine Ireland has to confront the evidence of rising incomes discussed in chapter 2. The Irish became wealthier, but according to a Malthusian model they acted as if they were poorer. Connell's solution to this problem was to point to the Land Acts, which he claimed enabled rural people to accumulate property for the first time. He said, in effect, that prior to the Land Acts the fruit of any foresight would accrue to the landlord, while after the Land Acts rural Irish people could sacrifice for material gain and be reasonably sure of keeping it.

Robert Kennedy (1973), in contrast, dismisses any important role for the land legislation, arguing that the timing of the Land Acts does not coincide with increases in celibacy. Instead, he stresses a related point, that rising material aspirations made Irish people more and more willing to sacrifice marriage and a family to the goal of achieving what they saw as a decent living. There is a basic similarity between Connell's and Kennedy's arguments. Both writers claim that Irish families became increasingly willing to put material goods before marriage and children, and each points to a historical change that reconciles the rising incomes with the Malthusian model. They differ only in the reason for that change.

Three features of Kennedy's argument can be criticized. First, his dismissal of the land legislation's role in Irish society misses the point Connell was making. Kennedy (1973, p. 158) rightly notes that land reform had not created many peasant proprietors until long after the surge in celibacy after 1871. Yet Connell refers not to proprietors but to the changes in landlord-tenant relations brought about by the Land Acts of 1870 and 1881. The 1870 statute gave tenant farmers certain protection against ejectment from their holdings, and the 1881 law regulated their rents. If pre–land reform tenures had been as insecure as Connell claimed, then these two acts would have put an end to "elastic rent." Thus Connell's timing is not so far off as Kennedy argued. The second curious feature of Kennedy's argument pertains to the nature of his evidence for changes in material aspirations at the end of the nineteenth century. This point is crucial to his explanation. If the Irish came to value houses and bicycles over marriage and children, then Kennedy would have strong support for his view. Yet he presents no direct evidence on such changes. He refers to another study that argues that changing English marriage patterns reflected changes in material aspirations in England (1973, p. 149).[1] Similar demographic trends in England and Ireland may have the same explanation, though not necessarily so. But as Kennedy himself notes, the trend away from marriage in England was not really all that similar to the trend in Ireland. The rise of celibacy in England was more muted than in Ireland, and was confined largely to women. And even if the demographic changes in England and Ireland were identical, there is no good reason to assume that the two changes had identical causes. Much preferable as support for this type of argument would be direct evidence for Ireland that material aspirations were increasing. Without such evidence Kennedy's argument is circular: the Irish refrained from marrying because they grew to care more for material goods, but we know about the change in material aspirations only because of the increases in celibacy.

Finally, Kennedy, like Connell before him, does not try to explain why the Irish reaction to increasing material aspirations was to refrain from marriage. One can imagine other reactions, and in fact we observe them under similar circumstances. An increase in the value attached to material consumption—and that is all we are talking about—might lead people to work more. Given its tradition of emigration, a change in material aspirations could easily be satisfied by leaving the country for more prosperous places.

There is also the question of why material aspirations would change. Problems of evidence aside, what could cause such a change in aspirations? Kennedy does not say. One plausible mechanism is through the information transmitted home from emigrants to Britain or the United States. The thousands of Irish people living in Britain and overseas wrote home regularly, describing their experiences and what was to be had in the countries to which they had moved. Emigrants often included concrete evidence of their success in the form of remittances. A brother in New York who wrote home annually, telling of the material wonders of his new home, of better food and housing, of fancier clothing and all the gadgets of nineteenth-century consumer society—such a brother might well induce a sense of dissatisfaction at the material conditions of those who remained in Ireland. Contemporaries blamed returned migrants for the spread of a vague materialism in Irish society (see, for example, Keep 1955, p. 385). Scholars of migration find this phenomenon in many situations, and there is no reason to doubt the impact of these information flows on Irish attitudes. Yet in other situations the transmission of desire for material goods is thought to induce even more people to migrate.

Kennedy's argument about increasing relative deprivation also conflicts with the pattern of real-wage convergence discussed earlier. Irish wages were lower absolutely, but the gap between real wages in Ireland and in the United States and between Ireland and Britain narrowed considerably during the second half of the nineteenth century. Thus the emigrant brother could write home of a better life to be had in the United States, but the degree to which the U.S. life was better had not increased during the period of sharply rising celibacy rates. Connell (1958, p. 4) provides a better rationale for Kennedy's argument, oddly enough, noting the penetration of peddlers and shops into the countryside, bringing with them concrete evidence of what money could buy. Liam Kennedy (1979) traces the development of these commercial networks in the late nineteenth century and shows that they eventually penetrated virtually every corner of the island. But even Connell's observation cannot answer the question raised by Robert Kennedy's argument: why would people react to a sense of deprivation by refraining from marrying? If a migrant's younger brother grew dissatisfied with his material lot in Ireland, why would he react by remaining in Ireland and not marrying, rather than by joining the brother in the emigrant stream?

Posing the question of marrying versus migrating brings us to a second basic problem with the Malthusian explanation. Emigrating required an up-front investment and imposed a personal cost, but most people who remained in Ireland could have left if they had wanted. As a logical matter the stem-family system Connell describes held out two alternatives for those who received neither farm nor dowry: remain a bachelor or spinster in Ireland, or emigrate. Patterns of celibacy in Ireland always reflected decisions about emigration as much as decisions about marriage. A bachelor or spinster living in Ireland in 1911 would not form part of Ireland's remarkable marriage patterns if he or she had either married or left Ireland. High levels of celibacy in Ireland can be viewed just as accurately as low levels of emigration. The Malthusian model implies people felt too poor to marry in Ireland. But the same model implies that they did not feel so poor in Ireland that they sought to leave. We can see these alternatives of migrating and marrying implicitly in table 7.1, which shows the proportion that never married by age in 1911 for the manuscript census samples and for the provinces of Ireland. Part of the decline in celibacy with age reflects men and women marrying and so switching from the "single" to the "married" category. But much of the decline in celibacy with age reflects the departure of single men and women from Ireland. To reinforce this point consider the cohort of people who were ages 5–14 in 1861. If we looked at this cohort in the 1911 census of Ireland, when its members were 55–64 years old, we would conclude that 22 percent of them had never married. But this is a misleading picture of the cohort's experience because we are only looking at those who stayed in Ireland. Imagine 100 males and 100 females who were 5–14 years old in 1861. Twenty years later, in 1881, not quite half of the males and somewhat more of the females were still living in Ireland. Some of those missing had died, but most had left Ireland. Adults who remained in Ireland in 1911 were a small minority, about 22 percent, of the original cohort. People who never married and remained in Ireland until 1911 were only 5 percent of the original cohort. The particulars differ for different cohorts, but much the same is true if we consider the people aged 5–14 in 1851, or in 1871.[2] Considering this point places a different cast on the entire question of celibacy in Ireland. If only 5 percent of adults in Ireland had never married, we would be amazed by how *little* celibacy the country had.

TABLE 7.1
Celibacy by Age, Irish Provinces and England, 1911

Ages	M	F	M	F	M	F	M	F	M	F	M	F
					Census Aggregates							
	Ireland		Leinster		Ulster		Munster		Connaught		England	
20–24	95	86	95	85	92	83	97	90	99	92	86	76
25–34	70	54	69	53	62	51	76	57	81	56	38	35
35–44	41	31	43	33	37	32	44	29	45	27	17	20
45–54	27	25	31	27	26	27	26	21	25	18	12	16
55–64	22	22	26	25	22	25	30	18	18	15	10	13
					Manuscript Census Sample							
	Clare		Meath		Wicklow		Mayo		Total			
20–24	100	96	96	79	98	86	99	84	98		87	
25–34	88	66	82	67	72	49	77	33	78		56	
35–44	53	25	59	39	39	19	37	16	48		24	
45–54	21	7	51	36	19	15	16	5	27		17	
55–64	29	12	42	19	25	19	6	6	22		13	
N	394	321	333	264	354	305	293	227	1,374		1,117	

Source: For aggregates: Great Britain (1912–1913a, table I; 1912–1913b, table XVIII).
Note: English figures include Wales. Lower panel includes all persons, regardless of relationship to household head.

Maps 7.1–7.4 display the geographic and temporal distribution of permanent celibacy in Ireland in 1881 and 1911. The patterns are similar for women and men. In 1881 levels of permanent celibacy greater than 15 percent of the age cohort were limited to areas in the north and east of Ireland. By 1911 permanent celibacy had become even more common in those areas. The pattern had spread westward, moreover, leaving counties that in 1881 had seen little change in marriage patterns with large numbers of bachelors and spinsters.

The geographic distribution of celibacy is instructive in two ways. First, the initial rise in celibacy occurred in some of the regions of Ireland where farms were largest and most commercialized (compare maps 2.1–2.3). This simple geographic correlation should caution against any interpretation that would equate Irish celibacy with hard-stricken peasants or poverty in any simple sense. Second, the areas of Ireland where celibacy remained rarest in the nineteenth and early twentieth centuries were the western counties where emigration was relatively most attractive, reinforcing the idea that Irish celibacy was closely connected to decisions about emigration.

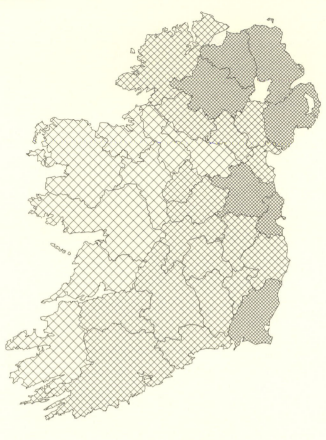

Percent never-married aged 45–54

⬚ Less than 5%	▨ 10% to 15%
▨ 5% to 10%	▧ More than 15%

Map 7.1 Never-married women, 1881. (*Source:* Census of Ireland, 1881, as abstracted in Vaughan and Fitzpatrick 1978, table 32.)

Who Were the Never-Married?

Neither Connell nor Robert Kennedy (1973) confronted the question of the identity of those who did not marry. But it is important that the stem-family account implies that people who did not marry were those denied land or dowry and who spent their adult lives as unmarried assistants on family farms. Was this true? Table 7.2 uses the 1911 census from my manuscript sample to look at this question. The composition of the un-

Percent never-married aged 45–54

⬚ Less than 5%		⬚ 10% to 15%	
⬚ 5% to 10%		⬚ More than 15%	

Map 7.2 Never-married men, 1881. (*Source:* Same as map 7.1)

married is different from age group to age group, partly because the sample is small for this degree of cross-classification. Some regularities are clear for those 45 and older, however. Connell was right in one sense. Many of the unmarried were the household head's siblings, although this role was more important for women than for men. Some unmarried women were also the head's daughter (in these cases the household head often being a widowed father or mother). These are the bachelors and spinsters we would expect from Connell's story. Even this is not sufficient, because we do not know why some preferred to remain in Ireland

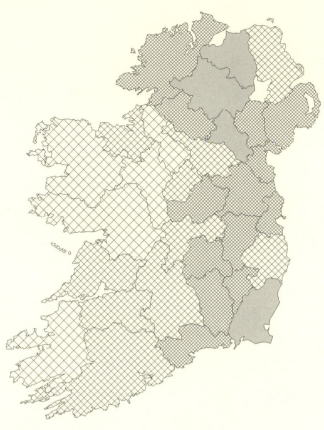

Percent never-married aged 45–54

⬚	Less than 20%	⬚	25% to 30%
⬚	20% to 25%	⬚	More than 30%

Map 7.3 Never-married women, 1911. (*Source:* Census of Ireland, 1911, as abstracted in Vaughan and Fitzpatrick 1978, table 33.)

when doing so meant forgoing a family—but at least this aspect of the stem-family account receives some support from the evidence.

The Malthusian account would not lead us to expect another important group of bachelors and spinsters, however: household heads. By age 55 over 40 percent of all unmarried males headed their households. In fact, the most startling feature of table 7.2 is the large number of men who had never married even though they headed their own households. Connell's story implies something different. In his view, men married when they took control of their parents' farms. The only barrier between

Percent never-married aged 45–54

▨	Less than 20%	▨	25% to 30%
▨	20% to 25%	▨	More than 30%

Map 7.4 Never-married men, 1911. (*Source:* Same as map 7.3)

a man and marriage was lack of land. When we examine this information in detail we find something even more puzzling. Table 7.3 shows the
proportion of older male household heads who did not marry, classified
by occupations and (for farmers) by farm value. This table shows that it
was not just the poor who did not marry. Depending on the census year
and age group, there were more single men among the wealthiest farmers
than among any other group. Moreover, it appears that laborers were no
less likely to marry than farmers, and—perhaps—that the wealthiest
farmers were less likely to marry than were their poorer neighbors.

TABLE 7.2
Relationship to Household Head of Those Never Married, 1911

Relationship	Age Groups				
	25–34	35–44	45–54	55–64	"All"
Never-Married Males					
Head	8.4	15.4	24.5	40.5	14.9
Son	69.3	53.7	37.5	2.9	57.1
Sibling	3.9	8.1	12.5	22.9	7.2
Other Relative	4.9	5.1	5.6	8.6	5.3
Not Related	13.6	17.6	19.4	17.1	15.6
Total Persons	309	136	72	35	552
Never-Married Females					
Head	3.9	6.3	19.4	13.6	7.0
Daughter	64.0	54.0	25.0	13.6	53.5
Sibling	11.2	11.1	41.7	50.0	17.7
Other Relative	10.7	6.3	5.6	0.0	8.4
Not Related	10.1	22.2	8.3	22.7	13.4
Total Persons	178	63	36	22	299

Source: Manuscript census sample.

Note: Figures are percentages of each age group. "All" column is for ages 25–64 only.

Farm Size and Celibacy

The pattern displayed in table 7.3 warrants close scrutiny. The table shows that many of the never-married in Ireland were by any measure prosperous, and that the probability of being married might have declined with increases in wealth. For our purposes the second finding is interesting but not necessary to support the argument below. Ó Gráda (1994, p. 217) has questioned whether the findings might reflect idiosyncratic features of the locales in my study, and presents evidence from a later period that contradicts the second finding. There are two ways to "interrogate" results of this sort. We can ask how the source may be misleading or how we could be misinterpreting it. We can also compare our finding with those of other historians to see whether we are the only ones to have come to this conclusion on the basis of this source.

Let us initially consider whether this finding could be something other than what it seems. There are two potential problems with table 7.3. One is that cross-tabulation is a crude way of addressing the question, because it does not hold constant some other factors (such as locale), and any age groupings used will be somewhat arbitrary. But this does not seem to be a problem in this case: the basic result, that increasing wealth does not increase the chance that a household head marries, is robust

TABLE 7.3
Male Household Heads and Celibacy

| | Household Heads Aged | | | |
| | 40–59 | | 60+ | |
Occupation by Census	Percentage	Number	Percentage	Number
1911 Census				
Farmers, by farm value				
£0–4	8.8	57	5.2	58
£4–30	15.2	105	5.4	74
£30+	14.3	28	25.9	27
Laborers	10.0	80	12.7	63
Others	8.7	80	17.0	47
All	11.2	350	11.0	269
1901 Census				
Farmers, by farm value				
£0–4	13.8	65	5.6	36
£4–30	7.9	89	8.5	59
£30+	24.1	29	28.6	28
Laborers	14.0	86	9.5	63
Others	5.7	87	16.0	50
All	11.4	367	12.5	236

Source: Manuscript census sample.

to these objections. In Guinnane (1991b) I developed and estimated an econometric model of the probability that a man would marry if he remained at home. The model allows us to control statistically for a variety of effects, including locale, and does not require the classification of age and wealth into what may be arbitrary groups. This model meets the objection noted and still supports the basic result noted in table 7.3. A wealthy farmer was no more likely to marry than was a poor farmer. A second concern is reasonable but easy to exaggerate. The measure of farm value used, the ratable valuation of land and buildings, is a rough measure of family wealth. Other assets such as financial holdings or even machinery are not included in this measure. Nor are farm debts. Some of the farms in the sample may be mortgaged, either explicitly to a lender or implicitly through obligations to siblings and retired parents. Thus some with valuable farms could have less wealth than it appears. For these problems to cause serious biases, however, it would have to be that only small farmers had financial assets, or only large farms, debts. This is implausible. The measure of farm value is imperfect, but we can reasonably assume that it is highly correlated with "true" farm value.[3]

One could also wonder whether the patterns represented in table 7.3 represent something unusual about the four locales in the sample. Are we looking at four places that happen to be idiosyncratic? The best way to address this worry is to compare the findings with information from other parts of Ireland. Unfortunately no other study to my knowledge presents information identical to that presented in table 7.3. But several other studies do present information that is at least analogous and can be used as a rough check. One study is somewhat different but seems not to support our finding. As part of the study of Thomastown (County Kilkenny), Silverman and Gulliver (1986) reported the conjugal status of males by occupation in 1901 for the two District Electoral Divisions of Thomastown and Jerpoint Church. They note that by age 55 most farm-ers (all but 9 percent) had married, but that many of those who remained farm laborers (about 33 percent) had not married. Thus farmers in their study area were more likely than farm laborers to marry. Yet this finding is not so at odds with my own as it might appear. They do not present any detail on farmers, so we cannot compare those with different farm sizes. And Silverman and Gulliver do not draw attention to the fact that only 3 percent of the category of "general laborers" never married (Silverman and Gulliver 1986, table 7). They do not provide the informa-tion necessary to check this claim, but it is also possible that by age 55 there are few farm laborers left. Fitzpatrick's (1983) study, also relying on the 1901 and 1911 census schedules, provides strong confirmation for the pattern in table 7.3 here. He reports the proportion of households that are "defective," or that do not include a married couple.[4] In both 1901 and 1911, and for nearly all of his five study locales, the proportion of defective households increases with farm size (Fitzpatrick 1983, table 7). Thus the wealthier the farming household, the less likely it was to have at its core a married couple. He notes that with one exception among his five locales, "large landholders always had a greater proportion of single male heads than had small holders" (Fitzpatrick 1983, p. 360, n. 46).

Combining the four locales in my manuscript census sample with the five locales in Fitzpatrick's provides strong confirmation for the fre-quency of celibate male household heads. Unfortunately this is the best that can be done for 1911 (and before). No published census prior to the 1926 census of the Irish Free State provided any detail on marital status by occupation. The 1926 census reported for the first time a great wealth of information on marital status, including detailed tables show-ing the marital status of men and women in various occupations and the marital status of farm residents by farm size. Several writers, including Kennedy (1973) and Ó Gráda (1994), have appealed to this information for an understanding of the development of permanent celibacy in nineteenth-century Ireland.[5] Yet there are reasons to be cautious about doing so. The omission of Northern Ireland from these tables is one problem, but we could remedy this shortcoming by focusing on differences between 1911 and 1926 within the twenty-six counties. More troubling is the implicit assumption that marriage patterns in 1926 would be identical to those in the period of interest, which is to assume that nothing in the economic and social environment changed between 1911 and 1926. We know this to be false. The country's partition is only part of the story. Irish farmers experienced great rural prosperity during the First World War, and the new Free State's economic policies prolonged that prosperity. The aggregate data on marital status, as we saw, shows consistent changes during the second half of the nineteenth century. Marital status in 1926 reflects decisions made during conditions that did not obtain in the 1890s.

A second reservation about the 1926 data is less serious but worth stating. The quality of farmland in Ireland varies enormously from area to area. Table 7.3 uses the taxable valuation of farms as the measure of farm size. The 1926 tables are presented only by acreage, and so are not directly equivalent. The value of an acre of land varies so much across Ireland that a small farm in one region can be worth more than a large farm in another. In 1926, to take some relevant examples, the total valuation of County Clare averaged about £0.4 per acre. The same figures for Mayo are £0.25, for Meath £0.96, and Wicklow £0.59.[6] The valuation figures here include all property, including nonagricultural buildings and land, but give an idea of the problem of making comparisons across farm sizes on the basis of acreage: with Meath land worth nearly four times as much as Mayo land, we would learn little by comparing a Meath farmer with 100 acres of prime grazing land with a Mayo farmer with 100 acres of windblown rocks. Because the primary comparisons here are within county, the variation is somewhat less, but there are some counties—Mayo being an example—where there were substantial variations in farm value from region to region within the county.

These reservations noted, let us turn to the 1926 data. Table 7.4 lists the marital status of farmers and farm laborers for the Free State and for the four counties that contain our study locales. In some ways the patterns are similar to those found in 1911. In Counties Wicklow and Meath we see the large proportions of farmers who are not married, and in these two counties (where laborers are the most numerous) there is no large difference between the chance that a laborer ever married and the chance that his employer ever married. The classifications of marital status for farmers by farm size modifies this impression somewhat. For both the Free State as a whole and for the four counties listed separately the proportion never married for farmers 45–64 decreases with an in-

TABLE 7.4
Farm Size and Celibacy, 1926: Percentage Never Married for Males Aged 45–64

		Farmers: Farm Size in Acres			
Area	Farm Laborers	1–10	15–30	30–50	100+
Ireland (26 counties)	29	23	18	17	17
Co. Meath	31	44	32	32	25
Co. Wicklow	30	42	24	24	16
Co. Clare	31	28	17	12	15
Co. Mayo	35	11	11	11	14

Source: Irish Free State (1926, volume XX, table 13).
Note: Farm laborers are those "not living in."

crease in farm size. Thus the 1926 census does not confirm table 7.3's suggestion that more wealthy farmers were less likely to be married. There are three possible explanations for the discrepancy. First, the nuptiality/farm size relationship may have changed from 1911 to 1926. Second, the 1926 census may not be comparable to the valuation data in the ways discussed above. Third—and this is Ó Gráda's concern—table 7.3 may be spurious in the sense that it simply reflects patterns in four idiosyncratic locales. The last possibility is the least likely, given the corroboration from a similar study of five other locales.

All this discussion of whether celibacy was more common among the wealthier farmers should not be allowed to obscure the central point: even the 1926 data provide no support for the Malthusian interpretation. Although marriage chances may increase slightly as farm size increases, even on the largest farms there were large numbers of never-married farmers. About one-quarter of Meath's wealthiest male farmers, for example, had never married. So the 1926 census confirms the most important conclusion drawn from the 1901 and 1911 evidence: being the head of a prosperous household did not necessarily mean that a farmer married.

Remaining without Marrying

Household heads are not the only uncomfortable issue for the Malthusian model. Connell's story implies that many siblings were denied land or dowry in Ireland and so faced a choice between emigration and living on the family farm as a dependent brother or sister. He did not offer much explanation regarding how or why these decisions would be made. Kennedy's argument about relative deprivation is even less able to account for such people. Table 7.2 shows that they were quantitatively significant. For the oldest age group, siblings are the largest group of never-married people of both sexes (next to household heads). There are also significant numbers of people not related to the household head at all. These people raise an important issue: why did they stay in Ireland?

Many of Ireland's bachelors and spinsters stayed in Ireland even though they must have known that remaining made marriage unlikely. Another considerable proportion of male celibates in Ireland were those who headed their own households, often farming households of some substance. The decisions these people made can tell us much about how they saw the world and their options, and undermines Malthusian explanations of the rise of permanent celibacy in Ireland. If we could interrogate the first group we would ask: if life in Ireland held such meager material prospects that you did not think you could marry there, why did you remain rather than join the emigrant outflow that took so many of your friends and family? And if we could interrogate the second we would ask: if it is in fact lack of access to material resources that keeps people from marrying, how can you explain the fact that you had your own household but never married? The explanation of Irish celibacy that I suggest at the end of this chapter is an effort to answer these questions and so understand the decisions these young people made.

INSTITUTIONAL EXPLANATIONS

Another explanation of Ireland's celibacy turns on impediments to marriage associated with the Match and its concomitant transfer of property. Like the Malthusian model, these ideas are not so much incorrect as applied too broadly or too simply. In chapter 5 we discussed the property transfers that occurred at the time of marriage. A wife brought with her a dowry used to settle claims on the family farm. Sources mention using the money for paying off debts (such as shop debts), but the dowry was primarily used to provide for the heir's siblings and parents. For siblings the dowry was a form of compensation for the farm they were now ceding to their brother and his new wife. Discussions of the dowry and the Match more generally often focus on keen bargaining between the two parties. Accounts stress that other issues, such as the wife's social status, health, and putative fecundity, were important, but if her other traits were satisfactory attention focused on the size of her dowry.[7] Careful statistical investigation in modern societies such as India shows that dowry sizes reflect the traits of the husband and wife as well as the relative numbers of men and women available to marry (Rao 1993a, b).

What role might dowry have played in the increasing celibacy of the nineteenth century? The institutional argument goes as follows. If there were no dowries, then the appointed heir (or his parents, since this was an arranged marriage) could search for a wife. Under this scenario a dowry would not be one of the considerations in this search. At the time of his marriage the heir would find ways to convince his siblings that it was time to leave the nest. Because of the dowry, however—which is to say because of the heir's obligations to those who were giving up their claims to the farm—the heir had to restrict his choice of mates to women wealthy enough to have an adequate dowry. A potential wife who had less than the required amount would place the new couple in the unenviable position of either living with disgruntled siblings or mortgaging the holding to raise the "portions" promised to the others. Such a woman had to be available for marriage, moreover, at just the point the heir was looking for a wife.

This claim contains an element of truth, but misplaces its emphasis. As a logical matter the argument assumes that for the siblings the portion is an all-or-nothing matter. Assume that there are four siblings, each of whom has been promised £25. According to this argument they can hold their brother the heir hostage to a dowry of £100. But why would the siblings want to do that? Yes, they would like more money rather than less. But if their brother does not marry at all (and so never brings in a dowry), the sibling's portion will be less or even nothing. Even if their insistence on the £100 dowry only forces their brother to wait a year or two to find the right mate, the siblings might still be acting against their own interest. Why not accept a slightly smaller portion to be able to emigrate and start a new life sooner? To place the dowry at the center of Irish celibacy is to assume that claimants on the dowry would prefer nothing rather than something smaller than they wanted. This may be true—both the heir and his siblings may have precise ideas of just what kind of woman (and dowry) will persuade them to break up their household and form a new one. But if this is true then the heir's desire to marry must be slight, and his sibling's desire to leave their natal household must be weak.

So at the level of the household, or the individual group of siblings, this story has little appeal. The dowry story also seems peculiar when we step back and consider this transfer's larger role in Irish society. In the system typical of Ireland after the Famine, where a male heir received the undivided farm and his siblings received some compensation in lieu of a piece of the farm, the dowry has twofold significance. Thus far we have focused on the dowry as the system's way of compensating siblings without dividing the farm. One implication of this feature of dowry is marital endogamy by class for farmers. Compensation for a valuable farm, that is, requires a large dowry, and only another wealthy family can afford that dowry. Fitzpatrick examined this hypothesis by comparing the wealth of brides' and grooms' families in three locales at the turn of the twentieth century. In the forty-eight instances in which he could establish the wealth of both spouse's families, he found that just under half (twenty-one cases) allied with families of similar economic status. Endogamy measured in this way was considerable but not complete. Many couples were willing to violate what is supposed to have been a strong social norm.[8] Dowry also has a related, second level of significance: the fact that an Irish farm could command a dowry (which is to say that a farmer could expect payment for the right to marry his son) means that land was scarce; the sizes of dowries reflected this scarcity.

If dowry was a serious impediment to marriage then we should expect changes in dowry over time, as celibacy became more common. We do not have sources that allow us to trace precisely trends in the sizes of dowries over the nineteenth century. Ó Gráda (1993, table 47) reports that daughters' shares of their parents' estates decreased from about 1870 through 1910. He interprets this trend as a decline in dowry sizes. The price of marrying a daughter into a comparable farm declined during this period because farmers had to be willing to accept less of rural women who had better options abroad. Viewed from the other side, Irish farmers had to accept an ever-smaller dowry in order to find a wife for their sons. Both the imperfect endogamy found by Fitzpatrick and the trend in dowry sizes discovered by Ó Gráda indicate that there was some flexibility to Irish pairings.

The Availability of Mates

Another popular argument turns on the relative numbers of men and women, or the availability of mates. This claim is popular in part because it has some resonance with discussions of demographic forces in modern societies. Some years ago popular publications in the United States discovered a "man shortage," a deficit in the number of young adult males relative to young adult females. This shortage of young men was thought to be contributing to a decline in marriage in the United States.[9] Perhaps motivated by this development, demographers turned their attention to the issue of marriage rates and sex imbalances. The demographic research on this topic is based on three strong regularities and an important assumption. First, in most societies males tend to marry women who are somewhat younger than themselves. Second, there are often year-to-year fluctuations in the number of children born over time. A "baby boom" for a few years will be followed a "baby bust" for a few years. Some young women will find themselves members of a relatively large group of baby boomers all trying to find the slightly older husbands who were born during a baby bust. Later on, marriage-minded men will find themselves competing for a relatively small group of younger women born just after the baby boom ceased. Third, in most societies marriage is endogamous by social class and sometimes by other traits, such as occupation, religion, or ethnicity. The number of people in the right categories of age, sex, religion, ethnicity, and so on, can be small indeed.

Finally, this research makes the strong assumption that the relative number of men and women in the "right" groups exercises a powerful influence over the possibility that men and women will marry. If men in a given society usually marry women four years younger, the argument goes, and if there are 10 percent more men than women in the relevant age groups when it comes time to marry, then many of those men should expect not to marry. A variant on this argument stresses that relative numbers of available mates may affect individual marriage chances even more if individuals restrict their search for a mate to some smaller social group. If, for example, there are more college-educated black women than college-educated black men, and if college-educated women usually marry a college-educated man of the same race, then some of the college-educated black women will not marry.

However intriguing it might be to think about the problems of searching for a spouse in such a society, neither logic nor evidence supports the notion that availability of mates played a major role in the celibacy we see in Ireland by 1911. First consider the argument as it pertains to recent experience in the United States. In one study Goldman and her coauthors, using contemporary U.S. data, argued that reduced marriage rates among educated whites was caused by the surplus of women over men at the socially acceptable ages (Goldman, Westoff, and Hammerslough 1984). If men and women can only marry within the categories Goldman and her colleagues describe as normal (for example, same race or similar educations and incomes) then in such a situation some will go unmarried. But the entire argument hinges on people of both sexes being quite rigid about whom they will marry. Faced with the prospect of not marrying at all, some men or women might decide to marry someone with a slightly lower income, slightly less education, or slightly older or younger than Goldman and her colleagues consider normal. If some men and some women remain unmarried, then the cause is not relative numbers, but the fact that some people remain unmarried rather than marry someone of the "wrong" traits—too old, not enough education, and so forth. Relative numbers are only part of the story: the marriage squeeze has the strongest results where the incentive to marry is weakest.

A famous historical example shows how easy it is to overestimate the importance of such numerical imbalances. The First World War killed 1.3 million French soldiers, roughly one-quarter of the military-aged men in prewar France. By the logic outlined above we would expect to see a huge increase in celibacy among women of corresponding ages. Yet nothing of the sort occurred. Henry (1966) noted that women of that devastated generation experienced only slight increases in permanent celibacy. How did this result, so contrary to the logic driving research such as that of Goldman and colleagues, come about? Faced with the alternative of never marrying, many French women adjusted their requirements in a mate. The likelihood that a divorced or widowed French male would remarry increased substantially; single French women became more likely to be second wives. The age differences between husbands and wives changed, with men marrying women more nearly their own age than had been typical in prewar France. And some French women married one of the many immigrants who came to France after the war to replenish the decimated labor force. The point is that this enormous war-induced imbalance in the number of men and women created only a tiny increase in permanent celibacy for women—less than a 1 percent increase over the cohorts before and after those affected by the war (Maison and Millet 1974, table 1).[10]

The French experience illustrates the general point about incentives. Thinking of those who marry as those who were able to leap some discrete hurdle (sufficient material resources in the case of the Malthusian model, finding the right mate in the present instance) will not get us far. In some circumstances people facing adverse marriage markets are willing to adjust their definition of an appropriate mate. Faced with the deaths of their first choices, French women married their second choices. In other circumstances not marrying is apparently preferable to the second choice. This alternative returns us to the original point. To know when people adjust their sights versus when they remained unmarried, we have to know how badly they want to get married.[11]

The closest analogy in the Irish historical case turns on the class endogamy implicit in discussions of dowry. If likes marry likes, then the relevant numbers in a region may be small indeed. A wealthy farmer's son especially could encounter difficulty in locating the daughter of a similarly wealthy farmer who was ready to marry at the same time. Take County Meath in 1901 as an example of a place with relatively many large farms. In that year there were some 1,260 farms valued at £100 or more. Even if we assume that those at the bottom and those at the top of this group would view one another's children as from the same social class, and even if as many as 5 percent of these farms would have a son or daughter seeking to get married at the same time, County Meath might seem like a very small place. But can this explain why so many of Meath's farmers did not get married? We have already seen that endogamy was far from perfect. The evidence also shows that wealthier people searched for mates over a wider geographical area. The manuscript census sample contains 640 married couples in 1911. Both husband and wife were born in the same Irish county in 82 percent of cases. This proportion is highest for laborers and lowest for farmers, and the wealthiest farmers have the lowest percentage of wives who were born in the same county. The mean value of farms among those whose wives were born in the same place was £14 (N = 323); farming couples born in different places occupied farms with a mean value of £26 (N = 25). Smyth (1983, table 3) reports a similar finding in his study of the parish of Clogheen-Burncourt as does Vincent (1984, pp. 182–186) in her study of Lisbellaw (South Fermanagh).

Yet the prevalence of out-migration leaves the nagging doubt that there might have been too many of one sex for monogamous marriage to have resulted in marriage for everyone. There have been historical situations in which this was the case, but nineteenth-century Ireland was not one of them. The proportion of never-married individuals among males and females was similar in the country as a whole. Cohort-depletion levels for males and females were roughly equal. There was no excess of males over females in individual cohorts. There were, however, regional imbalances in celibacy. In rural areas men were more likely to be celibate; in cities spinsters were more common than bachelors. But even when the proportion of males who never married exceeded that of females, there were so many unmarried females in the area that marriage of all unmarried females would have resulted in low rates of celibacy for males. Brettell (1986, p. 138) makes a similar point in her study of Portugal. In the district she studied so many men emigrated that women outnumbered men by a large margin. But there were still unmarried men; lack of potential mates in the simple sense was not the problem. Anderson and Morse (1993b, table 4) do not interpret their evidence entirely the same way, but they note something similar in Scotland's Crofting and Border Counties in 1911. There, the proportions of never-married women aged 45–49 were high indeed, ranging from one-quarter to one-third. Male celibacy was somewhat less common, but there were still plenty of never-married men. In Argyll, where 31 percent of women aged 45–49 had never married, 31 percent of men that age had not married, either. In Ireland's County Clare in 1911, for example, there were about three never-married males aged 45–54 for every two never-married females in the same age group. If every single male had married one of the single women, then only 11 percent of males would have never married. Reworking the example assuming that males marry younger women or permitting widowed persons to remarry only reinforces the point that sex ratios alone cannot be the source of so many never-married persons. Using more formal econometric techniques, I investigated whether the ratio of men to women in a county had any appreciable effect on celibacy once other important factors had been held constant. Even after experimenting with a wide variety of definitions of the sex ratios and other variables, I could find no evidence of such an effect for people in their forties and fifties in 1911 (Guinnane 1991b, table 12). Walsh (1970a, p. 155) found a similar lack of association and offered the appropriate interpretation. The imbalances reflected rather than caused the decline in marriage. Single women found cities more appealing than the countryside.

Too Old to Marry? Waiting for Farms and Waiting to Marry

Another element of the folk wisdom of Irish nuptiality holds that many men never married because their fathers, or more often their widowed mothers, refused to turn over the family farm until the son was too old to marry. This is the tale told in Kavanagh's poem "The Great Hunger." Other claims to this effect can be found in Arensberg (1968, p. 98) or Hayes (1953, p. 157). This argument has an important kernel of truth in it once we place the argument in proper context, but cannot apply to women and is too simple as applied to men. Imagine a simple model. Assume that there is some age A^* beyond which a man cannot marry. (What "too old to marry" might mean is considered below.) Assume also that potential heirs cannot marry until both parents die. In this simple world if both parents die before the heir is A^* years old, then he marries, and otherwise, not. This model is at odds with evidence discussed in chapter 5 because it assumes that the heir is more passive than we found to be the case. But it is instructive to consider what the model would imply if it really were an adequate characterization of why men did not marry in Ireland.

The model implies that remaining in Ireland and waiting for the farm was a gamble on the life of one's parents. What type of gambles are most people willing to accept? Usually they involve some outcome that is good if the gamble pays off, but that is not terribly costly if the gamble does not pay off. Lotteries are a good example: the chance of winning a million dollars is low, but losing means parting with only one or two dollars. In situations involving risk where the bad outcomes are serious, such as a house burning down, people are generally not willing to take the gamble. In fact, they pay someone else (an insurance company) to take most of the risk for them. The analogy to Ireland is imperfect, admittedly, but still underscores an important point. Most potential heirs probably wanted to marry and to raise their own families on the family farm. Still, they could not have viewed the alternative as so horrible as to be unacceptable. Otherwise they would have been unwilling to remain and accept that the chance that their fate would be that of Kavanagh's Maguire.

An individual's age at inheritance may explain why he in particular did or did not marry, but to understand the willingness of sons to endure such waits and the ability of parents to make them endure such waits, we first have to understand why young men viewed the gamble on never marrying as acceptable. Finally, what does it mean to be "too old to marry"? If bearing a large family is a primary goal of marriage then women can become too old to marry as their child-bearing years are circumscribed by the onset of menopause. But this argument is usually made about men, because it is they who needed the farm to marry. What does it mean for a man to be too old to marry? If he wants children to help him on his farm and to care for him in his old age, then it is possible that even by marrying a younger woman he could reach an age at which marriage would no longer be worthwhile. If Maguire had indeed married at age 65 he might not have lived to see his children reach adulthood. But this age is well beyond that of the 40- and 50-year-old bachelors referred to in these discussions. Perhaps what made a man too old to marry was not his age itself, but the fact that in living his life without wife and family for so many years he had arrived at ways of socializing and organizing his time that made marriage less attractive to him at age 45 than it might have been at age 30. The next section discusses some ethnographic evidence to this effect.

In a related vein, one might also wonder about the effect of growing up in a country where so many young people left Ireland. Some young people would be undecided about leaving, and while undecided they might be unwilling to make commitments (such as marriage) that would preclude or necessitate leaving. Thus as long as a young man or woman thought he or she might want to emigrate, marriage would be put off. Just how this results in permanent celibacy is unclear, however, unless we invoke the "too-old-to-marry" idea noted above.

CULTURAL AND RELIGIOUS EXPLANATIONS

The third style of explanation is different in that it attributes widespread celibacy to religion, personality, and culture. This "preferences" explanation is discussed in three steps. First the role of the Roman Catholic Church in the creation of celibacy in Ireland is considered. Second, the discussion turns to authors who have focused more on sexual repression and related motives as explanations of Irish celibacy. Third, we consider evidence sometimes invoked by those who take a "cultural" line on Irish celibacy: even emigrants from Ireland tended not to marry, in contrast to the native stock of the countries to which they went.

Religion and Marriage

One persistent claim is that the Catholic Church had much to do with the decline of marriage in Ireland. Ireland's historians have flatly denied the claim, but it crops up from time to time. For example, Jackson (1984, p. 1012) claims that "[t]he Catholic Church propagated this system of marriage and household formation." The irony of blaming the Catholic Church for Ireland's celibacy was noted earlier. The Church encourages marriage, considering it one of the sacred sacraments. We also discussed the considerable limitations on the Catholic Church's influence over its flock. How could Catholicism have acted as a brake on marriage? Catholic restrictions on divorce (and especially remarriage) are sometimes advanced as one reason. Because a regretted marriage could not be remedied through divorce and perhaps remarriage, the argument goes, people would be less likely to marry in the first instance. This view is largely based on an anachronism, as it posits the implications of a prohibition on divorce for a society such as our own. Fitzpatrick's (1987a) corrective discussion of divorce in Ireland emphasizes two points. First, rural marriages were primarily partnerships for running households and carrying on the generations. Even after marriage husbands and wives continued to spend much if not most of their socializing time with members of their own sex. The failure to find personal satisfaction that lies at the heart of much marital breakdown in modern western society may be painful to those involved, but the Irish were not raised in a society where emotional intimacy was seen as the primary reason for marriage. Second, the rural Irish did have informal mechanisms for contending with failed marriages. Arensberg and Kimball (1968, pp. 137–138) discuss the "country divorce" that might ensue after a marriage proved infertile. The wife returned to her parental home and neither she nor her husband would ever remarry. The result of these informal divorces were much the same as never getting married in the first place, so it is difficult to understand how the canon law prohibition on divorce could increase the number of never-married people. More recent history is also unkind to this view; only now has the Republic of Ireland moved to permit divorce, but celibacy rates have declined considerably in recent decades.

Walsh (1969, p. 14) notes that some have suggested the Church may have encouraged permanent celibacy in another way, by banning the practice of contraception. Devout Catholics had to anticipate that their families would be large, making greater demands on their personal resources and in effect raising the cost of marrying. This view may be relevant to religious differences in marriage and other demographic behaviors that emerged later in the twentieth century. There is little evidence for the nineteenth century, however, of the much larger Catholic families this argument presumes. Marital fertility is discussed further in the next chapter, but for now it suffices to say that the evidence available does not support the view that Irish Catholics had significantly larger families at the turn of the twentieth century.

Connell advanced a more subtle view of the Church's role in lay celibacy. Irish priests were largely from the farming classes and carried with them all the attitudes of that class toward property, family, and marriage. Whatever the Church's formal teachings, these priests would communicate a sense that lay celibacy was somehow admirable. This argument probably has some element of truth to it. But Connell viewed Catholicism primarily as something that helped young people to reconcile themselves to a life that was necessitated by other forces. It was not causal: "[T]he peasant's Catholicism, it may be, was the most pervasive, the most persuasive, of the agencies reconciling the young to their curious marriage" (1968, p. 121). The Church in Connell's argument was an institution that took sons of the farming classes and put them in positions of influence throughout the country. They could just have well been teachers or doctors if those professions had enjoyed as much esteem as the priesthood.

Whatever its logical merits, there is also a simple empirical weaknesses to the Catholicism argument. If Catholicism were an important consideration in Ireland's celibacy, we should expect to see large differences in the marital status of Catholics and Protestants. Unfortunately the published census never cross-tabulated marital status by religion during the nineteenth century, and my own sample contains too few Protestants to allow detailed comparisons. (My sample, however, shows no clear-cut religious difference. In 1911, among males aged 45–64, 25 percent of the Catholics had never married [N = 395] versus 22 percent of the Protestants [N = 32]. Among females of the same age, 14 percent of the Catholics had never married [N = 340] and 29 percent of the Protestants [N =35]. For these comparisons to be more informative we would have to be able to break the religious groups into the finer categories explored above, for example, comparing Catholic farmers to non-Catholic farmers. And for that the number of Protestants in the sample is too small.) The first published Irish census to cross-tabulate religion by marital status was the 1946 census of the Irish Republic. In that year the differences in proportions of never-married individuals between Catholics and others at ages 45–54 were small. Kennedy (1973, table 52) notes that in 1946, women in the Irish Republic's small Protestant minority were less likely than Catholic women to have married. The religious differences were larger in Northern Ireland at that time.

More troubling for this view is a related and by now familiar observation. The Catholic Church prohibited divorce among its adherents everywhere. As noted earlier, rural areas of the Canadian province of Québec were overwhelmingly Catholic but also had low levels of celibacy. Why did this prohibition only lead to elevated celibacy levels in Ireland? The answer could well be "because Irish Catholicism is distinctive." But is Irish Catholicism distinctive for some independent reason, or is it distinctive because it is the major religion in a country where many people end up living out their days without marrying and having children?

Sexual Repression?

Another set of views on Irish marriage emphasizes supposed personality traits that make Irish people unwilling to marry. (The Catholic Church is also implicated here, as well, although in principle this is a distinct explanation.) The tone of these discussions can portray these personality differences as either relatively benign or as something quite sinister, involving elements of misogyny and psychosis. Some discussions begin with the observation that rural society enforced strong sexual divisions in virtually all activities. As we have seen, within the household boys and girls were viewed as distinct groups. Men and women not only had different tasks in farm and other operations, they socialized separately and even walked separately on roads to and from church and town. Married couples spent little time together. As Arensberg and Kimball described Clare society in the 1930s,

> Men and women are much more often to be seen in the company of other members of their own sex than otherwise, except in the house itself. Except upon ceremonial occasions in family life or in the considerable affluence of owning a gig or a trap or a motorcar, in Clare at least they go to mass, to town, or to sportive gatherings with companions of their own sex. Till recently and even now in remote districts, a conventional peasant woman always kept several paces behind her man, even if they were walking somewhere together. (Arensberg and Kimball 1968, p. 196)

Others point to the role of Catholic priests and nuns in keeping young unmarried men and women separate. Supposedly the priests went to great lengths to discourage even the most innocent meetings of young men and women, out of concern for sexual chastity. Some of the most colorful statements to this effect come from the mid-twentieth century (for example, O'Faolain 1953; Messenger 1969, p. 69), but the same appears in recollections and comments from the nineteenth century. Mary Fogarty remembered "once seeing a number of boys and girls dancing at the cross-roads on a summer Sunday, but this diversion was strictly forbidden by priests and parents, who had a great dread of young people falling in love" (Carbery 1937, p. 46). The efforts of priests to regulate contact between the sexes bothered Plunkett (1970 [1904], p. 117), who claimed with atypical overstatement that "no man can get into the confidence of the emigrating classes without being told by them that the exodus is largely due to a feeling that the clergy are, no doubt from an excellent motive, taking innocent joy from the social side of home life." The supposed result of this clerical vigilance was that by the age at which most men and women would marry, Ireland's young adults had established a comfortable social life that did not involve emotional intimacy with members of the opposite sex, much less sexual relations per se. Messenger (1969, pp. 68–69) comments:

> The marriageable man in his late twenties and thirties . . . has established a routinized existence, and has male companions for whom he feels affection and with whom he shares numerous work and recreational activities. Some men who have been promised or willed land, and who have consenting parents and brides-to-be, will balk at a match because they are "too happy with the lads," and, if persuaded to marry, they will attempt to retain as much of their bachelor role as possible within marriage—"The men run with the boys before marriage and carry on the same afterward."

Separation of the sexes and disinterest in marriage has a more unhealthy cause in the eyes of some other observers. The one distinctive characteristic of marriage, as opposed to any same-sex friendship, is sexual intercourse and reproduction.[12] The ellipsis in the passage quoted above gives Messenger's real view on why people did not marry: "The marriageable man in his late twenties and thirties is usually repressed to an unbelievable degree" (Messenger 1969, pp. 68–69).

Scheper-Hughes (1979) took this style of argument a step further. Her book concerns the unusual frequency of severe mental illness, especially schizophrenia, in twentieth-century Ireland. But part of her argument concerns the frequency of bachelors and spinsters. Neurotic family lives, it seems, made large number of Irish people psychotic: "Marriage in Ireland is, I suggest, inhibited by anomie, expressed in a lack of sexual vitality; familistic loyalties that exaggerate latent brother-sister incestuous inclinations; an emotional climate fearful of intimacy and mistrustful of love; and an excessive preoccupation with sexual purity and pollution, fostered by an ascetic Catholic tradition" (p. 111). Schizophrenia is in her view at least partly due to celibacy, which in turn she traces to the factors quoted above. What can we make of such assertions? We should note first, in fairness to their authors, that they base their writings on fieldwork in Ireland in the twentieth century (Messenger in the 1960s, Scheper-Hughes in the 1970s). Scheper-Hughes in particular sees her research in part as an effort to trace the evolution of family life in Ireland since Arensberg and Kimball's "definitive" work. To the extent that Messenger and Scheper-Hughes advance their discussions as explanations of nineteenth-century developments it is only by ignoring history, thereby implying that the patterns of interest were unchanging. Neither Messenger nor Scheper-Hughes seems entirely clear on the point that celibacy in Ireland was common at least fifty years earlier than the date of their own research. Celibacy in Ireland as a whole declined between 1926 and 1960. To clarify their discussion these authors might have at least ventured a guess on the question of whether the Irish had been repressed or mentally ill all that time, or if the reasons for widespread celibacy had changed. What seems particularly odd about the views of both Scheper-Hughes and Messenger is that both are anthropologists but both commit the classic error of judging another society by the standards of their own. Anderson and Morse (1993b, p. 330) allude to this error in commenting that "[i]t is thus wrong to see the thousand who stayed and remained single as the frustrated relics of an overpopulated society." They were referring to Scotland, of course. One wonders what Scheper-Hughes would have made of a society with high celibacy rates but less Catholicism.

The chief weakness with this sort of tale as a historical explanation is a lack of evidence. What do we truly know about sexual attitudes in the nineteenth century? It would be bold indeed to assert that fieldwork done in the late twentieth century can tell us about how Irish men and women thought about sex in the nineteenth century. For all the claims about Catholic priests smothering sexual desire, we also have quite specific claims to the contrary. In *Tarry Flynn*, Kavanagh suggests that Church efforts along these lines were formidable but mostly counter-productive. The sexes sat on different sides of the chapel, but the protagonist remarks that "[t]he congregation was in danger of becoming squint-eyed from this arrangement. Even plain women look pretty in church" (1948, p. 11).

One of the more amusing incidents in *Tarry Flynn* takes place when the priest decides that the parish, which was "comprised of old unmarried men and women," "was in danger of boiling over in wild orgies of lust." This crisis requires a Mission under the auspices of the Redemptorists, "specialists in sex sins." The protagonist's reaction to the Mission is to speculate with excitement on meeting new girls at the Mission. More generally, all the talk of sex by the Redemptorists backfires: "The second Missioner was hearing Confessions during the sermon and the transformation he was effecting in the minds of the penitents was astonishing. Men who had forgotten what they were born for came out of the confessional . . . 'ready to bull cows.' This was the effect the Mission was having on all minds." One concrete outcome of the mission is to motivate an old neighboring bachelor to pursue, somewhat ridiculously, the protagonist's sister.[13] *Tarry Flynn* is of course fiction, but Kavanagh's story points out that clerical proclamations may not have the intended result. Vèrriere (1979, p. 472) makes the telling point that Irish literature of the time contains little evidence of psychological crisis. Presumably if a new and more virulent Oedipal virus had made its appearance in Ireland in the 1860s, someone would have drawn attention to the fact, even if, pre-Freud, there was no proper diagnosis of the disease. Can we really say that we know these attitudes changed during the nineteenth century, or that in 1861 people in County Meath were more repressed than those in County Mayo, as the relative celibacy levels would imply? To date there has been no in-depth study of sexual attitudes in Irish history. Lacking independent evidence, we are faced with the circular argument that Irish people did not marry because of extreme sexual repression, a problem we know about because so many did not marry.

Scheper-Hughes's specific claim about schizophrenia and Irish celibacy is plainly false. The disease has a biochemical basis, and the connection to marital status reflects not causality but the difficulties people with this disease have in convincing someone else to share their lives. A modern psychiatry textbook raises the line of reasoning Scheper-Hughes applied to Ireland but only to debunk it (Kaplan and Sadock 1995, p. 908). Earlier editions of this and other standard works—that is, textbooks available at the time Scheper-Hughes wrote—interpret the relation between marital status and schizophrenia in the same way.[14]

Most interestingly, given the respect accorded their book in some quarters, advocates of the sexual repression thesis overlook Arensberg and Kimball's clear disagreement with the proposition. Their statement refers to County Clare in the 1930s, and so strictly speaking is not ethnographic evidence on either "Ireland" or the nineteenth century. Still, it warrants consideration for being in blunt disagreement with claims of sexual repression:

> Yet these [puritanical] attitudes [about sex] coexist together with other very hearty, casual, and sometimes ribald attitudes which make their appearance in banter, joke, and repartee even between speakers of different sex. These even take the form of taunts about prowess and mild ridicule for the possession of a greater relish than is meet, or fanciful recitation of past magnificent misdeeds. This is particularly true in the recitations of stories and adventures of persons in the ken of the community, where details of amorous desire and accomplishment are given with considerable gusto, and greeted and reiterated again and again amid hearty laughter. (1968, p. 199)

If Arensberg and Kimball's study was in fact "definitive," then we are faced with inconsistent evidence. County Clare already had some of the highest celibacy levels in Ireland by the time the anthropologists did their fieldwork. Yet at that point the sexual repression Scheper-Hughes associated with celibacy *later* had not made its appearance.[15]

Just stating the second objection risks tedium: if we are to believe that sexual repression (with or without schizophrenia) caused the rise of permanent celibacy in Ireland, then we have to look for a correlation between the extent of repression and the extent of celibacy. We have to believe that Irish people became more repressed through the nineteenth century, but less so starting in the mid-twentieth century. We have to believe that in the 1870s people in County Meath were more repressed than people in County Mayo, but that the good people of Mayo caught up, morally speaking, in the early twentieth century.

A third objection returns to the problem of comparative history. Permanent celibacy, as noted several times already, was a regular feature of the European marriage system well into the twentieth century. Ireland had more celibates than most other European societies, and the evidence suggests that the Irish were less likely to engage in sex outside of marriage. But no one in Ireland was living a life that did not have a counterpart elsewhere in Europe, in prior centuries or in other peasant regions of Europe during the nineteenth century. Thus to attribute Irish marriage patterns to sexual repression or Oedipal complexes is to imply that pre-Famine Irish had enjoyed uniquely good mental health, since they were so much more likely to marry; that Alpine peasants had similar psychological problems, since their marriage patterns were rather like the post-Famine Irish; that seventeenth-century England had an outbreak of mental illness, perhaps a particularly virulent Oedipal reaction to the decapitation of a symbolic father in the person of Charles I; and that the United States, where nineteenth-century celibacy was comparatively less common, was a place free from sexual repression.

Marriage Patterns among the Irish Overseas

Another way to assess the effects of Irish culture, as opposed to the circumstances in which Irish people found themselves, is to study people born and raised in Ireland but who lived in another society—that is, Irish emigrants. Several authors have noted that Irish-Americans tended to marry late and that many did not marry, in effect mimicking marriage patterns in Ireland.[16] The problem with these discussions is that they compare the marriage patterns of Irish migrants to marriage patterns of U.S. natives who are quite unlike the Irish in many other respects. Failing to control for these other differences—failing to compare like with like—exaggerates the difference between Irish immigrants and the native stock.

The best way to study this question for the United States at least is to draw on the large public use samples that have been compiled from the federal censuses of the nineteenth and early twentieth centuries. By using these micro sources we can cross-tabulate birthplace and parents' birthplace by age and marital status (something the published census never did), and also introduce finer controls, such as for rural/urban residence and occupation. Here I discuss results from the 1910 census only, although qualitatively similar findings come from the censuses of 1880 and 1900. This discussion will focus on permanent celibacy, restricting its attention to people aged 45–49 years in 1910. About 22 percent of Irish-born males and 16 percent of Irish-born females in the United States had never married in 1910 (N = 257 and 293). Note that the Irish-born in the United States were more likely to marry than were those of the same cohorts who remained in Ireland. Among native whites of native parentage in the United States, the comparable figures are 10 percent and 9 percent (N = 4,127 and 3,943). The Irish celibacy figures are also higher than for most other major immigrant groups in the United States, although lower than for men born in Scotland (26 percent, N = 62) and not much higher than for Swedish-born men (20 percent, N = 159). Irish-born women in the United States had much higher never-married proportions than their men, making Irish women more distinctive than Irish men.[17] This is the comparison made in other studies, and seems to supports the view that the Irish remained "marriage-shy" even when not in Ireland. But is this the right comparison? People who lived in large urban centers in the United States were less likely to have married regardless of their birthplace. Given that 45 percent of the Irish-born lived in the ten largest U.S. cities in 1910 and that another 21 percent lived in the next fifteen largest cities, it seems more appropriate to compare the Irish-born with the native white urban population. Among native whites of native parentage in the ten largest cities, 17 percent of men and 23 percent of women (N = 244,240) had never married. In other words, when we restrict our attention to the Irish-born in the ten largest cities of the United States, the Irish marriage patterns do not seem at all peculiar. Of Irish-born men 18 percent had not married (N = 101), and for women the figure is lower at 15 percent (N = 123). The Irish in the United States seem exotic only because they were compared with some hypothetical "typical" American, and not with those who most nearly resembled them in other respects.

Comparisons of this sort are more difficult to interpret than they at first seem. One could ask whether the Irish who left Ireland are a fair representation of Irish culture. If the rebels left, as Connell claimed, then what we see in the comparisons above is only a fringe element of Irish culture. We should also attempt to control for influences other than urban/rural residence. The Irish differed from the native white population in other ways, including occupational status. This second problem can be addressed using statistical models that hold constant a number of causal variables such as ethnicity, education, occupation, and so forth. Formal statistical tests of Irish/native differences that do control for other factors such as occupational attainment still show that the Irish in the United States were less likely to marry, but the difference is much smaller than is implied by the raw percentages cited above.[18]

This brief examination using the census of the United States cannot really settle the issue. Irish emigrants to the United States were less likely to marry than were comparable whites born in the United States. Yet much of the difference reflects other differences in their lives. Unlike most native whites, the Irish tended to live in large cities and to have unskilled occupations, traits that are correlated with permanent celibacy in the entire U.S. population. The celibacy of Irish-Americans is poor evidence of an antimarriage attitude among the Irish.

UNDERSTANDING IRISH CELIBACY

None of the dominant explanations accounts for the historical evidence discussed in this and earlier chapters. Each makes telling points, but only succeeds as an explanation once a relatively weak desire to marry is assumed. Here I propose what is less a theory than a perspective on marriage in nineteenth-century Ireland. At an analytical level this perspective is complementary to the Malthusian and institutional explanations and explains the facts better. My discussion will tie marriage more strongly to elements of the social and economic environment and in so doing allow us to view changing marriage patterns in post-Famine Ireland as reactions to the situations in which young Irish people found themselves. The argument can be summarized in a few words. The remainder of this chapter adds historical flesh to the argument.

1. Marriage has costs as well as benefits.
2. For many of marriage's benefits there are other ways of achieving the same ends. I will call these "marriage substitutes."
3. The costs and benefits of marriage, as well as the costs of marriage substitutes, depend on a person's wealth, occupation, and other characteristics.
4. Thus the balance of costs and benefits, and so the incentive to marry, will vary across individuals and in historical time; and differences in these costs and benefits imply differences in the incentive to marry.

For the time being I abstract from any noneconomic reasons to marry. This is only a rhetorical device intended to focus attention on key parts of the argument. I consider the personal and emotional implications of marriage below. In addition, the argument will be outlined with only passing references to gender. After laying out the entire argument I return to the important implications of the differences in the way marriage affected men and women.

Marriage as a Decision

A central idea concerning marriage needs emphasis: marriage is a decision, and the outcome of marriage reflects motivation. At one level this view is an extension of the ideas of orthodox economic theory into another aspect of life. The most influential advocate of this type of thinking, Gary Becker, tends to see most or even all human action in terms of an economic paradigm of maximizing individual well-being in the face of constraints.[19] As already noted, this paradigm need not require complete information or complete selfishness, as some critics claim. A more specific critique of this kind of model is implicit in much anthropological and other writing on Ireland. Can we truly call arranged marriages, as in Ireland, the product of choice? Young men and women had the right to refuse a specific match but did not necessarily have the right to marry the man or woman they loved—the beloved might not have appealed to their parents. In other instances men and women may have turned down marriage opportunities because to do so would mean abandoning their parents or parental farm, something they might have felt guilty about doing. These constraints do not obviate the basic contention that people made decisions about marriages; rather, they imply that for many people the choices were more constricted than they might have liked. Saying that celibacy rates were high because people refused to marry anyone other than their first choice is a matter already discussed above.

Choice in marriage is fundamental to the western European household-formation system. Charles Darwin, to take a famous example, deliberated at some length over whether to marry his cousin Emma Wedgwood (MacFarlane 1986, pp. 3–5). Darwin wrote out a list of the advantages and disadvantages of marriage (or, as MacFarlane says, the costs and benefits of marriage), and in the end decided that the benefits outweighed the costs. Darwin married Emma in January of 1839. MacFarlane sees in this calculation a feature fundamental to the institutions Malthus described: "What Malthus was in fact describing was a situation where those contemplating marriage had to make a choice. Marriage was . . . something to be chosen, a conscious decision which could be made early or put off, and there were costs and benefits in any solution" (MacFarlane 1986, p. 11). Malthus, it is true, emphasized the strength and constancy of "the passion between the sexes," and seemed to believe that without impediments nearly all people would marry at ages that were quite young for western European populations. But he also emphasized the strength and diversity of those impediments to marriage, some of which turn on "reason" or the ability to contemplate the economic and social consequences of marriage.

Thinking about marriage as an implicit comparison of what life would mean after following one of two different courses of action pays several dividends. The Malthusian model cannot explain three facts of Irish celibacy. First, many people who never married were heads of prosperous households. Second, many who remained and did not marry could have emigrated and have had a decent life overseas. Third, to explain the increase in celibacy in the decades 1851–1911, the Malthusian model must turn the undeniable fact of rising rural incomes into a perception of relative poverty. The central weakness of the Malthusian view is its implicit assumption of a trade-off between two objectives, personal consumption and marriage and a family. Connell argued that the pre-Famine Irish married on low incomes because they did not face this trade-off. The land system, in his view, robbed them of the fruits of any forbearance on marriage, and a large family was one of the few sources of security. Connell's post-Famine Ireland is a place where marriage became unpopular because landlords had been tamed and the Malthusian trade-off had reasserted itself. That reassertion underlies Lee's famous comment about "the primacy of economic man over the Irish countryside" (Lee 1973a, p. 5). But this argument begs the question of how and why marriage is a threat to living standards and how the relation between marriage and living standards might change over time.

This perspective also yields insight into the institutional view's limitations. The explanation points quite reasonably to features of rural Irish society that would make it more difficult for marriage-minded men and women to locate one another and make the property arrangements that were part of the institution of marriage as they knew it. Yet claiming that these difficulties were the cause of celibacy amounts to saying that the difficulties amounted to absolute prohibitions, which they did not. It would take very serious impediments indeed to produce, single-handedly, cohorts in which 25 percent of people never married. Impediments are only meaningful in a relative context. The institutional view is missing an understanding of the incentives to marry.

Means and Ends

Economic objectives may be thought of under two headings. The "living standard" that Malthus stressed consists of the economic well-being an individual could expect in normal times, while able to work. And we shall use "security" to refer to the well-being one could expect during times of adversity, such as illness, old age, or crop failure. My argument concerns the effect of marriage and family on both of these objectives. First, Malthus emphasized that marriage and children are expensive, which is undeniable. He did not emphasize that some of the costs of marriage would be offset by labor performed by spouses or children in household operations such as a farm. The costs of children depend on economic and social circumstances. Second, the cost of marriage and family brings a return in the form of security. People must, in general, trade off their living standard and their security. In today's society we usually sacrifice our current well-being to purchase assets such as insurance policies or annuities that will protect us in adversity or old age. In other societies that trade-off might be better managed through forming ties to other people.[20]

We can think of each young adult in rural Ireland as faced with a situation that amounts to a set of "endowments." The most important endowments are employment and land and other forms of wealth. As noted in chapter 2, rural labor markets were often characterized by underemployment or unemployment, especially at off-peak times. Employment was never certain for those whose holdings did not occupy them fully. Continuous income could depend on a regular position as a shepherd or laborer for a more substantial farmer. The implications of land were more complicated. Depending on its size, a holding acted as a guarantor of employment, although many holdings were too small to fully occupy a man let alone a husband, wife, and children. Thus even smallholders could be underemployed if they did not find regular work for neighboring farmers. Land also had an asset value. Even for most tenants that value was guaranteed after 1881 by law, if not before by custom.

Other endowments are actually rights associated with membership in a family group or community. As we have already seen, numerous commentators, including Arensberg and Kimball, believe the obligations of kinship in rural Ireland to be especially strong. The frequency of brother-sister households suggests a degree of closeness and commitment that would imply security even when not required by the terms of a father's will. Like all endowments, however, the importance of kin ties depends on the number and characteristics of those kin. At least according to the Vice-Regal Commission most aged people in Irish workhouses had no kin in Ireland. Another and perhaps surprising endowment was the system of public support. The Irish Poor Law provided meager relief and what it did provide was often invested with stigma. The terrible (and usually well-deserved) reputation of Poor Law workhouses and hospitals can easily mask the fact that the system guaranteed that no one in Ireland need starve. In 1908 the Old Age Pensions Act added a new and more generous level to the system of public support.

Implications of Marriage

Consider first an individual who has the material resources to marry—most concretely, a son favored to inherit the family farm—and examine the implications of marriage for him. Below we examine the second part of the question, why an individual would remain in Ireland knowing that he or she would probably never marry. Marriage entailed relationships to two new sets of people, a spouse and children. As Malthus emphasized, raising a family was expensive, meaning that the man who marries would be able to keep less of his income for personal use. Just how expensive, however, depends on factors sometimes overlooked. Most discussions follow Malthus in emphasizing the role of class and social rank in determining how expensive children would be. A prosperous farmer would ordinarily spend more on his children's food, clothing, and education than would a laborer, so the former's children would be more expensive. There is another dimension to this issue of cost, however. Family members, including children, played a large role in the operation of small farms. A farmer's son or daughter might not be able to fully pay for himself or herself, but the ability to guarantee some employment for children meant that children were cheaper for landholders. Laborers and others who could not guarantee employment for their children would, as noted in chapter 6, bear the full cost of their rearing until the child left home. A wife's labor was if anything more important on the farm. Women bore primary responsibility for some farms tasks and provided crucial extra hands at times of special labor needs, such as hay making. Employment opportunities for women off the farm were not good and often depended on the presence of businesses likely to hire women, such as a pub or a shop. At the same time, a wife's independent income-generating activities such as poultry rearing could raise and diversify the household's total income. The implications of marriage and family for living standards are not as simple as the Malthusian model implies. For some the labor provided by spouses and children substituted for labor that would otherwise be provided through the labor market.

Marrying and rearing children brings a return primarily through security. The economic and demographic literature on the value of children is quite large, but most of it focuses on a question narrower than that relevant here. Many studies ask whether the value of child labor was greater or less than the cost of raising the child. We want to interpret the "value of children" more broadly to mean what it would cost to replace the services provided by children by some other means. This enhanced definition emphasizes marriage and children as providers of security. For the poorest Irish parents children might be seen as a tickets in a peculiar lottery: if the child emigrated, and if the child did well, and if the child decided to share that wealth with family back in Ireland—a long string of "ifs"—the child could return to his parents far more than it cost to raise him or her. For more substantial people not willing to take this strange risk, children were not a very satisfactory savings instrument. There were other, more conventional financial vehicles for savings, in addition to investments in land. A dense system of commercial banks and government-backed Post Office savings banks gave rural people adequate, low-risk ways to save their money by the 1870s.[21]

Children were also potentially useful providers of insurance. Contending with the risks of disease and incapacitation—making sure that in the event of illness or infirmity, someone will provide for one's basic needs—is an important issue in any society. Under the retirement arrangements discussed in chapter 5, the heir (or the heir and his wife) provided not only income (by working the farm) but also the services necessary to assist aged people. Physical decline in old age was not the only potential worry. The prevalence of tuberculosis, with its ability to disable people it did not ultimately kill, was an ever-present concern.

Another form of uncertainty affects the relationship between the costs of children and what they might return in the form of economic security. Children are a risky investment, one that may not pay off at all. Children may themselves die or fall victim to accidents or disease, requiring their parents to care for them. They may also simply fail to honor their parents' expectations—they may default on the implicit contract linking them to the older generation. Landholders possessed an important mechanism for guaranteeing their investment in children. Farmers could use the land to secure old-age support through the formal agreements discussed earlier.

Marriage Substitutes

Marriage, because of relationships to a new spouse and the creation of children, was both expensive and an important mechanism for providing for the future and for bad times. These functions are managed in other ways in modern economies. Rural Irish people of the post-Famine period also had alternatives to marriage. These marriage substitutes took three primary forms. One was to live with kin, perhaps even of the opposite sex, but not in a conjugal relationship. Some never-married male household heads lived with their sisters. Others were either the sibling or some other close relative of the household head. Forty percent of never-married women aged 45–64 in the manuscript census sample were the household head's sister. Viewed the other way, about 33 percent of never-married male household heads in that age group had at least one resident never-married sister. These sibling households reproduced many features of a conjugal household, including a sexual division of labor and at least as much personal affection as one might expect under the Match. Birdwell-Pheasant (1993, p. 28) notes that these households were also a type of family: "I would maintain, and I think the Irish would agree, that a household consisting of unmarried brother(s) and sister(s) is still very much a family household." In her study area of Ballyduff, one-third of farmers had a brother or sister who remained at home, unmarried (1993, p. 25). These arrangements had a clear virtue in that they did not result in the large families typical of a married couple. In 1911, households headed by married males aged 50–59 include on average 6.4 family members ($N = 137$); households headed by never-married males of the same ages, 2.3 ($N = 15$). Living with a sibling enabled a household head to share risk and household services without assuming the burden of child rearing. These arrangements were apparently quite durable. Of households headed by the same never-married man in 1901 and 1911, more than three-quarters of sisters present in 1901 remained to 1911.[22] These households are not that numerous, but they suggest an ability to form and sustain households that did not revolve around a conjugal couple.

In the mid-twentieth century Noonan (1953) argued that these arrangements played an important role in Ireland's celibacy levels. Although as a Catholic priest Noonan had no first-hand knowledge of marriage, he might well have been a better-informed and more detached observer on such matters: "Frequently it is the man in possession of all the normal comforts of life who emerges into confirmed bachelorhood. He does not require a wife to cook his meals or to keep his home in order. He can pay a maid, or he may have a loyal unmarried sister. In his eyes marriage is more of a disability than a blessing. While terminating his gay independence, it makes demands on his generosity and self-sacrifice" (pp. 45–46). Noonan hints at a related alternative to marriage, which is to hire someone to do various household tasks. As a priest Noonan was probably quite familiar with this sort of domestic arrangement.

A second marriage substitute was other people's children. Child rearing was a central function of rural Irish marriages. But one could also form relationships with members of the younger generation without actually procreating them. Another person's son could not be one's heir in the figurative, emotive sense of that word, but another person's son could carry out many if not all of the economic functions of heirship. An unmarried farmer might rely on wage labor, arranging for the services needed to run a farm and household, or he might enter into a long-term relationship with a local youth, treating him as an "heir substitute." In fact, finding an heir this way is in a real sense less risky, given that there is no chance of a sterile marriage and one can choose as heir a local youth with demonstrated aptitude for farming. In his study of the parish of Clogheen-Burncourt (Tipperary), Smyth (1982, table III) found that 6.5 percent of all farm transfers between 1851 and 1900 went to nephews, more than to any other category save married sons and widows. Birdwell-Pheasant (1992, p. 218) found that 85 percent of unmarried farmers in Ballyduff succeeded in passing their farm to a family member. One household in the manuscript census sample appears to undergo just this change. In 1901 this household consists of an aged man living alone, and in 1911 it contains the older man, his nephew, and the nephew's new wife and children. Arensberg and Kimball (1968, pp. 132–133) also discuss arrangements made by farmers who lacked heirs. The anthropologists' point is to stress that when possible, family continuity was preserved on the land by passing the farm to a relative, and their account agrees with that of others (such as Smyth 1983, p. 29) who point out that even when a farm was "sold," it was expected that distant relatives would be given some preferential access to the holding. Yet from our viewpoint the formation of this surrogate heir relationship is little affected by the fact that the younger person is, in fact, a relative. From the elder's viewpoint the heir surrogate might be better or worse than his own child. The surrogate would not know the farm as well, but broader choice might yield a better farmer. A long-term relationship (leading to the younger person's inheriting the farm) would minimize incentive problems; why would the younger party want to run down a holding that would one day be his? No less practical, one might also be able to drive a harder bargain with someone other than one's own child. This use of land to secure a surrogate heir suggests the final substitute, wealth and particularly land itself. Wealthier individuals were able to contract for the services that others could only obtain by procreating children.

The Poor Law, and much later the Old Age Pensions Act, was another form of marriage substitute. The Poor Law had such a vile reputation for many Irish people that it might seem strained to claim that someone would look to it as a source of security. But the context is important. For the very poorest, marrying and raising a family would mean a life of privation and hardship. No sensible person would look forward to reliance on the Poor Law in old age. But for some the existence of this guarantee would reduce the desire to provide for their old age in other ways.

How can these marriage substitutes account for the marriage patterns discussed above? We have reviewed both a set of costs and a set of benefits, and traced how they might differ across people in different economic and social circumstances. There are those for whom marriage might not be an intolerable burden, but for whom returns are comparatively low. They had little need of children and family for security, because their farms and wealth were better guarantors of their future than children. Their farms could rely on hired labor, and would be attractive to a surrogate heir. Marriage had a stronger economic rationale for small farmers. They needed household labor to run their holdings. Smallholders could expect their emigrant children to help them, and needed their own heir to remain out of filial piety on a holding that had few other attractions. At the other end, there were those for whom marriage was a sacrifice. Some made the sacrifice because it was the best way to arrange their lives. For others, it was better to avoid the burden and fall on the dubious mercies of the Poor Law.

Emigration or Marriage

And what about those who did not migrate—the brothers and sisters for whom marriage in Ireland was unlikely, but who stayed anyway? The decision to emigrate implies that one's expected lifetime well-being was greater elsewhere than in Ireland. Ireland's emigration rates imply that many preferred emigration. Yet enough persons without evident resources in Ireland remained, as we saw earlier, to make up over half of all never-married persons. What accounts for these decisions? Most young people would enjoy a higher consumption level if they emigrated. The answer once again is found in the dimension of security. Ireland offered the security of family and kin: both in concrete individuals and, according to some observers, in an ethos that placed greater stress on familial obligations. Social and cultural historians have argued that the aged in the nineteenth-century United States were despised as weak and parasitical. To rely on one's children for old-age support in such a place seems unwise. One returned emigrant told of an Irish acquaintance in the United States who had reared ten sons. "It was better for him that he had reared ten pigs. [It] is only too typical of parental indifference among children in America."[23] Schrier (1958, p. 26) quotes a 1905 letter from Patrick McKeown to his sisters: "Old people are thought very little of in this country, especially poor ones that have made no provision for old age. Not even their own families have any regard for them when they become played out from age and my own is no exception." Siblings who remained with an unmarried brother in Ireland might be in dependent positions socially, but they shared in household resources. State institutions for the support of the poor and aged also differed between Ireland and potential destination countries. The United States in particular had no comprehensive Poor Law during the nineteenth century. Individual states and communities had various relief systems, but these varied in rules and generosity. Without making the Irish Poor Law out to be a more benevolent institution than is justified, we should note that the Poor Law and associated medical relief provided a floor beneath which the material well-being of anyone in Ireland could not fall. In this respect migration to Britain was different. Britain was easier to return from (if one became, for example, seriously ill) and had a poor law.[24]

The importance of other people as substitutes for spouses points to an important interaction in this process. Every brother who decided not to marry created a place for an unmarried sister, and every sister who remained "loyal," to use Father Noonan's phrase, reduced the importance of marriage for her brother. Historical changes that made emigration less attractive increased nonmarriage in Ireland by retaining surplus siblings who both remained unmarried themselves, and whose presence reduced the incentive to marry for their heir brothers. A related and more complicated mechanism ties the brother-sister pairs to the marriage market. Assume that a brother and a sister live together. Each would like to marry, but each prefers living with his sibling to living alone, and each feels a commitment not to accept an offer of marriage unless the sibling receives a simultaneous offer to marry. We could view this commitment as a form of mutual insurance against the possibility of being left with neither spouse nor sibling, or as part of the emotional bond between siblings. In either case such commitments would make matches much more complicated affairs, given that simultaneous offers are much less likely than any single offer. One could even imagine siblings remaining together in Ireland rather than one emigrating precisely because this implicit insurance agreement made life in Ireland more attractive than life overseas. This point once again presumes that there is something desirable about being an unmarried person in Ireland, something overlooked in the historiography. Historical changes that reduced the incentive to marry for male heirs increased nonmarriage in Ireland both through these unmarried household heads and by making life as an unmarried sibling in Ireland more attractive for those who would otherwise have emigrated.

The Noneconomic Implications of Marriage

Not even economists think marriage, even an arrangement such as the Match, concerns economic matters alone. So far we have ignored anything else. What do the noneconomic implications of marriage mean for our argument? At the simplest level, three motivations play a role. The term "sex" should require no further explanation. Marrying and having one's own family also meant a respected position in the community and household, and the satisfaction of continuing a lineage—"keeping the name on the land." This sort of motivation may be termed "lineage." Finally, marriage may entail emotional closeness and companionship.

From what we know about the issue, and the evidence is only indirect, people who did not marry in Ireland were not ordinarily sexually active.[25] For sexual relations—unlike in modern society—marriage in rural Ireland had no substitute. So what does this mean? Nothing in particular: to the extent that sexual relations mattered, an individual would be willing to shoulder more of the cost of rearing a family and expect a smaller security return to do so. If sex was not a strong motivation to marry, even fewer would have done so. From the vantage point of the late twentieth century it is easy to make a mistake similar to the one Fitzpatrick argues underlies the psychosis version of the culture argument. Many, post-Freud and the products of a society in which adult virginity is often considered evidence of a personality disorder, claim not to be able to imagine a fulfilling life that does not involve sexual relations. Whether or not this is true even for society today, it remains true that for centuries many Europeans did not marry. And while they might not all have been as chaste as the rural Irish, it would be rash to assert that those celibates were either afraid of the opposite sex or viewed their lives as hopelessly defective. We must be careful not to project modern-day attitudes backward in time. The lineage motivation for marriage has similar implications for my argument. To the extent that people wanted emotional bonds with children, or community status, or to keep the name on the land, and to the extent that these sources of satisfaction depended on marrying, people would be more likely to marry given a particular economic circumstance. Without belaboring the point, it is worth noting again that Arensberg and Kimball (1968, p. 132) state that transferring a farm within the family is sufficient to satisfy the desire for family continuity. In other words, marriage was not even necessary to keep the name on the land. Finally, would people marry to have the emotional closeness and companionship now associated with marriage? The evidence discussed certainly does not rule out this possibility, but it suggests that love-pairings were unusual and that Irish spouses hoped to like each other but looked elsewhere for their emotional satisfaction.

Even if we believe that noneconomic motivations to marry were important, we must be careful about claiming that they could explain the historical patterns at issue. It is one thing to say that such things matter to people, and quite another to say they matter to people to different degrees. To use these noneconomic motivations to explain the marriage patterns observed, the argument has to be able to explain the data. We would have to claim that the desire for sex declined during the nineteenth century, or that people in the eastern provinces of Ireland were less sexually vigorous than those in the west. Both claims strain credulity.

Men and Women

I have not yet discussed the different implications of marriage for men and women. This was done in order to emphasize the features that are similar, and not to imply, as Ó Gráda (1994, p. 218) complained about an earlier statement of the argument, that men were making all the decisions about marriage. There were important differences in the implications of marriage for men and for women, and these differences doubtless helped shape nuptiality over the nineteenth century. The Match and its associated property transfers imply important differences that made marriage less attractive to women than to men. Ordinarily a wife came from another household to live with a man and his family whom she did not know well.[26] Many accounts, including Arensberg and Kimball's, speak of conflict between new wives and their mothers-in-law. Such conflicts are likely in any situation where a young person abruptly displaces an older person, but in the close quarters of family life they are apt to be more serious. There were probably more than a few new Irish wives who wished they had remained an unmarried Irish sister on this account alone.

There is a darker side to this image of a wife's life in rural Ireland. Chapter 4 noted that Irish women had unusually poor mortality, and that one explanation for this was an unequal distribution of resources within the household. We do not know whether sisters were treated better than wives; Bourke's image of Irish wives as "The Best of All Home Rulers" implies not. The role of repeated risk of death in childbirth does not seem a major factor in female mortality in Ireland, at least not directly, but it is also true that unmarried sisters never faced this risk and that women who emigrated tended to have much smaller families. Other accounts convey a sense of emotional loss in an Irish marriage. In *The Green Fool* Kavanagh includes a brief episode of a 21-year-old woman's marriage to a 60-year-old farmer. One onlooker remarks that the wedding reception had the feel of a wake, and at the end of the evening the new bride begins to cry. The episode once again shows Kavanagh's preoccupation with very old bridegrooms, but the young bride's mixed feelings at marrying an older man she did not know were probably shared in many cases.[27] Mary Fogarty was born in County Limerick in 1858. She provided an even darker view of an Irish woman's place in a rural marriage that hints at why so many young women left the country rather than take their chances with the Match: "In those days young girls had nothing to look forward to but a loveless marriage, hard work, poverty, a large family and often a husband who drank. Small wonder that when they could they escaped to America" (Carbery 1937, p. 47). Many rural women wanted a large family, of course, and were no strangers to either hard work or poverty. But emigration offered possibilities foreclosed by rural Irish marriage.

The nature of property transfers associated with the Match also differed for men and for women. The favored son received an asset that was immovable. The bride's contribution to the Match was something completely movable, cash. The substantial dowries paid for marriage into farms by the late nineteenth century would go a long way elsewhere—in training for one of the few professions open to women, or in a country where women were not expected to bring dowries to marriage. The willingness to pay such dowries speaks of the strong sentiment for families to settle their daughters in Ireland. Viewed from the male's perspective, the immovable nature of land meant less freedom of action. One example of this is the "conditional inheritance" that Mogey (1947, p. 45) thought was an important reason for permanent celibacy when he wrote in the 1940s. In the example he presents, a son received his parents' farm in return for looking after his "simple" sister. Mogey thought this sister's presence prevented the heir from marrying. His argument is once again too simple—the sister might make the farm seem less attractive to an incoming wife, but it is hard to see how it could be an absolute bar to a man who wanted to marry—but this arrangement does highlight the way the gender specificity of inheritance could tie men to the countryside in ways their sisters were not.

These considerations all imply that marriage was less appealing to women than to men, but they do nothing to explain the rise of celibacy over time. The rising emigration rates for Irish women in the later nineteenth century are one side of Irish women's ability to reject what Irish life held for them. Rising celibacy rates for women and men is the other side of that rejection. Ó Gráda's finding of declining dowry sizes implies that fewer daughters had both the cash for a dowry and the willingness to accept these conditions, relative to the number of men with farms. There is little reason to think that conditions for Irish wives worsened absolutely during this period, but with falling fertility in the United States (even among the Irish-born there, as we shall see in chapter 8) life as an Irish wife might have become less attractive relative to life as an emigrant.

These differences between the implications of marriage for men and marriage for women in Ireland suggest that Irish women were central to the institution's decline during the nineteenth century. Women assumed many of the most onerous burdens of marriage and a family. Given the mobility of their patrimony and the relative freedom of emigration, women could afford to be choosier about marriage in Ireland. This put them in a stronger bargaining position in the Match, as Ó Gráda's (1993) data on wills suggest, and also placed them in a strong bargaining position within their marriages as well. The growing number of never-married women reflects their ability to reject what their mothers might have accepted, and the growing number of never-married men reflects a male preference for celibacy over marriage on terms less favorable to males. Changes in the alternatives available to women reduced the attraction of marriage to both sexes.

The Rise of Nonmarriage during the Nineteenth Century

So how do we explain the rise of permanent celibacy in Ireland in the decades between the Famine and the First World War? There are two important changes during this period that do not fit comfortably into a Malthusian model, but that are central to the analysis outlined above. The first change, the Land Acts, is difficult to assess, in part because historians do not yet agree on how substantial the change really was. The implications of the statutes would be clear enough. Change in landlord-tenant relations in Ireland first made tenancies secure property and then increased the value of the tenancies by regulating the rents below market levels. These changes shifted wealth from landlords to tenants, as Solow (1971) has argued, but also changed the role of land in the rural Irishman's portfolio. Because farmsteads could be treated as property, they could form the basis for intergenerational compacts. Farms became a better and better substitute for families in the production of security. And because they were more valuable, waiting for an Irish tenancy, one's parents' or another's, became more attractive relative to emigration. The weak point in this account is that we do not know with much certainty the degree of difference the Land Acts really made. Vaughan (1994, p. 98) argues that the Land Act of 1870 strengthened the legal position of tenants, and the Land Act of 1881 reduced their rents. But Connell's assessment was certainly based on an exaggerated notion of the land legislation's importance.

This interpretation of the Land Acts' role in Irish demographic patterns sounds similar to Connell's, but there are important differences. Connell argued that peasants always lusted for land, and that only the Land Acts made it possible to satisfy that lust. He quoted a folklore informant: "Let any man go down to hell and open an Irishman's heart . . . the first thing writ across it was land" (Connell 1958, p. 5). Connell's explanation, for all his historical and cultural sensitivity, boils down to fascination with something long denied. My argument stresses an element present only as a subtext in his work: the role of land, both as a store of value and as part of a relationship linked to labor services capable of providing more security than possible with families alone. What Connell views as a young man's increased willingness to tolerate his father's power because his father now controls something writ in the son's heart, my argument interprets as the younger man's reasoned evaluation of the future prospects connected to emigration versus waiting for the family farm.

A second change was the development of a poor relief system and later the old-age pension, both of which substituted to some degree for family and children in the provision of security. As noted, this substitute was most important for the poor: the wealthier could do better than the Poor Law. The Poor Law was a manifest failure during the Famine, mostly because it was asked to do something for which it was not intended. But after the Famine the poor-relief system expanded and became slowly more generous throughout the century. The first change made it possible to receive relief without surrendering all land. A later alteration in the outdoor-relief rules greatly expanded the numbers receiving this form of support. Outdoor relief was especially important because it allowed people to retain some independence and dignity but still receive public support. At the very end of the post-Famine period, the Old Age Pensions Act made old-age support available to all, regardless of family status.

The agricultural crises of the 1870s and 1880s were a third contributor to the rise of celibacy during this period. Again, this argument sounds Malthusian but the logic is different. Price collapses and bad harvests from the late 1870s on contributed to serious distress in some parts of Ireland, especially the west. These crises, in fact, played no small part in the agitation leading up to the 1881 Land Act. By Turner's estimate, the total value of Irish agricultural output peaked in 1876 at £48 million and fell rapidly to £32 million in 1887 (Turner 1996, table 4.2). Emigration rates during the 1880s were at levels higher than at any time since the Famine. But the crisis was comparatively brief—the value of output per capita increased significantly between 1871 and 1891 (Turner 1995, table 5.3). Yet celibacy had been rising even before the 1880s, and became more and more common into the twentieth century. How did this crisis contribute to the long-term surge in celibacy? A cohort of men and women came to marrying age during a period of crisis. The development of the alternatives to marriage discussed earlier meant that they were willing to sacrifice less of their living standard for the benefits of marriage. The experience of those coming of age during the 1880s contributed even more to the development of these alternatives, making marriage less and less attractive for those who followed, even in the comparatively prosperous decades ahead.

SUMMARY

Explanations for the rise of celibacy in Ireland between the Famine and the First World War have stressed three elements: economic limitations on marriage (which usually means an overly effective Malthusian preventative check), institutional limitations thrown up by the inheritance and dowry system, and cultural factors that amount to a lack of interest in the opposite sex. Historians have never taken the last explanation very seriously, but it forms a staple of other accounts. The Malthusian and institutional explanations of Irish celibacy make important points but can neither explain all the empirical patterns at hand nor serve as internally consistent accounts. Missing in both is an appreciation that impediments to marriage are only meaningful when compared with how badly someone wants to get married. Economic and institutional change in Ireland might have increased the difficulty of marrying as the Malthusian and institutional views imply, but those changes also reduced the incentive to marry. The rise of celibacy in post-Famine Ireland reflects slow, long-term changes in the economic significance of one form of the institution of marriage.

Chapter 8

MARITAL FERTILITY AND FERTILITY DECLINE

> I used to hear people saying that God never sends a mouth
> but he sends something to fill it. A true saying only that it
> seemed to me—God sometimes sent the mouthful to
> the wrong address.
> —Patrick Kavanagh, *The Green Fool*

AT THE TURN of the twentieth century the typical married woman in Ireland bore many more children than her counterparts in England, France, or Germany. Ireland's marital fertility forms the linchpin of older demographic histories. If a population stubbornly refuses to use contraception, the story goes, then demographic adjustment—in this case, population decline—can only take place through reduced marriage, increased emigration, or increased mortality. I have already questioned this view, implicitly at least, in earlier chapters. Here I consider Ireland's marital fertility more directly. There are two purposes in this inquiry. First, just how high was Ireland's marital fertility, and how does it compare with fertility in other countries? Did the Irish really refuse to practice contraception at all? Second, what are the reasons for Ireland's distinctiveness in this regard?

The fertility of Irish marriages is so famous as to verge on stereotype. Table 8.1 suggests why by summarizing the fertility of women in the manuscript census sample who had been married at least twenty years as of 1911. The table uses a special survey included with the 1911 census. Women who were married at the time of the census were asked how long they had been married, how many children they had borne, and how many survived. About half of the women had given birth to between five and nine children by the time they had been married twenty years, and about 30 percent of women had ten or more children. Fitzpatrick (1983, table 6) reports similarly high fertility. In four of his five locales women married twenty years as of 1911 had borne on average at least seven children.

The similarity of the census for England and Wales, Scotland, and Ireland makes it convenient and instructive to compare the fertility of Irish marriages with that of marriages in Great Britain. For virtually any subgroup in 1911, whether rural or urban, and regardless of at what age

TABLE 8.1
Distribution of Number of Children Born and Surviving, Manuscript Census
Sample

Number of Children	Clare	Meath	Wicklow	Mayo	All
Zero					
Born	6.85	7.14	9.38	2.38	6.08
Surviving	6.85	7.14	10.94	3.52	8.19
1–4					
Born	13.70	9.52	14.06	7.14	11.08
Surviving	23.29	14.29	17.19	16.67	18.25
5–9					
Born	47.95	57.14	53.13	52.38	52.09
Surviving	57.53	69.05	62.50	69.05	64.26
10 or more					
Born	31.51	26.19	23.44	38.10	30.80
Surviving	12.33	9.52	9.38	10.71	10.65
Number of Women	73	42	64	84	263

Source: Manuscript census sample.
Note: Limited to women married at age 35 or earlier and married at least twenty years in 1911.

and how long married, Irish couples had more children than comparable couples in either England or Scotland. To take one example, a woman born in England who married at age 25–29 and had been married for twenty to twenty-five years in 1911 had on average 3.9 children. Her Scottish counterpart had on average 4.6 children. Her rural Irish counterpart had 5.9 children; her urban Irish counterpart had 4.8 children (Anderson 1996, table 1, from census data). (Urban-rural breakdowns are not available for England or Scotland.) These comparisons hold, roughly speaking, for most age and marital-duration groups in 1911. English fertility was much lower than in either Scotland or Ireland. Rural Irish fertility was much higher than fertility for Scotland as a whole. Urban Irish fertility, however, approximated the fertility of Scotland taken as a whole, being slightly higher. We shall see that rural Ireland's position within the United Kingdom in this regard was similar to its position in Europe overall. Rural Irish fertility was unusually high by 1911. But the fertility of the urban Irish had declined considerably, and though not as low as in some European cities elsewhere bore a closer resemblance to places outside Ireland than to rural Ireland.

In contrast to other aspects of Ireland's demographic history, marital fertility has received little formal attention from historians. This omission may reflect agreement with the most common interpretation—that the Church forbade contraception, and Irish Catholics obeyed their Church—which, once accepted, requires little elaboration. This chapter

questions this view by placing Ireland in a European context and by discussing new evidence that suggest an Irish fertility transition at the end of
the nineteenth century. Systematic discussions of Irish fertility tend to
focus on either the pre-Famine period or the twentieth century. The
omission of the period between 1850 and 1911 reflects a lack of comparative perspective. Irish families were large by European standards even
before the Famine, true enough, but Irish fertility became most distinctive during the late nineteenth century when fertility fell dramatically in
most of western Europe

Ireland's moderate fertility transition is consistent with a different
view of the entire matter, which this chapter will advance and substanti-
ate. Irish people had available to them in this period contraceptive methods that were sufficiently effective to account for the observed moderate
declines in marital fertility. Use of some of these methods contradicted
the teachings of the Roman Catholic Church, but not all did, and however much the Church might disapprove, its views in this area were not
always relevant and not always decisive. Ireland's late and moderate
fertility transition, and the fact that even though Irish couples were willing to use contraception they still wanted families larger than was true in
other European societies, indicates that fertility patterns in Ireland reflected choices about contraception and family sizes and not strict adherence to canon law. There is thus reason to doubt the older view that
made high marital fertility a deterrent to marriage and forced Irish population adjustment to take other forms.

To appreciate the distinctive features of Ireland's fertility patterns we
must set Irish behavior in the context of fertility in Europe as a whole.
The decline of fertility in nineteenth-century Europe has received extensive scrutiny. That research has yet to produce a consensus on the causes
of historical fertility transitions, but demographic historians have at least
identified broad empirical contours. Perhaps more usefully, there are
well-defined, competing explanations for Europe's experience. These explanations can frame the discussion of Ireland's fertility here. This chapter begins with some comments on what is meant by a fertility transition
and by a review of what is known about fertility transitions and contraceptive practices elsewhere in Europe. We then turn back to Ireland.

WHAT IS A FERTILITY TRANSITION?

One of the reasons historians and social scientists do not agree on the
best explanation for a fertility transition is that they do not always agree
on what needs to be explained. A fertility transition implies that women
bear fewer children, but many demographers do not characterize the
onset of fertility decline in terms of family size alone. Rather, demogra-

phers often characterize a population's fertility patterns as either "natural" or "controlled." The distinction between natural and controlled fertility pertains not to family size but to the conscious adoption of behaviors that reduce family size. The fertility transition by this account is the period in history when a significant proportion of couples begin to control their fertility. Like many economic historians I have serious reservations about this approach, because it posits an artificial distinction between behaviors that consciously reduce fertility and those that are supposedly unconscious.

What constitutes a conscious effort to regulate family size? Scholars do not agree. Many behaviors can reduce the chance that a woman becomes pregnant. Demographers tend to argue that we should not interpret changes in all of these behaviors as motivated by the desire to avoid having children. Breast-feeding, as noted earlier, is a mild contraceptive, and historically at least some European populations were well aware of this effect. A woman could breast-feed her children for a long time to reduce the chances of becoming pregnant after bearing a child. But prolonged breast-feeding could reflect other concerns, such as the child's health. Knodel (1988, app. F), for example, argues that breast-feeding practices in Germany were strongly affected by local customs.[1]

Demographic historians usually must infer the presence or absence of deliberate fertility control from quantitative information about the number and timing of births. In the absence of direct information on motives, demographers have tended to follow Henry (1961) in saying that "post-transitional populations are ones in which many couples decide not to have any additional children before the end of the childbearing years" (Alter 1992, p. 14). Henry called this a lack of "parity-dependent fertility control." This somewhat awkward phrase means that if a couple is taking steps to reduce the chance of having a child, those steps are essentially the same, regardless of how many children the wife has already borne. That is, Henry's definition of fertility control requires that contraceptive efforts be greater, the greater the number of children a woman has already had. Santow notes the potentially odd implication of Henry's definition of fertility control: "Strict application of [Henry's definition] means that populations with average completed family sizes of twelve, six, or even four children . . . can be grouped together under the rubric of natural fertility, just so long as their patterns of childbearing show no evidence of parity-dependent control: if there is birth control, then it is practised without regard to parity" (Santow 1995, p. 21). Discussions of Henry's definition of fertility control have become more common in recent years, and several scholars have suggested that adherence to this definition has led to erroneous understandings of some historical fertility transitions. This view, which amounts to saying that much historical fertility control was not parity-dependent, is one that has much merit. But that debate is beyond the scope of our discussion.[2]

A further distinction arises in comparing Ireland with other countries. Suppose that in a specific country I_g falls from 700 to 500, that is, fertility falls from about 70 percent of Hutterite levels to about 50 percent. (I_g, discussed in chapter 4, is an index of marital fertility defined in reference to the fertility of the Hutterites, a religious group with very high levels of fertility.) This decline could come about in several ways. Virtually all couples could be using contraception, that is, behaving in ways that will result in family sizes consistent with an I_g of 500. Or fertility control could be restricted to a minority. Perhaps some couples are having very small families while most couples are still having very large families. The I_g index cannot, unfortunately, distinguish between the extent of control (how many couples are controlling their fertility) and the degree of control (the family sizes of controlling couples). But this distinction clearly matters. One would expect that if I_g declined in a country with considerable moral opposition to contraception, that decline would be confined to a small minority. This seems a reasonable expectation for Ireland, and makes overall indices such as I_g especially problematic there. Below I discuss evidence based on a different measurement scheme, one better suited to detecting fertility control among minorities.

THE FERTILITY TRANSITION IN NINETEENTH-CENTURY EUROPE

At one time many demographers of modern populations thought that understanding Europe's fertility transitions would help leaders design policies to foster fertility reductions in developing countries. This interest in the European fertility transition led to a large-scale project at Princeton University under the direction of Ansley Coale. Commonly called the European Fertility Project (EFP), Coale and his collaborators produced monographic studies for the majority of western European countries. The project's summary volume, Coale and Watkins (1986), includes several cross-national interpretive essays. Teitelbaum (1984), the project's volume on Great Britain, primarily concerns England and Wales, but includes some discussion of Ireland. It reported that Ireland's fertility transition did not take place until the 1920s, well after most European countries had experienced their fertility transition (Coale and Treadway 1986, table 2.1).

A central feature of the Princeton project was its reliance on a common methodology for most of the monographic studies. The common methodology permitted fairly precise comparisons across countries with different types of historical sources. The Princeton authors divided each country into a number of "provinces" or administrative areas and computed the measures I_f, I_g, and so forth for each of these provinces. (In Ireland the "provinces" are the thirty-two counties, not the four provinces of Leinster, Munster, Ulster, and Connaught.) Thus the unit of analysis was not women or couples, but an administrative district. Most country studies found that before the fertility transition there were large differences across provinces in the level of I_g. The Princeton studies interpreted differences in the level of I_g as reflecting breast-feeding practices and other behaviors that they did not think were related to intentional fertility control. Thus the project does not define the onset of a fertility transition by the value of I_g at a given date. Rather, the definition adopted by the Princeton studies places the fertility transition at the first date where I_g has fallen by 10 percent or more.

The Princeton project's findings have been interpreted as supporting what Carlsson (1969) has called the "innovation/diffusion" interpretation of the fertility transition. According to this view, a fertility transition reflects a change in attitudes toward using contraception and limiting family size. This change in attitudes can take several forms. For some people, contraception might seem immoral, and thus only with changes in theology or the declining importance of religion ("secularization") are couples willing to control their fertility. For others the new idea might not be so much that contraception is moral as that it is possible. Ariès (1978, pp. 37–38) has argued that the fertility transition reflects a new understanding of the natural world, one in which human beings can control outcomes such as births.[3] A change in ideas occurs somewhere in a population—among the urban-dwellers, or the elite—and these individuals begin to control their fertility. This change diffuses throughout the rest of the population as others accept the new behavior.

The competing style of explanation for the fertility transition is called the adjustment, or adaptation, view.[4] The adaptation view holds that reduced fertility reflects changes in the costs and benefits of having children. As social changes alter the way people work and live, children become more costly and rearing children has less direct economic benefit. For example, as industrialization changes work patterns children become more expensive because mothers must forgo factory work to look after their children. The adaptation view is not limited to narrowly economic developments, however. Changes in educational requirements for middle-class occupations might make schooling more expensive and lead parents to want fewer children.

Economic explanations of fertility decline are usually classified as adaptation arguments, although they need not be. Most economic models of fertility are based on Becker's theory of the demand for children. In this model children are much like expensive consumer durables, and the factors affecting their demand are prices and incomes, as with any other good. One of Becker's purposes in writing down his model was to show that just because family sizes usually fall with increases in incomes does not mean that children are an "inferior" good. The costs of children include direct costs such as food, clothing, and education, and indirect costs such as the opportunity cost of their parents' time in child care. The more parents can earn in the labor market, the more expensive are their children. Thus if the major source of income is through working in the labor market, higher-income parents will in fact have fewer children. Later elaborations of this kind of thinking have expanded on its central ideas. Economic explanations of fertility transition also encompass elements of the innovation/diffusion model. For example, economists would not be at all surprised to find parents changing their behavior with the introduction of a more effective or less costly form of contraceptive method. This kind of change fits comfortably into a Becker-style model. Similarly, economic models of the diffusion of innovations are often based on the idea that what a person knows depends in part on whom she talks to and what that person knows.

Evidence on the European Fertility Transition

The Princeton project's support of the innovation/diffusion argument rests on two observations. One implication of the project's findings is that the fertility transition in most European countries occurred within a very narrow time span. The project dates the fertility transition in Belgium at 1881; Germany, 1888; England and Wales, 1892; and The Netherlands, 1897 (Coale and Treadway 1986, table 2.1). Given that at any one time the countries of Europe were at different levels of economic and social development, the argument goes, the onset of the fertility transition could not reflect adjustment to common changes in the costs and benefits of having children. England's fertility transition occurred at about the same time as the transition in Hungary, then one of the least-developed areas of Europe (Alter 1992, p. 21). This argument from the apparently simultaneous fertility transitions has been called into question, however. Guinnane, Okun, and Trussel (1994) show that the measures used to date the fertility transition, I_g included, do a poor job of identifying the initial stages of the change. Under reasonable assumptions nearly a third of couples can be controlling their fertility without I_g registering a 10 percent decline (Guinnane, Okun, and Trussell 1994, fig. 1). Thus an important decline in fertility could be under way without being detected by the Princeton project's I_g-based definition. Unfortunately the problems in I_g are not such that we can safely assume it is always off by a certain percentage, or always dates a fertility transition twenty years too late or fifteen years too early. England's transition could have predated Hungary's by several decades and we would not know that on the basis of the Princeton project's methods.

A second type of evidence drawn from the Princeton project supports the innovation hypothesis more directly. In several countries, the fertility transition occurred in fairly tight geographical clusters. In Belgium, the southern, French-speaking areas experienced their transition before the Flemish areas. Southern Germany experienced its transition after much of northern Germany, while the eastern parts of Prussia were even later than the southern German. Northern Norway's fertility declined after southern Norway's.[5] The Belgian case is the most striking. Lestaeghe compared pairs of villages in which one village was French-speaking, the other, Flemish. Each pair was close together and matched for similar size, economic activities, and so on. In each case, the French-speaking village had its fertility transition earlier than its Flemish counterpart (Lestaeghe 1977, pp. 111–114). Lestaeghe interprets these linguistic clusters as reflecting shared ideas and shared culture.

Ireland and the European Fertility Project

Ireland, considered only as part of Teitelbaum's (1984) study of fertility in Great Britain, played a small role in Coale's project. Teitelbaum computed the basic fertility measures used throughout the project for the counties of England and Wales, Scotland, and Ireland. He then conducted a statistical analysis of the correlates of the fertility transition in Great Britain and examined the effect of social and cultural variation on the changes in fertility. He did not extend his statistical analysis to Ireland. Although he found large differences in the level of I_g across Ireland's counties, his estimates did not show the required 10 percent decline in marital fertility, and he reasonably concluded that there was no need for statistical analysis of the correlates of an Irish fertility transition that he thought had not occurred (Teitelbaum 1984, pp. 153–154). Teitelbaum's estimates of I_g for Ireland cannot be trusted, unfortunately. He based his estimates on uncritical acceptance of the numbers reported by the birth-registration system, which, as noted in chapter 4, was badly flawed in its early years. Here I use an alternative set of I_g estimates for 1881 and 1911 that Ó Gráda prepared from more reliable sources. The Ó Gráda estimates of I_g were formed by using the number of children reported to the census, corrected for the number of children who would have died by the time of the census, to estimate the number of births. These estimates can also be criticized, but are definitely preferable to Teitelbaum's.[6] The refined estimates do not show the Princeton

TABLE 8.2
Marital Fertility (I_g) for Ireland and Other Populations

	I_g			
	1841	*1881*	*1911*	*1931*
Ireland	868	841	769	570[a]
Co. Dublin	649	615	586	596[a]
Co. Mayo	866	910	929	676[a]
Co. Clare	893	961	858	648[a]
Co. Antrim	820	742	602	433[a,b]
England and Wales		674	467	292
London		611	460	282
Scotland		733	565	404
France		460	315	273
Germany[c]		735	542	264
Berlin		594	303	152
Niederbayern		913	835	473
East Prussia		794	692	384

Sources: Ireland, 1841–1911, Ó Gráda (1993, table A5); Ireland, 1931, Coale and Treadway (1986; app. A). All others, Coale and Treadway (1986, app. A).

Note: All-Ireland estimates for 1841–1911 are unweighted means for the thirty-two counties.

[a] 1936.

[b] Antrim-Down-Belfast combined.

[c] German estimates for 1880 and 1910 are for contemporary territory. Figure for 1933 is the "Germany minus Alsace-Lorraine" variant. Dates for Germany are 1880, 1910, and 1933.

project's 10 percent decline in fertility, either, but they come closer and warrant more scrutiny.

Given the Princeton project's influence, it is useful to think about how Ireland might have fit into that account. Table 8.2 reports values of I_g for Ireland and for several other European countries and subdivisions of countries between 1881 and 1931. This table confirms the view that Irish fertility was high by European standards. Yet it also cautions against exaggerating the difference between fertility in Ireland and elsewhere. The table singles out the Bavarian *Regierungsbezirk* of Niederbayern, but there were others. Some of Ireland's high-fertility counties truly were unusual by European standards. Few places in Europe had I_g's over 900 in the early twentieth century, as did Galway, Mayo, and Sligo. But there were several regions of Europe in which the rest of Ireland would be unremarkable. Some of these regions are by now familiar; for example, several Bavarian provinces had I_g's in the 700s and even 800s at the end of the nineteenth century, and in Niederbayern the index has a value of

Ó Gráda's I_g for 1911

⬚	Less than 700	⬚	More than 800
⬚	700 to 800		

Map 8.1 Levels of I_g, 1911. (*Source:* Ó Gráda 1993, table A5.)

900 until 1900. The differences between Ireland and its neighbors in this respect were by no means as dramatic as the differences in the proportions of those never married. Maps 8.1 and 8.2 are Irish versions of a central analytical tool of the European Fertility Project. Map 8.1 shows levels of I_g in 1911. The pattern is now familiar: fertility was extremely high along the Atlantic seaboard, falling as we move east across the country. But the level of I_g was less important to the Princeton project than changes in the level of I_g. The reasoning here is that levels of fertility reflect breast-feeding and other behaviors not necessarily associated with

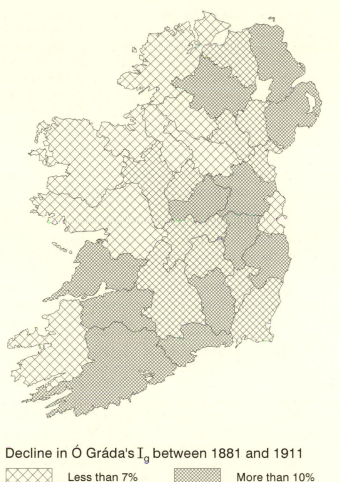

Decline in Ó Gráda's I_g between 1881 and 1911

⊠ Less than 7%	▨ More than 10%
⊠ 7% to 10%	

Map 8.2 Percentage decline in I_g, 1881–1911. (*Source:* Calculated from Ó Gráda 1993, table A5.)

deliberate fertility control, while declines in marital fertility probably reflect deliberate control. Map 8.2 shows the extent to which I_g declined in each of the thirty-two counties between 1881 and 1911. The map shows nine counties that experienced a 10 percent decline in I_g and so fit the EPI criterion for a fertility transition. The map also shows a further eleven counties that experienced a decline in I_g of 7 to 10 percent between 1881 and 1911. The nine counties with a 10 percent decline in I_g made up 34 percent of the total population in 1911 (45 percent if we include

Dublin).[7] Moreover, most of the country had experienced a smaller but still nonnegligible decline in I_g. Thus using the EFP methodology with more appropriate data has the effect of mitigating Teitelbaum's finding that Ireland's fertility transition did not take place until the 1920s.

The clustering in the Irish map is less pronounced than in several other countries and has little interpretative value. Language in Ireland was not an important factor by 1911. Although the western counties had the most Irish-speakers, by 1911 there were few monolingual speakers of Irish anywhere. Many counties that did not experience a fertility decline had proportionately as few Irish-speakers as those that did. A more general cultural interpretation is equally problematic. Historical geographers have demonstrated tremendous variations in local Irish cultures. Some regions, such as the west, were clearly perceived as being different from the rest of Ireland. Few would object to the claim that Counties Mayo and Wicklow had different local cultures, and the same could be said for the northeast region, with its majority of non-Catholics and much greater preponderance of industry. Few would claim that language and culture were a complete explanation for geographical patterns of the fertility transition anywhere. In Ireland that argument is very difficult to sustain as an explanation for the difference between, say, Queen's and Wicklow.

Recent research on Scotland provides a useful perspective on Ireland's experience. Scotland's fertility declined more rapidly between 1881 and 1911 than was the case in Ireland, and in fact meets the Princeton project's criterion of a 10 percent decline in I_g. But the Scottish experience was like Ireland's in that fertility in 1911 was still relatively high. Anderson and Morse (1993a, pp. 16–17) note that the average value of I_g for Scotland in 1911 was equal to the value of that index for the highest-fertility English county at that date, Durham. In both Ireland and Scotland we cannot deny that an important change was taking place, but neither should we exaggerate the degree of change in fertility behavior.

Contraception in Nineteenth-Century Europe

Central to virtually any definition of a fertility transition is the idea of reduced fertility brought about consciously with the intention of having fewer children. How do we know the decline of fertility in Europe reflected such choices, rather than some other force? Nineteenth-century observers, noticing that family sizes were becoming smaller, sometimes attributed the change to factors other than contraception. Reed (1984, p. 5) mentions several hypotheses, including poor nutrition, corsets, and the spread of venereal disease. How did nineteenth-century couples control their fertility at all? Many birth-control methods used today were unknown in the nineteenth and early twentieth centuries. A brief discussion of the methods of fertility control is important to establish that the fertility declines noted in figure 8.1 below reflect voluntary behavior rather than underlying biological or other changes.

Historians have shown for several European populations that at least some couples knew of and used a variety of simple methods to limit the number of children they would have.[8] This is not to say that nineteenth-century contraceptive techniques were as safe or convenient as those used today. Most methods had relatively high failure rates or interfered with sexual pleasure, and some were even medically unsafe. Some were based on dubious medical information and were at best useless. So why did couples use these methods? If we are to understand why nineteenth-century couples behaved as they did, we must understand how their motivations for contraception differed from many motivations for contraceptive use today. Two differences are particularly important. First, the discussion here refers to the relevant use of contraception by married couples. Most nineteenth-century couples wanted at least some children, so a contraceptive failure—an unintended pregnancy—simply meant having one more child, and perhaps earlier, than planned. Rudimentary contraceptive methods were also used by those having sexual relations outside of marriage in the nineteenth century, but were obviously less satisfactory for this purpose than are more modern methods. Second, contraceptive methods are often used today to plan births to fall into fairly narrow time periods defined by educational or career goals. Such precise timing was less important in a world where mothers in particular were not trying to hold market jobs and obtain higher education. A fertility transition implies only that couples try to reduce the number of children below the number they would have had in the absence of contraception. For that goal, even fairly unreliable methods are still useful.

There are to date no historical studies that establish which contraceptive methods were known to Irish couples in the nineteenth century. Ó Gráda and Duffy (1989) discuss the influence of Marie Stopes's English birth-control clinic on Irish women during the twentieth century, but they could not establish from their evidence how much knowledge was available to women in Ireland even at that time. Some letters from the period 1918–1940 suggest striking ignorance of the basic facts of human reproduction (Ó Gráda 1994, p. 219). Kennedy (1973, p. 183) thought that abstinence (both periodic and permanent) was the most common method used in Ireland, but he admits to having no direct evidence. In other European countries the two most common contraceptive methods were periodic abstinence and withdrawal. Santow (1995) argues that withdrawal was widely used even before the fertility transition.[9] Santow (1993) cites several other studies to the effect that withdrawal was widely used in the early twentieth century. Given the flow of migrants between Great Britain and Ireland one wonders whether the Stopes clinic's Irish correspondents were just especially ignorant.

Withdrawal and the rhythm method today have the deserved reputation of being unacceptably unreliable. Could they really have accounted for the fertility declines we see in European history? David and Sanderson (1986) investigate this question by using a mathematical model to study the effect of using one of these rudimentary methods for many years. Their model estimates the number of children a woman could expect to bear during a twenty-year marriage if she used one of these contraceptive methods. The model relies on reasonable assumptions about some key behaviors (such as how often the woman has intercourse) and combines these assumptions with biological data taken from modern studies of contraceptive effectiveness. The model's implications demonstrate the power of these rudimentary contraceptive methods. Consider as the baseline a case in which a couple who practiced no contraception during their reproductive life would have 9.4 children. That is, given their sexual practices, the woman's fecundity, and so on, the expected number of births to this couple is 9.4 in a twenty-year span. If the couple used withdrawal, they would have only 5.3 children, even if they failed to use this method in one out of every five times they had intercourse. (Of course, if they used withdrawal more regularly, or used some other, more effective method, they could have an even smaller family.) Five children is still a large family by modern standards, but the reduction from nine children is more than sufficient to produce the declines in I_g already discussed. Using the method more consistently—omitting use only once in twelve times—would reduce the number of children to 3.35.[10] Santow's (1993, pp. 770–772) review of several studies of twentieth-century populations shows that withdrawal, though not nearly as effective as recent methods such as the pill, is better than even the diaphragm and not appreciably worse than condoms. There is no need to appeal to the effect of corsets or any more plausible biological phenomenon. The late nineteenth-century Irish had available to them contraceptive methods that would account for fertility reductions of the magnitudes observed.

AN IRISH FERTILITY TRANSITION?

What we might term the conventional view of Irish fertility, then, consists of two parts. Before most European countries had undergone their fertility transition, Ireland's marital fertility was relatively high. More important, Ireland, unlike most of its neighbors, seems not to have experienced a fertility transition at the end of the nineteenth century. Is this consensus view justified? The revised I_g estimates discussed earlier demand some rethinking. And several recent studies rely on more refined methods to produce stronger evidence for the beginnings of a fertility transition in Ireland by 1911. Two of these studies use a measurement technique called Cohort Parity Analysis (CPA), devised by Paul David and his associates (David et al. 1988). CPA compares the number of children ever born for women in two populations: one thought not to be practicing contraception (the "model population") and a population whose possible contraceptive practices are under study (the "target population"). Unlike I_g, which pertains to the fertility of all women in a specific year (that is, it is a "period" measure) CPA considers the fertility of a group of women throughout their lifetimes. David and Sanderson (1988) used the rural Irish (as defined by the 1911 census) as their model population, in effect assuming little or no fertility control in rural Ireland. To account for the effects of length of marriage and the age at which a woman marries, CPA compares women who married at similar ages and who have been married about the same number of years. If the number of children born to the target population is significantly lower than for the standard population, CPA interprets the difference as evidence of fertility control.[11] The CPA method has its doubters, and Okun (1994) argues that the results obtained from CPA are sensitive to the choice of a "model" population. At the very least, however, CPA results for Ireland are congruent with other evidence and further undermine the notion that Irish fertility did not decline in the late nineteenth century.

The CPA method has a clear analytical advantage over a measure such as those used by the European Fertility Project. I_g can only tell us that couples are having fewer children during a specific time period; CPA, in contrast, can in theory decompose that decline in the number of children into the extent and degree of control. That is, CPA can tell us whether the number of births fell because a few couples had no children and the remainder had many children, or because most couples in the population reduced their fertility. (Note that CPA's ability to make this distinction relies on the structure it puts on the observed data.) This distinction is extremely important in a situation such as Ireland's. If the Irish fertility transition was feeble because most couples refused to practice contraception, then we would expect to find the observed decline in fertility to be traceable to large changes among a small minority of couples. But if most couples simply wanted to have four or six children, rather than eight or ten, then we should expect to find a large proportion of couples controlling their fertility but not averting many births.

Table 8.3 summarizes the results of two CPA studies of Irish fertility in 1911. The lower-bound and upper-bound estimate of the proportion controlling are not statistical confidence bands. They conform to two dif-

TABLE 8.3
CPA Results for Ireland, 1911

			Proportion of Women Controlling Fertility	
Population	Age at Marriage	Marital Duration	Lower Bound	Upper Bound
Urban Women	20–24	5–9	20.6	30.7
		15–19	21.6	32.6
Urban Women	30–34	5–9	31.9	40.3
		15–19	37.6	50.9
Rathgar (suburban Dublin)	25–29	5–9	67.5	87.4
Rural County Tyrone	25–29	5–9	31.9	40.3

Sources: Urban women: David and Sanderson (1988, table 1); Rathgar and Tyrone: Ó Gráda (1991, table 7).

Note: "Urban" women are those living in one of the six county boroughs: Dublin, Belfast, Cork, Londonderry, Limerick, and Galway, Ó Gráda's estimates are from micro-samples taken from the 1991 Irish census.

ferent versions of the basic model. Consider first the results for urban women. We have focused on rural people, but for the study of fertility urban women are particularly important. In most populations, fertility control was first initiated by those in urban areas. For example, Knodel shows that the fertility transition took place in urban Prussia about ten years prior to the rural fertility transition (Knodel 1974, table 3.3). The Irish were no exception to this generalization. David and Sanderson's (1988) estimates show evidence of large minorities of birth controllers in the urban population. In the group shown in table 8.3, controllers amount to at least one-fifth of the population, and among women who married later in life an even higher proportion were controlling their fertility. Like Kennedy (1973, p. 179) before them, David and Sanderson draw particular attention to the fact that fertility control was most common among women who married rather late. This result does not amount to saying that late-marriers have fewer children because their reproductive lives are shorter. CPA compares women who married at similar ages and who have been married for similar lengths of time. Nearly half of urban women who had married at ages 30–34, the CPA estimates imply, were controlling their fertility.

Ó Gráda employed the CPA method with two other groups of Irish women, including a sample of rural women, producing more startling results. The Dublin suburb of Rathgar in 1911 was populated by the middle class, many of them government officials or managers and their families. Ó Gráda's findings show that among these people fertility control was the norm rather than an exception. At least two-thirds had initiated fertility control by the time they had been married five to nine years. These people are precisely those we would expect to initiate a fertility transition, but the CPA results are surprising nonetheless, given the old view of marital fertility. Still more surprising are Ó Gráda's results from rural County Tyrone. This region was religiously mixed and though primarily a farming area had some textile employment in 1911. Here about one-third of couples were controlling their fertility.

David and Sanderson used the "rural Irish" as their natural fertility standard. For purposes of the 1911 census's fertility survey, rural Ireland consisted of the entire population except those living in the six county boroughs. As such, the rural Irish include a substantial number of people living in smaller cities and towns and is not completely "rural." One could ask whether the rural Irish, as defined in the published census, included an appreciable number of women who were controlling their fertility. To investigate the issue more thoroughly, Ó Gráda used micro samples from the 1911 census for parts of County Clare as the natural fertility model, and the published rural Irish data as the target population. This exercise suggests that in rural Ireland as a whole some 20 to 25 percent of couples were controlling their fertility in 1911 (Ó Gráda 1991, table 7). These last results have two implications. David and Sanderson's results probably underestimate the degree of fertility control in urban Ireland. If the "model" population includes many couples who are really controlling their fertility, as Ó Gráda's results suggest for the David-Sanderson study, then CPA will underestimate the degree of control in the target population. Most important for our interests, many couples in rural Ireland were, according to Ó Gráda's findings, controlling their fertility by 1911.

Anderson (1996) used CPA to reanalyze some of the published data on Ireland and to compare this with data for Scotland, where a similar fertility survey was included in the 1911 census. He finds that some features of the Irish fertility control discussed here were also true in Scotland, although Scottish couples who controlled their fertility tended to have smaller families than birth-controllers in Ireland. But the fertility decline in Scotland shares the important feature of not implying very small families for those who used contraception.

Some of these same findings are echoed in another study that uses the 1911 fertility survey but different methods to study which couples were limiting fertility, and by how much. Ó Gráda and Duffy (1995) use regression methods to study the effects of age at marriage, occupation, and other variables on fertility early in marriage in three areas of Ireland. They find once again that older-marrying women were more likely to limit fertility. These authors are also able to provide an estimate of the effect of child mortality on fertility. We would expect that couples who experience the loss of a child, and who had in mind some idea of how many children they wanted in their family, might alter their fertility control behavior to compensate for the child's death. This behavior, which demographers call the "replacement effect," is one way to test whether couples are controlling their fertility. In a natural-fertility population infant mortality rates will not affect fertility. Ó Gráda and Duffy (1995) confirm the presence of strong replacement effects in Ireland in 1911, although the magnitude of those effects varies with the estimation method they employ.

The discussion of replacement effects raises a related issue. If differences in infant mortality rates are large, then similar replacement effects could produce differing levels of marital fertility. As noted in chapter 4, we do not know how much infant mortality varied by the parents' occupation or social class in Ireland. But geographical differences in infant mortality, especially between urban and rural areas, could be large indeed. The probability of a child dying before age 2 was about 50 percent higher in Ireland's cities than in rural areas in the early twentieth century (Preston and Haines 1991, table 5.2).[12] Note, however, that replacement effects cannot explain the lower fertility in Irish cities. Higher infant mortality would imply, if parents were trying to make up for the deaths of infants, higher marital fertility in Irish cities.

What is to be made of all this? We can hardly deny that Ireland was undergoing a fertility transition by the turn of the twentieth century. Changes in marital fertility as measured by I_g were modest but real, and the CPA estimates imply substantial minorities making important changes in behavior. The transition seems to have started with the urban population, but at least some members of the rural population had also begun to limit their fertility. There is no denying that the reduction in family sizes in Ireland was much smaller than those in England or France. But Ireland's larger family size may reflect a desire for relatively large families more than a refusal to use contraception. That is, the CPA estimates suggest that the relatively high levels of marital fertility in Ireland in 1911 reflect many couples who were controlling their fertility but still having four or five children. Why have historians for so long accepted the view that the Irish refused to control their fertility? Part of the answer lies in table 8.1. The European Fertility Project has been very influential, and Teitelbaum's I_g estimates are still better known than Ó Gráda's preferable estimates. Part of the old view's power also lies in the discussion of concepts and measurement techniques above: there is an analytical difference between adopting fertility control and having a very small family. The Irish fertility transition did not lead to marital fertility levels as low as in England or in most other European countries. As Robert Kennedy (1973, p. 181) has noted, it remained uncommon for an Irish couple to have no children. Many Irish couples continued to have four to six children into the 1960s, when families of this size had become rare elsewhere. The Irish fertility transition consisted, it seems, of couples reducing their families from seven to nine children down to four to six, a number very high by contemporary European standards but demonstrating fertility control nonetheless.

NONMARITAL FERTILITY

Another distinctive feature of Ireland's fertility patterns was its very low levels of extramarital fertility. The Princeton project's index of extramarital fertility, I_h, probably suffers from flaws similar to those for I_g for Ireland. But it is the best source we have to compare extramarital fertility in Ireland with elsewhere. Comparisons based on I_h show that Ireland's extramarital fertility was as low as its marital fertility was high. In 1911 this index had a value of 10 in Ireland (out of a possible 1000). In England and Wales in that year the index was 19, and in Scotland, 31. By United Kingdom standards Ireland had very few births to unwed mothers, and by some standards it had practically none. The index I_h has a value of 59 for Germany as a whole in 1910, and for the Bavarian province of Niederbayern the index was 112 in that year (Coale and Treadway 1986, app. table A). In another comparison, the number of illegitimate births per thousand unmarried women of child-bearing age was nearly six times as high in Sweden as in Ireland in the late nineteenth century (Sklar 1977, table 2). Within Ireland illegitimacy levels conformed to the patterns typical elsewhere, with I_h higher in cities than in rural areas. Connolly (1979) used a selection of Catholic parish registers to study illegitimacy in Ireland in the early nineteenth century. His findings are subject to some doubt about the quality of the records, as he notes, but he also finds that illegitimacy in Ireland was relatively rare. Connolly is also able to examine how many Irish pregnancies were prenuptial. In many parts of Europe it was common for women to become pregnant before marriage but to marry prior to the child's birth, saving the child from the label of illegitimacy. Connolly's parish registers suggest that prenuptial pregnancy in Ireland was uncommon.

The information available suggests that the unmarried Irish were either remarkably chaste or remarkably careful when not chaste. Visitors to Ireland sometimes puzzled over this fact.[13] The impression of chastity outside marriage may be a bit exaggerated, however. The estimates of extramarital fertility with which we make these comparisons are probably flawed, perhaps seriously so. In a country such as Ireland, where illegitimacy was considered shameful, women who gave birth but were not married might find many ways to avoid reporting the fact to the authorities. Mary Fogarty tells the story of a young unmarried neighbor whose father threw her out of the house when she became pregnant. The father relented only after the baby had died and the girl had contracted rheumatic fever from sleeping outside (Carbery 1937, pp. 49–50). Part of the high reported rates of illegitimacy in a Bavaria or a Sweden must reflect the great social acceptance of the phenomenon there; women who bore children out of wedlock would be less likely to hide the fact. Furthermore, the statistics on extramarital births in Ireland may be correct but still not reflect the extent of extramarital sexual unions among the Irish. Connell (1968, p. 119) remarks that some Irish seasonal laborers might have fathered children in Great Britain; that abortion and infanticide were not unknown in the Irish countryside; that illegitimate conceptions sometimes resulted in marriages, and so legitimate births; and that some pregnant, unmarried Irish women probably traveled to England to have their babies and so contributed to that country's illegitimacy statistics. The same might be true for emigrants to North America and beyond.[14] Still, as Connell notes, these reservations cannot fully explain the differences between Ireland and England, much less Ireland and Bavaria. Extramarital sexual relations were, it seems, rarer in Ireland than in other places.

Why was illegitimacy so rare in Ireland? Sklar (1977, pp. 362–365) offers two explanations that together probably capture the truth. In a society that placed great emphasis on lineages and the intergenerational transfer of property, illegitimate children complicated matters enormously. Their dubious inheritance rights are only part of the problem. The presence of illegitimate offspring in a family places the identity of fathers in doubt and clouds the possibility that by bringing in a daughter-in-law a family would definitely be propagating its own line. Rural Ireland also had in place a number of institutions well suited to making sure such complications did not arise. The Catholic Church's teachings on sex outside of marriage dovetailed neatly with the peasant's economic interests in this case. Sklar also notes that rural Ireland's relatively cohesive social structure made it more likely that sexual transgressions would be detected and sanctioned.

INTERPRETATIONS OF IRISH FERTILITY

Does Irish fertility simply reflect, as the conventional wisdom would have it, the influence of the Roman Catholic Church? Ireland's marital fertility has received relatively little systematic attention because the explanation seemed self-evident: the Church discouraged contraception and the Irish accepted the Church's teaching. But there are clear reasons to doubt that religious teaching can fully explain Ireland's fertility patterns. The fertility decline documented earlier in this chapter is inconsistent with the idea of universal obedience. In discussing the Church's influence we are in familiar territory, first explored in chapter 3 and again in chapter 7. Kennedy (1973, chap. 8) has raised two now-familiar objections to the "Catholicism" explanation of Irish fertility. Other Catholic countries had fertility transitions. France was in fact the first European country to experience a fertility transition. One could respond that French Catholicism is not Irish Catholicism, but that is precisely the point. We cannot simply invoke Catholicism as a set of beliefs and institutions; we must explain why, if Catholicism really is the answer, Irish couples accepted this facet of their Church's teaching. Kennedy also notes that Irish Catholics did not obey several other aspects of Church teaching on marriage and sexuality.

More generally, we need both a more refined view of Catholic teaching on contraception and the authority of the Catholic Church in nineteenth-century Ireland. Church objection to contraception has always been on the grounds of the act rather than its consequences. The Church is not so much concerned to encourage large families—unlike some sects, such as the Church of Jesus Christ of the Latter-Day Saints, which advocates large families on theological grounds—as to discourage sexual practices it views as contrary to natural law. The Church has no strictly theological objection to abstinence, periodic or otherwise, nor does it advocate maximizing fertility. This point is important, because in discussing Catholic teaching observers tend to lose sight of the fact that some contraceptive methods commonly used in the nineteenth century were acceptable in the eyes of the Roman Catholic Church.[15] If married Irish Catholics were indeed using abstinence to limit the size of their families, as Kennedy (1973) has suggested, they were not violating any Church teaching. The niceties of canon law, of course, do not necessarily survive the attitudes and day-to-day teachings of individual priests or nuns. Some priests may not have understood or cared about the fine distinction between "use no artificial contraception" and "maximize fertility." Still others may have confused their own views with the Church's and ended up teaching couples that the Church wanted large families. But the Church's teaching, strictly understood, would not stand in the way of a fertility transition. At most, the inability to use some effective methods available elsewhere (such as condoms) or reliance on abstinence might account for some of the feebleness of Ireland's fertility decline. But even the use of withdrawal, which was clearly condemned by the Church, would be difficult for priests to detect and condemn, especially if the resultant families were as large as have been recorded.

We should also bear in mind a point raised before: many Irish people were not Catholic. If fertility in 1911 was high just because Ireland was so heavily Catholic, then we should expect to find substantially lower fertility among the religious minority in Ireland. The evidence on fertility differentials by religion is thin, but does not show large differences during the period we are discussing. The first published census to provide details on fertility by religion for the twenty-six counties shows, in 1946, significant differences between Irish Catholic and Irish Protestant fertility (Kennedy 1973, table 64). Yet even at that late date, Protestant families in the Republic of Ireland were large relative to family size in England. Factors other than religion must be at work. Formal statistical analysis of the effect of religion in 1911 suggests that the Catholic/Protestant differential in fertility was of recent origin. Using microsamples from the 1911 census, Ó Gráda studied marital fertility in a confessionally mixed area near Londonderry city. Once he had taken account of the fact that Catholics were more likely to be laborers (laborers had higher fertility, regardless of their religion), he found that Catholic wives had, on average, only about 0.4 children more than non-Catholic wives (Ó Gráda 1985, table 3). Catholics and Protestants differed, but the difference was not so large as to account for the differences between Ireland and less Catholic countries such as England. Religious affiliation had much less effect on fertility behaviors than did other factors such as social and economic status. A similar study yielded more ambiguous results. There were virtually no religious differences in fertility in rural County Tyrone, while in Rathgar Catholics again had families somewhat larger than those of Protestants (Ó Gráda and Duffy 1995, tables 1a and 1c). Even where the Catholic/Protestant fertility difference is statistically significant, as in the Londonderry study, the difference is so small that it cannot explain the difference between Irish fertility and other countries' fertility in 1911.

The last two studies mentioned pertain to small areas of Ireland, leading one to ask how general their results might be. Unfortunately aggregate data on Irish fertility are not well suited to studying differential fertility by religion. Protestants tended to live in certain regions of Ireland and to be similar in other respects that make it difficult to separate the effect of religion from that of other influences. This is the statistical problem of multicollinearity, the same problem that makes hazardous any monocausal explanation of the geographic clustering of the Princeton project's maps. Consider another exercise by Ó Gráda. He used aggregate data from the thirty-two counties of Ireland to study the determinants of the decline in I_g between 1881 and 1911. His regression model showed that the higher the proportion of people in a county who were Catholic, the smaller the fertility decline, and the larger the average farm size, the larger the fertility decline (Ó Gráda 1991, table 2). That is, religion mattered, but so did economic structure. Results of this sort tend to be fragile. There are only thirty-two counties, which makes multicollinearity a potentially serious problem, and specific findings tend to be sensitive to how one defines the variables. Moreover, the Catholic variable "explains" little of the variation in the fertility-decline variable. Using Ó Gráda's definitions and similar data, I found that the Catholic variable alone only explains 15 percent of the variation in the fertility variable. Dummy variables for Ireland's four provinces alone explain 18 percent of the variance in fertility, which should place this entire exercise in context: the province in which a county is located accounts for more of the variation in the fertility decline variable than does the Catholic variable. Given the much smaller effect of religion found in the studies noted above, and the inability of the Catholic variable to explain much in this regression on its own, Ó Gráda (1991, p. 537) is probably right to suggest that the religion variable in these county-level regressions is proxying for something not included in the analysis.[16]

Marital Fertility, Migration, and Marriage

The evidence on religious differentials in fertility in Ireland lends little support to the view that Ireland's marital fertility patterns reflect the influence of the Catholic Church alone. Yet fertility within Ireland is not the only place to look for evidence on this question. Catholic teaching in particular, and social attitudes about fertility more broadly, might have had a more direct role in Irish fertility patterns by influencing the decision to emigrate or to marry if one remained in Ireland. Suppose one is unwilling to flout Church teaching, but also unwilling to have eight or nine children. In post-Famine Ireland, one could simply leave and have a smaller family elsewhere, or remain but not have any family at all. That is, we can identify two mechanisms through which Church teaching on contraception could have influenced Irish fertility, not by affecting the family sizes of those who married and remained in Ireland, but by leading some not to marry at all and others to leave Ireland.

Emigration from Ireland was at some level a rejection of what life there held. Many Irish women no doubt welcomed the expectation of a large family. For others, however, this feature of rural life might have been unappealing. Women least willing to have large families would be most likely to leave the countryside. That is, contraception might have been acceptable to some women who knew that it would be difficult to have a small family in rural Ireland. If this interpretation is correct, then Irish fertility in Ireland was relatively high in part because the potential birth-controllers were likely to have left. This is another form of the selection of migration mentioned in chapter 7 in connection with marriage. Selectivity of migration by fertility goals has been noted in several other contexts. One reason urban fertility fell earlier than rural fertility in other European countries was that migrants to the cities tended to have smaller families.[17]

I cannot claim that this selectivity hypothesis is supported, for Ireland, by the weight of evidence. But several empirical patterns are at least consistent with this hypothesis. David and Sanderson's (1988) results for urban Ireland are consistent with selectivity, because they show an urban fertility decline before the rural fertility decline. Couples who wanted smaller families might have moved from rural areas to the cities. But there are also other plausible explanations; the adaptation hypothesis suggests that urban couples have smaller families because the costs of children are higher in cities. To study the question properly one would want to be able to compare the fertility of women born in Dublin or Belfast with that of women who migrated from rural Ireland. The published census does not make this sort of study possible, and I am not aware of any research on Irish cities that addresses this question. Better evidence comes from the fertility of Irish emigrants overseas. One study of fertility in the United States does address this point. Morgan, Watkins, and Ewbank (1994) found that Irish-born women in the United States in 1910 were more likely to control their fertility than many other immigrant groups. Irish-born women, in fact, were more likely to practice contraception than were native-born whites. The result is consistent with the hypothesis that Ireland's fertility transition was comparatively late and modest because many of the women most likely to control fertility had left Ireland. The authors do not interpret their finding this way, and mine is only one possible interpretation of the result. But the low fertility of Irish-born women in the United States does raise the question of whether Ireland's feeble fertility transition reflects another, subtle effect of emigration.

Another form of selectivity is equally plausible but even harder to assess given the available sources. We have seen that by 1911 women who married and remained in Ireland were a very small fraction of the cohort into which they had been born. Suppose fertility desires was one of the factors encouraging some women who remained in Ireland not to marry. Of two women in similar economic and social circumstances, with the same dowry, prospective husbands, and so on, the one less willing to have the large family expected of an Irish wife would be more likely to remain unmarried but in Ireland. This implies, once again, that Irish wives were the subset of their birth cohort most interested in having a large family. Note that both forms of selectivity, by migration and by decision to marry, imply that Ireland's fertility transition was feeble in part because those most likely to control their fertility were not married and in Ireland or not in Ireland at all.

Clearly there is reason to question the monolithic role of Catholic social teachings in producing Ireland's weak fertility transition. Church teaching on the matter is more ambiguous than is often supposed, and religious comparisons in Ireland show smaller Catholic/Protestant differences than one would expect. As an alternative we consider interpretations more consistent with the evidence that Irish women were willing to control their fertility, but wanted relatively large families anyway. The adaptation interpretation of fertility transitions holds that the number of children a couple wants to bear depends at least in part on the perceived costs and benefits of rearing those children. The costs of children range from the expense of food and clothing, to the problem of providing them with the education or assets that allow the children to establish themselves as independent adults, to the lost earnings associated with parental—usually female—child-minding responsibilities. Economic explanations of historical fertility transitions in other countries emphasize one or the other of these factors; either the cost of maternal time or the difficulty of setting children up in an independent life.

Before considering specific costs of children, we should note that for the sizes of families we are discussing there are elements of per-child costs that decline with an increase in family size. That is, each successive child is cheaper. Two forces work to produce this result. The first is fixed costs. Some things that children need must be provided for the first child but can be used by all subsequent children. A good example would be a child's suit of clothing, assuming it does not wear out with heavy use. If a family has one child and the clothing costs C dollars, then this element of the child's cost is C. But if the family has K children then this element of the children's cost, on a per-child basis, would be only C/K. A second reason per-child costs decline with the number of children is that older children can help care for their younger siblings. In families of the size we are discussing here, the last few children born would enter a household that had adolescents able to free their mother from baby-minding and allow her to devote her time and energy to other tasks.

Figure 8.1 sketches stylized cost and benefit schedules for children in Irish circumstances and in circumstances labeled, for concreteness, English. The English scenario is intended to represent urbanites in western Europe. The figure assumes that the return to children in Ireland and England was identical. (I will argue to the contrary, but higher returns to children in Ireland would only reinforce the point made here.) In Ireland marriage involved a large fixed cost: for men and women alike, the Match required obtaining farm or dowry, locating a mate, and clearing the holding of excess relatives. Once this fixed cost was paid (which is to

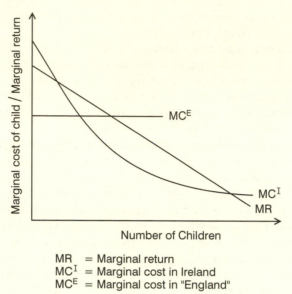

MR   = Marginal return
MC^I = Marginal cost in Ireland
MC^E = Marginal cost in "England"

Figure 8.1 Convex costs, marriage, and fertility

say, once a couple married) the marginal cost of each child was small, and probably declining. The English curve, in contrast, is drawn to reflect less costly marriage but a higher cost of each child. English couples did not face the problem of dowries and farms in getting married, but the housing, clothing, and food required for each child were more expensive. The English curves are drawn so that the marginal cost of each child is constant, but the argument here only requires that the cost not decline too rapidly. The optimal number of children is the point where the marginal cost curve intersects the marginal return curve from below.[18] An Irish family would be larger than an English family, which follows directly from the argument about child costs. More important, this figure illustrates a simple microeconomic explanation for the fact that many Irish did not marry, while most of those who did had very large families. With a high fixed cost of marriage and rapidly declining marginal costs of each child, this is precisely what we would expect.

Women's Work and Women's Time

One of the most important changes during the industrial revolution pertains to changes in women's work roles. Increased opportunities for factory and other market work gave women a more central role in generating income for their households. The increased opportunities made women's time more valuable. And the increased value of women's time made children—those most time-intensive of goods, especially for women—more expensive for their parents. Women whose work is confined to homes (whether household production or "housework") can combine child-minding with their other activities. A rural woman can watch her children while churning butter. The combination may not be best for the child or the butter, but it is possible. A woman working in a factory cannot. As factory work came to be increasingly important in women's work lives elsewhere, couples faced a choice between having a large family and using the wife's earning power to contribute income to the household budget. Households contributed more time to the labor market and used their higher cash incomes to purchase items they had previously made for themselves.

Change in the female labor force was important in the fertility transition in several European contexts. Crafts (1989), for example, shows that in England in 1911, women who lived in towns with more employment opportunities for females had significantly lower fertility than did other women. Teitelbaum (1984, table 7.2) found that women's employment hastened the timing of the fertility transition in England.[19] And what of Ireland? We have already noted that Ireland had relatively little industry and especially little nonfarm rural employment. Employment for women was particularly problematic. Poor rural earnings opportunities for women doubtless played a significant role in the large female emigrations of the late nineteenth century. Developments in the Irish economy had the effect of reducing income-earning chances for rural women, either by reducing the demand for a product usually made by female hands or by reorganizing production so that men replaced women. These changes actually lowered the costs of child rearing in rural Ireland, taking from the Irish an incentive to control fertility that had led other Europeans to want smaller families. Part of Ireland's famous fertility may be a straightforward reflection of a lower cost of child rearing.

Family Size, Farms, and Heirs

Chapter 5 mentioned the problem of trying to keep the "name on the land," or passing farms down to family members. Maintaining a patriline seems to have been important, although some behaviors—such as not marrying at all—were inconsistent with maintaining the patriline. Maintaining a patriline is not easy even with large families. There is always some chance that a couple will have only girls, or that any sons will die before old enough to take over the farm. Of course the larger the family, the less likely it is to lack a male heir. Table 8.1 shows that, despite the very large average family size, about 3.5 percent of Mayo couples in the manuscript census sample could expect to have no surviving children after twenty years of marriage.

Given that an extra child was so inexpensive in rural Ireland, is it possible that couples wanted large families to insure against the possibility of not having any surviving sons? Given the right data we can ask this question quite precisely. A preference for sons is a well-documented phenomenon in several societies, and demographers have reliable ways to establish son preference from information on births. Even in the absence of such information, the plausibility of this reason for high fertility can still be illustrated. Wrigley (1978) reports simulations that show, for a given family size and mortality patterns, the chance that a couple would not have a surviving male heir to inherit the farm. In the simulation most relevant to Ireland, a couple with four children has a 20 percent chance of lacking a male heir. Having nine children—not unrealistic in the high-fertility counties of western Ireland—reduces that chance to about 2.5 percent.[20] The desire to have a male heir probably has little to do with family sizes of nine or ten, but may explain why many rural Irish couples continued to have five or six children long after average family sizes shrank below that level elsewhere.

Emigration and Fertility

Emigration played a similar role in reducing the costs of child rearing for rural Irish couples. Most Europeans knew by 1900 that providing their children with a decent start in life required basic education and perhaps additional training, costs the parents would have to bear for each child who survived. Rural parents faced the inheritance dilemmas discussed in chapter 5. Yet Irish parents also knew that for the price of passage to Britain, North America, or Australia they could settle their children in any of several robust economies with a large Irish community. The desirability of emigration for young people meant that Irish parents could spend less on each child than would other European parents, secure in the knowledge that they could help the child acquire a start in a life at least as good as the one his parents had known.[21]

For the poorest couples, children might not have been just cheap, but were one way to ensure that the rent would be paid and that there would be an income in old age.[22] In counties where I_g remained above 900 in 1911—counties such as Kerry, Galway, and Mayo—parents might have viewed children as so many tickets in a fairly generous lottery. The value of children as sources of remittances figures heavily in several discussions of Irish fertility that reject the primacy of religious belief (for example, Ó Gráda 1993, chap. 5; Fitzpatrick 1984, p. 40). For this to be a reasonable cause of high fertility, of course, parents must be able to bear the costs of children now, in the hope of some payoff later. Ó Gráda's county-level fertility regressions, mentioned earlier, suggest that high emigration rates and high fertility went together.

Historical demographers have noted a similar correlation in other times and places: where emigration rates were high, fertility was also high. Knodel (1974, pp. 200–201) found this pattern in nineteenth-century Germany. To some this is evidence in favor of the theory of "multi-phasic demographic response" (Davis 1963; Friedlander 1969), which views emigration and fertility decline as two ways of relieving demographic "pressure." This theory is really a variant on Malthus. The argument made here is different and only remotely related to Davis's argument. In my view, high emigration rates altered the costs and benefits of rearing children, and so gave some Irish couples an incentive to continue to have large families long after the practice had ceased in many parts of Europe.

SUMMARY AND CONCLUSIONS

So what do we know about Ireland's marital fertility record? The simplest way to summarize all this evidence is to say that by the end of the nineteenth century many Irish couples were having families that were smaller than would have been the case if they were not trying to limit their fertility, but that were not all that small by contemporary standards. We must modify the older view, reinforced by the European Fertility Project, that Ireland did not experience a fertility transition until the 1920s. A variety of evidence from 1911 does show fertility control. Compared with most other countries in western Europe, fertility control was not as common, and couples who did practice contraception continued to have large families. But the evidence points to a modest fertility transition all the same.

Historical demographers do not agree on the nature and causes of fertility transitions anywhere, so we should not expect definitive explanations or universal agreement on Ireland. What can be said is that the influence of the Church on Irish fertility is not as clear-cut as is often argued. Many Irish were not Catholics. The Church might have discouraged some forms of contraception, but had no formal objections to abstinence, which seems to have played an important role in fertility transitions elsewhere. Catholicism's impact on the decline of fertility was important but cannot explain the entire story. We are on firmer ground focusing our attention on why Irish couples had so little desire to have smaller families, instead of assuming that couples were forbidden to do so by their Church.

These questions about the traditional portrait of Irish fertility behavior once again cast doubt on older interpretations of post-Famine population decline. A stubborn refusal to practice fertility control has formed a cornerstone of exceptionalist views of Irish demographic history. At the simplest level the Irish were not as extraordinary has often been assumed. Moreover, once we admit the possibility of population adjustment through marital fertility control, the other aspects of Ireland's demographic regime become more interesting simply because they were not dictated by inflexible patterns of marital fertility.

APPENDIX 8A
ALTERNATIVE ESTIMATES OF I_g FOR IRELAND

The Irish vital registration system was established in 1864. During its first decades of operation the system achieved only poor coverage, particularly in the remote areas of the west. Many vital events (births, deaths, marriages) were never registered. As coverage improved, the uncorrected birth-registration statistics imply an increase in marital fertility. Michael Teitelbaum's contribution to the EFP series, *The British Fertility Decline* (1984), does not correct for significant underregistration of births during the first years of the Irish birth-registration system's operation. His estimates show large, implausible increases in I_g for most western counties between 1881 and 1911. For example, by Teitelbaum's reckoning I_g increased from 696 to 878 between 1881 and 1911 in County Mayo, and from 687 to 852 in Sligo. Overall his estimates imply an increase in I_g for eighteen of Ireland's thirty-two counties between 1881 and 1911. As Ó Gráda (1991) argues, the lack of a decline in Teitelbaum's I_g between 1881 and 1911 most likely reflects a decline in actual fertility coupled with an improvement in the coverage of the birth-registration system, which together produced an inaccurate picture of stasis. Teitelbaum was well aware of the potential biases caused by undercounts in the birth-registration statistics (1984, pp. 127–132). But for reasons he does not explain he did not avail himself of a correction method similar to Ó Gráda's.

Teitelbaum's monograph contains an appendix by Ansley Coale and Edith Pantelides that describes their efforts to contend with a different problem in estimating I_g for Ireland. In 1871 and 1881 the counties defined for census purposes (from which we derive the proportions married, used in the denominator of the I_g index) did not always have the same geographic borders as the counties used for the purposes of the vital-registration system. Correcting for this problem as Coale and Pantelides describe makes the 1871 and 1881 estimates somewhat more sensible. Their corrections do not, however, bear on the larger and more significant problem of the underregistration of births. No adjustment was ever made to account for the underregistration of births in Ireland (Coale and Treadway 1986, app. C, p. 166).[23]

Ó Gráda's (1991) method for calculating Irish I_g uses the census to approximate the number of births, and so does not require reliance on the flawed birth-registration system and does not encounter the boundary-disparity problem discussed by Coale and Pantelides. He estimates the number of births in the year prior to the census by taking the number of children up to 4 years of age in the census and using reasonable guesses about infant and child mortality to estimate the number who were originally born to these cohorts. This alternative estimate of the number of births forms the numerator in his I_g. The method is not ideal— Ó Gráda has to make some unverifiable assumptions about infant and child mortality—but produces estimates that are better than can be obtained using the birth-registration system. Fitzpatrick's unpublished estimates of I_g, mentioned in the text but not employed, try to correct the number of births reported by the vital-registration system. His estimates are broadly similar to Ó Gráda's; for example, the zero-order correlation between the two sets of estimates is .75 in 1881 and .82 in 1911. The Fitzpatrick estimates imply less fertility decline than Ó Gráda's between 1881 and 1911, although precise comparison is difficult because Fitzpatrick's estimates pertain to entire decades rather than to single years.

Chapter 9

CONCLUSION

> History, Stephen said, is a nightmare
> from which I am trying to awake.
> —James Joyce, *Ulysses*

IRELAND'S population history elicits an odd fascination from both contemporaries and historians. Some of this fascination centers on truly remarkable developments and some stems from misperceptions. Here we have traced Ireland's demographic transformation from the Great Famine to World War I. This was the period of greatest depopulation, and the period in which Irish population patterns were most distinctive. This final chapter draws together major themes, highlighting major points, and then very briefly summarizes population changes during the twentieth century. Irish demographic behavior has changed considerably, especially in the last few decades, and the Irish are now much more like their European neighbors than they were in 1914. Present-day changes only underscore what this book has suggested, that the demographic patterns of the late nineteenth and early twentieth centuries were transitional phenomena driven by adjustments to world economic conditions and Ireland's place in the world economy. I conclude with some thoughts on Ireland's demographic distinctiveness.

OLD VIEWS AND NEW APPROACHES

This book owes much to the work of earlier scholars, but at many points has disagreed with their conclusions. The simplest way to contest any position is to present evidence inconsistent with that position. Much of my debate with earlier views depends on just this sort of procedure, drawing on both my own research and on secondary works. Two examples are especially important. Earlier discussions of Irish nuptiality lacked detailed empirical foundation. Relying on published censuses, Connell and others could not examine the identities of those who did not marry but remained in Ireland. Using census and land records from the turn of the century, and drawing on other studies that used similar sources, the preceding chapters have shown that many of the bachelors and spinsters in rural Ireland did not fit comfortably into Connell's story. Many were, as Connell suggested, the brother or sister of a household head. But many celibates were inconsistent with his account; they were male farmers who controlled a farm, often relatively valuable, but who never married. This empirical weakness in the Malthusian account, combined with the problem of rising incomes mentioned earlier, led to the rethinking described in chapter 7. Another example of an empirical response is this book's discussion of marital fertility. The brief discussion of Irish marital fertility that Teitelbaum included in his study of the British fertility decline did much to sanctify the view that the Irish were stubborn in their avoidance of contraception. More recent studies of marital fertility in Ireland suggest that Teitelbaum's study is incorrect on this point. The decline of marital fertility in Ireland was late and modest by the standards of France or England, but by the First World War a substantial minority of Irish couples were taking steps to avoid having large families.

Other responses consist of rethinking old evidence. Take marital fertility once again. Why were the Irish slower to adopt fertility control than other European populations? The obvious answer, that a large majority of Irish were Catholics, has a seductive appeal. Fertility decline in the Republic of Ireland has occurred over a period of declining influence for the Catholic Church there. And many people in developed countries, Catholic or not, perceive the modern Church as an institution that expends considerable energy to discourage the use of contraceptives and abortion. But the evidence on sectarian differences in fertility at the turn of the century does not support the view that religion was a major motivating factor in Ireland's late fertility decline. The Catholic Church's teachings were most likely to be followed when the Church was telling people to do what they wanted to do anyway. Thinking about the economic and social changes that led to fertility decline in England and on the Continent, and the relative absence of such changes in Ireland, led to a different interpretation. The changes in the costs of children that caused German or French parents to want fewer births simply had not occurred to the same degree in Ireland at the end of the nineteenth century. The Irish were willing to limit births, but most lacked a reason to do so.

A related but more pervasive response works best with arguments that presume Irish uniqueness. Ireland was not an industrializing, urbanizing society like England. Comparing it with England usually tells us little more than we already know. To believe that because Ireland was different from England it was unique is absurd. Claims about Ireland's exceptionalism usually fly in the face of similar institutions, problems, and population developments in other regions of Europe. As we have seen throughout, Irish population trends reflect not just adjustment to common external economic forces but behaviors that were widely adopted in other places. The combination of demographic behaviors that led to depopulation in Ireland was unusual, but none of the elements of that combination was unusual.

Malthusian Models and Their Drawbacks

This book's most consistent disagreement has been with Malthusian interpretations of Irish history. Malthusian models enjoy great popularity in demographic history. The most serious recent defense of a Malthusian position in Irish history comes from Robert Kennedy (1973), who argues that Irish people viewed themselves as increasingly poor during the last quarter of the nineteenth century because their incomes were not growing as rapidly as they wished. His position has echoes in other historical writings and is not so much incorrect as incomplete. Our discussion of the implications of marriage stresses the missing element. Kennedy's view is that Irish people became more willing to give up marriage because what they could get in return—material consumption—meant more to them. The problem with this view is that it presumes that giving up marriage has little or no economic consequence for the people involved. Our story stresses the declining economic significance of marriage: Irish people became more willing to give up marriage because what it had to offer meant less to them. Understanding how marriage affected people, and thus what they were willing to give up to marry, requires an understanding of the institutions of Irish society, institutions that play no role in simple Malthusian accounts. This is bad enough. A more general weakness of the Malthusian model is that it provides no guidance on how a population adjusts to changing economic circumstances. How important will emigration be? Permanent celibacy? Malthusian thinking is unhelpful because it provides no guidance on our fundamental question: why did Irish depopulation come about in the way that it did?

A Different Approach

Connell's account has the considerable merit of trying to integrate specific institutional and historical features into an explanation of what occurred in Ireland. Yet we can raise the same question about his stem-family account as we did about the more general Malthusian argument. The number of emigrants and unmarried adults depends on whether the excess siblings stay or leave. How are we to think about that? What are we to make of the underlying "problem" of large families? Yet a remark Connell made about the Poor Law and marriage before the Famine actually suggests a more fruitful way to think about these issues. Connell suggested that in a country lacking a poor law families might be valued as a social safety net, making marriage especially important. Poor people would marry in Ireland on an income that would not lead an English person to marry, because in Ireland the only guarantee against starvation was a spouse and kin. This remark raises the entire issue of a return to marriage, which forms the central argument in chapter 7 and naturally leads to the notion that in some dimensions there will be alternatives to marriage. There is something ironic about "Malthusian" arguments about marriage in historical demography. My argument—which I have, here and elsewhere, posed as a counter to Malthusian models in historical demography—seems to me more consistent with the central tendency of Malthus's own analysis of marriage. To Malthus the decision to marry reflected the interplay between instinct (in the form of the "passion between the sexes") and reason:

> The preventative check, as far as it is voluntary, is peculiar to man, and arises from that distinctive superiority in his reasoning faculties which enables him to calculate distant consequences . . . man cannot look around him and see the distress which frequently presses upon those who have large families; he cannot contemplate his present possessions or earnings, which he now nearly consumes himself . . . without feeling a doubt whether, if he follow the bent of his inclinations, he may be able to support the offspring which he will probably bring into the world.[1]

Malthus shied away from the full implications of his argument. Underlying marriage is sex, a biological desire. Children are in his argument just the regrettable by-product of sexual relations, and marriage has little economic consequence beyond those children. This simplistic view is inconsistent with Malthus's own emphasis on reason. If man is such a reasoned being, why does he not consider all the implications of marriage, including those that have little to do with sexual gratification: the formation of links to children and other kin; the provision of labor for running, and eventually inheriting, a family farm; and, as Connell noted, as a sort of insurance policy in a society lacking any social security system? The reason, one suspects, is that for all his interest in other societies, an interest that motivates successively larger parts of the later editions of the *Essay*, Malthus was reluctant to acknowledge the implications of institutions different from those he viewed as the norm in England. Once we consider that marriage and household formation might be part of complex strategies in which people attempt to provide for their various needs (and not just as the only form of sexual union tolerated by the parson Malthus) then we arrive at a much richer, and ultimately more useful, understanding of the relation between population and economic resources. Marriage is not just everyone's favorite good, to be purchased if one can afford it. The incentive to marry depends in complex ways on an individual's social and economic circumstances.

This approach, I have argued, provides a more intellectually satisfying account of Ireland's demographic odyssey between the Famine and the First World War. But a more careful integration of microeconomic analysis and institutional detail would be a useful addition to demographic history in other contexts, as well. Thinking about population in its proper economic and institutional context will pay two dividends. First, we will find explanations for otherwise anomalous changes such as increasing numbers of unmarried people in an increasingly prosperous country. If we remain glued to Malthus, we must invent theories of why the Irish increasingly shunned marriage at any price or try to convince ourselves that however well the Irish economy was performing, the Irish came to believe they were poorer and poorer. Second, considering the consequences of marriage gets us away from simple notions of real wages and whether someone can "afford" to marry and forces us to appreciate the full implications of marriage, fertility, and other demographic behaviors for the lives of historical people.

One of the ironies of modern demographic historiography is that many of those who criticize orthodox economic theory for being reductionist cling to Malthusian models, which are the most reductionist of all economic models of population. Economic historians and others who emphasize the role of the economy in population dynamics ignore much of what is interesting and important about historical economic development. Some of the factors emphasized in this book—the development of institutions, the role of households in the economy, the relationship between market and nonmarket means of satisfying human needs—are central to nondemographic studies of economic development. Other scholars who emphasize cultural differences and cultural change counterpose their views to a reductionist model of the relationship between population and the economy. Taking a broader view of the economy and its role in population change would not undermine the role of culture; it would sharpen and focus the role of culture in demographic behavior. This book can be viewed as an extended argument that economic and institutional details have profound implications for demographic history, and that the Malthusian model has no systematic way to account for those details.

Irish Population Developments since the First World War

In some respects Irish demographic patterns today differ from those of other Europeans. But the differences now are much smaller than they were in the early twentieth century, and recent changes hint that in relatively few years Irish demographic patterns will be completely unremarkable. Space does not permit a discussion of the entire twentieth century or even present developments in any degree of detail. But for understanding earlier events it is instructive to trace recent changes.

The Irish did not vanish, whatever O'Brien's fears. Depopulation during the twentieth century was slow compared with the 2-million-person decline from 1851 to 1911. The six counties of Northern Ireland experienced steady if slow population growth throughout the twentieth century, with the exception of a small decline during the 1970s. The population of the twenty-six counties that are now the Republic of Ireland continued to decline until 1961, but after some dips increased into the 1990s. The island's total population, which was about 8.2 million just before the Famine and 6.5 million just after, reached its minimum at about 4.2 million in 1926 and again in 1961. This is only 200,000 fewer than the population in 1911. Just as during the period studied in earlier chapters, these changes in population sizes reflect complex changes in marriage, in marital fertility, and in migration rates. The greatest single change, until recently, was in emigration rates. For most of the post-Famine period Ireland's overall birthrate was not unusual, but it was too low to offset Ireland's very high emigration rates. Birthrates have climbed some during the twentieth century, and more dramatically, emigration rates have dropped. Recently increased emigration and lower fertility has once again brought depopulation, although how long that will persist will depend on rapidly changing economic conditions both inside and outside Ireland.[2]

Marriage patterns in Ireland are much less remarkable now. Ireland still has many bachelors and spinsters, but the extent of permanent celibacy peaked at mid-century and has fallen considerably since. The latest available figures show that 15 percent of men and 10 percent of women aged 45–59 in the Irish Republic had never married. Levels of permanent celibacy for Northern Ireland are comparable. The 1980s saw an increase in the numbers of never-married people once again, but Ireland has not returned to the levels of nonmarriage that emerged in the late nineteenth century. Age at marriage has also fallen considerably since the mid-twentieth century. By 1986 the average age at marriage was only slightly higher than in the United Kingdom and several other western European countries.[3]

The fertility transition begun at the end of the nineteenth century continued into the twentieth century and to the present day. The Irish continue to have somewhat larger families than is typical of other western Europeans, but Irish families have become much smaller all the same. In 1992 the average woman in Ireland bore only 2.2 children, barely more than her counterparts in the United States (2.0) or the United Kingdom (1.9). The slightly higher Irish fertility rates reflects not lower levels of childlessness, but the continued greater tendency for Irish women to have more than two children.[4]

Another twentieth-century development in Irish demographic patterns is a divergence in the behavior of Catholics and Protestants. We saw for the post-Famine period that sectarian differences in demographic behavior were present, but small and difficult to disentangle from sectarian differences in wealth and occupation. Such differences became larger during the twentieth century. By 1961 Catholics had significantly larger families than Protestants of the same social group, both in the Republic of Ireland and in Northern Ireland. Among Irish Catholics those in Northern Ireland usually had larger families, making the Catholic/Protestant differences larger in that province than in the Republic. As of 1970 Catholics were less likely than Protestants to marry in both parts of the island, although lacking details by occupation we cannot know how much of this reflects the fact that Protestants have different occupations and social status. In recent years the Catholic/Protestant differential in fertility has begun to decline. The more detailed information on fertility and religious affiliation available now shows that Catholic fertility, though generally higher than the fertility of Protestants, has fallen much more rapidly in recent decades. In Northern Ireland Catholic marital fertility was about 70 percent higher than for Protestants in 1971, but by 1991 had fallen to a level approximately 40 percent higher. The fertility of Protestants in Northern Ireland fell considerably too; Catholic fertility simply declined more rapidly. The gap between Catholic and Protestant fertility in the Republic of Ireland narrowed considerably from 1961 to 1981. If anything, Catholics in Northern Ireland are now the most distinctive group in this respect in Ireland. The fertility of Northern Ireland's Catholics is not only higher than that of their Protestant neighbors, it exceeds by a good bit the fertility of Catholics in the Republic.[5]

A further change in Irish fertility patterns has been the recent rise of births outside marriage. Illegitimacy in nineteenth-century Ireland was rare. This has changed dramatically, especially in the past two decades. In 1990, about 15 percent of all births in the Irish Republic were to unmarried women, and provisional estimates for 1992 place the figure at

18 percent. Irish illegitimacy rates remained substantially lower than in the United Kingdom, but were actually higher than illegitimacy rates in the Netherlands and some other European countries.[6] Ireland's low illegitimacy rates in the nineteenth century were at least in part the product of efforts to conceal extramarital conceptions, either through misreporting or by having pregnant but unmarried women emigrate. Just how much of the increase in illegitimacy reflects changes in reporting or reduction in the emigration of pregnant women, and how much is a real change in behavior, is unknown. Access to medical contraceptives remains restricted in the Irish Republic, and medical abortions are illegal in virtually all circumstances. These policies are under intense scrutiny now as the Republic struggles to make its law compatible with the principles laid down by the European Union. In the 1990s, events such as the forced return to the Republic of Ireland of a 14-year-old girl who had gone to Britain for an abortion after being raped have led to serious discussion of changing the law. There is an interesting historical parallel here. In the nineteenth century, the ability to reject Irish life for life abroad helped support institutions such as the Match that otherwise might have come under severe pressure to change. People in the Irish Republic are increasingly aware that laws restricting contraceptives and abortion have been tolerated in part because contraceptives and abortion were easily available in Britain.

Emigration continues to be a major force in Irish demographic patterns and in Irish social and political life. A recent report on Irish emigration notes the historical sensitivity of Irish people to this phenomenon:

> [E]migration has frequently occupied centre stage in political, economic, and social debate in this country. The huge population losses through emigration, which occurred between the middle of the last century and the early 1960s, fueled an ongoing debate as to how the tide might be stemmed. One of the primary influences which underpinned and maintained the drive for independence was a perception that emigration could be eliminated once we had control of our own affairs. Many of the economic initiatives undertaken since Independence involved the elimination of emigration as a primary objective.[7]

Recent experience shows independent Ireland's inability to stem the outflow and the reason for considerable anguished debate in Ireland. Annual emigration rates have never returned to the levels of the 1880s, when 16 per thousand Irish people emigrated each year. But the 1950s came close, with about 14 per thousand emigrants each year, and in the last half of the 1980s the net emigration rate was higher than in the decade 1901–1911. More ominously, emigration in the late 1980s was extensive enough to exceed the Irish birthrate, portending, at least briefly, a return to the depopulation of the nineteenth century.

Whether emigration will remain at these levels seems unlikely. What is clear is that the character of Irish emigration has changed considerably since the nineteenth century. First, the major destination for Irish emigrants today is not the United States, as in the nineteenth century, but Britain.[8] This change reflects in large measure the restriction of migration to the United States and the open labor markets that now obtain among the member states of the European Union. Second, significant return migration has become and will probably remain a feature of Irish demographic patterns, one not observed in the nineteenth century. Convenient and inexpensive air travel makes possible sojourns in countries that pay higher wages while one waits for conditions to improve at home. In the 1970s, a period of remarkable prosperity in Ireland, return migrants actually outnumbered emigrants. But even in the 1980s, when the Irish Republic lost over 200,000 people on net to emigration, this net flow reflected about one returnee for every three emigrants.[9] Third, the Irish emigrant is now more skilled than in the past. We saw that in the nineteenth century most Irish emigrants were unskilled. As late as the 1950s unskilled workers, male and female, still dominated the outflow. Now Irish emigrants are broadly representative of the levels of education and skill of the Irish people as a whole. There is even a troubling tendency for those with university-level education to be more likely than others to emigrate. This emigration of highly educated workers has raised debate in Ireland about policies that might help to retain such people in Ireland, rather than have Irish taxpayers support universities to educate workers for the Silicon Valley and other foreign high-technology areas.

One feature of Irish demographic patterns that remain in flux is the difference between the Irish Republic and Northern Ireland. This demographic question echoes more general questions about the extent to which the partition of Ireland has created two genuinely distinct societies. Watkins (1991) has argued that the twentieth century has witnessed a process of "demographic convergence" all over Europe. She notes that in the nineteenth century most European countries had considerable internal demographic heterogeneity. This heterogeneity had largely disappeared by the 1960s; that is, in 1960 the French resembled one another much more in their demographic behavior than they had in the nineteenth century. Her analysis of Ireland suggests that Northern Ireland and the Republic have become for all purposes two distinct countries. Demographic differences between the six counties and the twenty-six counties were insignificant in the nineteenth century, but grew during the twentieth century. In 1926 and again in 1971, marital fertility and marriage behavior within the six counties was relatively homogeneous, as it was within the twenty-six counties. But the North differed considerably from the Republic. These results suggest "a hardening of the demographic boundary between these two areas" (Watkins 1991, pp. 131–134). The boundaries of Northern Ireland are not simply a religious boundary, as she notes, because while the Republic's Protestant minority is small (6 percent in 1971), Northern Ireland's Catholic minority is large (31 percent in 1971). The sources of this hardening are unclear, and the more recent study by Ó Gráda and Walsh (1995) suggests a murkier picture of Republic-Northern Ireland differences. But the demographic differences between the Republic and Northern Ireland remain.

What is more clear is Ireland's struggle to reconcile cherished beliefs and customs with new social and legal realities. In Northern Ireland these struggles tend to be overshadowed by larger questions of political violence and that province's constitutional status. The Republic of Ireland, in contrast, has confronted at least some of these issues directly. A recent referendum on divorce was as intriguing to outsiders as it was painful to many in the Republic. By the slimmest of margins (about nine thousand votes, or a victory with only 50.28 percent of votes cast), the people of the Irish Republic approved a constitutional amendment that will permit divorce in Ireland for the first time. The result was a startling turnabout, given that in 1986 the people had soundly defeated a different proposal to legalize divorce (Irish *Times*, November 27, 1995). Just what accounts for the narrow approval is unclear. The proposal requires an ungainly addition to the Republic's constitution, and in any event severely restricts divorce. Some Irish commentators interpret the vote's outcome as a slap in the face for the Roman Catholic Church, which had opposed the measure; others viewed the outcome as a reluctant effort to ease the suffering of those trapped in failed marriages. Whatever the reasons for this vote, it further advances Ireland along a path that makes the country's demographic distinctiveness a thing of the past.

Archaic Demographic Patterns?

Ireland's recent demographic experience, especially with regard to marital and extramarital fertility, suggests the country is converging to demographic patterns that have been more common elsewhere in Europe. But in a curious respect some features of Ireland's nineteenth-century depopulation have strong parallels to the modern world. The parallels should not be pushed too far, because they are not complete, but noting them is interesting nonetheless. The most obvious parallel is the decline of marriage as a social institution. Ireland in the nineteenth century became an extreme example of the western European marriage pattern of delayed marriage with high proportions of the population ultimately remaining single. This marriage pattern changed in much of western Europe during the early twentieth century. Traditionally the United

States had a relatively low proportion of people who never married. Marriage booms in several western European countries during the mid-twentieth century brought European experience more in line with the American. For several generations Europeans departed from their traditional demographic patterns and the unmarried seemed an increasingly peculiar group. No longer. The age at which people first marry has climbed steadily in most western countries in recent decades, and the fraction of people who are not married has increased with it. In the early 1980s, for example, about one-third of Swedish and U.S. men aged 35–39 and about one-quarter of Swedish and U.S. women of the same ages were not married (Davis 1985, table 1.2). During the period 1970–1988 alone, the percentage of U.S. men who had ever been married fell by 10 percent, and the figure for women declined almost as much (Schoen and Weinick 1993, table 1).

There is no literal parallel between the rise of permanent celibacy in Ireland and the decline of marriage in industrialized societies today. Many unmarried people now are divorced, not never-married as in nineteenth-century Ireland. Extramarital sexual unions were socially unacceptable in Ireland. Today census bureaus find it expedient to invent new categories to classify households with unmarried couples, and many who are not living with a sexual partner are sexually active nonetheless. The relation between marriage and child rearing has also changed. Many unmarried women now have children openly, even deliberately. At the same time, the desire to have children may be one of the other factors distinguishing cohabiting couples from married couples today. Yet there is a thought-provoking parallel nonetheless: the Irish grew increasingly to organize and to conduct their lives in household units that were not centered on a married couple. The same is increasingly common in the modern world. Why?

One explanation popular today says that changes in social and economic life have meant that single people can have many of the benefits of marriage without assuming the burdens of a life-long commitment. The reorganization of sex roles has made women less economically dependent on men. Schultz (1995) shows that the decline of marriage in the United States in recent years is strongly correlated with the rising wage-earning opportunities of women. The effect of such changes is complicated. Better earning opportunities, because they increase one's economic status as a single person, make marriage relatively less attractive to women. Increasing women's wages can increase the total income of married couples, but may also reduce men's bargaining position within the household and thus reduce the attractiveness of marriage for men. This kind of argument should sound familiar, because it is very similar to the explanation offered for the rise of permanent celibacy in post-Famine Ireland. The decline of marriage today is another example of a retreat from an institution that no longer offers what it did in the past.

The decline of marriage today also reflects changing attitudes toward sex and childbearing. In post-Famine Ireland sexual relations and child rearing were important reasons to marry. Taboos against extramarital sexual activity and extramarital childbearing have eroded dramatically in modern societies, making these activities less important reasons to marry. Survey data on sexual activity show that now, unlike Ireland in the nineteenth century, being unmarried does not require sexual abstinence. Cohabitation or "consensual unions" are common among young unmarried people. And a recent survey in the United States found that 70–75 percent of people who are not married or even living with someone have had at least one sexual partner in the past twelve months (Laumann et al. 1994, table 5.1A). Fertility patterns also suggest the declining importance of marriage. So many women now have children without marrying the father that (whether the practice is advisable, which is another question entirely) marriage no longer seems a prerequisite for parenthood. Social scientists continue to debate the reasons for rapidly changing family patterns in present-day society, and as yet there is nothing like a consensus on these issues. But the parallel with post-Famine Ireland is fascinating: increasingly, men and women seem to think marriage is not worth the sacrifices it entails. In this respect the post-Famine Irish were very modern.

INSTITUTIONS, HISTORY, AND DEMOGRAPHIC DECISIONS

The topic here has been Ireland's depopulation and the demographic behaviors that brought about depopulation. Throughout economic and institutional developments have been stressed as the forces underlying demographic change. In this emphasis I am only agreeing with most Irish historians of these issues, who, however much I have criticized them in other ways, are correct in thinking that cultural differences and cultural change did not play a large role in Irish demographic patterns. From a slightly more distant perspective, however, Ireland's demographic history suggests that to the historian the distinction between culture or institutions or economics is a bit artificial. That Irish people would make difficult decisions in the face of the changes that overtook them in the period between the Great Famine and the First World War is hardly surprising. More interesting is the character of those changes. Why were Irish demographic adjustments similar to those of parts of Scotland and some other countries, and so unlike the adjustments under way in the major industrial countries of Europe? This has been a background theme, and I have sought to provide specific answers. In closing it is worth restating at a general level some of the factors that made Ireland differ from, for example, England.

Some aspects of Irish demographic adjustment reflect historical facts that predate the Famine and, in some cases, the nineteenth century. One such fact is the nature of landholding in Ireland. Irish historians long stressed supposed defects in Ireland's tenurial system as a reason for Irish poverty. Most scholars today downplay this kind of reasoning, and this study joins in that revisionism. Surely the more important feature of Irish land tenure was not the existence of landlords or the lack of leases, but the fact that most agriculturalists in Ireland were peasants or relatively small farmers. The prevalence of these people among Ireland's agrarian classes was only strengthened by the Famine and subsequent developments, as the cottiers and laborers who had been so important prior to the Famine virtually disappeared from the countryside. This is very different from England's agrarian structure, where most agriculturalists were landless laborers working for farmer-entrepreneurs. In this respect England was the unusual case for Europe; peasantries dominated the land in large regions of Europe throughout the nineteenth century. In Ireland, for those holding land or related to those holding land, virtually every demographic decision reflected ties to this specific asset. Leaving Ireland meant settling claims to land, or cashing in one's potential claim to the land. Marrying meant acquiring land, by inheritance or dowry. And the existence of these small farms promoted, in ways discussed earlier, transitional household forms in which adults would not leave Ireland but would not marry and carry on the generations themselves.

Ireland might have gone the way of Bavaria or other peasant regions if not for a specific historical event: the Famine. Some historians have tried to downplay the Famine's significance, and some have advanced misleading interpretations of the Famine's impact on later demographic change. But the Famine was a watershed, and the Famine did shape later events. O'Rourke's (1991a) conclusion about the impact of the Famine on Irish labor markets points to one effect on later demographic adjustment. By driving so many from Ireland in a short time, the Famine solidified an already-strong emigrant tradition. Young people growing up after the Famine could easily leave to join friends or relatives overseas. Thriving overseas communities could finance emigration to a degree otherwise impossible in such a poor society. Once started, this emigration process meant that Ireland would remain a country of emigrants, as it has, and that virtually any economic crisis would lead to a heightened outflow, as in the 1880s. Emigration at this level, moreover, would have the profound effects on marriage, household formation, and marital fertility that were documented in earlier chapters. Other impacts of the

Famine are more subtle but probably just as important. To take one: some historians, including Connell, implied that rural people felt at fault for the Famine, that their lack of foresight had left them vulnerable to disaster. He saw in changing post-Famine marriage patterns a chastened people finally learning to live within their means. This interpretation seems unwarranted. Ireland's historians have not yet concluded their efforts to place blame for the Famine, but there is little reason to think that those who survived thought they were responsible. Indeed, those who survived the Famine had bitter and first-hand knowledge of what happened when Nature turned on a rural people, and would impart that knowledge to their children. A lasting effect of the Famine would be an attachment to the institutions and relationships that could insure against disaster in the future.

And what of a distinct Irish culture, or a culture that changed over the post-Famine decades and so became more distinctive? Culture and cultural change play a central part in much recent demographic historiography, including the Princeton Fertility Project. The emphasis on culture in demographic history reflects wider trends in historical research, which in recent years has given cultural differences and cultural change pride of place in historical writing. Some of this stress on culture in demographic history is ahistorical. Ireland's experience points to the need to view culture as itself the outcome of historical processes, processes that might be driven by economic change. Culture to the economist usually connotes systematic variations in individual behavior associated with preferences: an Englishman and a Frenchman faced with identical prices and incomes behave differently because they have preferences similar to those of their own group but different from those of other cultures. This way of thinking about the role of culture yields a certain clarity, but also enforces an artificial distinction that matters a great deal when considering a historical process such as Ireland's post-Famine adjustment. The limitations of the orthodox economic view were clear to Alfred Marshall: "[A]lthough it is man's wants in the earliest stages of his development that give rise to his activities, yet afterwards each new step upwards is to be regarded as the development of new activities giving rise to new wants, rather than of new wants giving rise to new activities" (Marshall 1920, p. 76). This essential interconnectedness of wants and their satisfaction underscores the role of history. Our present actions may, within the economic framework, reflect our best efforts to use the resources at hand to satisfy our wants. But both our wants and the actions we currently view as feasible are the products of a long history of human development. One would not expect vigorous disagreement about this claim, nor about the specific findings along these lines discussed in earlier chapters. Yet many works of historical demography attempt to refute "economic" explanations, which are arrayed as the alternative to "cultural" explanations. The unfortunate apposition of culture and economics obscures the central role of history in the behavior of the Irish or any other population.

Something similar can be said about the role of history in the formation of institutions. Much of my criticism of Malthusian thinking concerns the lack of institutional context in that model. Institutions such as the Match or the Poor Law or even the organization of labor markets are not just important to demographic decision making, they are the products of historical individuals and their efforts to grapple with the exigencies of their own lives. I have suggested that in a country where one-fourth of all adults were bachelors and spinsters it would be relatively easy to be a bachelor or spinster. Patterns of socialization, of care for the aged, of farm transfers from the childless—all would arise from and become regularized out of the practices of earlier generations. These institutions, the products of one generation's demographic decisions, would remain to influence the next generation's demographic decisions. Some of this influence worked through "economic" mechanisms, but some worked by shaping attitudes toward particular demographic behaviors such as permanent celibacy.

Irish demographic history is a powerful example of what economic historians such as Paul David have termed "path dependence": where we are now reflects not just what happened yesterday, but what happened long before yesterday, the cumulative effects of each period of history limiting and directing what takes place in the next. The power of the Atlantic economy, then, may explain why Ireland changed over the nineteenth century, but the particular form of that change was rooted in earlier Irish history. A full appreciation of history's role highlights the deeper irony of posing culture and economics as alternative explanations for events in human history. Ireland's history produced the particular economic and demographic changes that followed the Famine. Those changes in turn presented young Irish adults with a set of alternatives that differed from those faced by their own parents, but that were in part the result of actions undertaken by their parents. The shared history of one generation presents itself to the next as a set of attitudes and desires, but also as a set of opportunities and constraints. Our demographic system, like our culture, our institutions, and our economies, is itself the product of history.

NOTES

CHAPTER 1
DEPOPULATION IN POST-FAMINE IRELAND

1. Rural population for Iowa defined as "nonmetropolitan." Data are from U.S. Commerce Department (1992, p. 29). The two Portuguese studies focused on small communities. Depopulation in Fontelas was confined to a relatively brief period at the beginning of the twentieth century (O'Neill 1984, p. 39). The parish of Lanhese lost population for the entire period 1864–1890 (Brettell 1986, table 1).

2. Weindling (1989) traces the development of the eugenicist movement in Germany during the nineteenth century and analyzes its role in the Nazi atrocities of the 1930s and 1940s.

3. The *Ulster Examiner* is quoted in Keep (1955, p. 380).

4. See, for example, Clément (1910, p. 30).

5. See the articles by James J. Walsh and M. V. Kelly in the Catholic magazine *America* in the 1920s and early 1930s.

6. "Neo-Malthusian" as noted, has also been used to signify advocacy of birth control. Throughout this volume I will use the meaning introduced in the text.

7. Important critiques include Kennedy (1984), Solar (1984), and McGregor (1989).

8. De Vries (1994) effectively uses this idea to analyze shifts in production and consumption during the British industrial revolution.

9. The first quotation is from M.P. John Francis Maguire. Both are quoted in Keep (1955, p. 382).

10. Wilde is quoted in Fitzpatrick (1984, p. 1). Ogle (1889, p. 207) made a similar argument about migration from England's rural areas: "There must always be going on what may be called a skimming of the cream from the rural population, to the obvious weakening and deterioration of the residue that remains at home."

11. For readable overviews of research on savings, inheritance, and the accumulation of wealth, see Modigliani (1988) and Kotlikoff (1988).

12. Calculated from Mitchell (1980, series B2).

13. See, for example, the volumes of essays comparing Ireland and France (Cullen and Furet 1981) or Ireland and Scotland (Cullen and Smout 1977). Much of the newer secondary literature discussed below has a strong comparative focus.

14. Although some have challenged Arensberg and Kimball's assertions on specific points, as we shall see.

15. Hannan (1979, p. 28). The passage pertains to implications that rural Ireland had not changed between the 1930s and the late 1970s; one could make the same remark with reference to using Arensberg and Kimball as evidence for periods earlier than their study.

16. Bourke (1993) and her related articles do not focus on demographic issues but set a high standard for the study of women in Irish history. Diner (1983) concerns Irish women in the United States. Nolan (1989) and Rhodes (1992) are more recent accounts of women in nineteenth-century Ireland. Ward (1991) is a selective review of the field of women's history in Ireland.

CHAPTER 2
THE RURAL ECONOMY IN THE NINETEENTH CENTURY

1. For more detailed treatment and the nuances of debates: Ó Gráda (1994) is a general economic history. Turner (1996) is the first comprehensive account of the agricultural economy in the period covered by this book. Foster (1989) and Hoppen (1989) are two recent surveys that devote more attention to political and social developments.

2. The Schumpeter-Gilboy index, reprinted in Mitchell and Deane (1962, p. 469), shows a price-level increase of 80 percent over the same period. I report the version of the index that excludes cereals prices.

3. Ogilvie and Cerman (1996) provide an excellent introduction to the large literature on European proto-industrialization. Clarkson (1996) discusses proto-industry and industry in Ireland.

4. The use of height as a proxy for economic well-being remains controversial. The authors of the relevant research caution that their results are consistent with other interpretations, as well.

5. Earlier estimates of post-Famine agricultural output include Solow (1971), Vaughan (1994, app. 9), and Ó Gráda (1993, table 30). The Sauerbeck-Statist price index (Mitchell and Deane 1962, pp. 474–475) suggests that Turner's increase in output from 1850 to 1914 is robust to changes in the value of money.

6. I thank Boyer, Hatton, and O'Rourke for sharing their unpublished real-wage series.

7. This index and another created by Fitzpatrick, discussed below, pertain to males only. Historical censuses usually do a poor job with women's labor-force activities, particularly for rural women whose household and farm duties are closely linked. I discuss women's labor-force activities below.

8. For France, see Postel-Vinay and Weir (1994, table 2). Dillwitz (1973) conveniently summarizes the structure of German agriculture from official sources.

9. Using the valuation data does not completely solve the problem, owing to inconsistencies in the way the valuation was performed. Solow (1971, pp. 58–66) discusses the primary valuation and problems with that effort.

10. Readers interested in more recent research on land tenure and land reform in Ireland may want to consult Guinnane and Miller (1996, 1997). Two other recent studies stress different but related aspects of the issues discussed in the text. Dowling (1997) studies the institution of tenant-right from its origins. Wilson (1994) studies land tenure among Irish immigrants to Canada and compares those arrangements with what the immigrants had left behind in Ireland.

11. Dowling (1997) traces the origins of the term "tenant-right" and the institution from its earliest history in the settlement of Ulster.

12. The original court was the Incumbered Estates Court, established in 1849. The powers of this body were transferred to a new Landed Estates Court in 1858.

13. The Irish calculation assumes a population of 8 million, which was obviously not accurate by the end of the Famine.

14. The literature on the Land War is very large. Jordan's (1994) study of the Land War in County Mayo is a recent contribution that discusses earlier accounts.

15. The Royal Commission reference is from Bourke (1993, p. 170). She discusses proposals for reforming poultry raising on pp. 172–186.

16. Crafts (1985, table 3.4). Britain was unusual in the very low proportion of its labor force in agriculture even in the eighteenth century.

CHAPTER 3
THE STATE AND THE CHURCHES

1. Private groups also made substantial contributions. The nature and adequacy of Famine relief is the subject of much controversy; for an overview, see Ó Gráda (1989).

2. This evidence is abstracted and discussed in Guinnane (1993, table 3).

3. Precise comparisons of the pension with weekly earnings, with the costs of upkeep for an aged person, and with total household income for poor households can be found in Guinnane (1993, pp. 273–274).

4. Budd and Guinnane (1991) discuss the misreporting of age in Ireland in more detail. The data suggest that many people in Ireland really did not know their true age, but also shows that when in doubt they erred on the side of the pension.

5. Figures are summarized by Akenson (1970, pp. 276–277, 321, 346) from parliamentary sources.

6. There is a considerable literature on education and the effects of basic literacy in economic history. Mitch (1992) is a recent discussion of literacy in Victorian England.

7. Newsinger (1995) is a recent review essay on aspects of the nineteenth-century Catholic Church in Ireland.

8. See Connolly (1982, app. B) for a discussion of the 1834 enumeration and of earlier attempts to count adherents to religious faiths in Ireland. One might reasonably ask whether the data on religion were inaccurate, either because people were unwilling to state their religion or because census-takers manipulated the replies. Although we cannot rule out this possibility absolutely, no serious historian has suggested that the religious inquiries produced significantly flawed answers.

9. The figures are discussed by Vaughan (1989, pp. 741–742), who also remarks on the role of rental incomes in the differences between Protestant and Catholic incomes.

10. Each decennial census from 1861 through 1911 reports this information.

11. The Penal Laws and discrimination against Catholics in British-ruled Ireland is a large and contentious issue that goes beyond the scope of our subject.

The interested reader should consult Connolly (1982, 1992). Connolly emphasizes the difference between the letter and practice of the Penal Laws. He also notes that many Catholics lacked certain rights (such as the right to vote) by virtue of the property qualifications for the franchise that affected both Catholic and Protestant. Vaughan (1989, p. 738) makes the telling point that by the 1870s at least, Ireland was by European standards a place relatively free from official disabilities on religious sects or their adherents.

12. Larkin (1972) is an early account of the Catholic devotional revolution. Miller (1975, pp. 83–87) took a closer look at the pre-Famine attendance figures and provides some correctives to Larkin's account.

13. Hempton and Hill (1992) is a history of the Irish Presbyterians in the nineteenth century. Miller (1978) is an analysis of Ulster Presbyterianism and social change associated with the industrial revolution.

14. Fitzpatrick (1987a) considers divorce in modern Ireland in some detail. I discuss the issue in chapter 7.

CHAPTER 4
THE DEMOGRAPHIC SETTING

1. Life table estimates from Boyle and Ó Gráda (1986, app. table 3). Ó Gráda (1989, p. 17) discusses the evidence on smallpox.

2. For a specific example, see Connell (1962a, p. 520), where he quotes without critical comment the Poor Inquiry's conclusion that in many counties most people married before their early twenties.

3. Appendix 4B defines I_g and shows its relation to the other Princeton indices I_f, I_h, and I_m. I am using I_g to follow the literature. Guinnane, Okun, and Trussell (1994) argue that I_g is much less sensitive to changes in marital fertility than had originally been thought, and is thus only really useful as a way of comparing studies all based on that measure. I_g is used in this book in that spirit.

4. The main point of Schellekens's (1993) paper is to argue, using stable population theory, that marital fertility alone could not produce the observed growth rates. This point is well taken and reinforces the sense that pre-Famine population growth rates are something of a mystery.

5. Mokyr (1980b) produced another set of national and, more ambitiously, county-level estimates of excess death rates.

6. I have estimated the figures in the text from Boyle and Ó Gráda (1986, app. table A1).

7. All changes from Vaughan and Fitzpatrick (1978, table 6), after the censuses of 1841 and 1851.

8. A simple calculation shows the point. Assume that the age-specific fertility of Irish women followed the Hutterite pattern. The number of children born in a single year to women with these fertility patterns and the marriage patterns obtaining in Ireland in 1911 could have been born to half as many women with the same fertility patterns but all of whom were married.

9. See Ó Gráda (1975) and especially Ó Gráda (1978, p. 70) for a discussion of the emigration statistics and their relation to regional patterns.

10. Connell (1962a, p. 520). He is more cautious on this point in his monograph *The Population History of Ireland, 1750–1845*.

11. Verrière (1979, fig. III-22) shows a large increase in the median age at marriage just after the Famine. He does not provide details of his computations, unfortunately. Ireland did experience increased ages at first marriage during the first half of the twentieth century (Walsh 1972).

12. I quote the relevant passage in chapter 5 below.

13. Chapter 9 briefly discusses demographic developments in Ireland during the twentieth century.

14. Computed from Canada (1893, vol. II, tables I-III). "Rural" is an approximation consisting of the province minus the two largest cities of Montréal and Québec.

15. See, for example, Cullen (1972, p. 136) or Lee (1973a, pp. 3–5). The problem may be related to the confusion over age at marriage and celibacy.

16. In preliminary work, Miller (1994) uses more refined published data to measure changes in marriage patterns over this period. His results are not fully consistent with the interpretation in the text and suggest caution about the Famine's direct impact, although it remains true that the lack of congruence between the simple celibacy figures and the areas of the Famine's greatest demographic impact show that the Cullen-Lee argument is too simple.

17. Dublin and Belfast computed from the 1911 census of Ireland, after Vaughan and Fitzpatrick (1978, tables 27 and 33).

18. German population and emigration figures from Marschalck (1984, tables 1.3 and 5.1). Irish figures from Vaughan and Fitzpatrick (1978, tables 3 and 54). For both countries the estimates are of *gross* emigration, which approximates net emigration well for Ireland, less so for Germany.

19. Appendix 4A discusses the problems with the counts of emigrants.

20. See O'Dowd (1991) for an extended history of these people.

21. Harris (1994) is a recent history of Irish migration to Britain.

22. Computed from summaries of emigration statistics reported in Commission on Emigration and Other Population Problems 1954, app. table 26. Ó Gráda's (1975) contention that emigrants to Britain were undercounted implies that the measured shares going overseas are too high.

23. Figures are from national censuses as reported by Commission on Emigration and Other Population Problems (1954, table 95).

24. Computed from Commission on Emigration and Other Population Problems (1954, table 95).

25. Computed from Commission on Emigration and Other Population Problems (1954, table 91).

26. Computed from Commission on Emigration and Other Population Problems (1954, table 90).

27. Although one should avoid exaggerations such as calling Ireland's emigration "basically a mass female movement" (Diner 1983, p. 30).

28. Hoy (1995) discusses one interesting facet of female emigration from Ireland, which was young women leaving to join religious orders overseas. Had they remained as nuns in Ireland, of course, these women would not have married in Ireland, but the size of this emigrant stream was small relative to the total.

29. Reported in the "Emigration Statistics of Ireland," 1902 (Great Britain 1903c). Other years show very similar occupational distributions.

30. Thomas (1973, app. tables 81 and 82). Part of this difference reflects relatively numerous Irish female emigrants. Women were less likely to report a skill in either population.

31. Several sources refer to women returning with dowries they had earned on their own. See, for example, Schrier (1958, pp. 130–131). I discuss dowries and their role in household dynamics in chapters 5 and 7.

32. Gould (1980, p. 56) estimates that in the early twentieth century 6 per hundred Irish emigrants to the United States would return home. This figure is far below his estimates of 12 for English, 22 for German, and 58 for Italian migrants to the United States. Verrière (1979, pp. 78–80) provides the higher estimate of 10 per hundred returnees for the period 1861–1901.

33. For a recent and particularly careful study of this type, see Wegge's (1995) analysis of emigration from the German state of Hesse in the mid nineteenth century.

34. Under the old system, 12 pence ("d.") equal one shilling ("s."), and 20 shillings equal £1.

35. The Registrar-General's reports on mortality provide estimates for the period 1870–1872 on. (They are summarized in Commission on Emigration and Other Population Problems 1954, table 79). Estimates from this source appear sensible, and show the rising expectations of life reported in table 4.6. But given the deficiencies in the death-registration system it would take considerable adjustment to create reliable life tables from that source. In unpublished work Fitzpatrick used the recorded death-registration data to estimate survivorship for people aged 15–55 by county and decade for the period from the Famine to 1910. His calculations make no correction for underregistration of deaths, but for this period of life underregistration was probably relatively minor. His estimates for Ireland as a whole are broadly consistent with the figures reported in table 4.6.

36. Data from the United Kingdom are from Local Government Board (1908, diagram 6) and Smith (1988, table 1). For evidence on declines in tuberculosis death rates in the United States and several western European countries during this period, see the dated but still useful Dubos and Dubos (1987 [1952], apps. A–C). One measure of a cause of death's quantitative importance is the number of years of life that would be added for the average person if that cause of death were eradicated. The "cause-deleted" life table for Ireland in 1951 shows that the elimination of respiratory tuberculosis would have added 1.2 years of life for the average male, slightly more for a female. In England the elimination of tuberculosis in 1951 would have added only about 6 months of life for males and less for females. Elimination of the disease in England and Wales in 1901 would have added 2.1 years of life for men and about 1.7 years for women. Comparable Irish estimates are not available for 1901. The notional impact of eliminating tuberculosis in Ireland falls considerably by 1961, reflecting energetic public-health interventions (Lyons 1973, p. 572). The relevant life tables are reported in Preston, Keyfitz, and Schoen (1972).

37. Old age as a cause of death is reported in Local Government Board (1908, diagram 1). The Registrar-General is quoted in Smith (1988, p. 21, n. 14).

38. Housing figures from Local Government Board (1908, table 18, p. 15). The report does not say, but these figures are most likely extracted from the 1901 census of the several countries. Comparative tuberculosis death rates in Irish cities from Local Government Board (1908, table 49, p. 46).

39. Kennedy's comments apparently struck a chord, as two recent studies of Irish women remark on these mortality patterns. Nolan (1989, p. 37) cites Kennedy, but Rhodes (1992, pp. 211–218) looks at the mortality data herself. Rhodes notes that the official mortality data are flawed, but argues that "the mortality data of the 1860s and 1870s is likely to be marred by under-registration but it is also expected that this under-reporting should not vary by gender" (p. 211). This is contrary to her own view of the place of women in Ireland. One would expect that women's deaths *were* under-reported relative to men's; if women are of lower social status, their deaths would be consider less worthy of note. In a personal communication David Fitzpatrick reports that he found just such greater under-reporting of female deaths. Differential reporting of this type implies that the life tables Rhodes discusses exaggerate female longevity and thus understate the relatively poor mortality of Irish women. The unpublished Fitzpatrick estimates mentioned in note 35 show better mortality for women than for men in some cases. But the difference is small (if we convert his estimates to estimates of the expectation of life at birth, using the Coale-Demeny "North" model life table, the difference in male and female expectations is usually less than two years) and is consistent with the view that Irish women had relatively poor mortality.

40. Nicholas and Oxley (1993) provide evidence for an earlier period that is not consistent with the explanation of mortality differences advanced in the text. They use the heights of prisoners transported to Australia to study gender differences in work and access to household resources for an earlier period (1795–1820). They find that Irish women in this period appear to have been treated better, relative to men, than were English women. The apparent discrepancy may reflect changes over time or, more likely, unusual features of the kind of people convicted of crimes and transported to Australia.

41. If I_g is used as our measure of fertility, in 1911 marital fertility in Ireland was 65 percent higher than in England and Wales. Overall fertility, which is the concept more appropriate to Akenson's suggestion that Irish women lived short lives because many died in childbirth, was only 14 percent higher in Ireland than in England and Wales. See table 4.5.

42. For statements about Italy, compare table 4.6 to Italian values reported by Coale and Treadway (1986). All statements about risks of death by cause supported by Preston, Keyfitz, and Schoen (1972).

43. Scotland as well as England and Wales also had somewhat higher general mortality for women at ages 5–19, but the difference is nothing like that in Ireland. And young women in other parts of the United Kingdom also had higher death rates from tuberculosis than boys and young men, but again, the sex differences are much smaller than in Ireland.

44. Computed from census data reported in Commission on Emigration and Other Population Problems (1954, table 3). Urban places are defined as those with 1,500 or more persons.

45. Non-Irish city growth computed from Mitchell (1980, series B4).

46. Guinnane (1992a, table 4) reports a rough measure of the ratio of those moving within Ireland from a county to those emigrating from the county, for the period 1871–1910. For County Wicklow this ratio is 1.07 for men and 2.01 for women.

47. Calculated from Fitzpatrick (1989a, app. tables 1 and 2).

48. For discussion of the 1821 and 1831 censuses, and for earlier estimates of Ireland's population size, see Mokyr and Ó Gráda (1984) and the references they cite.

49. The German *Ortssippenbücher* used by Knodel (1988) and Imhof (1990) are also based on parish registers. The *Ortssippenbuch* is a village genealogy compiled during the twentieth century, but the underlying source is largely the parish register(s) for the area in question.

50. Morgan and Macafee (1984) and Macafee (1987) discuss some apparent shortcomings in Irish parish registers caused by failure to record all demographic events. Daultrey, Dickson, and Ó Gráda (1981) discuss the hearth tax and attempts to use it as the basis of population counts.

51. The quotation is from the Registrar-General's First Annual Report, as reported in Walsh (1970a, p. 150). I discuss the problem of underregistration in chapter 7.

52. Guinnane, Okun, and Trussell (1994) argue that the index I_g cannot reliably date the start of a fertility transition, its principal use in the Princeton project. The index remains valuable for comparisons to other published studies, as used here.

53. The Hutterite schedule as used in the Princeton Project is .3 for women aged 15–19, .55 (20–24), .502 (25–29), .447 (30–34), .406 (35–39), .222 (40–44), and .061 (45–49).

54. Murphy (1981, p. 125), for example, refers to "the destruction of Irish census schedules in 1922." A non-exhaustive list of studies based wholly or in part on the 1901 and 1911 manuscript census includes Ó Gráda and Kennedy for the study of farm inheritance (Ó Gráda 1980; Kennedy 1991); Ó Gráda on Catholic-Protestant fertility differentials (Ó Gráda 1985); Ó Gráda more generally on fertility control (Ó Gráda 1991); Mary Daly on class structure in Dublin (Daly 1982); Gibbon and Curtin, Fitzpatrick, myself, and Birdwell-Pheasant on household structure and related demographic issues (Gibbon and Curtin 1978; Fitzpatrick 1983; Guinnane 1991b, 1992a, b; Birdwell-Pheasant 1992). My own interest in this source was stimulated by an article pointing out that manuscript census schedules had been underused (Royle 1978), and by the example and encouragement of Fitzpatrick and Ó Gráda.

55. Some studies use explicitly name-based schemes to get around this problem. For example, Joseph Ferrie (1994) has linked passenger lists to the manuscript census of the United States for several years. He purposely chose rare names to reduce the problem of too many "John Smiths."

56. The sample includes every household in the District Electoral Divisions (DEDs) of Scarriff (County Clare); Drummin, Bundorragha, Erriff, Owennadornaun, and Kilgeever (County Mayo); Newtown, Staholmog, and Cruicetown (County Meath); and Coolattin, Coolboy, and Shillelagh (County Wicklow). The census schedules are located in the Public Record Office, the Four Courts, Dublin. Valuation records are kept at the Valuation Office, Ely Place, Dublin.

57. Valuation matches are of equally high quality, although I should register one caveat: some farmers held more one plot, and if a plot was in a DED outside the one in which the household was located, the second plot would not be part of the valuation records I employed. As a simple check on this, I searched the valuation information of neighboring DEDs. That check did not suggest that this problem was quantitatively important.

CHAPTER 5
HOUSEHOLDS AND THE GENERATIONS

1. Berkner and Mendels (1978) discuss inheritance systems and fertility and provide references to other works.

2. Laslett (1972) describes this classification system, which was later elaborated in more detail in Hammel and Laslett (1974). Lee and Gjerde (1986) are among the critics of the Hammel-Laslett classification scheme.

3. As Laslett notes, who heads such a household is irrelevant. Consider a household consisting of a man and wife, their children, and his widowed mother. The household is "extended" regardless of whether the man or his widowed mother is listed as household head (Laslett 1972, p. 29).

4. Elsewhere Birdwell-Pheasant (1993, table 4) reports that the wealth/complexity relationship is stronger in 1911 than in 1901.

5. Here as before I follow Laslett's definitions in dividing the extended-family households into subtypes.

6. Young people in particular in the 1901 and 1911 census manuscripts tend to say that their relation to the household head is "visitor," but their occupation is farm servant. The term visitor as used in the Irish census is ambiguous. Fitzpatrick (1983, n. 27) argues that visitors were kin of the household head. I discuss servants in detail in the next chapter.

7. Berkner (1972, p. 405). Berkner (1975) extends this discussion. The statistical studies reported in Wachter, Hammel, and Laslett (1978) are largely motivated by Berkner's critique.

8. Alter (1988) for Belgium and Janssens (1993) for the Netherlands are two recent studies relying on population registers. Brown, Guinnane, and Lupprian (1993) discuss a similar system used by the city of Munich in the late nineteenth century.

9. The binary probit regression is reported and discussed in more detail in Guinnane (1992b, table 5).

10. Birdwell-Pheasant (1992) came to a similar conclusion concerning Ireland. My own version of the argument is further detailed in Guinnane (1992b).

11. This perspective also informs both Guinnane (1992b) and Kennedy

(1991). Recent thinking at some level simply revives an older understanding of the economic significance of farm inheritance, drawing out themes absent in Connell's writings but present in reports such as those of the Poor Law inspectors (Great Britain 1870a). There is also a rich central European literature on the subject, for example, Brugger (1936).

12. Patrick Kavanagh, "The Great Hunger," in *Collected Poems* (1992).

13. Most reports also note that the landlords—who could block the execution of these arrangements—generally only objected if the deal called for subdivision of the farm. The reports are contained in Great Britain (1870a).

14. I thank David Fitzpatrick for drawing my attention to this letter and the Local Government Board's report.

15. The following discussion is based on casual reading through the "Memorials of Wills, Deeds, and Admons," Registry of Deeds, Dublin. Because these documents are "memorials," the original agreements often contain conditions which are only mentioned, but not described, in the memorial.

16. "Memorial of Wills," 1911, vol. 171, no. 160.

17. Brien's sister Eliza could leave at any time, for any reason, and take with her a further £10 charged on the farm. "Memorial of Wills," 1911, vol. 171, no. 205.

18. "Memorials of Wills," 1911, vol. 3, no. 168.

19. The income-maximization assumption is harmless. If the family redistributes income among its members (which it did, in the form of payments to outgoing siblings, and so on), then income maximization is in the interest of all.

20. Guinnane (1992b) illustrates this argument with a simple diagram. Kimhi (1994) presents a formal model of my argument.

21. I will examine age at leaving home in more detail in the next chapter.

22. Kennedy (1991, table 3) could not determine the birth order of some 25–33 percent of all heirs in his samples. But the corroboration of the other studies suggests that the missing information would not overturn his result.

23. Ó Gráda's families are drawn from three areas in Counties Clare (including the region studied by Arensberg and Kimball), Cork, and Waterford. His method is subject to some limitations. The 1911 census usually only reports marital duration for currently married couples, so his sample of "gaps" is limited to households where both parents are still alive in 1911. Thus widows with sons waiting to succeed are excluded from this evidence. And as he concedes, there is no guarantee that a gap of five years means a family has passed over an elder son in favor of a younger. Some families might have had only girls during that period. Given the parallel results from other studies these limitations do not seem severe.

24. The 1926 census of the Irish Free State cross-tabulated farm sizes by marital status, and so permits a rough look at the same issue for the twenty-six counties. I have some reservations about the comparability of these data to the 1901–1911 censuses (discussed in chapter 7), but it is worth noting here that they suggest a somewhat more complicated picture. For the Free State as a whole, and for most individual counties, the proportion of all farmers aged 45–64 who are (female) widows is largest for the smallest farm size (1–10 acres), then declines to a minimum at about 15–30 acres, before rising again. Excepting the smallest farms, that is, widowed females were more likely to be listed as

farmers, the larger the farm. This is consistent with the argument made in the text. Their presence on smaller farms (1–10 acres) is not consistent with my argument, and probably reflects the difficulty in persuading any male heir to remain on such holdings. The statistical test alluded to in the text is the Mann-Whitney nonparametric test for differences in the means of two samples. In the first case, the z-score is 1.23 (P(z) = 0.1); in the second, the z-score is 6.11 (P(z) < .0001).

25. The Mann-Whitney test confirms formally that large farmers did marry later than small farmers (z = 2.5, P < .01).

26. In the article mentioned above, Ó Gráda (1980) does not report information on the relationship between heirship and farm size, but he did anticipate the point that heirs would be older on larger farms.

27. Ó Gráda (1988, chap. 5) is an important exception.

28. Johnston was arguing for a relaxation of the pension rules so that aged people who received such support would not be denied benefits. He might have been exaggerating to make the problem seem more serious. See Great Britain (1919, Q8425).

29. Figures computed from the Census of Ireland 1901, General Report tables 18 and 136, and the Census of Ireland 1911, General Report tables 66 and 115. We are looking at those aged 75 or more in 1901 and those aged 75 or more in 1911; we are not following a cohort through time.

30. Royal Commission (1910c, Q5080).

31. O'Neill (1984, table 4.1) reports that 65 percent of farming families and 77 percent of laboring families had simple households.

CHAPTER 6
COMING OF AGE

1. A very incomplete list of studies of age at leaving home would include Schofield (1970), Modell, Furstenberg, and Hershberg (1975), Wall (1978, 1987), Galenson (1987), Steckel (1988), Stevens (1990), and Guinnane and Gutmann (1992). In addition, there is a related, growing literature on the social and cultural history of youth. For leading examples of this genre, see Ariès (1962), Demos (1970, chap. 10; 1986).

2. The table assumes that a child left home if the child is present in 1901, absent in 1911, and resided in a household returned in both the 1901 and the 1911 censuses. Below I will discuss a check on this definition of leaving home.

3. See table 8.1. Marital fertility is discussed at length in chapter 8.

4. In the 1880 U.S. census the figure was 60 percent for Irish-born men aged 15–54 (number of men aged 15–54 = 6,936). The figure for 1900 was similar (61 percent, N = 638). The 1910 census suggests some improvement in Irish-American men's occupational status (49 percent are laborers or operatives, N = 1,494) although this change may reflect changes in occupational definitions. These figures are computed from the public use samples of the U.S. federal censuses of 1880, 1900, and 1910.

5. That is, migration in some circumstances is an investment made in conditions of uncertainty. See Burda (1995) for a recent effort to model this idea.

6. Censuses tend to undercount children, and that tendency may be greater for girls than for boys. The information discussed below, however, shows that the larger number of boys reported in table 6.2 is not purely due to such undercounting.

7. The term 'head' as used in table 6.3 includes 'co-heads,' or wives. None of the female heads aged 25–29 in table 6.3 is never-married.

8. The comparable figure for women is 3.5 percent ($N = 142$). Both figures pertain to the 1911 census.

9. Computed from the 1901 and 1911 censuses of Ireland. The comparable figure for males is 19 percent. The percentage of women who left home to marry between 1901 and 1911 cannot be estimated from the manuscript sample, because the data tell us only that someone has left the household and not why they did so.

10. Domestic service, a somewhat different institution, is discussed below.

11. See, for example, *The World We Have Lost*, or more specifically Laslett (1977, pp. 29–35).

12. Berkner notes that this family cycle was described by A. V. Chayanov, a Russian sociologist of peasant life.

13. See Kavanagh's *The Green Fool*, pp. 144–167, for his fictional account. O'Dowd (1991, pp. 129–226) discusses the treatment of temporary farm workers, which was probably worse than conditions for farm servants hired on long-term contracts.

14. In table 6.6 a servant is anyone who states his relationship to the household head as "servant," "employee," and so on. The "relationship" definition of servant agrees with a definition based on stated occupation for 93 percent of individuals aged 15–19 in 1911 who state an occupation. For present purposes the distinction between farm servants and domestic servants is irrelevant, so no attempt has been made to distinguish them here.

The only indicator of internal migration in either census is the individual's birthplace, given as county for those born in Ireland. The four locales were chosen deliberately to be on or near county borders to maximize the birthplace variable's sensitivity to short-distance migration. There is, unfortunately, no way to know how many of the servants in each locale were born outside the subsample locale but within that county.

15. This comment is quoted in Fitzpatrick (1989a, p. 625).

16. Guinnane (1992a) explains the statistical problem posed by the fact that heirs would ordinarily never leave home.

CHAPTER 7
THE DECLINE OF MARRIAGE

1. The study in question is J. A. Banks, *Prosperity and Parenthood* (1965). Vèrriere (1979, p. 469) also claims that Ireland was invaded by "the coldest materialism" and "a substitution of calculation for sentiment," but provides no evidence.

2. Calculations here are all from the censuses of 1861, 1881, and 1911, as reported in Vaughan and Fitzpatrick (1978, tables 25 and 27).

3. This is a problem common to many economic studies, historical and modern. Wealth variables usually rely on measures reported to tax authorities (or, less often, to census-takers), and these are usually gross of debts. The valuation measures here have the virtue of not being self-reported, so at least we do not have to worry about the possibility of tax evasion polluting the measure.

4. A defective household may be headed by a widowed woman whose son is still waiting to inherit the farm. So Fitzpatrick's table also includes some households that would be excluded from table 7.3 here, because the household head was not male.

5. See Kennedy (1973, table 54) and discussion. Ó Gráda (1994, p. 217) uses the 1926 data to question the pattern shown in table 7.3.

6. Computed from the Census of the Irish Free State, 1926, vol. I, table 6.

7. Breen (1984, p. 287) summarizes some of these discussions.

8. Fitzpatrick notes, correctly, that his research also raises a question of the standard of proof for the existence of endogamy. The data mentioned in the text and his comment are both from personal communications.

9. For an example of this media attention, see "Too Late for Prince Charming?" *Newsweek*, June 2, 1986, pp. 54–61.

10. Similarly, William Julius Wilson (1987, pp. 83–92), among others, argues that declining job opportunities for unskilled African-American men has left African-American women with a shortage of suitable partners. Wilson is certainly right, but only because he is also right in his unstated assumptions about the options facing African-American women: they either cannot or will not marry men of another race, and prefer to not marry at all if their options are men with low incomes.

11. *Newsweek* understood this point. In the article cited in note 9 the magazine interviewed women who were involved with men who did not belong to the categories conventional for them, such as a man younger than themselves.

12. I know of no discussions of homosexuality in nineteenth-century Ireland. Although it would be wrong to claim it did not exist and was not in fact a component of some of the same-sex friendships discussed here, it would be equally wrong to assume that these friendships were usually homosexual relationships.

13. The Mission episode takes place on pages 26–30 of *Tarry Flynn* (Kavanagh 1948).

14. For an example of an earlier textbook account of schizophrenia and its relation to marital status, see Gregory (1968, p. 460). The second edition of Kaplan and Sadock was published in 1976, or three years prior to Scheper-Hughes's book. This edition of the psychiatry textbook gives more credence to psychological theories of the etiology of schizophrenia, but interprets the marital status of schizophrenics in the same way as the 1995 edition discussed in the text.

15. Arensberg and Kimball (1968, p. 199) did remark that some in the community thought puritanical outlooks on sexual matters had become more common in the last generation.

16. See, for example, Walsh (1969), who quotes Heer (1961). Schellenberg (1991) extends this argument using more recent data from both the United States and Britain.

17. The U.S. census at this time asked about birthplace but not ethnicity. The whites of native parentage mentioned in the text probably include some people of Irish ethnicity. Akenson (1985, pp. 42–46) stresses this limitation of the U.S. census for the study of the Irish in the United States.

18. Those tests, reported in Guinnane (1987, chap. 6), use the Public Use Sample from the 1900 Census of the United States. Guinnane and Rouse-Foley (1994) extends this research to the 1880 and 1910 censuses.

19. Becker's original paper on marriage was published in 1973, and is reprinted as chapter 11 in Becker (1976). In Becker (1981) he draws out a more complete picture of household behavior based on this type of thinking.

20. My notion of "security" conflates two ideas that are usually kept distinct: risk aversion and time preference. One purchases insurance against the risk of undesirable events, and one saves to make sure of consumption in the future. Because the institutions for transferring wealth across states of the world and through time are to some extent the same in this case, the added complication of the risk-aversion/time-preference distinction does not seem worthwhile.

21. I return to the costs and benefits of children in Ireland in the next chapter.

22. There are seventeen households of this form in the 1901 census.

23. "Sidelights on Irish Emigrant Life," *Ireland's Own*, February 21, 1912.

24. See Fischer (1978, chap. 3) on attitudes toward the aged in the United States. Katz (1983) discusses poverty policy in the United States. The aged and poor-relief policy are both areas of active research, and the statements made in the text are intended as general characterizations only.

25. Births out of wedlock were comparatively rare. Prostitution was not unknown, judging from the records of prosecution for this crime and from the incidence of venereal diseases among troops stationed in Ireland. But the available evidence does not support meaningful inferences about how many Irish men had sex with prostitutes.

26. In some cases daughters inherited the family land, in which case the groom brought a dowry. In my census sample this occurred only in cases where there were no sons available to inherit.

27. The episode is in Kavanagh (1939, pp. 206–211).

CHAPTER 8
MARITAL FERTILITY AND FERTILITY DECLINE

1. Wrigley (1978, pp. 135–136) notes that some of these taboos might reflect "group rationality," that is, they may be adaptive because they enhance child survival or reduce fertility. However true this may be, the historiography usually defines the fertility transition in terms of individual fertility decisions.

2. The drawback to Henry's "stopping" definition is that it rules out birth spacing, a form of fertility control well suited to couples who do not have access to modern methods of contraception. Several rudimentary contraceptive methods such as coitus interrruptus ("withdrawal") or periodic abstinence (the

"rhythm method") result in longer intervals between births throughout the couple's reproductive life. Santow (1993, 1995) discusses fertility control in the past, and notes that the methods most frequently used in Europe are not necessarily compatible with Henry's approach. Bean, Mineau, and Anderton (1990) is one extended critique of the notion that fertility control in historical populations took the form of stopping only.

3. In Ansley Coale's famous phrase, some societies see contraception as "beyond the calculus of conscious choice." Knodel and van de Walle (1986, p. 404) discuss this idea and provide references. For secularization and its role in the fertility transition, see Lestaeghe and Wilson (1986).

4. Carlsson's term was "adjustment." Bean, Mineau, and Anderton (1990) use the term "adaptation," and I am following their usage.

5. See Coale and Watkins (1986, map 2.1), and the individual country studies.

6. See Appendix 8.A, which discusses Ó Gráda's preferred alternative estimates of I_g. The weakness in Teitelbaum's estimates is *not* the problem addressed by Coale and Pantelides in their appendix to Teitelbaum's book. Throughout this book I use the corrected estimates published in Ó Gráda (1993), which supersede those published in his 1991 paper. Fitzpatrick has also prepared a set of alternative estimates of I_g for Ireland. His unpublished estimates, which are based on a different method but generate results broadly similar to Ó Gráda's, are not employed here but are discussed in Appendix 8A.

7. County Dublin had an I_g of 615 in 1881 and 586 in 1911 (Ó Gráda 1993, table A5). Thus it did not experience the 10 percent decline used by the EFP authors. Below I discuss other evidence that shows a substantial fertility decline in Dublin prior to 1911.

8. Himes (1963) is a classic survey of contraception since antiquity. Reed (1984) discusses contraception in the United States. Teitelbaum (1984, pp. 200–210) discusses the dissemination of contraceptive information in Great Britain, which is probably most relevant to the Irish case. Santow (1995) discusses contraceptive methods used before and during the fertility transition in Europe.

9. Santow's argument is in part a suggestion that fertility before the so-called fertility transition was not as "natural" as Henry suggested.

10. David and Sanderson (1986, table 7.8) present a range of estimates for the effectiveness of these methods. The example cited in the text assumes a mid-range value for the number of times the couple has intercourse in each month. Other examples produce the same qualitative result.

11. A full exposition of CPA is beyond the scope of this chapter. See David et al. (1988) for the original description. Okun (1994) presents a simpler way to understand the method and discusses some of the assumptions that underlie its results.

12. Fitzpatrick has prepared a set of estimates of infant mortality that rely on uncorrected reports of the civil registration system. His estimates confirm the urban/rural differential.

13. See the observations quoted by Diner (1983, p. 21).

14. Sklar (1977, note 33) offers an estimate of the number of illegitimate conceptions in Ireland that became illegitimate births in England and Wales. The estimates imply that Connell's suspicions about emigration of pregnant girls would not much alter the picture of low illegitimacy in Ireland.

15. Bean, Mineau, and Anderton (1990, pp. 61–67) offer a succinct comparison of the teachings of major religions concerning contraception. O'Reilly (1975) is a brief introduction to Church teaching on the subject. Noonan (1986) is a detailed history of Church views on contraception. Smith (1991), in her discussion of the modern encyclical *Humanae Vitae*, emphasizes the diversity of Catholic theological views on contraception.

16. My regression exercise differs from Ó Gráda's in that I omit the counties of Dublin and Antrim (with Belfast). This difference does not affect the results noted in the text.

17. Brown, Guinnane, and Lupprian (1993, table 7), for example, found this pattern in the fertility transition in Munich. Moch (1992) is a recent discussion of the role of migration in the fertility transition.

18. Thus at the first intersection of the Irish cost curve and the marginal return curve, the total cost of having children exceeds the total return. This is not an optimum.

19. Haines (1992) surveys the relation between male occupations and fertility in England in 1911.

20. As Wrigley notes, his simulations are simplified but convey the basic flavor of the issue.

21. This discussion of emigration and fertility owes much to earlier views. See, for example, Fitzpatrick (1984, p. 40) or Ó Gráda (1993, pp. 194–197).

22. Recall that in chapter 4 we discussed quantitative evidence on the amount of remittances home to Ireland.

23. Walsh (1970a, p. 152, and table 3) noted the underregistration problem. He makes no reference to the boundaries problem discussed by Coale and Pantelides.

CHAPTER 9
CONCLUSION

1. Malthus (1927, II: p. 12). The omitted passage refers to the necessity of dividing the income among several children.

2. Population data are for census years; sources are Ireland (1993, table 2.1) and Great Britain (1994, table 2.1).

3. Statements documented in Walsh (1972, table 1) and Creton (1991, table 1).

4. The Irish fertility figures pertain to the Republic only, and are the Total Fertility Rate (TFR), which is defined as the number of children born to a hypothetical woman who, as she passed through each age, experienced the age-specific fertility rates currently applying to that age group. TFRs from UN Development Program (1994, table 45). In 1987 about 43 percent of all births in Ireland were to a woman who already had two or more children. The comparable figure for the United Kingdom is 24 percent (Creton 1991, table 1).

5. Sources are Walsh (1970b, table 4) and Ó Gráda and Walsh (1995, pp. 263–279).

6. See Ireland (1993, table 2.8) and Creton (1991, table 1).

7. NESC 1991, p. 43.

8. Source is NESC (1991, table 2.6). Emigration here is the *gross* outflow. Emigrants to Great Britain were probably undercounted in both periods, but more so in the nineteenth century.

9. NESC 1991, table 2.6.

REFERENCES

Akenson, Donald H. 1970. *The Irish Education Experiment: The National System of Education in the Nineteenth Century.* London: Routledge and Kegan Paul.

———. 1985. *Being Had: Historians, Evidence, and the Irish in North America.* Port Credit, Ont.: P. D. Meany.

———. 1988. *Small Differences: Irish Catholics and Irish Protestants, 1815–1922.* Kingston, Ont.: McGill-Queen's University Press.

Alter, George. 1988. *Family and the Female Life Course: The Women of Verviers, Belgium, 1849–1880.* Madison: University of Wisconsin Press.

———. 1992. "Theories of Fertility Decline: A Nonspecialist's Guide to the Current Debate." In John R. Gillis, Louise A. Tilly, and David Levine, eds., *The European Experience of Declining Fertility, 1850–1970.* Cambridge, Mass.: Blackwell Publishers.

Anderson, Michael. 1980. *Approaches to the History of the Western Family, 1500–1914.* London: Macmillan.

———. 1988. *Population Change in North-Western Europe, 1750–1850.* London: Macmillan.

———. 1996. "The Scottish Fertility Decline: Evidence from the 1911 Census of Fertility." Working paper.

Anderson, Michael, and Donald J. Morse. 1993a. "High Fertility, High Emigration, Low Nuptiality: Adjustment Processes in Scotland's Demographic Experience, 1861–1914, Part I." *Population Studies* 47(1): 5–25.

———. 1993b. "High Fertility, High Emigration, Low Nuptiality: Adjustment Processes in Scotland's Demographic Experience, 1861–1914, Part II." *Population Studies* 47(2): 319–343.

Anderson, Robert Andrew. 1983. *With Plunkett in Ireland: The Co-op Organiser's Story.* Dublin: Irish Academic Press. Reprint of 1935 edition.

Arensberg, Conrad. 1968. *The Irish Countryman.* Garden City, N.J.: Natural History Press.

Arensberg, Conrad, and Solon T. Kimball. 1968. *Family and Community in Ireland.* 2nd ed. Cambridge, Mass.: Harvard University Press.

Ariès, Philipe. 1962. *Centuries of Childhood: A Social History of Family Life.* Translated by Robert Baldick. New York: Vintage Books.

———. 1978. "La contraception autrefois." *L'Histoire* 1: 36–44.

Banking Commission. 1926. (Irish Free State). *Banking Commission: Second, Third, and Fourth Interim Reports.* Dublin: Stationery Office.

Banks, J. A. 1965. *Prosperity and Parenthood.* London: Routledge and Kegan Paul.

Beames, M. R. 1987. "Rural Conflict in Pre-Famine Ireland: Peasant Assassinations in Tipperary, 1837–1847. "Reprinted in C.H.E. Philpin, ed., *Nationalism and Population Protest in Ireland.* New York: Cambridge University Press, pp. 264–283. Originally published in 1978.

Bean, Lee, Geraldine P. Mineau, and Douglas L. Anderton. 1990. *Fertility Change on the American Frontier: Adaptation and Innovation*. Berkeley: University of California Press.

Becker, Gary S. 1976. *The Economic Approach to Human Behavior*. Chicago: University of Chicago Press.

————. 1981. *A Treatise on the Family*. Cambridge, Mass.: Harvard University Press.

Beckett, Samuel. 1963. *Murphy*. London: Picador.

Bellettini, Athos. 1981. "Les remariages dans la ville et dans la campagne de Bologne au dix-neuvième siècle." In Jacques Dupâquier, E. Hélin, P. Laslett, M. Livi-Bacci, and S. Sogner, ed., *Marriage and Remarriage in Populations in the Past*. New York: Academic Press, pp. 259–272.

Ben-Porath, Yoram. 1980. "The F-Connection: Families, Friends, and Firms and the Organization of Exchange." *Population and Development Review* 6(1): 1–30.

Berkner, Lutz K. 1972. "The Stem Family and the Developmental Cycle of the Peasant Household: An Eighteenth-Century Austrian Example." *American Historical Review* 77(2): 398–418.

————. 1975. "The Use and Misuse of Census Data for the Historical Analysis of Family Structure." *Journal of Interdisciplinary History* 5(4): 721–738.

————. 1976. "Inheritance, Land Tenure and Peasant Family Structure: A German Regional Comparison." In Jack Goody, Joan Thirsk, and E. P. Thompson, eds., *Family and Inheritance in Rural Western Europe, 1200–1700*. Cambridge: Cambridge University Press, pp. 71–95.

Berkner, Lutz K., and Franklin Mendels. 1978. "Inheritance Systems, Family Structure, and Demographic Patterns in Western Europe, 1700–1900." In Charles Tilly, ed., *Historical Studies in Changing Fertility*. Princeton: Princeton University Press, pp. 209–224.

Bernheim, B. Douglas, Andrei Shleifer, and Lawrence H. Summers. 1985. "The Strategic Bequest Motive." *Journal of Political Economy* 93(6): 1045–76.

Bertillon, Jacques. 1911. *La dépopulation de la France*. Paris: F. Alcan.

Birdwell-Pheasant, Donna. 1992. "The Early Twentieth-Century Irish Stem Family: A Case Study from County Kerry." In Marilyn Silverman and P. H. Gulliver, eds., *Approaching the Past: Historical Anthropology through Irish Case Studies*. New York: Columbia University Press, pp. 205–235.

————. 1993. "Irish Households in the Early Twentieth Century: Culture, Class, and Historical Contingency." *Journal of Family History* 18(1): 19–38.

Birrell, Augustine. 1937. *Things Past Redress*. London: Faber and Faber.

Bittles, A. H., and J. J. McHugh. 1986. "The Irish Famine and Its Sequel: Population Structure Changes in the Ards Peninsula, Co. Down, 1841–1911." *Annals of Human Biology* 13(5): 473–487.

Black, R. D. Collison. 1960. *Economic Thought and the Irish Question, 1817–1870*. Cambridge: Cambridge University Press.

————. 1972. "The Irish Experience in Relation to the Theory and Policy of Economic Development." In A. J. Youngson, ed., *Economic Development in the Long Run*. London: Allen and Unwin.

Blum, Jerome. 1978. *The End of the Old Order in Rural Europe*. Princeton: Princeton University Press.

Blythe, Ronald. 1969. *Akenfield: Portrait of an English Village*. New York: Pantheon.

Bolger, Patrick. 1977. *The Irish Co-operative Movement: Its History and Development*. Dublin: Institute of Public Administration.

Bourgeois-Pichat, Jean. 1987. "The Unprecedented Shortage of Births in Europe." In Kingsley Davis, Mikhail S. Berstam, and Rita Ricardo-Campbell, eds., *Below-Replacement Fertility in Industrialized Societies: Causes, Consequences, Policies*. New York: Population Council, pp. 3–25.

Bourke, Joanna. 1987. "Women and Poultry in Ireland, 1891–1914." *Irish Historical Studies* 25(99) (May): 293–310.

———. 1989. " 'The Health Caravan': Domestic Education and Female Labor in Rural Ireland, 1890–1914." *Eire-Ireland* 24(4): 21–38.

———. 1990. "Dairywomen and Affectionate Wives: Women in the Irish Dairy Industry, 1890–1914." *Agricultural History Review* 38(2): 149–164.

———. 1991. "Working Women: The Domestic Labor Market in Rural Ireland, 1890–1914." *Journal of Interdisciplinary History* 21(3): 479–499.

———. 1993. *Husbandry to Housewifery: Women, Economic Change, and Housework in Ireland, 1890–1914*. New York: Oxford University Press.

Bourke, P. M. Austin. 1965. "The Agricultural Statistics of the 1841 Census of Ireland: A Critical Review." *Economic History Review* 18(2): 376–391.

Boyer, George R. 1989. "Malthus Was Right after All: Poor Relief and Birth Rates in Southeastern England." *Journal of Political Economy* 97(1): 93–114.

Boyer, George R., Timothy J. Hatton and Kevin J. O'Rourke. 1994. "The Impact of Emigration on Real Wages in Ireland, 1850–1914." In Timothy J. Hatton and Jeffrey G. Williamson, eds., *Migration and the International Labour Market, 1850–1939*. London: Routledge, pp. 221–239.

Boyle, Phelim P. and Cormac Ó Gráda. 1986. "Fertility Trends, Excess Mortality, and the Great Irish Famine." *Demography* 23(4): 543–562.

Breen, Richard. 1982. "Farm Size and Marital Status: County and Provincial Differences in Arensberg and Kimball's Ireland." *Economic and Social Review* 13(2): 89–100.

———. 1983. "Farm Servanthood in Ireland, 1900–1940." *Economic History Review*, 2nd ser., 26(1): 87–102.

———. 1984. "Dowry Payments and the Irish Case." *Comparative Studies in Society and History* 26(2): 280–296.

Brettell, Caroline B. 1986. *Men Who Migrate, Women Who Wait: Population and History in a Portuguese Parish*. Princeton: Princeton University Press.

Brody, Hugh. 1973. *Inishkillane: Change and Decline in the West of Ireland*. London: Jill Norman and Hobouse.

Brown, John C., and Timothy W. Guinnane. 1991. "Fertility Decline in Nineteenth-Century Munich: Background, Issues, and Some Preliminary Results." Paper presented at the annual meeting of the Social Science History Association, New Orleans.

Brown, John C., Timothy W. Guinnane, and Marion Lupprian. 1993. "The Munich *Polizeimeldebögen* as a Source for Quantitative History." *Historical Methods* 26(3): 101–118.

Brugger, P. 1936. *Der Anerbe und das Schicksal seiner Geschwister*. Berlin: Verlagsbuchhandlung Paul Parey.

Budd, John W., and Timothy W. Guinnane. 1991. "Intentional Age-Misreporting, Age-Heaping, and the 1908 Old Age Pensions Act in Ireland." *Population Studies* 45(3): 497–518.

Burda, Michael C. 1995. "Migration and the Option Value of Waiting." Center for Economic Policy Research Discussion Paper no. 1229.

Bureau of the Census. 1994. *Statistical Abstract of the United States, 1994*. Washington, D.C.

Caldwell, John. 1982. *Theory of Fertility Decline*. New York: Academic Press.

Canada. 1893. *Second Census of Canada, 1890–91*. vol. 2. Ottawa: S. E. Dawson.

Carbery, Mary. 1937. *The Farm by Lough Gur*. London: Longman, Green and Co.

Carlsson, Gösta. 1969. "The Decline of Fertility: Innovation or Adjustment Process." *Population Studies* 20(2): 149–174.

Carney, Francis J. 1981. "Household Size and Structure in Two Areas of Ireland, 1821 and 1911." In Louis M. Cullen and François Furet, eds., *Ireland and France: Towards a Comparative Rural History*. Paris: Éditions de l'École des Hautes Études en Sciences Sociales, pp. 149–165.

Carr, Edward Hallet. 1961. *What Is History?* New York: Vintage Books.

Chaunu, Pierre. 1988. "Die Verantwortung der Europäer." In Bruno Heck, ed., *Sterben Wir Aus? Bevölkerungsentwicklung in der Bundesrepublik Deutschland*. Freiburg im Bresgau: Herder.

Clark, Samuel. 1979. *Social Origins of the Irish Land War*. Princeton: Princeton University Press.

Clarkson, Leslie. 1985. "Population Change and Urbanization." In Liam Kennedy and P. Ollerenshaw, eds., *An Economic History of Ulster, 1820–1939*. Manchester: Manchester University Press, pp. 137–157.

Clarkson, Leslie. 1996. "Ireland 1841: Pre-industrial or Proto-industrial; Industrializing or De-industrializing?" In Sheilagh C. Ogilvie and Markus Cerman, eds., *European Proto-industrialization*. Cambridge: Cambridge University Press, pp. 67–84.

Clément, Henry. 1910. *La dépopulation en France*. Paris: Bloud.

Coale, Ansley J. 1986. "Demographic Effects of Below-Replacement Fertility and Their Social Implications." In Kingsley Davis, Mikhail S. Bernstam, and Rita Ricardo-Campbell, eds. *Below-Replacement Fertility in Industrialized Societies: Causes, Consequences, Policies*. New York: Population Council, pp. 203–216.

———. 1991. "Excess Female Mortality and the Balance of the Sexes in the Population: An Estimate of the Number of 'Missing Females.'" *Population and Development Review* 17(3): 517–524.

Coale, Ansley J., and Roy Treadway. 1986. "A Summary of the Changing Distribution of Overall Fertility, Marital Fertility, and the Proportion Married in the

Provinces of Europe." In Ansley J. Coale and Susan Cotts Watkins, eds., *The Decline of Fertility in Europe: The Revised Proceedings of a Conference on the Princeton European Fertility Project.* Princeton: Princeton University Press, pp. 31–181.

Coale, Ansley J., and Susan Cotts Watkins, eds. 1986. *The Decline of Fertility in Europe.* Princeton: Princeton University Press.

Cole, J. W., and Wolf, E. R. 1974. *The Hidden Frontier: Ecology and Ethnicity in an Alpine Valley.* New York: Academic Press.

Commission on Emigration and Other Population Problems. 1954. *Reports.* Dublin: Stationery Office.

Connell, Kenneth H. 1950. *The Population of Ireland, 1750–1845.* Oxford: Clarendon Press.

———. 1957. "Peasant Marriage in Ireland after the Great Famine." *Past and Present* 12: 76–91.

———. 1958. "The Land Legislation and Irish Social Life." *Economic History Review*, 2nd. ser., 11(1): 1–7.

———. 1962a. "Peasant Marriage in Ireland: Its Structure and Development since the Famine." *Economic History Review*, 2nd. ser., 14(3): 502–523.

———. 1962b. "The Potato in Ireland." *Past and Present* 13: 57–71.

———. 1968. "Catholicism and Marriage in the Century after the Famine." In Connell, *Irish Peasant Society: Four Historical Essays.* Oxford: Clarendon Press, pp. 113–161.

Connolly, Sean J. 1979. "Illegitimacy and Pre-Nuptial Pregnancy in Ireland before 1864: The Evidence of Some Catholic Parish Registers." *Irish Economic and Social History* 6: 5–23.

———. 1982. *Priests and People in Pre-Famine Ireland, 1780–1845.* New York: St. Martin's Press.

———. 1985. *Religion and Society in Nineteenth-Century Ireland.* Studies in Irish Economic and Social History, no. 3. Dundalk: Economic and Social History Society of Ireland.

———. 1992. *Religion, Law, and Power: The Making of Protestant Ireland, 1660–1760.* Oxford: Clarendon Press.

Cousens, S. H. 1961. "Emigration and Demographic Change in Ireland, 1851–1861." *Economic History Review*, 2nd ser., 14(4): 275–288.

———. 1964. "The Regional Variations in Population Changes in Ireland, 1861–1881." *Economic History Review*, 2nd ser., 17(2): 301–321.

Crafts, Nicholas F. R. 1985. *British Economic Growth during the Industrial Revolution.* New York: Oxford University Press.

———. 1989. "Duration of Marriage, Fertility, and Women's Employment Opportunities in England and Wales in 1911." *Population Studies* 43: 325–335.

Crawford, E. M. 1984. "Dearth, Diet, and Disease in Ireland: A Case Study of Nutritional Deficiency." *Medical History* 28(20): 151–161.

Creton, Dominique. 1991. "Fertility Changes and the Irish Family." *Geography* 76(2): 154–157.

Crotty, Raymond. 1966. *Irish Agricultural Production: Its Volume and Structure.* Cork: Cork University Press.

Cuddy, Michael, and Chris Curtin. 1983. "Commercialisation in West of Ireland Agriculture in the 1890s." *Economic and Social Review* 14(3): 173–184.

Cullen, Louis M. 1968. "Irish History without the Potato." *Past and Present* 40: 72–83.

———. 1972. *An Economic History of Ireland since 1660.* London: Batsford.

———. 1981. *The Emergence of Modern Ireland, 1600–1900.* London: Batsford Academic and Educational.

———. 1989. *Eason & Son: A History.* Dublin: Eason & Son Ltd.

Cullen, Louis M., and François Furet. 1981. *Ireland and France: Towards a Comparative Rural History.* Paris: Editions de l'École des Hautes Études en Sciences Sociales.

Cullen, Louis M., and T. C. Smout. 1977. *Comparative Aspects of Scottish and Irish Economic and Social History, 1600–1900.* Edinburgh: Donald.

Curtis, L. P. 1980. "Incumbered Wealth: Landed Indebtedness in Post-Famine Ireland." *American Historical Review* 85(2): 332–367.

Daly, Mary E. 1981. "Late Nineteenth and Early Twentieth Century Dublin." In David Harkness and Mary O'Dowd, eds., *The Town in Ireland.* Belfast: Appletree Press, pp. 221–252.

———. 1982. "Social Structure of the Dublin Working Class, 1871–1911." *Irish Historical Studies* 23(90): 121–133.

———. 1984. *Dublin: The Deposed Capital—A Social and Economic History, 1860–1914.* Cork: Cork University Press.

Danzer, Paul. 1943. *Geburtenkrieg.* 4th ed. Berlin: J. F. Lehmanns Verlag.

Daultrey, Stuart, David Dickson, and Cormac Ó Gráda. 1981. "Eighteenth-Century Irish Population: New Perspectives from Old Sources." *Journal of Economic History* 41(3): 601–628.

David, Paul A., and Thomas A. Mroz. 1989. "Evidence of Fertility Regulation among Rural French Villagers, 1749–1789: A Sequential Econometrics Model of Birth-Spacing Behavior (Part 2)." *European Journal of Population* 5(2): 173–206.

David, Paul, Thomas Mroz, Warren Sanderson, Kenneth Wachter, and David Weir. 1988. "Cohort Parity Analysis: Statistical Estimates of the Extent of Fertility Control." *Demography* 25(2): 163–188.

David, Paul A., and Warren S. Sanderson. 1986. "Rudimentary Contraceptive Methods and the American Transition to Marital Fertility Control, 1855–1915." In Stanley L. Engerman and Robert E. Gallman, eds., *Long-Term Factors in American Economic Growth.* Chicago: University of Chicago Press, pp. 307–390.

———. 1987. "The Emergence of a Two-Child Norm among American Birth-Controllers." *Population and Development Review* 13(1): 1–41.

———. 1988. "Measuring Marital Fertility Control with CPA." *Population Index* 54(Winter): 691–731.

———. 1990. "Cohort Parity Analysis and Fertility Transition Dynamics: Reconstructing Historical Trends in Fertility Control from a Single Census." *Population Studies* 44(3): 421–445.

Davis, Kingsley. 1963. "The Theory of Change and Response in Modern Demographic History." *Population Index* 29(4): 345–366.

———. 1985. "The Future of Marriage." In Kinglsey Davis, ed., *Contemporary Marriage*. New York: Russell Sage Foundation, pp. 25–52.

Demos, John. 1970. *A Little Commonwealth: Family Life in Plymouth Colony*. New York: Oxford University Press.

———. 1986. "The Rise and Fall of Adolescence." In Demos, *Past, Present, and Personal: The Family and the Life Course in American History*. New York: Oxford University Press.

De Vries, Jan. 1994. "The Industrial Revolution and the Industrious Revolution." *Journal of Economic History* 54(2): 249–270.

De Waal, Alexander. 1989. *Famine That Kills: Darfur, Sudan, 1984–1985*. New York: Oxford University Press.

Dickler, Robert A. 1975. "Organization and Change in Productivity in Eastern Prussia." In W. N. Parker and E. L. Jones, eds., *European Peasants and Their Markets: Essays in Agrarian Economic History*. Princeton: Princeton University Press, pp. 269–262.

Dillingham Commission. *See* United State Immigration Commission.

Dillwitz, Sigrid. 1973. "Die Struktur der Bauernschaft von 1871 bis 1914: Dargestellt auf der Grundiage der deutschen Reichsstatistik." *Jahrbuch für Geschichte* 9: 47–128.

Diner, Hasia R. 1983. *Erin's Daughters in America: Irish Immigrant Women in the Nineteenth Century*. Baltimore: Johns Hopkins University Press.

Dixon, Ruth. 1971. "Explaining Cross-Cultural Variations in Age at Marriage and Proportions Never-Marrying." *Population Studies* 25(2): 215–233.

———. 1978. "Late Marriage and Non-Marriage as Demographic Responses: Are They Similar?" *Population Studies* 32(3): 449–466.

Donnelly, James S. 1975. *The Land and the People of Nineteenth-Century Cork: The Rural Economy and the Land Question*. London: Routledge and Kegan Paul.

Dowling, Martin W. 1997. *Tenant Right and Agrarian Society in Ulster 1600–1870*. Dublin: Irish Academic Press.

Drake, Michael. 1963. "Marriage and Population Growth in Ireland, 1750–1845." *Economic History Review* 16(2): 301–313.

Dubos, René, and Dubos, Jean. 1987. *The White Plague: Tuberculosis, Man, and Society*. New Brunswick, N.J.: Rutgers University Press. Reprint of 1952 edition.

Dumont, Arsène. 1990. *Depopulation et civilisation: étude démographique*. Paris. Reprint of 1890 edition.

Dupâquier, Jacques. 1981. "Les Aventures démographiques de la France et de l'Irlande." In Louis M. Cullen and François Furet, eds., *Ireland and France: Towards a Comparative Rural History*. Paris: Editions de l'École des Hautes Études en Sciences Sociales, pp. 167–180.

Dyrvik, Stale. 1981. "Gagne-pain ou sentiments? Trait du remairiage en Norvège au dix-neuvième siècle." In Jacques Dupâquier, E. Hélin, P. Laslett, M. Livi-Bacci, and S. Sogner, eds., *Marriage and Remarriage in Populations in the Past*. New York: Academic Press, pp. 297–306.

Eckberg, Douglas Lee. 1995. "Estimates of Early Twentieth Century U.S.

Homicide Rates: An Econometric Forecasting Approach." *Demography* 32(1): 1–16.

Ehmer, Josef. 1991. *Heiratsverhalten, Sozialstruktur, ökonomischer Wandel: England und Mitteleuropa in der Formationsperiode des Kapitalismus.* Kritische Studien zur Geschichtswissenschaft 92. Göttingen: Vandenhoeck & Ruprecht.

Engerman, Stanley. 1978. "Economic Perspectives on the Life Course." In Tamara K. Hareven, ed., *Transitions: The Family and the Life Course in Historical Perspective.* New York: Academic Press, pp. 271–286.

Erickson, Charlotte. 1989. "Emigration from the British Isles to the USA in 1841: Part I. Emigration from the British Isles." *Population Studies* 43(3): 347–367.

Eversley, David. 1981. "The Demography of the Irish Quakers, 1650–1850." In J. M. Goldstrom and L. A. Clarkson, eds., *Irish Population, Economy, and Society: Essays in Honour of the Late K. H. Connell.* Oxford: Clarendon Press, pp. 57–58.

Fahey, Tony. 1992. "State, Family, and Compulsory Schooling in Ireland." *Economic and Social Review* 23(4): 369–395.

Farley, Desmond. 1964. *Social Insurance and Social Assistance in Ireland.* Dublin: Institute of Public Administration.

Fauve-Chamoux, Antoinette. 1985. "Vieillesse et Famille-Souche." *Annales de Démographie Historique,* 111–125.

———. 1987. "Vieillesse et Famille-Souche." *Annales de Démographie Historique,* 242–262.

Ferenczi, I., and W. F. Wilcox. 1929. *International Migrations.* Vol. 1: *Statistics.* New York: National Bureau of Economic Research.

Ferrie, Joseph P. 1994. "The Wealth Accumulation of Antebellum European Immigrants to the U.S., 1840–1860." *Journal of Economic History* 54(1): 1–33.

Fischer, David Hackett. 1978. *Growing Old in America.* New York: Oxford University Press.

Fitzpatrick, David. 1980. "The Disappearance of the Irish Agricultural Labourer, 1841–1912." *Irish Economic and Social History* 7: 66–92.

———. 1982. "Class, Family, and Rural Unrest in Nineteenth-Century Ireland." In P. J. Drudy, ed., *Irish Studies,* vol. 2. Cambridge: Cambridge University Press.

———. 1983. "Irish Farming Families before the First World War." *Comparative Studies in Society and History* 25(2): 339–374.

———. 1984. *Irish Emigration, 1801–1921.* Studies in Irish Economic and Social History, no. 1. Dundalk: Economic and Social History Society of Ireland.

———. 1985. "Marriage in Post-Famine Ireland." In Art Cosgrove, ed., *Marriage in Ireland.* Dublin: College Press, pp. 116–131.

———. 1986. " 'A Share of the Honeycomb': Education, Emigration, and Irishwomen." *Continuity and Change* 1(2): 217–234.

———. 1987a. "Divorce and Separation in Modern Irish History." *Past and Present* 114: 172–196.

———. 1987b. "The Modernization of the Irish Female." In Patrick O'Flanagan, Paul Ferguson, and Kevin Whelan, eds., *Rural Ireland, 1600–1900: Modernization and Change*. Cork: Cork University Press, pp. 162–180.

———. 1989a. " 'A Peculiar Tramping People': The Irish in Britain, 1801–70." In W. E. Vaughan, ed., *A New History of Ireland*. Vol. 5: *Ireland under the Union, I, 1801–1870*. Oxford: Clarendon Press, pp. 623–660.

———. 1989b. "A Curious Middle Place: The Irish in Britain, 1871–1921." In Roger Swift and Sheridan Gilley, eds., *The Irish in Britain, 1815–1939*. London: Pinter Publishers, pp. 10–59.

———. 1989c. "Emigration, 1801–1870." In W. E. Vaughan, ed., *A New History of Ireland*. Vol. 5: *Ireland under the Union, I, 1801–1870*. Oxford: Clarendon Press, pp. 562–619.

———. 1990. "Was Ireland Special? Recent Writing on the Irish Economy and Society in the Nineteenth Century." *Historical Journal* 33(1): 169–176.

———.1994. *Oceans of Consolation: Personal Accounts of Irish Migration to Australia*. Ithaca: Cornell University Press.

Flandrin, Jean-Louis. 1979. *Families in Former Times: Kinship, Household, and Sexuality*. Translated by Richard Southern. Cambridge: Cambridge University Press.

Flinn, Michael, ed. 1977. *Scottish Population History: From the Seventeenth Century to the 1930s*. Cambridge: Cambridge University Press.

Flinn, Michael. 1981. *The European Demographic System, 1500–1820*. Baltimore: Johns Hopkins University Press.

Foster, R. F. 1989. *Modern Ireland, 1600–1972*. New York: Viking Penguin.

Francome, Colin. 1992. "Irish Women Who Seek Abortions in England." *Family Planning Perspectives* 6: 265–268.

Freedman, Alfred M., Harold J. Kaplan, and Benjamin J. Sadock. 1976. *Modern Synopsis of Comprehensive Textbook of Psychiatry, II*. 2nd ed. Baltimore: Williams and Wilkins.

Friedlander, Dov. 1969. "Demographic Response and Population Change." *Demography* 6(4): 359–381.

Galenson, David. 1987. "Economic Determinants of the Age at Leaving Home: Evidence from the Lives of Nineteenth-Century New England Manufacturers." *Social Science History* 11(4): 355–378.

Gaunt, David. 1983. "The Property and Kin Relationships of Retired Farmers in Northern and Central Europe." In Richard Wall, Jean Robin, and Peter Laslett, eds., *Family Forms in Historic Europe*. Cambridge: Cambridge University Press, pp. 249–280.

Gibbon, P., and C. Curtin. 1978. "The Stem Family in Ireland." *Comparative Studies in Society and History* 20(3): 429–453.

Gjerde, Jon. 1985. *From Peasants to Farmers: The Migration from Balestrand, Norway, to the Upper Middle West*. New York: Cambridge University Press.

Goldman, Noreen, Charles F. Westoff, and Charles Hammerslough. 1984. "Demography of the Marriage Market in the United States." *Population Index* 50(1): 5–25.

Goldschmidt, Walter, and E. J. Kunkel. 1971. "The Structure of the Peasant Family." *American Anthropologist* 73(5): 1058–76.

Goldstrom, J. M. and L. A. Clarkson, eds. 1981. *Irish Population, Economy, and Society: Essays in Honour of the Late K. H. Connell*. Oxford: Clarendon Press.

Gould, J. D. 1980. "European Inter-Continental Emigration: The Road Home—Return Migration from the USA" *Journal of European Economic History* 9(1): 41–112.

Great Britain. 1836. "Third Report of the Commissioners for Inquiring into the Condition of the Poorer Classes in Ireland." House of Commons Sessional Papers, vol. 30.

———. 1870a. "Reports from Poor Law Inspectors in Ireland as to the Existing Relations between Landlord and Tenant in Respect of Improvements on Farms." House of Commons Sessional Papers, vol. 14.

———. 1870b. "Returns Showing the Number of Agricultural Holdings in Ireland, and the Tenure by Which They Are Held by the Occupiers." House of Commons Sessional Papers, vol. 56.

———. 1873. "Seventh Annual Report of the Registrar-General of Marriages, Births, and Deaths in Ireland. 1870." House of Commons Sessional Papers, vol. 20.

———. 1890. "27th Detailed Annual Report of the Registrar-General (Ireland) (1890)." House of Commons Sessional Papers, vol. 23.

———. 1892. "Return Relating to In-Door and Out-Door Relief in Ireland." House of Commons Sessional Papers, vol. 68.

———. 1895. "Royal Commission on the Financial Relations between Great Britain and Ireland. Report." House of Commons Sessional Papers, vol. 36.

———. 1896. "Royal Commission on the Financial Relations between Great Britain and Ireland. Final Report with Evidence and Appendices." House of Commons Sessional Papers, vol. 33.

———. 1897. "Report from the Select Committee on Money Lending." House of Commons Sessional Papers, vol. 11.

———. 1898a. "Report of the Select Committee on Money Lending." House of Commons Sessional Papers, vol. 10.

———. 1898b. Committee on Old Age Pensions. "Report." House of Commons Sessional Papers, vol. 45.

———. 1900. "Report of the Departmental Committee Appointed to Report on the Financial Aspects of the Proposals made by the Select Committee of the House of Commons of 1899 about the Aged Deserving Poor." House of Commons Sessional Papers, vol. 10.

———. 1901. "Tenth Report of the Congested Districts Board for Ireland." House of Commons Sessional Papers, vol. 60.

———. 1903a. "Bill to Amend the Law Relating to the Occupation and Ownership of Land in Ireland and for Other Purposes Relating Thereto, and to Amend the Labourers (Ireland) Acts." House of Commons Sessional Papers, vol. 2.

———. 1903b. "Report of Mr. W. R. Baley, Legal Assistant Commissioner, an Inquiry into the Present Conditions of Tenant Purchasers under the Land Purchase Acts." House of Commons Sessional Papers, vol. 57.

———. 1903c. "Emigration Statistics of Ireland, 1902." House of Commons Sessional Papers, vol. 82.

————. 1905. "Second Report of Mr. Wilson Fox on the Wages, Earnings, and Conditions of Employment of Agricultural Labourers in the United Kingdom." House of Commons Sessional Papers, vol. 97.

————. 1908a. "A Bill to Provide for Old Age Pensions." (As amended on Re-Committal.) 8 Edward 7. House of Commons Sessional Papers, vol. 3.

————. 1908b. "Royal Commission on Congestion in Ireland. Seventh Report (with Appendices and Evidence)." House of Commons Sessional Papers, vol. 40.

————. 1909a. "Savings Banks (Ireland). Return." House of Commons Sessional Papers, Vol. 79.

————. 1909b. "Statistical Memoranda on Public Health and Social Conditions." House of Commons Sessional Papers, vol. 111.

————. 1910. "Estimated Irish Contribution to the True Revenue of the Year 1909–1910 in Respect of New and Additional Taxation Imposed by the Finance (1909–10) Act, 1910." House of Commons Sessional Papers, vol. 59.

————. 1911a. "A Bill to Amend the Old Age Pensions Act, 1908." 1 George 5. House of Commons Sessional Papers, vol. 4.

————. 1911b. "47th Detailed Annual Report of the Registrar-General (Ireland) (1911)." House of Commons Sessional Papers, vol. 11.

————. 1911c. Registrar's statistics for 1910.

————. 1911d. "Emigration Statistics, Ireland. 1910." House of Commons Sessional Papers, vol. 60.

————. 1911e. "Seventeenth Abstract of Labour Statistics (1915)." House of Commons Sessional Papers, vol. 61.

————. 1913a. Commissioners of His Majesty's Customs and Excise. "Report for the Year Ended 31st March, 1913." House of Commons Sessional Papers, vol. 19.

————. 1913b. "Return as to the Old Age Pensions in Ireland . . ." House of Commons Sessional Papers, vol. 41.

————. 1913c. "Memorandum on the Estimated True Irish Contribution to the Revenue of the Year 1912–13 in Respect of New and Additional Taxation Imposed by the Finance (1909–1910) Act, 1910." House of Commons Sessional Papers, vol. 41.

————. 1913d. "Irish Land Purchase Acts. Return." House of Commons Sessional Papers, vol. 53.

————. 1913e. "Old Age Pensioners and Aged Pauperism." House of Commons Sessional Papers, vol. 55.

————. 1913f. "Savings Banks (Ireland). Return." House of Commons Sessional Papers, vol. 272.

————. 1914a. "Report of the Departmental Committee on Agricultural Credit." House of Commons Sessional Papers, vol. 13.

————. 1914b. "Seventeenth Abstract of Labour Statistics (1915)." House of Commons Sessional Papers, vol. 61.

————. 1919. Departmental Committee on Old Age Pensions. "Report." House of Commons Sessional Papers, vol. 27.

————. 1920a. "Report of the Estates Commissioners." House of Commons Sessional Papers, vol. 20.

Great Britain. 1920b. "Report of the Irish Land Commissioners." House of Commons Sessional Papers, vol. 20.

——. 1920c. "Twenty-Seventh Report of the Congested Districts Board for Ireland." House of Commons Sessional Papers, vol. 20.

——. 1994. *Annual Abstract of Statistics, 1994.* Central Statistics Office, London.

Gregory, Ian. 1968. *Fundamentals of Psychiatry.* Philadelphia: Saunders.

Grigg, D. B. 1980. *Population Growth and Agrarian Change: An Historical Perspective.* Cambridge: Cambridge University Press.

Guinnane, Timothy W. 1987. "Migration, Marriage, and Household Formation: The Irish at the Turn of the Century." Ph.D. dissertation, Department of Economics, Stanford University.

——. 1991a. "Land and Credit in Late-Nineteenth Century Ireland." Paper presented to the 1991 annual meetings of the Economic History Association, Montreal, Canada.

——. 1991b. "Economics, History, and the Path of Demographic Adjustment: Ireland after the Famine." *Research in Economic History* 13: 147–198.

——. 1992a. "Age at Leaving Home in Rural Ireland, 1901–1911." *Journal of Economic History* 52(3): 651–674.

——. 1992b. "Intergenerational Transfers, Inheritance, and the Rural Irish Household System." *Explorations in Economic History* 29(4): 456–476.

——. 1993. "The Poor Law and Pensions in Ireland." *Journal of Interdisciplinary History* 34(2): 271–291.

——. 1994a. "A Failed Institutional Transplant: Raiffeisen's Credit Co-operatives in Ireland, 1894–1914." *Explorations in Economic History* 31(1): 38–61.

——. 1994b. "The Great Irish Famine and Population: The Long View." *American Economic Review Papers and Proceedings* 84(2): 303–308.

Guinnane, Timothy W. and Myron P. Gutmann. 1992. "Leaving Home in Nineteenth-Century Texas." Paper presented to the 1992 annual meetings of the Social Science History Association.

Guinnane, Timothy W., and Ronald I. Miller. 1996. "Bonds without Bondsmen: Tenant-Right in Nineteenth-Century Ireland." *Journal of Economic History* 56(1): 113–142.

——. 1997. "The Limits to Land Reform: The Land Acts in Ireland, 1870–1909." *Economic Development and Cultural Change,* forthcoming.

Guinnane, Timothy W., Barbara S. Okun, and James Trussell. 1994. "What Do We Know about the Timing of Fertility Transitions in Europe?" *Demography* 31(1): 1–20.

Guinnane, Timothy W., and Mark Rouse-Foley. 1994. "Did Irish Marriage Patterns Survive the Emigrant Voyage?" Working paper.

Habakkuk, H. J. 1955. "Family Structure and Economic Change in Nineteenth-Century Europe." *Journal of Economic History* 15(1): 1–12.

Haines, Michael. 1992. "Occupation and Social Class during Fertility Decline: Historical Perspectives." In John R. Gillis, Louise A. Tilly, and David Levine, eds., *The European Experience of Declining Fertility, 1850–1970.* Cambridge, Mass.: Blackwell Publishers, pp. 193–226.

Haire, David N. 1980. "In Aid of the Civil Power, 1868–90." In F.S.L. Lyons and R.A.J. Hawkins, eds., *Ireland under the Union: Varieties of Tension— Essays in Honor of T. W. Moody.* Oxford: Clarendon Press, pp. 115–147.

Hajnal, John. 1953. "Age at Marriage and Proportions Marrying." *Population Studies* 7(2): 111–136.

———. 1965. "European Marriage Patterns in Perspective." In D. V. Glass and D.E.C. Eversley, eds., *Population in History: Essays in Historical Demography.* London: E. Arnold, pp. 101–148.

———. 1982. "Two Kinds of Preindustrial Household Formation System." *Population and Development Review* 8(3): 449–494.

Hammel, Eugene A. 1972. "The *Zadruga* as Process." In Peter Laslett and Richard Wall, eds., *Household and Family in Past Time.* Cambridge: Cambridge University Press.

———. 1990. "A Theory of Culture for Demography." *Population and Development Review* 16(3): 455–486.

Hammel, Eugene A., and Laslett, Peter. 1974. "Comparing Household Structure over Time and between Cultures." *Comparative Studies in Society and History* 16(1): 73–109.

Handley, James E. 1945. *The Irish in Scotland, 1798–1845.* Cork: Cork University Press.

———. 1947. *The Irish in Modern Scotland.* Cork: Cork University Press.

Hannan, Damian F. 1979. *Displacement and Development: Class, Kinship, and Social Change in Irish Rural Communities.* Economic and Social Research Institute Paper no. 96. Dublin: Economic and Social Research Institute.

Harris, Ruth-Ann M. 1994. *The Nearest Place That Wasn't Ireland: Early Nineteenth-Century Irish Labor Migration.* Ames: Iowa State University Press.

Hatton, Timothy J. and Jeffrey G. Williamson. 1993. "After the Famine: Emigration from Ireland, 1850–1913." *Journal of Economic History* 53(3): 575–600.

———. 1994. "What Drove the Mass Migrations from Europe in the Late Nineteenth Century?" *Population and Development Review* 20(3): 533–560.

Hayes, John M. 1953. "Stemming Flight from the Land." In John A. O'Brien, ed., *The Vanishing Irish: The Enigma of the Modern World.* New York: McGraw-Hill, pp. 133–148.

Hearn, Mona. 1989. "Life for Domestic Servants in Dublin, 1880–1920." In Maria Luddy and Cliona Murphy, eds., *Women Surviving: Studies in Irish Women's History in the Nineteenth and Twentieth Centuries.* Dublin: Poolbeg Press, pp. 148–179.

Heer, David M. 1961. "The Marital Status of Second Generation Americans." *American Sociological Review* 26(2): 233–241.

Held, Thomas. 1982. "Rural Retirement Arrangements in Seventeenth- to Nineteenth-Century Austria: A Cross-Community Analysis." *Journal of Family History* 7(3): 227–254.

Helmut, Otto. 1939. *Volk in Gefahr: Der Geburtenrückgang und seine Folgen für Deutschlands Zukunft.* Berlin: J. F. Lehmanns Verlag.

Hempton, David, and Myrtle Hill. 1992. *Evangelical Protestantism in Ulster Society, 1740–1890.* London: Routledge.

Henry, Louis. 1961. "Some Data on Natural Fertility." *Eugenics Quarterly* 8(1): 81–91.

———. 1966. "Perturbations de la nuptialité résultant de la guerre 1914–18." *Population* 21(2): 273–332.

Himes, Norman E. 1963. *A Medical History of Contraception.* New York: Gamut Press.

Hoare, H. J. 1915. *Old Age Pensions: Their Actual Working and Ascertained Results in the United Kingdom.* London: P. S. King and Son.

Hoffman, Elizabeth, and Joel Mokyr. 1983. "Peasant, Poverty, and Potatoes: Transactions Costs in Pre-Famine Ireland." In Gary Saxonhouse and Gavin Wright, eds., *Technique, Spirit, and Form in the Making of the Modern Economy: Essays in Honor of William N. Parker.* Greenwich, Conn.: Greenwood Press, pp. 115–145.

Honahan, W. A. 1960. "The Population of Ireland." *Journal of the Institute of Actuaries* 86(1): 30–49.

Hooker, Elizabeth R. 1938. *Readjustments of Agricultural Tenure in Ireland.* Chapel Hill: University of North Carolina Press.

Hoppen, K. Theodore. 1989. *Ireland since 1800: Conflict and Conformity.* London: Longman.

———. 1991. "Landownership and Power in Nineteenth-Century Ireland: The Decline of an Elite." In Ralph Gibson and Martin Blinkhorn, eds., *Landownership and Power in Modern Europe.* New York: Harper Collins Academic, pp. 164–180.

Horvath, Robert A. 1981. "Le développement des remariages en Hongrie de 1890 à 1977." In Jacques Dupâquier, E. Hélin, P. Laslett, M. Livi-Bacci, and S. Sogner, eds., *Marriage and Remarriage in Populations in the Past.* New York: Academic Press, pp. 325–334.

Houston, R. A. 1992. *The Population History of Britain and Ireland, 1500–1750.* London: Macmillan.

Hoy, Suellen. 1995. "The Journey Out: The Recruitment and Emigration of Irish Religious Women to the United States, 1812–1914." *Journal of Women's History* 7(1): 64–98.

Huttman, John P. 1972. "The Impact of Land Reform on Agricultural Production in Ireland." *Agricultural History* 46 (3): 353–368.

Imhof, Arthur E. 1990. *Lebenserwartungen in Deutschland vom 17. Bis 19. Jahrhundert.* Weinheim: VCH, Acta humaniora.

Ireland. 1993. *Ireland: Statistical Abstract.* Dublin: Central Statistics Office.

Irish Free State. 1926. *Census of the Irish Free State* Dublin: Stationery Office.

———. 1928. *Agricultural Statistics, 1847–1926.* Dublin: Department of Industry and Commerce.

———. 1931. Central Statistics Office. *Statistical Abstract of Ireland.* Dublin.

Jackson, Pauline. 1984. "Women in Nineteenth Century Irish Emigration." *International Migration Review* xviii(4): 1004–1020.

Janssens, Angelique. 1993. *Family and Social Change: The Household as a Process in a Community.* Cambridge: Cambridge University Press.

Johnson, David S., and Liam Kennedy. 1991. "Nationalist Historiography and the Decline of the Irish Economy: George O'Brien Revisited." In Seán Hutton and Paul Stewart, eds., *Ireland's Histories: Aspects of State, Society, and Ideology*. New York: Routledge, pp. 11–35.

Johnson, James H. 1967. "Harvest Migration from Nineteenth-Century Ireland." *Transactions of the Institute of British Geographers* 41: 97–112.

Johnson, James H. 1990. "The Context of Migration: The Example of Ireland in the Nineteenth Century." *Transactions of the Institute of British Geographers*, 15: 259–276.

Johnson, Paul. 1985. *Saving and Spending: The Working-Class Economy in Britain, 1870–1939*. Oxford: Clarendon Press.

Jordan, Donald E., Jr. 1994. *Land and Popular Politics in Ireland: County Mayo from the Plantation to the Land War*. New York: Cambridge University Press.

Joyce, James. 1986. *Ulysses*. Gabler edition. New York: Vintage Books.

Kaplan, Harold I and Benjamin Sadock, eds. 1995. *Comprehensive Textbook of Psychiatry*. 6th ed., vol. 1. Baltimore: Williams & Wilkins.

Katz, Michael B. 1983. *Poverty and Policy in American History*. New York: Academic Press.

Kavanagh, Patrick. 1939. *The Green Fool*. New York: Harper and Brothers.

———. 1948. *Tarry Flynn*. London: Pilot Press.

———. 1992. *Collected Poems*. Manchester: Carcanet Press.

Keating, Mary Frances. "Marriage-shy Irishmen." In John A. O'Brien, ed., *The Vanishing Irish: The Enigma of the Modern World*. New York: McGraw-Hill, pp. 170–182.

Keep, G.R.C. 1955. "Some Irish Opinion on Population and Emigration, 1851–1901." *Irish Ecclesiastical Record*, 5th ser., 84: 377–386.

Kelly, Richard. J. 1908. *Old Age Pensions Act, 1908*. Dublin: Sealy, Bryers, and Walker.

Kennedy, Liam. 1977. "A Sceptical View on the Reincarnation of the Irish 'Gombeenman.'" *Economic and Social Review* 8(3): 213–222.

———. 1978. "The Early Response of the Irish Catholic Clergy to the Co-operative Movement." *Irish Historical Studies* 21: 55–74.

———. 1979. "Traders in the Irish Rural Economy, 1880–1914." *Economic History Review* 32(2): 201–210.

———. 1981. "Regional Specialization, Railway Development, and Irish Agriculture in the Nineteenth Century." In J. M. Goldstrom and L. A. Clarkson, eds., *Irish Population, Economy, and Society: Essays in Honour of the Late K. H. Connell*. Oxford: Clarendon Press, pp. 173–193.

———. 1984. "Why One Million Starved: An Open Verdict." *Irish Economic and Social History* 11: 101–106.

———. 1991. "Farm Succession in Modern Ireland: Elements of a Theory of Inheritance." *Economic History Review*, 2nd ser., 44(3): 477–499.

Kennedy, R. E. 1973. *The Irish: Emigration, Marriage, and Fertility*. Berkeley: University of California Press.

Kerr, Donal A. 1982. *Peel, Priests, and Politics: Sir Robert Peel's Administration and the Roman Catholic Church in Ireland, 1841–1846*. Oxford: Clarendon Press.

Kimhi, Ayal. 1994. "Optimal Timing of Farmstead Transferal from Parent to Child." *American Journal of Agricultural Economics* 76(2): 228–236.

Kinealy, Christine. 1989. "The Poor Law during the Great Famine: An Administration in Crisis." In E. Margaret Crawford, ed., *Famine: The Irish Experience, 900–1900—Subsistence Crises and Famines in Ireland*. Edinburgh: John Donald, pp. 157–175.

King, Miriam, and Steven Ruggles. 1990. "American Immigration, Fertility, and Race Suicide at the Turn of the Century." *Journal of Interdisciplinary History* 20(3): 347–369.

Knodel, John. 1974. *The Decline of Fertility in Germany, 1871–1939*. Princeton: Princeton University Press.

———. 1986. "Demographic Transitions in German Villages." In Ansley J. Coale and Susan Cotts Watkins, eds., *The Decline of Fertility in Europe*. Princeton: Princeton University Press, pp. 337–389.

———. 1988. *Demographic Behavior in the Past: a Study of Fourteen German Village Populations in the Eighteenth and Nineteenth Centuries*. New York: Cambridge University Press.

Knodel, John, and Mary Jo Maynes. 1976. "Urban and Rural Marriage Patterns in Imperial Germany." *Journal of Family History* 1(2): 129–168.

Knodel, John, and Etienne van de Walle. 1986. "Lessons from the Past: Policy Implications of Historical Fertility Studies." In Ansley J. Coale and Susan Cotts Watkins, eds., *The Decline of Fertility in Europe*. Princeton: Princeton University Press, pp. 390–419.

Komlos, John. 1989. "The Age at Menarche in Vienna: The Relationship between Nutrition and Fertility." *Historical Methods* 22(4): 158–163.

Kotlikoff, Lawrence J. 1988. "Intergenerational Transfers and Savings." *Journal of Economic Perspectives* 2(2): 41–58.

Kussmaul, Ann. 1981. *Servants in Husbandry in Early Modern England*. New York: Cambridge University Press.

Lane, Roger. 1979. *Violent Death in the City: Suicide, Accident, and Murder in Nineteenth-Century Philadelphia*. Cambridge, Mass.: Harvard University Press.

Larkin, Emmet. 1972. "The Devotional Revolution in Ireland, 1850–1870." *American Historical Review* 77(3): 625–652.

Laslett, Peter. 1972. "Introduction: The History of the Family." In Peter Laslett and Richard Wall, eds., *Household and Family in Past Time*. Cambridge: Cambridge University Press, pp. 1–90.

———. 1977. *Family Life and Illicit Love in Earlier Generations: Essays in Historical Sociology*. Cambridge: Cambridge University Press.

———. 1984. *The World We Have Lost: England before the Industrial Age*. 3rd ed. London: Methuen.

Laumann, Edward O., John H. Gagnon, Robert T. Michael, and Stuart Michaels. 1994. *The Social Organization of Sexuality: Sexual Practices in the United States*. Chicago: University of Chicago Press.

Le Bras, Hervé. 1991. *Marianne et les lapins: L'obsession démographique*. Paris: Olivier Orban.

Lee, Joseph. 1973a. *The Modernization of Irish Society, 1848–1918*. Dublin: Gill and Macmillan.

————. 1973b. "The Ribbonmen." In T. Desmond Williams, ed., *Secret Societies in Ireland*. Dublin: Gill and Macmillan, pp. 26–35.

Lee, James, and Jon Gjerde. 1986. "Comparative Household Morphology of Stem, Joint, and Nuclear Household Systems: Norway, China, and the United States." *Continuity and Change* 1(1): 89–112.

Lees, Lynn Hollen. 1979. *Exiles of Erin: Irish Migrants in Victorian London*. Ithaca: Cornell University Press.

LePlay, Frédéric, 1874. *L'organisation de la famille selon le vrai modèle signalé par l'histoire de toutes les races et de tous les temps*. Paris.

Lesthaeghe, Ron. 1977. *The Decline of Belgian Fertility, 1800–1970*. Princeton: Princeton University Press.

Lesthaeghe, Ron, and Chris Wilson. 1986. "Modes of Production, Secularization, and the Pace of Fertility Decline in Western Europe, 1870–1930." In Ansley J. Coale and Susan Cotts Watkins, eds., *The Decline of Fertility in Europe*. Princeton: Princeton University Press, pp. 261–292.

Livi-Bacci, Massimo. 1971. *A Century of Portuguese Fertility*. Princeton: Princeton University Press.

————. 1977. *A History of Italian Fertility during the Last Two Centuries*. Princeton: Princeton University Press.

————. 1981. "On the Frequency of Remarriage in Nineteenth Century Italy: Methods and Results." In Jacques Dupâquier, E. Hélin, P. Laslett, M. Livi-Bacci, and S. Sogner, eds., *Marriage and Remarriage in Populations in the Past*. New York: Academic Press, pp. 347–362.

Local Government Board (Ireland). 1904. "Annual Report for the Year Ending 31 March 1903." House of Commons Sessional Papers, vol. 27.

————. 1908. *Tuberculosis in Ireland*. His Majesty's Stationery Office.

————. 1909. "Annual Report for the Year Ending 31 March 1909." House of Commons Sessional Papers, vol. 30.

————. 1910. "Annual Report for the Year Ending 31 March 1910." House of Commons Sessional Papers, vol. 40.

————. 1911. "Annual Report for the Year Ending 31 March 1911." House of Commons Sessional Papers, vol. 33.

————. 1912–13. "Annual Report for the Year Ending 31 March 1912." House of Commons Sessional Papers, vol. 37.

————. 1914. "Annual Report for the Year Ending 31 March 1914." House of Commons Sessional Papers, vol. 39.

Longstaff, G. B. 1893. "Rural Depopulation." *Journal of the Royal Statistical Society* 56: 380–433.

Lyons, F.S.L. 1973. *Ireland Since the Famine*. London: Fontana.

Macafee, William. 1987. "Pre-famine Population in Ulster: Evidence from the Parish Register of Killyman." In Patrick O'Flanagan, Paul Ferguson, and Kevin Whelan, eds., *Rural Ireland, 1600–1900: Modernization and Change*. Cork: Cork University Press, pp. 142–161.

MacCárthaigh, Domhnall. 1942. "Marriage and Birth Rates for Knockainy Parish, 1882–1941." *Journal of the Cork Historical and Archaeological Society* 47: 4–8.

McCleary, George F. 1937. *The Menace of British Depopulation*. London: George Allen and Unwin.

McDowell, R. B. 1964. *The Irish Administration, 1801–1914*. London: Routledge and Kegan Paul.

———. 1975. *The Church of Ireland, 1869–1969*. London: Routledge and Kegan Paul.

MacFarlane, A. 1986. *Marriage and Love in England, 1300–1840: Modes of Reproduction, 1300–1840*. New York: Blackwell.

McGregor, Patrick P. L. 1989. "Demographic Pressure and the Irish Famine: Malthus after Mokyr." *Land Economics* 65(3): 228–238.

McKenna, E. E. 1978. "Age, Region, and Marriage in Post-Famine Ireland: An Empirical Examination." *Economic History Review* 31(2): 238–256.

McLeod, Hugh. 1981. *Religion and the People of Western Europe, 1789–1970*. Oxford: Clarendon Press.

McNeill, D. B. 1969. *Irish Passenger Steamship Services. Vol. 1: North of Ireland*. Newton Abbot: David and Charles.

———. 1971. *Irish Passenger Steamship Services. Vol. 2: South of Ireland*. Newton Abbot: David and Charles.

Macourt, Malcolm P. A. 1978. "The Religious Inquiry in the Irish Census of 1861." *Irish Historical Studies* 21(82): 168–187.

Maison, D., and E. Millet. 1974. "La nuptialité." *Population*, numéro special, pp. 31–50.

Malthus, Thomas R. 1927. *An Essay on the Principle of Population*. Everyman Library Edition, 2 vols. New York.

Marschalck, Peter. 1984. *Bevölkerungsgeschichte Deutschlands im 19. und 20. Jahrhundert*. Frankfurt aM: Suhrkamp.

Marshall, Alfred. 1920. *Principles of Economics*. 8th ed. London: Macmillan.

Matthews, R.C.O., C. H. Feinstein, and J. C. Odling-Smee. 1982. *British Economic Growth, 1856–1973*. Stanford: Stanford University Press.

Mendels, Franklin. 1972. "Proto-industrialization: The First Phase of the Industrialization Process." *Journal of Economic History* 32(1): 241–261.

Messenger, John C. 1969. *Inis Beag: Isle of Ireland*. New York: Holt, Rinehart and Winston.

Micks, William L. 1925. *An Account of the Constitution, Administration, and Dissolution of the Congested Districts Board for Ireland from 1891–1923*. Dublin: Eason & Son.

Miller, David W. 1975. "Irish Catholicism and the Great Famine." *Journal of Social History* 9: 81–98.

———. 1978. "Presbyterianism and 'Modernization' in Ulster." *Past and Present* 80: 66–90.

———. 1994. "Fertility and Social Change in Ireland, 1841–1861." Paper presented at the 1994 annual meetings of the Social Science History Association, Atlanta, Georgia.

Miller, Kerby. 1985. *Emigrants and Exiles: Ireland and the Irish Exodus to North America*. New York: Oxford University Press.

———. 1990. "Emigration, Capitalism, and Ideology in Post-Famine Ireland."

In Richard Kearney, ed., *Migrations: The Irish at Home and Abroad*. Dublin: Wolfhound Press, pp. 91–108.

Mitch, David F. 1992. *The Rise of Popular Literacy in Victorian England: The Influence of Private Choice and Public Policy*. Philadelphia: University of Pennsylvania Press.

Mitchell, B. R., ed. 1980. *European Historical Statistics, 1750–1975*. 2nd ed. New York: Facts on File.

Mitchell, B. R., and Phyllis Deane. 1962. *Abstract of British Historical Statistics*. Cambridge: Cambridge University Press.

Mitterauer, Michael. 1990. "Servants and Youth." *Continuity and Change* 5(1): 11–38.

Mitterauer, Michael, and Reinhard Sieder. 1982. *The European Family: Patriarchy to Partnership from the Middle Ages to the Present*. Translated by Karla Osterveen and Manfred Hörzinger. Chicago: University of Chicago Press.

Moch, Leslie Page. 1992. "The History of Migration and Fertility Decline: The View from the Road." In John R. Gillis, Louise A. Tilly, and David Levine, eds., *The European Experience of Declining Fertility, 1850–1970*. Cambridge, Mass.: Blackwell, pp. 175–192.

Modell, John, Frank Furstenberg, and Theodore Hershberg. 1975. "Social Change and Transitions to Adulthood in Historical Perspective." *Journal of Family History* 1(1): 7–32.

Modigliani, Franco. 1988. "The Role of Intergenerational Transfers and Life Cycle Saving in the Accumulation of Wealth." *Journal of Economic Perspectives* 2(2): 15–40.

Mogey, John M. 1947. *Rural Life in Northern Ireland*. New York: Oxford University Press.

Mokyr, Joel. 1980a. "Industrialization and Poverty in Ireland and the Netherlands." *Journal of Interdisciplinary History* 10(3): 429–458.

———. 1980b. "The Deadly Fungus: An Econometric Investigation into the Short-Term Demographic Impact of the Irish Famine, 1846–1851." *Research in Population Economics* 2: 237–277.

———. 1981. "Irish History with the Potato." *Irish Economic and Social History* 8: 8–29.

———. 1985. *Why Ireland Starved: A Quantitative and Analytical History of the Irish Economy, 1800–1850*. London: Allen and Unwin.

Mokyr, Joel, and Cormac Ó Gráda. 1984. "New Developments in Irish Population History, 1700–1850." *Economic History Review*, 2nd ser., 37(4): 473–488.

———. 1988. "Poor and Getting Poorer? Living Standards in Ireland before the Famine." *Economic History Review*, 2nd ser., 41(2): 209–235.

———. 1994. "The Heights of the British and Irish c. 1800–1815: Evidence from Recruits to the East India Company's Army." In John Komlos, ed., *Stature, Living Standards, and Economic Development: Essays in Anthropometric History*. Chicago: University of Chicago Press, pp. 39–59.

Morgan, S. Philip, Susan Cotts Watkins, and Douglas Ewbank. 1994. "Generating Americans: Ethnic Differences in Fertility." In Susan Cotts Watkins, ed.,

After Ellis Island: Newcomers and Natives in the 1910 Census. New York: Russell Sage Foundation, pp. 83–124.

Morgan, Valerie, and William Macafee. 1984. "Irish Population in the pre-Famine Period: Evidence from County Antrim." *Economic History Review*, 2nd ser., 37(2): 182–196.

Morineau, Michel. 1970. "La pomme de terre au XVIIIe siècle." *Annales Économies, Sociétés, Civilisations* 25(6): 1767–85.

Murphy, Cliona. 1995. "Review of Joanna Bourke, *Husbandry to Housewifery: Women, Economic Change, and Housework in Ireland, 1890–1914.*" *American Historical Review* 100(3): 906–907.

Murphy, Maura. 1981. "The Economic and Social Structure of Nineteenth Century Cork." In David Harkness and Mary O'Dowd, eds., *The Town in Ireland.* Belfast: Appletree Press, pp. 125–154.

National Economic and Social Council, Ireland. 1991. *The Economic and Social Consequences of Emigration.* Dublin: National Economic and Social Council.

National Research Council. 1986. *Population Growth and Economic Development: Policy Questions.* Washington, D.C.: National Academy Press.

NESC. *See* National Economic and Social Council, Ireland.

Newsinger, John. 1995. "The Catholic Church in Nineteenth-Century Ireland." *European History Quarterly* 25(2): 247–267.

Nicholas, Stephen, and Deborah Oxley. 1993. "The Living Standards of Women during the Industrial Revolution, 1795–1820." *Economic History Review* 46(4): 723–749.

Nicholls, George. 1856. *A History of the Irish Poor Law.* London: John Murray.

Nolan, Janet A. 1989. *Ourselves Alone: Women's Emigration from Ireland, 1885–1920.* Lexington, Ky.: University of Kentucky Press.

Noonan, John T. 1986. *Contraception: A History of Its Treatment by the Catholic Theologians and Canonists.* Enl. ed. Cambridge, Mass.: Harvard University Press.

Noonan, Patrick. 1953. "Why Few Irish Marry." In John A. O'Brien, ed., *The Vanishing Irish: The Enigma of the Modern World.* New York: McGraw-Hill, pp. 42–49.

O'Brien, George A. P. 1921. *The Economic History of Ireland from the Union to the Famine.* London: Longman, Green.

O'Brien, John A. 1953. "The Irish Enigma." In John A. O'Brien, ed., *The Vanishing Irish: The Enigma of the Modern World.* New York: McGraw-Hill, pp. 3–10.

Ó Danachair, Caoimhin. 1985. "Marriage in Irish Folk Tradition." In Art Cosgrove, ed., *Marriage in Ireland.* Dublin: College Press, pp. 99–115.

O'Dowd, Anne. 1991. *Spalpeens and Tattie Hokers: History and Folklore of the Irish Migratory Agricultural Worker in Ireland and Britain.* Dublin: Irish Academic Press.

O'Faolain, Sean. 1953. "Love among the Irish." In John A. O'Brien, ed., *The Vanishing Irish: The Enigma of the Modern World.* New York: McGraw-Hill, pp. 111–122.

Ogilvie, Sheilagh C., and Markus Cerman. 1996. "The Theories of Proto-industrialization." In Sheilagh C. Ogilvie and Markus Cerman, eds., *European Proto-industrialization.* Cambridge: Cambridge University Press, pp. 1–11.

Ogle, William. 1889. "The Alleged Depopulation of the Rural Districts of England." *Journal of the Royal Statistical Society* 52(2): 205–232.

Ó Gráda, Cormac. 1973. "Seasonal Migration and Post-Famine Adjustment in the West of Ireland." *Studia Hibernia* 13: 48–76.

———. 1975. "A Note on Nineteenth-Century Irish Emigration Statistics." *Population Studies* 29(1): 143–149.

———. 1978. "Some Aspects of Nineteenth-Century Irish Emigration." In L. M. Cullen and T. C. Smout, eds., *Comparative Aspects of Scottish and Irish Economic and Social History, 1600–1900.* Edinburgh: John Donald, pp. 65–73.

———. 1980. "Primogeniture and Ultimogeniture in Rural Ireland." *Journal of Interdisciplinary History* 10(3): 491–498.

———. 1985. "Did Ulster Catholics Always Have Larger Families?" *Irish Economic and Social History* 12: 79–88.

———. 1989. *The Great Irish Famine.* Hampshire: Macmillan.

———. 1990. "Irish Agricultural History: Recent Research." *Agricultural History Review* 38(II): 165–173.

———. 1991. "New Evidence on the Fertility Transition in Ireland, 1880–1911." *Demography* 28(4): 535–548.

———. 1992. "Corrigenda." *Demography* 29(4): iv.

———. 1993. *Ireland before and after the Famine: Explorations in Economic History, 1808–1925.* 2nd ed. Manchester: Manchester University Press.

———. 1994. *Ireland: A New Economic History, 1780–1939.* New York: Oxford University Press.

Ó Gráda, Cormac, and Niall Duffy. 1989. "Fertility Control in Ireland and Scotland c. 1880–1930: Some New Findings." University College, Dublin.

———. 1995. "Fertility Control Early in Marriage in Ireland a Century Ago." *Journal of Population Economics* 8: 423–431.

Ó Gráda, Cormac, and Kevin O'Rourke. 1995. "Migration as Disaster Relief: Lessons from the Great Irish Famine." Working paper.

Ó Gráda, Cormac, and Brendan M. Walsh. 1995. "Fertility and Population in Ireland, North and South." *Population Studies* 49(2): 259–280.

Okun, Barbara S. 1992. "How Much Can Indirect Estimation Techniques Tell Us About Marital Fertility Control?" Ph.D. dissertation, Princeton University.

———. 1994. "Cohort Parity Analysis: An Exposition." *Historical Methods* 27(2): 53–60.

Oldham, C. H. 1914. "The Incidence of Emigration on Town and Country Life in Ireland." *Journal of the Statistical and Social Inquiry Society of Ireland* 94: 207–218.

O'Neill, Brian Juan. 1987. *Social Inequality in a Portuguese Hamlet.* Cambridge: Cambridge University Press.

O'Neill, Kevin. 1984. *Family and Farm in Pre Famine Ireland: The Parish of Killashandra.* Madison: University of Wisconsin Press.

O'Neill, T. P. 1989. "The Food Crisis of the 1890s." In E. Margaret Crawford, ed., *Famine: The Irish Experience, 900–1900: Subsistence Crises and Famines in Ireland.* Edinburgh: John Donald, pp. 176–197.

O'Reilly, James. 1975. *The Moral Problem of Contraception*. Chicago: Franciscan Herald Press.

O'Rourke, Kevin H. 1989. "Agricultural Change and Rural Depopulation: Ireland, 1845–1876." Ph.D. dissertation, Department of Economics, Harvard University.

―――― 1991a. "Did the Great Irish Famine Matter?" *Journal of Economic History* 51(1): 1–22.

―――― 1991b. "Rural Depopulation in a Small Open Economy: Ireland, 1856–1876." *Explorations in Economic History* 28(4): 409–432.

O'Rourke, Kevin. 1992. "Why Ireland Emigrated: A Positive Theory of Factor Flows." *Oxford Economic Papers*, n.s., 44(2): 322–340.

O'Rourke, Kevin. 1995. "Emigration and Living Standards in Ireland since the Famine." *Journal of Population Economics* 8: 407–421.

Orr, Alastair. 1984. "Farm Servants and Farm Labour in the Forth Valley and South-East Lowlands." In T. M. Devine, ed., *Farm Servants and Labour in Lowland Scotland: 1770–1914*. Edinburgh: John Donald, pp. 29–54.

Piore, Michael J. 1979. *Birds of Passage: Migrant Labor and Industrial Societies*. Cambridge: Cambridge University Press.

Plunkett, Horace. 1970. *Ireland in the New Century*. Dublin: Kennikat Press. Reprint of 1904 edition.

Pollak, Robert A. 1985. "A Transactions Cost Approach to Families and Households." *Journal of Economic Literature* 23(2): 581–608.

Pollak, Robert A., and Susan Cotts Watkins. 1993. "Cultural and Economic Approaches to Fertility: Proper Marriage or *Mésalliance*?" *Population and Development Review* 19(3): 467–496.

Pomfret, John E. 1930. *The Struggle for Land in Ireland, 1800–1923*. Princeton: Princeton University Press.

Postel-Vinay, Gilles, and David R. Weir. 1994. "Frenchman into Peasants: Myths and Realities of Agricultural Labor Markets in France, 1862–1929." Working paper.

Preston, Samuel, and Michael Haines. 1991. *The Fatal Years: Child Mortality in Late Nineteenth Century America*. Princeton: Princeton University Press.

Preston, Samuel, Nathan Keyfitz, and Robert Schoen. 1972. *Causes of Death: Life Tables for National Populations*. New York: Seminar Press.

Rao, Vijayendra. 1993a. "Dowery 'Inflation' in Rural India: A Statistical Investigation." *Population Studies* 47(2): 283–294.

―――― 1993b. "The Rising Price of Husbands: A Hedonic Analysis of Dowry Increases in Rural India." *Journal of Political Economy* 101(4): 666–677.

Redford, Arthur. 1976. *Labor Migration in England: 1800–1850*. 3rd ed. Manchester: Manchester University Press.

Reed, James. 1984. *From Private Vice to Public Virtue: The Birth Control Movement and American Society since 1830*. New York: Basic Books.

Rhodes, Rita M. 1992. *Women and the Family in Post-Famine Ireland: Status and Opportunity in a Patriarchal Society*. New York: Garland.

Richards, Toni. 1977. "Fertility Decline in Germany: An Econometric Reappraisal." *Population Studies* 31(3): 537–553.

Roebuck, P. 1981. "Landlord Indebtedness in Ulster in the Seventeenth and Eighteenth Centuries." In J. M. Goldstrom and L. A. Clarkson, eds., *Irish Population, Economy, and Society: Essays in Honour of the Late K. H. Connell*. Oxford: Clarendon Press, pp. 135–154.

Rose, M. E. 1986. *The Relief of Poverty, 1834–1914*. London: Macmillan.

Royal Commission on the Aged Poor. 1895a. "Report." House of Commons Sessional Papers, vol. 14.

———. 1895b. "Evidence." House of Commons Sessional Papers, vol. 14.

———. 1896. "Evidence." House of Commons Sessional Papers, vol. 15.

Royal Commission on the Poor Laws and the Relief of Distress. 1909. "Report on Ireland." House of Commons Sessional Papers, vol. 38.

———. 1910a. "Appendix Vol. XXV (England and Wales)." House of Commons Sessional Papers, vol. 50.

———. 1910b. "Appendix Vol. X." House of Commons Sessional Papers, vol. 53.

———. 1910c. "Appendix Vol. XXXI (Ireland)." House of Commons Sessional Papers, vol. 54.

Royle, Stephen A. 1978. "Irish Manuscript Census Records: A Neglected Source of Information." *Irish Geography* 11: 110–125.

Ruggles, Steven. 1987. *Prolonged Connections: The Rise of the Extended Family in Nineteenth-Century England and America*. Madison: University of Wisconsin Press.

Ryan, W.J.L. 1955. "Some Irish Population Problems." *Population Studies* 9(2): 185–188.

Salaman, Redcliffe. 1985. *The History and Social Influence of the Potato*. Cambridge: Cambridge University Press. Reprint of 1949 edition.

Santow, Gigi. 1993. "*Coitus Interruptus* in the Twentieth Century." *Population and Development Review* 19(4): 767–792.

———. 1995. "*Coitus Interruptus* and the Control of Natural Fertility." *Population Studies* 49(1): 19–44.

Schellekens, Jona. 1993. "The role of Marital Fertility in Irish Population History, 1750–1840." *Economic History Review* 46(2): 369–378.

Schellenberg, James A. 1991. "Patterns of Delayed Marriage: How Special Are the Irish?" *Sociological Focus* 24(1): 1–11.

Scheper-Hughes, Nancy. 1979. *Saints, Scholars, and Schizophrenics: Mental Illness in Rural Ireland*. Berkeley: University of California Press.

Schoen, Robert, and Robin W. Weinick. 1993. "The Slowing Metabolism of Marriage: Figures from 1988 U.S. Marital Status Life Tables." *Demography* 30(4): 737–746.

Schofield, R. 1970. "Age-Specific Mobility in an Eighteenth-Century Rural English Parish." *Annales de Démographie Historique*, 261–274.

Schrier, Arnold. 1958. *Ireland and the American Emigration, 1850–1900*. Minneapolis: University of Minnesota Press.

Schultz, T. Paul. 1995. "Eroding the Economic Foundations of Marriage and Fertility in the United States." Department of Economics, Yale University.

Shannon, H. A. 1935. "Migration and the Growth of London, 1841–1891: A Statistical Note." *Economic History Review* 5(2): 79–86.

Sheehan, James J. 1989. *German History, 1770–1866*. New York: Oxford University Press.

Shorter, Edward. 1980. "Illegitimacy, Sexual Revolution, and Social Change in Modern Europe." In Robert I. Rotberg and Theodore K. Rabb, eds., *Marriage and Fertility: Studies in Interdisciplinary History*. Princeton: Princeton University Press, pp. 85–120.

Sieder, R. 1987. *Sozialgeschichte der Familie*. Frankfurt aM: Suhrkamp.

Silverman, Marilyn, and P. H. Gulliver. 1986. *In the Valley of the Noire: A Social History of Thomastown, County Kilkenny, 1840–1983*. Dublin: Geography Publications.

Sklar, June. 1977. "Marriage and Nonmarital Fertility: A Comparison of Ireland and Sweden." *Population and Development Review* 3(4): 359–376.

Slater. 1894. *Slater's Royal National Directory of Ireland*. 9th ed. London: Kelly and Co.

Smith, Adam. 1976. *An Inquiry into the Nature and Causes of the Wealth of Nations*. Chicago: University of Chicago Press. Reprint of the Cannan Edition.

Smith, Frank B. 1988. *The Retreat of Tuberculosis, 1850–1950*. London: Croom Helm.

Smith, Janet E. 1991. *Humanae Vitae: A Generation Later*. Washington, D.C.: Catholic University of America.

Smyth, William J. 1982. "Nephews, Dowries, Sons, and Mothers: An Analysis of the Geography of Farm and Marital Transactions in a South Tipperary Parish." Paper presented to the Franco-Irish Conference on Rural Communities, Paris.

———. 1983. "Landholding Changes, Kinship Networks and Class Transformation in Rural Ireland: A Case-Study from County Tipperary." *Irish Geography* 16: 16–35.

Solar, Peter. 1984. "Why Ireland Starved: A Critical Review of the Econometric Results." *Irish Economic and Social History* 11: 107–115.

———. 1987. "Growth and Distribution in Irish Agricultural before the Famine." Ph.D. dissertation, Stanford University.

———. 1995. "Poor Relief and English Economic Development before the Industrial Revolution." *Economic History Review* 48(1): 1–22.

———. 1996. "The Potato Famine in Europe." Working paper.

Solow, B. L. 1971. *The Land Question and the Irish Economy, 1870–1903*. Cambridge, Mass.: Harvard University Press.

Somerville, Alexander. 1994. (Reprint) *Letters from Ireland during the Famine of 1847*. Edited by K.D.M. Snell. Dublin: Blackrock. Reprint.

Steckel, Richard. 1988. "The Age at Leaving Home: A View from Families Matched in Census Manuscript Schedules." Working paper, Ohio State University.

Stevens, D. 1990. "New Evidence on the Timing of Early Life Course Transitions: The United States from 1900 to 1980." *Journal of Family History* 15(2): 163–178.

Sundstrom, W. A., and P. A. David. 1988. "Old-Age Security Motives, Labor Markets, and Farm Family Fertility in Antebellum America." *Explorations in Economic History* 25 (2): 164–197.

Symes, David G. 1972. "Farm Household and Farm Performance: A Study of Twentieth Century Changes in Ballyferriter, Southwest Ireland." *Ethnology* 11(1): 25–38.

Tapinos, Georges. 1974. *L'économie des migrations internationales*. Paris: Presses de la Fondation Nationale des Sciences Politiques.

Teitelbaum, M. 1984. *The British Fertility Decline: Demographic Transition in the Crucible of the Industrial Revolution*. Princeton: Princeton University Press.

Tennstedt, Florian. 1981. *Sozialgeschichte der Sozialpolitik in Deutschland*. Göttingen: Vandenhoeck & Ruprecht.

Thomas, Brinley. 1973. *Migration and Economic Growth: A Study of Great Britain and the Atlantic Economy*. 2nd ed. Cambridge: Cambridge University Press.

T'Hart, Marjolein. 1985. "Irish Return Migration in the Nineteenth Century." *Tijdschrift voor Econ. en Soc. Geografie* 76(3): 223–231.

Trussell, T. James, and Timothy W. Guinnane. 1993. "Techniques of Event-History Analysis." In David S. Reher and Roger Schofield, eds., *Old and New Methods in Historical Demography*. New York: Oxford University Press, pp. 181–205.

Turner, Michael E. 1987. "Towards an Agricultural Prices Index for Ireland, 1850–1914." *Economic and Social Review* 18(2): 123–136.

————. 1991. "Agricultural Output and Productivity in Post-Famine Ireland." In B.M.S. Campbell and M. Overton, eds., *Land, Labor, and Livestock: Historical Studies in European Agricultural Productivity*. Manchester: Manchester University Press, pp. 410–438.

————. 1996. *After the Famine: Irish Agriculture, 1850–1914*. Cambridge: Cambridge University Press.

United Nations. 1990. *Demographic Yearbook*. New York.

United Nations Development Program. 1994. *Human Development Report*. New York: Oxford University Press.

United States Bureau of the Census. 1913. *Thirteenth Census of the United States*. Vol. 1: *Population*. Washington, D.C.: Government Printing Office.

————. 1975. *Historical Statistics of the United States: Colonial Times to 1970*. Washington, D.C.: Government Printing Office.

————. 1994. *Statistical Abstract of the United States, 1994*. Washington, D.C.

United States Commerce Department. 1992. *Statistical Abstract of the United States*. Washington, DC.

United States Immigration Commission (The Dillingham Commission). [1907–1910] 1970. *Reports*. Reprint. New York: Arno Press.

United States Senate. 1913a. *Agricultural Credit and Cooperation in Germany*. U.S. Senate Document number 17, 63rd Congress, 1st Session.

————, 1913b. *Agricultural Cooperation and Rural Credit in Europe*. Senate Document number 214, 63rd Congress, 1st Session.

Van de Walle, Etienne, and Helmut V. Muhsam. 1995. "Fatal Secrets and the French Fertility Transition." *Population and Development Review* 21(2): 261–280.

Vann, Richard T., and David Eversley. 1992. *Friends in Life and Death: The*

British and Irish Quakers in the Demographic Transition, 1650–1900. Cambridge: Cambridge University Press.

Van Zanden, J. L. 1991. "The First Green Revolution: The Growth of Production and Productivity in European Agriculture, 1870–1914." *Economic History Review*, 2nd ser., 44(2): 215–239.

Vaughan, W. E. 1984. *Landlords and Tenants in Ireland, 1848–1904.* Studies in Irish Economic and Social History, no. 2. Dundalk: Economic and Social History Society of Ireland.

———. 1989. "Ireland c. 1870." In W. E. Vaughan, ed., *A New History of Ireland. Vol. 5: Ireland under the Union, I, 1801–1870.* New York: Oxford University Press, pp. 726–802.

———. 1994. *Landlords and Tenants in Mid-Victorian Ireland.* New York: Oxford University Press.

Vaughan, W. E., and A. J. Fitzpatrick, eds. 1978. *Irish Historical Statistics: Population, 1821–1971.* Dublin: Royal Irish Academy.

Verdon, Michel. 1979. "The Stem Family: Towards a General Thesis." *Journal of Interdisciplinary History* 10(1): 87–105.

Verrière, Jacques. 1979. *La population de l'Irlande.* Paris: Mouton.

Viazzo, Pier Paolo. 1989. *Upland Communities: Environment, Population, and Social Structure in the Alps Since the Sixteenth Century.* Cambridge: Cambridge University Press.

Vice-Regal Commission. 1906a. "Report of the Poor Law Reform Commission (Ireland)." House of Commons Sessional Papers, vol. 51.

———. 1906b. "Appendix to the Report of the Poor Law Reform Commission (Ireland)." House of Commons Sessional Papers, vol. 52.

Vincent, Joan. 1984. "Marriage, Religion, and Class in South Fermanagh, Ireland, 1846–1920." In Owen M. Lynch, ed., *Culture and Community in Europe: Essays in Honor of Conrad M. Arensberg.* Delhi: Hindustan Publishing Corp., pp. 175–193.

Wachter, Kenneth W., Eugene Hammel, and Peter Laslett. 1978. *Statistical Studies of Historical Social Structure.* New York: Academic Press.

Wall, Richard. 1978. "The Age at Leaving Home." *Journal of Family History* 3(2): 181–202.

———. 1987. "Leaving Home and the Process of Household Formation in Preindustrial England." *Continuity and Change* 2(1): 77–101.

———. 1989. "Leaving Home and Living Alone: An Historical Perspective." *Population Studies* 43(3): 369–389.

Wall, Richard, Jean Robin, and Peter Laslett. 1983. *Family Forms in Historic Europe.* Cambridge: Cambridge University Press.

Walsh, Brendan M. 1969. "A Perspective on Irish Population Patterns." *Eire-Ireland* 9(3): 3–21.

———. 1970a. "Marriage Rates and Population Pressure: Ireland, 1871 and 1911." *Economic History Review*, 2nd ser., 23(1): 148–162.

———. 1970b. "Religion and Demographic Behavior in Ireland." Economic and Social Research Institute (Dublin), Paper no. 55.

———. 1972. "Trends in Age at Marriage in Postwar Ireland." *Demography* 9(2): 187–202.

———. 1985. "Marriage in Ireland in the Twentieth Century." In Art Cosgrove, ed., *Marriage in Ireland*. Dublin: College Press, pp. 132–150.

———. 1989. *Ireland's Changing Demographic Structure*. Dublin: Gill and Macmillan.

———. 1995. "Marriage and Fertility in Modern Ireland." Working paper.

Ward, Margaret. 1991. *The Missing Sex: Putting Women into Irish History*. Dublin: Attic Press.

Watkins, Susan Cotts. 1986. "Regional Patterns of Nuptiality in Western Europe, 1870–1960." In Ansley J. Coale and Susan Cotts Watkins, eds., *The Decline of Fertility in Europe*. Princeton: Princeton University Press, pp. 314–336.

———. 1991. *From Provinces into Nations: Demographic Integration in Western Europe, 1870–1960*. Princeton: Princeton University Press.

Watkins, Susan Cotts, and Jane Menken. 1985. "Famines in Historical Perspective." *Population and Development Review* 11(4): 647–675.

Wegge, Simone. 1995. "Chain Reactions: Information and Nineteenth-Century European Migration." Working paper.

Weindling, Paul. 1989. *Health, Race, and German Politics between National Unification and Nazism, 1870–1914*. Cambridge: Cambridge University Press.

Weir, David R. 1982. "Fertility Decline in Rural France, 1740–1829." Ph.D. dissertation, Stanford University.

———. 1984. "Better Never than Late: Celibacy and Age at Marriage in English Cohort Fertility, 1541–1871." *Journal of Family History*, 9(4): 340–354.

———. 1993. "Family Reconstitution and Population Reconstruction: Two Approaches to the Fertility Transition in France, 1740–1911." In David S. Reher and Roger Schofield, eds., *Old and New Methods in Historical Demography*. New York: Oxford University Press, pp. 145–158.

West, Trevor. 1986. *Horace Plunkett: Co-Operation and Politics, an Irish Biography*. Washington, D.C.: Catholic University of America Press.

Whelan, Kevin. 1986. "The Famine and Post-Famine Adjustment." In William Nolan, ed., *The Shaping of Ireland: The Geographical Perspective*. Dublin: Mercier Press, pp. 151–164.

Whyte, J. H. 1960. "The Influence of the Catholic Clergy on Elections in Nineteenth-Century Ireland." *The English Historical Review* 75(295): 239–259.

Wilcox, Walter F., ed. 1929. *International Migrations. Vol. I: Statistics*. New York: National Bureau of Economic Research.

Williamson, Jeffrey G. 1986. "The Impact of the Irish on British Labor Markets during the Industrial Revolution." *Journal of Economic History* 46(3): 693–720.

———. 1988. "Migrant Selectivity, Urbanization, and Industrial Revolutions." *Population and Development Review* 14(2): 287–314.

———. 1990. *Coping with City Growth during the Industrial Revolution*. New York: Cambridge University Press.

———. 1994. "Economic Convergence: Placing Post-Famine Ireland in Comparative Perspective." *Irish Economic and Social History* 21: 5–27.

Wilmoth, John R., and Patrick Ball. 1992. "The Population Debate in American Popular Magazines." *Population and Development Review* 18(4): 631–668.

Wilson, Catherine Anne. 1994. *A New Lease on Life: Landlords, Tenants, and Immigrants in Ireland and Canada*. Montreal: McGill-Queen's University Press.

Wilson, William Julius. 1987. *The Truly Disadvantaged: The Inner City, the Underclass, and Public Policy*. Chicago: University of Chicago Press.

Woods, C. J. 1980. "The General Election of 1892: The Catholic Clergy and the Defeat of the Parnellites." In F.S.L. Lyons and R.A.J. Hawkins, eds., *Ireland under the Union: Varieties of Tension—Essays in Honor of T. W. Moody* Oxford: Clarendon Press, pp. 289–319.

Wrigley, E. A. 1978. "Fertility Strategy for the Individual and the Group." In Charles Tilly, ed., *Historical Studies in Changing Fertility*. Princeton: Princeton University Press, pp. 135–154.

Wrigley, E. A., and R. Schofield. 1981. *The Population History of England, 1541–1871: A Reconstruction*. Cambridge, Mass.: Harvard University Press.

INDEX

age at marriage. *See* marriage patterns
age misreporting, 289n.4
agricultural output, 38–40
Akenson, Donald H., 64–65, 118–19
Anderson, Michael, 214, 257
Arensberg, Conrad, 30, 222, 235

Beames, M. R., 52
Becker, Gary, 18, 226, 246–47
Berkner, Lutz, 138, 143, 178
Birdwell-Pheasant, Donna, 140, 158, 165, 295n.10
Bourke, Joanna, 54–55
Boyle, Phelim, 86
breast feeding: as contraceptive, 244; and pre-Famine population growth, 85
Breen, Richard, 179
Brettell, Caroline B., 214

canon law, 217, 261
Carlsson, Gösta, 246
celibacy. *See* marriage patterns
Church of Ireland, 50, 75
Church of Jesus Christ of the Latter-Day Saints, 261
Coale, Ansley J., 245, 270
cohort depletion, 183–85; defined, 127–28. *See also* migration
Cohort Parity Analysis (CPA), 255–57
Cole, J. W., 138
Congested Districts Board, 47, 50–51, 66. *See also* land tenure
Connell, Kenneth H., 15–16, 82, 91–94, 195
Connolly, Sean J., 259
contraception, 217–18, 252–54; Roman Catholic teaching on, 261
cooperatives, 73
Cousens, S. H., 88–89
Crafts, Nicholas F. R., 267
Cullen, Paul Cardinal, 69
Curtin, C., 134

Darwin, Charles, 226
David, Paul A., 254–56, 286
depopulation, 3–9; in the twentieth century, 277

divorce: ban on, as impediment to marriage, 217; informal, 217; referendum on, 281; and Roman Catholic Church, 76
dowry: as impediment to marriage, 209–11; uses of, 157–58
Drake, Michael, 82–84
Duffy, Niall, 253, 257

education, 64–65; gender differences in, 55; and leaving home, 171–72
emigration. *See* migration
European Fertility Project, 245; and definition of fertility indices, 128–29; and Ireland, 248–52
Ewbank, Douglas, 264

Famine. *See* Great Irish Famine
Ferrie, Joseph P., 294n.55
fertility: Catholic compared to Protestant, 262–63, 278; and emigration, 263–64; estimates of marital fertility levels, 270–71; before the Famine, 81–85; illegitimate, 259–60, 278–79; in Ireland, compared to England and Wales, and Scotland, 242; reasons for high marital fertility in Ireland, 264–68; in twentieth-century Ireland, 278. *See also* contraception; fertility transition; European Fertility Project
fertility transition, 243–52; defined, 243–45; economic analysis of, 246–47; in Ireland, 254–59
First World War: effects of, on French marriage patterns, 212–13
Fitzpatrick, David, 53, 94–95, 141, 206, 271, 292n.35, 299n.8
Flandrin, Jean-Louis, 139
Fogarty, Mary, 236, 260

gender differences: in age at leaving home, 186–92; in education, 55; in emigration rates, 105–6; in implications of marriage, 235–37; in mortality, 117–21; in work patterns, 54–55
Gibbon, P., 134
Goldman, Noreen, 212

Great Irish Famine, 37–38; and impact on population, 85–88; and marriage patterns, 98–99; and Poor Law, 61; violence during, 52; as watershed, 284
Gulliver, P. H., 206

Habakkuk, John, 139
Hajnal, John, 13, 177–78
Hammel, Eugene A., 144
Hannan, Damian F., 165
heirs. *See* inheritance
Henry, Louis, 213, 244, 300n.2
Hoffman, Elizabeth, 36–37
homosexuality, 299n.12
households and household structure, 134–38, 162–65, chapter 5 *passim*; and classification systems, 139; and developmental cycle, 143; and extended family, 142–43; household succession in, 154–56; and nuclear family, 136–37; and Old Age Pension, 140; relation to wealth and occupation, 141–42; and stem family, 134–37, 165
Hutterites, 84

illegitimate fertility. *See* fertility
inheritance: and age at marriage, 215–16; gender differences in, 236–37; heirs, 146–49; and the Land Acts, 139; law of, 139; partible and impartible, 138–39; and primogeniture, 151–54; and substitute heirs, 231–32; and treatment of non-heirs, 156–60. *See also* intergenerational relations
intergenerational relations, 149–51, 160
Irish Folklore Commission, 134

Kavanagh, Patrick, 95, 149
Kennedy, Liam, 44, 73, 154
Kennedy, Robert E., 26, 117–21, 196, 253, 256, 258
Kimball, Solon T. *See* Arensberg, Conrad

laborers, 41–42
land reform. *See* land tenure
land tenure, 48–52, 288n.10; and land reform, 48, 50, 139; and subdivision of farms, 42–43, 139
Land War, 53, 72
Larkin, Emmet, 70
Laslett, Peter, 136, 144, 178
leaving home, chapter 6 *passim*; age at,

186–92; and emigration, 181–85; and internal migration, 179–80
Lee, Joseph, 52
LePlay, Frédéric, 136
Lesthaeghe, Ron, 248
life expectancy. *See* mortality
Local Government Board for Ireland, 62, 119–24

MacFarlane, A., 226
Malthus, Thomas Robert, 12. *See also* Malthusian models
Malthusian models: in Irish history, 13–15; of Irish marriage patterns, 195–209
marriage patterns 94–97, chapter 7 *passim*; age at marriage and delayed inheritance, 215–16; before the Famine, 82–84; and connection to emigration, 198, 208–9, 233–234; decline of marriage in modern western societies, 282–83; dowry as impediment to marriage, 209–11; gender differences in implications of marriage, 235–37; geographical variation in, 199; identity of permanent celibates, 200–208; increases in permanent celibacy, 96–97, 195–209, 238–39; in Ireland in the twentieth century, 277–78; of Irish in the United States, 223–25; of Irish, compared to elsewhere, 97–98; and numbers of possible mates, 211–15; and religion, 217–19; and sex, 234–35; widowhood and remarriage, 99–101
marriage squeeze, 212
Marshall, Alfred, 49, 285
The Match, 92–94. *See also* marriage patterns; households and household structure
Menken, Jane, 87–88
Messenger, John C., 220
migration, 22–24, 101–11; chain, 108–11; and characteristics of emigrants, 104–8, 181–83; cohort depletion measure of emigration, 101, 183–85; costs of, 109–10; emigration after the Famine, 101–4; emigration before the Famine, 81; emigration and leaving home, 181–85; emigration as reason for high fertility, 263–64; emigration in the twentieth century, 279–80; enumeration of migrants, 127; financial assistance to emigrants, 110; to Great Britain, 103; internal, 122–25, 179–80; and marriage patterns, 22–24, 198, 208–9, 214, 233–34; seasonal, 102–3

Miller, David W., 291n16
Miller, Ronald I., 49
Mokyr, Joel, 36–37, 80–81, 84
Morgan, S. Philip, 264
Morse, Donald J., 214
mortality: before the Famine, 81; gender
    differences in, 117–21; of infants, 258;
    post-Famine, 111–21; due to tuberculo-
    sis, 113–17, 119–21

National Schools, 64–65, 171. *See also*
    education
nuclear-family households. *See* households
    and household structure

Ó Gráda, Cormac, 26, 57, 80, 84, 86, 158,
    204, 248, 253, 256–59, 262, 271
Okun, Barbara S., 247, 255
Old Age Pensions Act of 1908, 25, 63–
    64; effect of, on household structure,
    140, 160–62; and implication for
    marriage patterns, 232; and Poor
    Law, 160–62
O'Neill, Kevin, 82
O'Rourke, Kevin, 38, 284

Pantelides, Edith, 270
Parnell, Charles Stewart, 72
path dependence, 286
Penal Laws, 69–70
Plan of Campaign, 53, 72
Plunkett, Horace, 219–20
Pollak, Robert A., 147
Pomfret, John E., 51
Poor Law, 60–63; implications of, for
    marriage patterns, 232; and Old Age
    Pension, 160–62
potato, 35–36, 47
Presbyterian Churches, 76
primogeniture. *See* inheritance
prostitution, 300n.25
Protestants, 74–76; compared to Roman
    Catholics, 67–69, 216–19, 262–63. *See
    also* Church of Ireland; Presbyterian
    Churches
proto-industry, 35–37

Quakers, 82–83

remarriage. *See* marriage patterns
remittances, 110
Rhodes, Rita M., 293n.39
Roman Catholic Church: on demographic

patterns, 10–11; and divorce, 217; insti-
    titional development of, 69–71; as leader,
    71–73; and Nationalist struggles, 53,
    73; priests and nuns of, 70, 291n.28;
    on sex and family life, 73–74, 76–77,
    219–20, 260–63; social basis of, 73.
    See also Church of Ireland; Presbyterian
    Churches
Roman Catholics: compared to Protestants,
    67–69, 216–19, 262–63

Sanderson, Warren C., 254, 256
Santow, Gigi, 244
Schellekens, Jona, 85
Scheper-Hughes, Nancy, 220–23
schizophrenia, 220–22, 299n.14
Schultz, T. Paul, 282
servants, 177–78; domestic, 55, 179–80
sex: and marriage, 234–35; repression of,
    219–23
Silverman, Marilyn, 206
singulate mean age at marriage (SMAM),
    94–95
Sklar, June, 260
Solar, Peter, 35
stem family. *See* households and household
    structure
Stopes, Marie, 253

taxation, 60
Teitelbaum, Michael, 245, 267
tenant right, 49. *See also* land tenure
Trussel, T. James, 247
tuberculosis. *See* mortality

Ulster, 33
Ulster Custom. *See* tenant right
United States of America: as destination for
    Irish emigrants, 103–4; marriage patterns
    among Irish migrants to, 223–25
urbanization, 121–25

Vaughan, W. E., 49–50

Wachter, Kenneth W., 144
wages: of agricultural workers, 40; conver-
    gence of, with other countries, 197
Walsh, Brendan M., 215
Watkins, Susan Cotts, 87–88, 264, 280–81
widows. *See* marriage patterns
Williamson, Jeffrey G., 57
Wilson, William Julius, 299n.10
Wolf, E. R., 138